Pronouncing Shakespeare's Words

Pronouncing Shakespeare's Words

A GUIDE FROM A TO ZOUNDS

DALE COYE

ROUTLEDGE
NEW YORK AND LONDON

Published in 2002 by
Routledge
29 West 35th Street
New York, NY 10001
www.routledge-ny.com

Published in Great Britain by
Routledge
11 New Fetter Lane
London EC4P 4EE
www.routledge.co.uk

Routledge is an imprint of the Taylor & Francis Group.

Printed in the United States of America on acid-free paper.
10 9 8 7 6 5 4 3 2 1

Library of Congress Cataloging-in-Publication Data
Pronouncing Shakespeare's words : a guide from A to Zounds / Dale Coye.
   p. cm.
   Includes index.
   ISBN 0–415–94182–2 (pbk. : alk. paper)
   1. Shakespeare, William, 1564–1616–Language–Glossaries, etc. 2. English language–Early modern, 1500–1700–Pronunciation–Dictionaries. I. Title.

PR3081 .C87   2002
822.3'3–dc21   2002009622

Contents

Preface

First, what this book is not: It is not about how Shakespeare might have pronounced his words four hundred years ago. It is a guide to how they are pronounced today. It is a book for students, actors, readers, and teachers of Shakespeare who find themselves wishing there were pronunciation notes for all of the unfamiliar words they otherwise must guess at or take the time to look up in a dictionary.

Readers of Shakespeare, especially those confronting him for the first time, often feel overwhelmed by his language. Much of this has to do with unfamiliar meanings, but part of the difficulty also arises from questions of pronunciation. This is something which actors obviously must struggle with, and this book is certainly intended for them, both at the amateur and professional levels, but by far the largest number of people reading Shakespeare do so in classrooms, usually with very little understanding of how to speak the lines or pronounce the unfamiliar words. One professor who read this manuscript commented that Shakespeare classes at the college level, and English courses in general, seldom include any effort on the part of the teacher to have students read out loud. Surely this is unfortunate, for when students are encouraged to speak the verse themselves, their experience inevitably becomes richer, more personal and immediate than would otherwise be the case if hearing the language only through lectures, films, or tapes. This *Guide* then, was written with students in mind, to help them confidently negotiate metrical and pronunciation difficulties on their own. But it was also written for teachers, both at the high school and college levels, who are themselves often uncertain about many of these archaic or literary words. Here they will find an authoritative, up-to-date, comprehensive guide to pronunciation. The hope is that this volume will encourage teachers to read with their students, helping them to discover the rhythms of the verse as they learn to savor the sound of the spoken word.

Anyone who has ever opened a volume of Shakespeare knows how quickly the barrage of unfamiliar words begins. Although obscure meanings are noted in any good edition, no Shakespeare glossary or edition of his work offers any consistent guidance to the pronunciation of obsolete or literary words, leaving the reader to struggle with the dictionaries. But dictionaries are not always very helpful. Some of these "Shakespearean" words are not listed in the average college dictionary or even in the thickest unabridged volumes. The *Oxford English Dictionary (OED)* lists nearly all of them with the British pronunciation, but for some archaic words gives only meanings without pronunciation guidance. Furthermore, proper names are not included in the *OED*, and if they are given in other dictionaries, it would be hopeless to expect that the many obscure people and places mentioned in Shakespeare would be listed.

Dictionaries can also be misleading. Consider Shylock's cry of triumph:

This is the fool who lent out money *gratis*. (MV 3.3.2)

Gratis is a literary word rarely used in our everyday, spoken language. Students seeking advice on its pronunciation would find different answers depending on where they looked (symbols have been translated to the system used in this volume).

From British sources:

Collins Cobuild English Language Dictionary, 1987	/GRAYT iss, GRAT iss, GRAHT iss/
English Pronouncing Dictionary, 14th ed., 1988	/GRAYT iss/, less commonly /GRAHT iss, GRAT iss/
Oxford English Dictionary, 2nd ed., 1989	/GRAYT iss, GRAT iss, GRAHT iss/
Longman Pronunciation Dictionary, 1990	UK /GRAT iss/, less commonly /GRAYT iss, GRAHT iss, -us/; US /GRAT iss/
BBC English Dictionary, 1992	/GRAT iss, GRAHT iss/

From American sources:

A Pronouncing Dictionary of American English, 1953	/GRAYT iss/
Webster's Third New International Dictionary, 1961	/GRAT iss, GRAYT iss/
The Random House Dictionary, 2nd ed., 1987	/GRAT iss, GRAYT iss/
The American Heritage Dictionary, 3rd ed., 1992	/GRAT iss, GRAHT iss, GRAYT iss/
Merriam-Webster's Collegiate Dictionary, 10th ed., 1993	/GRAT iss, GRAYT iss/

In this case, the dictionaries generate more questions than they answer: Are all three pronunciations really used today, and if so, by whom? Are some of them old-fashioned? Is one pronunciation more often heard in England and another in the United States? What method did each of these dictionaries use to determine which pronunciations are actually in use?

To give another example, a reader seeking the pronunciation of *quietus* in Hamlet's "To be or not to be" soliloquy will find only one pronunciation given in nearly every dictionary, /kwī EE tus/, although two other variants are commonly used by scholars and actors, /kwī AY tus/ and /kwee AY tus/. What are the implications of this discrepancy? Is there a right and wrong way to pronounce it?

Then there is the question of *bade.* Whenever a group of students or even a company of professional actors rehearses a Shakespeare play there is always an argument over the pronunciation of this word, as well as of *wont, adieu, wassail, zounds* and many others commonly found in Shakespeare's works. In all of these cases an appeal to the authority of the dictionaries will only yield a list of variants without further comment.

Recordings are also of limited value as sources. First, because most of them were produced in Great Britain, reinforcing the unfortunate tendency of North American students to shift into their notion of a British accent whenever they speak Shakespeare's lines. Second, because actors on recordings sometimes use obsolete or even incorrect pronunciations. *Peize* in one recording of *King John* was pronounced to rhyme with *size*, rather than as /peez/ or /payz/. *Counterfeit* ends in /-feet/ in some of the recordings, an unusual pronunciation in the United Kingdom today and unheard of in the United States.

This volume is unique in its use of a survey of American, Canadian, and British Shakespearean scholars who were asked for their recommendations on how to pronounce over 300 of Shakespeare's words. The results from the Survey show, for example, in the case of *gratis,* that the form common to most dictionaries, /GRAY tiss/, is virtually non-existent today, while the pronunciation least cited, /GRAH tiss/, is now used more often than /GRAT iss/ in the United States and the United Kingdom. The Survey also shows that even among the experts great uncertainty exists in some instances. Over half of the Shakespearean scholars in the United States said they were not sure how to pronounce *oeillades, artere,* and *gimmal. Puissance* was given eleven different pronunciations; *importune* had eight. This multiplicity of forms usually boils down to a question of traditional pronunciations vs. innovations based on spelling, a distinction that is often poorly understood by students, actors, and scholars alike.

There are other sources of pronunciation difficulty in Shakespeare, some arising from the verse form of the plays. Many readers are unaware that the iambic verse sometimes demands a shift in stress for some common words (*access, exploit, princess*) while others are expanded or compressed. Then there are the proper names and foreign phrases liberally scattered throughout the plays. Again, many of these names are not listed in any ordinary dictionary, while the glossaries that do exist, like Helge Kökeritz's *Shakespeare's Names* (1959), though valuable, are sometimes out-of-date or incorrect in their American vs. British distinctions.

Together these factors make reading Shakespeare a frustrating experience for many beginning students, while even seasoned Shakespearean actors and teachers find themselves baffled at times over choices of pronunciation. Other works in this field, like Kökeritz's *Shakespeare's Pronunciation* (1953), Viëtor's *Shakespeare's Pronunciation* (1906), and Cercignani's *Shakespeare's Works and Elizabethan Pronunciation* (1981), all focus on the development of the Elizabethan sound system and are decipherable only by the philologist. Some recent studies are helpful in understanding how the demands of verse affect pronunciation and line readings, notably Wright's *Shakespeare's Metrical Art* (1988), Spain's *Shakespeare Sounded Soundly* (1988), and Linklater's *Freeing Shakespeare's Voice* (1992), but none of these discuss pronunciation comprehensively or serve the reader in the line-by-line difficulties that arise from the text.

In this volume the reader and actor will find a straightforward guide to the pronunciation of the "hard" words in Shakespeare's plays. The hope is that it will add to the enjoyment of the casual reader, professional actor, or Shakespeare scholar as it removes some of the obstacles inherent in working with a form of speech that is four centuries old.

This book would not have been possible without the assistance of the many scholars who took time to answer the postal questionnaire and the email surveys. I'm grateful to all who contributed. In addition I owe special thanks to R. Whitney Tucker, best known for his work with ancient Greek, but whose knowledge of Latin is also formidable. His assistance in determining the pronunciation of the Latin entries, particularly the Anglo-Latin variants, was invaluable.

I would also like to mention two Shakespeare scholars at my alma mater, St. Lawrence University. The first, Stanley Holberg, taught Shakespeare classes that everyone wanted to take and that I was fortunate enough to be a part of my senior year. The idea for this volume was born in his classroom. The second, Thomas Berger, was kind enough to recommend my work to Jane Garry at Greenwood Press where the hardcover edition encompassing the complete plays and poems was published in 1998. I'm grateful to both Tom and Jane for their support.

The present volume of the twenty-one best-known plays owes its existence to the hard word of Rick Balkin, my assiduous agent, and Bill Germano, editor at Routledge, who was interested in bringing this work to a larger audience. Without them this edition would have been impossible.

Further inspiration came from my friends and family. I'm grateful to Nan and Ian Twiss for reading through long lists of words, and to Jamie Horton and Isabel Tourneau for encouraging me to just do it. Thanks finally to Leah for your Prospero, to Adria for your Titania, to Ben for your Lysander, to Julie for the many nights of reading the comedies together, and Bev for letting me disappear so often in order to immerse myself in the world of vowels and consonants.

Pronunciation Key

Word Stress (accent) is shown with uppercase letters: /SHAYK speer/

a, ă- bat	ī- high	oy- boy
ah- mama	ih- divide	p- pay
ah^n- French sans	ĭr- mirror	r- road
air- pair	j- jump	s- so
ăir- marry	k- kill	sh- shell
a^n - French fin	l- lose	t- tea
ạr, ar- car	ł- little	ţh- that
âr- war	m- moon	t̶h̶ - thin
aw- law	n- no	U, Ŭ- but
ay- bay	ṇ- listen	u, ŭ- about
b- bad	ng- sing	ụ- bull
c, ck- duck	o- old	ü- French vu,
ch- chill	ŏ- hot	German müde
d- dead	ö- French peu, Germ.	uh- about
e- bet	Goethe	UR- fur
EE- bee	oh- boat	ur- under
ee- very	oh^n- French bon	v- vow
eer- peer	oo- mutual	w- will
ĕr- merry	o͞o- wood	wh- why
f- fill	o͞o- moon	y- yell
g, ĝ- give	oor- tour	z- zoo
h- how	or, ōr- or	zh- measure
i- bit	ow- how	

Abbreviations

THE WORKS OF SHAKESPEARE

AC	Antony and Cleopatra	MM	Measure for Measure
AW	All's Well That Ends Well	MND	A Midsummer Night's Dream
AYL	As You Like It		
Cor	Coriolanus	MV	The Merchant of Venice
CE	The Comedy of Errors	MWW	The Merry Wives of Windsor
Cym	Cymbeline		
E3	Edward III	O	Othello
Ham	Hamlet	P	Pericles
1H4	Henry IV part one	R2	Richard II
2H4	Henry IV part two	R3	Richard III
H5	Henry V	RJ	Romeo and Juliet
1H6	Henry VI part one	T	The Tempest
2H6	Henry VI part two	TA	Titus Andronicus
3H6	Henry VI part three	TC	Troilus and Cressida
H8	Henry VIII	TGV	The Two Gentlemen of Verona
J	King John		
JC	Julius Caesar	TmA	Timon of Athens
L	King Lear	TN	Twelfth Night
LLL	Love's Labor's Lost	TNK	The Two Noble Kinsmen
M	Macbeth	TS	The Taming of the Shrew
MA	Much Ado About Nothing	WT	The Winter's Tale

REFERENCE WORKS

EPD	*English Pronouncing Dictionary*	*RH2*	*Random House Dictionary, 2nd ed.*
LPD	*Longman Pronunciation Dictionary*	*W3*	*Webster's Third New International Dictionary of the English Language*
OED2	*Oxford English Dictionary, 2nd ed.*		

OTHER ABBREVIATIONS

adj.	adjective	mod.	modern
adv.	adverb	n.	noun
Am.	American	no.	number
angl.	anglicized	pl.	plural
Ang.Lat.	Anglo-Latin	prep.	preposition
App.	Appendix	Q	quarto
cf.	compare	RP	Received Pronunciation
Class.Lat.	Classical Latin		(Standard British)
CN	Canada	Shk	Shakespeare
ed.	editor	sing.	singular
F	folio	Sp.	Spanish
Fr.	French	s.v.	sub verbo (under that word)
Germ.	German	UK	United Kingdom
Gk.	Greek	US	United States
Ital.	Italian	v.	verb

Introduction

USING THE *GUIDE*

This edition of the *Guide* lists all the words in Shakespeare's most famous plays which the average college student or actor might find difficult to pronounce. The words are listed by act, scene, and line in the order they appear in each play.

> **Before turning to the individual plays readers should first become familiar with the two lists on pp. 29–36:**
>
> **"The Most Common 'Hard' Words in Shakespeare"**
> **"The Most Common Reduced Forms"**

Knowing the pronunciation of these words is an absolute prerequisite for anyone attempting to speak Shakespeare's lines. They will not be found in the scene-by-scene listings because they appear so often that including them would have meant repeating the same words many times throughout the *Guide*.

The Basic Text: *The Riverside Shakespeare*

The Riverside Shakespeare (1974) edited by G. Blakemore Evans provides the basic text, and line numbers refer to this edition.[1] However the *Guide* is intended as a companion volume for any modern text edition of Shakespeare a reader may be using. *Riverside's* line numbers will not correspond exactly to those in other editions, but they will help place a word generally and will be especially useful when a scene or play is read from beginning to end. In general, the longer a scene and the more prose passages, the greater will be the discrepancy between line numbers of different editions. In some cases the way scenes are divided will differ from edition to edition. This poses a more serious difficulty to finding the word, but it is relatively rare, and if the reader is reading the scenes in order, the words will still occur in their proper sequence. The scene divisions of one other edition, Wells and Taylor's *The Complete Oxford Shakespeare* (1987), have been included in parentheses where they differ from *Riverside*.

Of the many editions of Shakespeare's works, *Riverside* was chosen as the basic text for several reasons. First, because it is usually considered the standard text for use in critical works on Shakespeare (Thompson, et al. 1992, 16). It also serves as the basis for Marvin Spevack's *Harvard Concordance to Shakespeare* (1973), an invaluable tool in any study of Shakespeare's language. Perhaps even more important is the conservative editing. Though *Riverside* is a modern spelling text, it does not modernize as many words as most other editions. Instead, it retains what it considers legitimate older forms which may indicate distinctive Elizabethan pronuncia-

---

[1] Line numbers are the same in the second edition of *Riverside* (1997) edited by Evans and J. J. M. Tobin.

tions (*Riverside* 1974, 39). In other words, the editor is trying to make it possible for the reader to experience more of the flavor of sixteenth- and seventeenth-century English by using older forms like *murther* for *murder*, *vild* for *vile*, and *bankrout* for *bankrupt*.

> **Readers should be aware that an edition other than *Riverside* may not contain every example listed in the *Guide* because the editor may have preferred another choice at that point. However, most of these alternatives have also been included.**

Riverside has been criticized for retaining too many archaic forms which may interfere with the reader's or listener's comprehension. It has also been criticized for including many inferior line readings (S. Wells 1979, 5; S. Wells 1984, 19–20; Thompson, et al. 1992, 16). Alternative readings are listed in *Riverside's* textual notes and the *Guide* includes some of these and others proposed by various editors. Specifically, the editorial choices of *The Complete Oxford Shakespeare* (1987) have been included for nearly all entries in the *Guide*.

But again a reminder: The *Guide* lists only those archaic words or alternative readings which would puzzle the average reader. *Shrowdly* vs. *shrewdly* appears because it is not clear whether the archaic form is pronounced with /ow/ or /oh/. However, *corse* vs. *corpse* is not listed because the pronunciation in either case is clear from the spelling.

Which Words Are Included?

Shakespeare's works are full of difficult words and, naturally, the more inexperienced the reader, the greater the number of unfamiliar words he or she will confront. The words in this *Guide* were chosen based on what an average college student might find difficult. Where to draw the line inevitably requires some arbitrary decisions. Some readers will wonder why *hie* or *deign* are included, but *adage* is not. It will be impossible to satisfy everyone on this score.

In general, words were included if they fell into one of the following categories:

1. Uncommon words whose pronunciation is not evident from the spelling: *gimmal, cerements, accompt, chough*
2. More common literary words whose pronunciation varies, or which are often mispronounced: *boor, bulwark, wassail, waft, heinous, jocund*
3. Words stressed differently in current English than in the line in question: *obscure, complete, frontier, antique*
4. Proper names whose pronunciation is not evident from the spelling, or whose pronunciation varies: *Holofernes, Thetis, Dunsinane, Bianca*
5. Foreign phrases

Common words which vary in today's English, either within one country's borders or between North America and the United Kingdom, are not included (*calm, either, often, hover, accomplish*), but some are listed in Appendix A. This is an important category of words to note because the influence of Standard British is so great that sometimes Americans make the mistake of assuming that the UK forms are the only correct ones for a Shakespeare play or poem.

Notation

The aim of the *Guide* is to allow readers to produce the correct pronunciation with minimal reference to a chart containing unusual symbols and diacritic marks. For that reason the International Phonetic Alphabet is not used, since it is unfamiliar to many potential users of the *Guide*. Instead, a system similar to that used by American dictionaries has been adopted in which letter symbols are keyed to simple, unambiguous vowels and consonants (see p. xi). The major difference from dictionary notation is, that diacritic marks over vowels have been avoided as much as possible, and word stress (accent), is indicated by uppercase letters rather than by a stress mark. For example, *bruited* is given as /BROOT id/ where the /OO/ indicates the vowel of *too* and carries the stress.[2]

Variants are listed according to syllable. For example,

methinks /mee-, mih ~~TH~~INKS/

indicates that the first syllable may be either /mih-/ or /mee-/. Variants that are used less frequently are given in square brackets [ ], and those specific to the United States, Canada, or the United Kingdom are indicated where appropriate.

One of the difficulties in writing a pronunciation guide for the English language is that there is no universally accepted standard on which to base it. Even within Standard British, which has been defined sound by sound and given the name Received Pronunciation (RP), there are accepted variations that reflect distinctive accents (J. C. Wells 1982, 2:279). This makes it difficult for a pronunciation guide to be accurate, comprehensive, and efficient at the same time. If the International Phonetic Alphabet were used, each national or regional variant would have to be listed for each word (cf. *LPD*), but using the key-word notation usually makes a more

---

[2] Since the goal is for the reader to be able to deduce a word's pronunciation correctly, the same sound may be symbolized in two different ways if it will increase the reader's likelihood of producing the correct pronunciation. /s/ in *gratis* is symbolized with a double *s*, /GRAT iss/, because if the final syllable were written /is/ readers might say /iz/. In other cases, primarily at the beginning of words, the single /s/ can be used unambiguously.

A diacritc mark is sometimes placed over or under a vowel to avoid ambiguity. For example, in a word like *bulwark*, there are two possibilities for the first syllable. The transcription /BUL work/ is ambiguous so diacritics are added: /BŬL wurk/ indicates the vowel of *dull*, and /BULL-/ is used for the variant with the vowel of *bull*.

Syllable division may seem inconsistent, but again the chief goal is to elicit the desired pronunciation. The various pronunciations of *adieu* are written with syllable breaks in different places (/uh DYOO, ad YOO /), with primary consideration given to avoiding potentially confusing notations like /a DYOO/ where a reader would be left wondering which value to give /a/ by itself.

efficient entry possible without sacrificing accuracy. Speakers will simply substitute the sounds of the key words as they normally pronounce them in whatever dialect they speak. This approach makes the *Guide* accessible to speakers anywhere in the English-speaking world, as long as care is taken in the choice of key words.

Pronunciation Variants within the United States

In a word like *apricot,* different vowels are used in different regions of the United States (/AYP rih kŏt/ vs. /AP rih kŏt/). Both sounds exist in the repertories of each group, but historical and social considerations have caused one to be favored over the other, giving rise to regional variation. Other examples of this sort are *bath* with the vowel of *bat* in most parts of America, and /ah/ in Standard British and parts of New England; *greasy* has /s/ in the northern and western United States and /z/ in the South. Americans living along the East Coast and in parts of the South pronounce words like *Morris, historical, Horace* with the vowel of *car*, while most other Americans use /or/. More and more Americans are pronouncing the /l/ in *calm, palm,* etc., but many speakers retain the older /l/-less pronunciation. These differences occur in a variety of common words and are important to note, especially for actors and directors who may not realize that theirs is a regional pronunciation, and consequently either less or more acceptable depending on their intended audience. The *Guide* points out some of these differences in common words in Appendix A, but variant forms are only included in the scene-by-scene lists for literary or unusual words like *lazar, satyr,* or *orison,* and it is usually difficult to ascertain whether a speaker's regional origin plays a role in these variations.

In some cases where a regional phonological feature is common to a category of words, geographical notations are made in the lists. The southern United States tends to preserve the glide /y/ in words like *duke, new, tune* (/dyo͞ok/, etc.) and this is carried over into some listed words like *importune.* Some speakers from eastern New England use the vowel /ah/ in *mask, bath, half,* and this applies to *masque, blasphemy,* etc. in the lists. On the eastern coast of the United States there are a number of vowel sounds before /r/ followed by another vowel which differ from the rest of the country and must be taken into account (*Harry: hairy* have different vowels on the East Coast, but are the same for most Americans). It should be noted, however, that regional factors are constantly changing, and when a variant in the *Guide* is given a label like "Eastern New England," the implication is not that all speakers from that area would use the given pronunciation, only that many do.

How the Pronunciations Were Determined

The pronunciations listed in this *Guide* were researched in two ways. First, the words were checked in the following dictionaries:

American
A Pronouncing Dictionary of American English, 1953
Webster's Third New International Dictionary, 1961
The Random House Dictionary, 2nd ed., 1987
The American Heritage Dictionary, 3rd ed., 1992

British
English Pronouncing Dictionary, 12th and 14th eds., 1964, 1988
Collins Cobuild English Language Dictionary, 1987
The Oxford English Dictionary, 2nd ed., 1989
Longman Pronunciation Dictionary, 1990, which contains both American and British pronun-
  ciations.
BBC English Dictionary, 1992

Those words which were not listed in any of these sources were checked in *Webster's New International Dictionary* (1934) and in Worcester's *A Universal Critical
and Pronouncing Dictionary of the English Language* (1856), both of which contain
many obscure Shakespearean entries.

A significant number of words are listed in these sources as having variant pronunciations. Sometimes they indicate that the differences are American vs. British.
Especially valuable in this regard is the *Longman Pronunciation Dictionary* (1990),
though at times the American entries are inaccurate.[3] In most dictionaries, however,
variants are simply listed without comment.

In order to ascertain whether these variant pronunciations still have any currency,
a survey was conducted of college professors of Shakespeare in the United States,
Canada, and the United Kingdom, asking them in a questionnaire how they would
recommend pronouncing these words and some others that were listed without variation in the dictionaries.[4] This was supplemented by a smaller survey of dramaturges
and literary consultants at theatres and drama schools in North America specializing
in Shakespeare performances. In addition, surveys were conducted via email discus-
sion groups which included classicists, historians, and professors of literature.[5]

---

[3] For example, *anybody* is listed only with /-bŏd ee/, omitting the common pronunciation
/-bŭd ee/. /ketch/ for *catch* is listed as non-standard, and words beginning with *wh-* are said to
be pronounced /hw/ in General American (770), a statement based on data that is now out of
date (Dale Coye, "A Linguistic Survey of College Freshmen: Keeping up with Standard
American English, " *American Speech* 69 (Fall 1994): 260–284.

[4] Ideally surveys would have also been conducted in other English-speaking countries, particularly Australia and New Zealand, but it was logistically difficult. Then too, once you begin
to report by nation, it is hard to know which countries to leave out. South Africa, India, and
Ireland, all deserve to be counted as well.

[5] The Carnegie Foundation for the Advancement of Teaching's *Classification of Institutions of
Higher Learning* (Princeton, 1994) was used as a base document to select American colleges
and universities for the main postal survey. After excluding specialty colleges (agriculture,
technology, the arts) every seventh college was selected from the lists in the following categories: Research Universities I and II, Doctoral Universities I and II, Master's Colleges and Universities I, Baccalaureate Colleges I. Telephone calls to those institutions determined the

Words that were included in any of these surveys are indicated by an asterisk. The results show that some variations in pronunciation are still in force, but others listed in the dictionaries appear to be extinct. In other cases pronunciations not listed in any source books are being used with great frequency.

When Is a Variant Pronunciation "Wrong"?

This raises the question of mispronunciation. Should every pronunciation found in the surveys (hereafter referred to as the Survey) or in a dictionary be listed and accorded the status of a correct, acceptable pronunciation? In other words, does the fact that somewhere a professor of English pronounces a word in a given way, define it as Standard English, or can they sometimes be "wrong"?

There are different schools of thought on mispronunciation. Some would have us believe that there are strict standards of pronunciation, defined by language experts and listed in source books that should serve as bibles to the uninformed. Others believe that the whole notion of what constitutes a mispronunciation is relative. *Webster's Third* defined standard speech in a way that has been largely accepted by American dictionary-makers. It rejected the idea of a single standard of pronunciation for the United States as a whole and defined the standard speech in any area as that used by a "sufficient number of cultivated speakers" (1961, 38a). In other words, when large numbers of well-educated people from Syracuse say *orange pajamas* as /ornj puh JAM uz/, while those in New York City say /AHR inj puh JAH muz/, neither group is incorrect. There are a number of words that vary in this way from region to region in the United States, and even more that differ between North American and British English (see Appendix A).

Orange is a word used regularly in daily life and the variations in its pronunciation

---

name of a professor teaching Shakespeare. In the United States 107 questionnaires were sent and 38 returned. A similar method was used for Canadian and British universities, with 12 questionnaires returned from Canada, and 19 from the UK (the source for the Canadian lists was the *Directory of Canadian Universities,* 29th ed., Association of Universities and Colleges of Canada, and for the UK *Commonwealth Universities Yearbook 1993,* Association of Commonwealth Universities). These numbers include only professors who are still teaching in the country where they learned English. Respondents' years of birth ranged from 1925 to 1966, with over one-third of the informants in each country falling in the years 1939–43. Over 300 words were asked in the US and UK surveys and slightly fewer for Canada. Because the word list was so long, it was divided seven ways (with some overlap) and distributed, with an additional 25 words of special interest sent to all informants. It was more difficult to engage the theatres, with only 7 responses from places such as the Stratford Festival in Ontario, New York's Public Theatre, and Julliard.

The email respondents came from various lists which serve as forums for professors, grad students, and others with an interest in the specific subject areas. For example, 38 names like *Atropos, Charon* were submitted to the classics list (asking for the pronunciation they would recommend if the name appeared in a work of English literature). Twenty-six responded from the US, 3 from Canada, and 7 from the UK. The 18th-century list was asked 50 literary words like *augury, environ, prerogative.* Forty-five responded from the US, 8 from Canada, and 13 from the UK.

arose through normal linguistic change, the same sorts of changes that created the differences between Old, Middle, and Modern English as the entire sound system shifted in various ways over the centuries, forming dialect regions that are sometimes radically different from each other. Book words—words that are found most often in writing but are rarely spoken—change as well but in a somewhat different way. When the communal memory of a word's pronunciation has been lost, or when speakers who have never heard a book word pronounced attempt it, then spelling will play a key role in determining the new pronunciation.

Bade is a case in point. This was once a much more commonly used word than it is today and was pronounced /bad/. In most dictionaries in the early part of the twentieth century this was the only pronunciation given, but at that time, as people became increasingly literate and the standard pronunciation faded from the collective memory, /bayd/, based on spelling and in existence for at least a century, rapidly gained ground. The Survey shows that in the United States /bayd/ is rarely used by those professors born before 1940 but is preferred by half of those born after that date. In keeping with this change among educated speakers, about twenty years ago dictionaries began to include /bayd/ alongside /bad/, it being now deemed an acceptable standard pronunciation, though some traditionalists would disagree.

Another word of this sort is *gyves* /jīvz/ 'fetters,' which was originally pronounced with /g/, not /j/. As the word fell out of use after the Elizabethan era, a new pronunciation based on the spelling arose and completely conquered the field by the end of the nineteenth century (*OED2*, s.v.). Similarly *avoirdupois* is listed as /AV ur duh poiz/ in many current dictionaries, but recently a bevy of spelling pronunciations based on French has made the older pronunciation obsolete.

Sometimes spelling pronunciations are applied to whole categories of words, for example, those ending in *-or*. *Mentor, orator* and other words of this class that are not commonly used in day-to-day life (including "Shakespearean" words like *servitor, proditor, paritor*) are often pronounced on- and off-stage with /-or/, but the traditional pronunciation is /-ur/, as found in most of our common words ending in *-or* (*actor, instructor, doctor*). Another example is found in a group of words containing *th*. *Apothecary, Arthur, author* were loaned into English from French with /t/, but sometime after the Elizabethan era were changed to /th/ because of their spelling (Kökeritz 1953, 320).

Conservatives often have little patience with spelling pronunciations. Spain calls the pronunciation of *bade* as /bayd/ a "gross mispronunciation" and deplores the practice in modern dictionaries of simply listing without comment the pronunciations which exist, even those "not worthy" of use (1988, 201, 210). Kökeritz scorned the spelling pronunciation of *Jaques* as /JAY kweez/ or as /JAY kwiz/, stating unequivocally that the pronunciation Shakespeare intended was /JAY kis/ (1959, 3). Despite his pronouncements /JAY kweez/ still dominates today.

The point for readers of Shakespeare is that there will always be an argument brewing over how certain words are pronounced. Conservatives and purists, looking to the history of the word, condemn spelling pronunciations outright and would have the reader adhere to traditional forms. On the other hand, many listeners will be unfamiliar with traditional pronunciations like /bad/, and may even believe that the performer is saying the word wrong.

The *Guide* reports which pronunciations are currently most in favor based on the Survey, pointing out which are traditional and which innovations based on spelling or analogy. Tension will always exist because the language changes and in some cases the choice between variants must be left to the reader. However, some basic guidelines can be set down. *Heinous*, for example, has traditionally been pronounced /HAY nus/ and is exclusively cited this way in nearly every dictionary,[6] but a small number of highly educated individuals, including professors from both sides of the Atlantic, use a newer pronunciation /HEE nus/. Generally a new pronunciation of a word based on spelling, like /HEE nus/, is subject to a collective displeasure in its infancy from those who pronounce it in the traditional way. In other words, if only a small segment of the educated population says /HEE nus/ it is easier to label it a mispronunciation. Those speakers who use the new pronunciation might agree that they were guessing from the spelling, and try to conform to the traditional form. Certainly high school students go through this process with some regularity in words like *epitome* which many meet first in print and pronounce /EP ih tohm/.

However, as more and more speakers use a new pronunciation, or as it acquires a base within a specific group (speakers within a geographic area, or younger speakers, for example), it becomes more difficult to call it incorrect. There comes a time when the linguist, if not the purist, must admit that a significant percentage of educated speakers does indeed say /bayd/ for *bade* and acknowledge it as an acceptable variant.

On the other hand, it is difficult to label fading traditional pronunciations incorrect until they are completely extinct. It is now possible to say that using a "hard" /g/ for *gyves* is wrong, but even if only one percent of the country were to say /bad/ for *bade*, would we be justified in calling it incorrect when it is the older, standard pronunciation? The *Guide*'s goal in these cases is to make the speaker aware that the conflict exists, and that until /bad/ disappears completely, it must still be considered acceptable. Using the *Guide*, readers can chose variants themselves.

However, the *Guide* offers some recommendations, generally urging readers to avoid newer, relatively rare, spelling pronunciations. /HAY nus/ is recommended, /HEE nus/ is not, which is another way of saying that the vast majority of educated speakers consider it non-standard.[7] Among other pronunciations not recommended are *doth* and *dost* with /ŏ/, and *choler* as /KOH lur/, all used by some of the professors in the Survey. Further, when an archaic word like *phthisic* has a wide variety of pronunciations, most of them based on guesswork from the spelling, tradition should be the deciding factor, making /TIZ ik/ the choice. Similarly when the educated community is divided over words like *bade, quietus,* and *liege,* the weight of history should tip the scales in favor of /bad/, /kwī EE tus/, and /leej/ for the student or actor trying to decide which pronunciation to use.

A final note is needed on RP (Received Pronunciation), the British standard pronunciation. Half a century ago RP had an undisputed prestige in England and was used in all formal situations, including Shakespeare recitations and performances.

---

[6] The exceptions are *W3* which lists "sometimes" /HEE nus/ or /HĪ nus/ and *LPD* which lists as non-standard /HEE nus/ and as incorrect /HAY nee us/.

[7] Though apparently in the UK the majority is not so vast. The Survey showed that in that country 4 out of 11 professors were using /HEE-/; in the US only 1 out of 17.

Daniel Jones's *English Pronouncing Dictionary* was the final arbiter on what was RP and what was not, today supplemented by the *Longman Pronunciation Dictionary* and others. Recently the situation has changed for Standard British as many regional features have crept into the sound system, creating variants that previously did not exist. Judging from the results of the Survey, many of the most highly educated members of society—the professors, lecturers and instructors at universities—use what *EPD* and *LPD* consider non-RP forms of English. To give two examples, the RP form of *satyr* is /SAT ur/ according to *LPD* and *EPD14,* but 30 percent of the professors surveyed from the UK say /SAY tur/. These dictionaries also report that the final syllable of *plantain* is RP /-tin/, but five out of six professors say /-tayn/. Perhaps the question, "what is the RP form" is of diminishing interest to the educated Briton. As in North America, the question should be: "what pronunciations are now being used by educated speakers, and are they different from older standard forms?" The *Guide* will indicate these discrepancies where they occur, again leaving the choice to the British reader.

Mannered Pronunciations and the Influence of British English in North America

Speaking Shakespeare's verse demands clear articulation, however there is a danger of going too far. For example, there is a tendency, sometimes encouraged by vocal coaches, to replace normal weak, unstressed vowels with full vowels in inappropriate places. In the United States *offend, opinion, official* are normally /uh FEND/, /uh PIN yun/, etc, yet in the theatre it is not uncommon to hear /oh FEND/, /oh PIN yun/. Other examples occur in words like *condemn, contempt*, pronounced with /kŏn-/ rather than normal /kun-/, *provide, pronounce* with /proh-/ rather than /pruh-/,[8] and *capitol* with /-tŏl/ instead of /-tł/. These are "mannered" or "stage" pronunciations. The speaker is altering the usual pronunciation of these words toward his or her perception of a correct standard of speech—a standard which in fact is used by virtually no one in real life. Mannered speech also affects some "Shakespearean" words. The final syllable of *recreant* and *miscreant* should be /-unt/, but actors sometimes use /-ant/ (cf. *important, significant, defiant*). *Vizard* should rhyme with *wizard*, yet it is sometimes given the vowel of *hard*. If no one but an actor says /oh POHZ/, then that pronunciation is an affectation and should be avoided (unless of course the actor is trying to make the character sound affected—Malvolio, for instance).[9]

There is a related problem specific to North America where Standard British (RP) has enormous influence when it comes to Shakespeare. Because recordings and films of Shakespeare's works are almost invariably produced with British actors us-

---

[8] *LPD* lists /kŏn-/ in these words as a non-RP form. It also labels *offend, provide* with /oh-/, /proh-/ as non-RP pronunciations.

[9] Note however that some unstressed vowels do vary normally. In American English *enough, eleven* may begin with either /ee-/ or /ih-/. Certain prefixes like *ex-* (*extend, explore*) vary between /eks-/ and a reduced form /iks-/.

ing RP, American actors, from superstars to neophytes, consciously or unconsciously, alter their pronunciation toward the British. It is very common to hear college students shifting to British accents, sometimes without realizing it, when reading Shakespeare. Some of these shifts are encouraged by speech teachers or directors in the name of "good" pronunciation, despite the fact that American pronunciations have as rightful a claim to historical legitimacy as their British counterparts. In acting schools in both North America and the United Kingdom actors are sometimes taught what is called a Mid-Atlantic Accent. This refers to a sort of pronunciation that is neither British nor North American, that is to say, an attempt is made to neutralize regional features to the point where an audience is unable to tell where the actor is from. It is certainly possible to cover up native speech patterns to a degree, but if an American actor starts moving his pronunciation in the direction of RP the audience will very likely be aware of it, and the effect is often a very stagey one. Some of the changes that American actors make in the direction of British are

1. Changing the vowel in *bath, ask, can't* etc. to /ah/. Often American amateur actors go too far, making the change in the wrong places, for example, in *can, and, had.*
2. Adding the glide /y/ in words like *new* /ny$\overline{oo}$/, *duke* /dy$\overline{oo}$k/, *tune* /ty$\overline{oo}$n/, *lute* /ly$\overline{oo}$t/,[10] instead of using the usual /n$\overline{oo}$, d$\overline{oo}$k/ etc.
3. /t/ between voiced sounds: The following pairs are homonyms in normal American English but not in British: *metal : medal, butting : budding*, and *letter* rhymes with *redder*. Yet on the stage or in readings Americans will usually pronounce the /t/ as the British would: unvoiced, with a slight puff of air.
4. Most importantly, the loss of /r/ at the end of a word or before a consonant. *Bark, far, ear, sure* are changed to /bahk/, /fah/, /ih-uh/, /sh$\overline{oo}$-uh/.[11]

Unless the play is being staged in a British setting (one of the histories for instance) with deliberately British accents, there is no reason American performers should alter any of their ordinary American vowel and consonant sounds, as long as they are following the patterns of the "cultivated" speakers in their region. Even in the case of a history play there is a good argument for using the North American accent. For if we are to lend color to the play by using British accents to portray British subjects, should we then use Scottish accents in *Macbeth* or Italian accents in *Romeo and Juliet*? We are not pronouncing the words as Shakespeare did in any case, nor did Shakespeare write in the language used by King John, or Richard II.

---

[10] In everyday American English /ny$\overline{oo}$, dy$\overline{oo}$k/, etc. are usually heard only in the South and even there it is becoming less frequent, see Betty S. Phillips, "Southern English Glide Deletion Revisited, " *American Speech* 69 (Summer 1994): 115–127. Elocutionists sometimes insist on the glide for the classical theatre, but it makes little sense to say /dy$\overline{oo}$k/ on the stage and /d$\overline{oo}$k/ in real life. /ly$\overline{oo}$-/ was once standard in the UK as well and used for the classics. Today however, many *lu-* words like *Luke, Lucy, Lucifer, lunacy* are no longer normally pronounced with /ly$\overline{oo}$-/ in Standard British, but simply as /l$\overline{oo}$-/, though some RP speakers may use /ly$\overline{oo}$-/ in other *lu-* words like *lubricate, lucid, lucrative, illuminate, lute,* and according to *LPD*, especially *lure, lurid,* and *alluring* (see the British dictionaries listed in the references, s.vv.).

[11] In some American dialects—parts of New York City, eastern New England, and the South—/r/ does not occur in these positions, but the vast majority of Americans naturally use /r/ and should do so on stage.

The audience is being asked to suspend disbelief and there is no reason why the American, Canadian, Australian, Irish, or South African languages may not serve as the medium as well as Standard British.

Lost Rhymes and Puns

> He is gone, he is gone,
> And we cast away moan (Ham 4.5.197–98)

When an Elizabethan Ophelia sang this song this was a true rhyme, probably with *gone* pronounced with the vowel of *go,* though *moan* may have been shortened (Cercignani 1981, 115). There are many other instances in Shakespeare of word pairs that no longer rhyme in modern English because of a shift in vowel sounds: *love-prove, come-doom, food-good-flood.* Some of these rhymes may have been only eye rhymes even in Shakespeare's day, poetic fossils from an earlier era (Kökeritz 1953, 31). Besides ignoring them and pronouncing the word in the modern manner, the reader is left with few options. In some cases it may be possible to nudge different vowels toward each other. For example, in the lines:

> He who the sword of heaven will bear
> Should be as holy as severe; (MM 3.2. 261–62)

it is not too difficult to alter the pronunciation of *bear* toward *severe* and vice-versa.

In other cases there is little the performer can do. For example, one of the most common types of rhyme in Shakespeare is illustrated in these lines:

> My ear should catch your voice, my eye your eye,
> My tongue should catch your tongue's sweet melody.
> (MND 1.1.188–89)

Nouns ending in *-y* and adverbs and adjectives in *-ly* were rhymed with either /ī/ or with /ee/ by Shakespeare, exhibiting a variation that goes back to Middle or even Old English. In the example given, presumably the Elizabethan performer would have said /MEL uh dī/, but today on stage, words in this class are always given their normal, modern pronunciation, and the rhyme is lost.

A similar problem affects some puns which are hopelessly lost because of pronunciation shifts. The following lines lose their resonance because the noun *ache* has lost its pronunciation as /aytch/, common until the eighteenth century:

> I had a wound here that was like a T,
> But now 'tis made an H. (AC 4.7.7–8)

In the *Guide* only those puns which require explanations will be pointed out, for example, *Person: pierce-one* LLL 4.2.82–84 (see Kökeritz 1953, 86–157 for a thorough description of puns in Shakespeare).

Proper Names

Many of the entries for proper names given in earlier glossaries are now out of date. For example, nearly every sourcebook gives *Laertes* as /lay UR teez/. This is indeed the traditional form, however the Survey found that two-thirds of American college professors today use /lay AIR teez/, a partially "restored" pronunciation (see p. 13). Comparing entries in Kökeritz's *Shakespeare's Names* (1959) to the current survey reveals a number of other differences, for example:

Table 1
Recommendations for the Pronunciation of Proper Names

	Kökeritz, 1959	Majority of UK professors in the current survey	Majority of US professors in the current survey
Adonis	/uh DOHN iss/	/uh DOHN iss/	/uh DŎN iss/
Bianca	/bee ANG kuh/	/bee ANG kuh/	/bee AHNG kuh/
Bolingbrook	/BŲLL ing brŏŏk, BŎL-/	/BŎL ling brŏŏk/	/BOHL ing brŏŏk, BŲLL-, BŎL-/
Dr. Caius	/keez/	/KĪ us/	/KAY us/
Dunsinane	/dun sih NAYN/	/DUN sih nayn/	/DUN sih nayn/
Eros	/EER ŏss, ĒR-/	/EER ŏss, ĔR ŏss, ĔR ohss/	/ĔR ŏss, -ohss/
Fleance	/FLEE unss/	/FLEE unss, FLAY-/	/FLEE ahnss, FLAY unss/

Probably as long as Shakespeare has been in print certain names have been given variant pronunciations. The *Guide* sorts through the variants and offers a truer picture of how these names are pronounced today. At the beginning of each play are two lists entitled "People in the Play" and "Places in the Play." Here the reader will find only those names which pose a difficulty for the average native speaker. The lists include names from the cast of characters, frequently mentioned places, and people not in the cast who are mentioned throughout the play.

Foreign Words and Phrases

Latin, Italian, and French words and phrases are common in the plays. Some guidance is given on how to pronounce these words, but the notation is unable to capture the sounds of these languages completely. The reader or actor must also bear in mind how the character speaking these lines would pronounce the phrase.

Pistol would probably pronounce French very badly, King Henry V might speak it better, and the Frenchmen and Frenchwomen perfectly. French pronunciations are often given without indication of word stress because in that language stress is variable. So if *Gerard de Narbon* is to be pronounced as in French in its only verse instance (AW 2.1.101), then *Gerard* could be stressed on either the first or second syllable and is given as /zhay rahr/. The meter dictates however that *Narbon* must be stressed on the first syllable, written as /NAHR boh^n/.

The pronunciation of Latin words is especially problematic. Up until the beginning of the twentieth century the normal pronunciation taught in all Latin classes and used by all English-speaking scholars was an anglicized Latin which was quite different from both classical Latin and that spoken on the continent (Allen 1978, 102–8). This Anglo-Latin has a long history dating from Middle English. It took part in the regular sound changes of English and is still used in many of the more common Latin names today, for example, *Caesar* /SEE zur/, *Cato* /KAY toh/, *Titus* /TĪ tus/. Latin phrases were commonly pronounced as though they were English: The tombstone inscription *hic jacet* (AW 3.6.62–63), 'here lies' in Anglo-Latin, was always /hick JAY sit/, while in classical Latin it would have been /heek YAH ket/.

At the end of the nineteenth century scholars began a campaign to rehabilitate these wayward vowels and consonants, claiming that, for example, that part of the brain known as the *pia mater* should no longer be /PĪ uh MAY tur/ as it had been for centuries, but /PEE ah MAH tĕr/, the pronunciation which was probably used in ancient Rome. The restoration of classical Latin sounds has been a great force in the last hundred years and has resulted in two competing pronunciations for Latin words, each with its own legitimacy. Sometimes there is a notable difference between North America and the UK, especially in the treatment of unstressed syllables. Names like *Lucius, Cassius, Ephesians,* and *Pallas* are most commonly /LOO shus, CASH us, ih FEE zhunz, PAL us/ in the United States, reflecting the normal development of these sounds in English (cf. *vicious, fictitious, vision, terrace*), while the majority of speakers in the United Kingdom have either tenaciously held on to forms from Middle and Early Modern English (and ultimately classical Latin or Greek) or restored them recently to /LOO see us, CASS ee us, ih FEE zhee unz, PAL äss/. To the American ear many of these restored forms sound overly precise or even bizarre.

Many of these words also show mixed forms with one syllable retaining an Anglo-Latin vowel, while the other has acquired the classical Latin. For example, the goddess *Ate* is traditionally /AY tee/, or in its restored form /AH tay/, but /AH tee/ was sometimes reported in the Survey as well. Similarly *quietus*, whose traditional form is /kwī EE tus/, sometimes has its second syllable restored but not its first: /kwī AY tus/. To add to the confusion, church Latin, based on the Italian version of classical Latin, is widely known in English-speaking countries through its use in singing. Choral groups are taught to say *excellcis*, for example, as /eks CHEL seess/, and many would guess that *hic jacet* should therefore be /heek YAH chet/.

The main point to be made is that using a restored, classical Latin pronunciation is not the only correct way to pronounce these words. For one thing, the reforms have not really restored the classical Latin sounds precisely. Typically only those sounds which already exist in English are used. Further, it is unthinkable to go back to the past and transform all the Latin words in English into their ancient Roman forms. This would mean altering words like *Caesar* to /KĪ sahr/. The reader must again decide what would be appropriate for the character speaking the lines, keeping in mind the audience's expectations. But again, the Anglo-Latin forms have the weight of an older tradition behind them, so when all else is equal, the recommendation is to choose the pre-restoration pronunciations for all names. Latin phrases are probably best pronounced as in classical Latin, at least in the United States.

French names in English also have a history of anglicization. Some of our common pronunciations of the French names that appear in Shakespeare are fully anglicized (*Paris, Verdun*), others only in part. Today, however, there is a tendency to pronounce some of these words with a full French pronunciation. This also applies to common English words that "feel" French. *Liege,* for example, is now most commonly heard in the United States as /leezh/, as in French, whereas *siege* is usually pronounced /seej/, though both share the same lineage. Other words of this sort are *nonpareil, adieu,* and *denier,* which in traditional English should be /nŏn puh REL, uh DYOO/, and /DEN yur/ or /duh NEER/,

Italian names also appear frequently in Shakespeare's plays. Some are typically pronounced as in Italian, while others have anglicized vowels: *Tranio* always has Italian /AH/, but in the United Kingdom *Bianca* usually is heard in its anglicized form /bee ANK uh/. Some directors prefer to give all names their modern Italian pronunciations. In that case a name like *Vincentio* becomes /veen CHEN tsee oh/, rather than the traditional /vin SEN shee yoh/. Both forms are listed in the *Guide*. Again it should be repeated that it is impossible to reproduce all of the phonetic nuances of a foreign language using the notation of this volume, or any other broad notation for that matter. For that reason the long French scenes in *Henry V* are not included. The best course for a performer who wants to pronounce these lines accurately is to consult a native speaker of that language.

Regional, Foreign, and Lower-Class Accents

Making fun of people with foreign accents was as popular in the Elizabethan era as it is today. Perhaps the most famous example in Shakespeare is the argument over the art of war in *Henry V* between the Scot, Jamie, the Irishman, MacMorris, and the Welshman, Fluellen. These accents are hinted at in Shakespeare's spelling, but by no means does he provide all the clues an actor would need to reproduce the dialect fully. Providing a notation for a regional or foreign accent is beyond the scope of this *Guide*. However some tips are given at the appropriate section in the line-by-line guide in order to help the reader decipher some of the spellings used in the text.

It is common on recordings and films of Shakespeare's plays to hear the kings, queens and courtiers speaking Standard British while the clowns and riff-raff speak with a Cockney or regional British accent. Again the reader should consider the play and the character. The gravedigger in *Hamlet* is a Dane, and since we are asking the audience to use its imagination and accept English as the language of communication, it should be able to accept American as well as British. In the United States there are also lower- and upper-class accents, and the pronunciation can be tailored to the character.   In any case Shakespeare provides only hints of these characters' accents which the actor or reader must then fill out in order to correctly reproduce whatever style of speech has been chosen.

ALTERING MODERN PRONUNCIATION TO FIT THE VERSE

Shakespeare wrote some scenes of his plays in prose, but most of them are written in verse using iambic pentameter as the metrical form.   The iamb is a weakly stressed syllable followed by a strongly stressed one.   Each iamb creates a foot, with generally five feet per line (*penta*—Greek 'five').   The normal iambic pentameter line can be illustrated using x to represent a weak stress and / a strong stress:

> x / x / x / x / x /
> The law hath yet another hold on you (MV 4.2.345)

> x / x / x / x / x /
> O, pardon me, thou bleeding piece of earth (JC 3.1.254)

There are several good studies available on reading iambic verse.[12]   For the purposes of pronunciation, it is important to recognize that the rhythmic requirements of these verse lines sometimes demand a pronunciation change for certain words, either by shifting the main stress to a different syllable, compressing the word, or adding an extra syllable.   In order to understand when these alterations should be made it is first necessary to become familiar with some of the common variations to the basic iambic pentameter line. [13]

Variations of the Basic Iambic Pentameter Line

1. **Inversion** of a foot, in which the strong stress precedes the weak one.   It may occur anywhere in the line except in the last foot where it is very rare, and it must be followed by a normal iambic foot with a strong final stress.   In other words, the inverted foot and the following foot form the pattern strong-weak-weak-strong.   Inversion is especially common in the first foot:

> / x   x / x / x / x /
> *Conscience* is but a word that cowards use (R3 5.3.309)
> *Dying* with mother's dug between its lips (2H6 3.2.393)

---

[12] Linklater 1992 and Wright 1988 are among the best.   The most important precept is beautifully summed up by Linklater: "The iambic pentameter is a pulse; it is the heartbeat of Shakespeare's poetry.   Like your pulse it does not keep a steady, dull pace; it races with excitement, dances with joy or terror, slows down in contemplation. . . . There is nothing mechanical about the rhythms of great poetry.   If they seem mechanical, *you* have made them so" (140).

[13]   See Sipe 1968, 32–35; Wright 1985, 366–67; Spain 1988, 10–21, 47–61 and especially Wright 1988, 116–206 for more details on these and other variations.

Here the fourth foot is inverted:

> That were our royal faiths *martyrs* in love (2H4 4.1.191)

However, if it occurs in the middle of a line it is most commonly found after a pause, as in this line with two inversions, one in the first foot, and one in the third:

> *Tamer* than sleep, *fonder* than ignorance (TC 1.1.10)

2. Some lines have an extra weak syllable at the end, the **feminine ending** or **double ending**:

> x /   x   /   x /   x /   x   / x
> How ill white hairs becomes a fool and jester! (2H4 5.5.48)

3. A **caesura**[14] is a break in mid-line, often, but not always, indicated by punctuation. Sometimes the regular iambic rhythm is not affected by the break:

> x   /   x/ x   / x / x   /
> O damn'd Iago! O inhuman dog! (O 5.1.62)

In other cases the caesura may be preceded and followed by a weak stress, giving the line two weak stresses in a row and eleven syllables instead of the usual ten. This is called an **epic caesura**. Its effect is to create a feminine ending before the break, with the iambic rhythm resuming on a weak stress with the next phrase:

> x   /   x / x   x   / x   / x   /
> Observe my uncle.   If his occulted guilt . . . (Ham 3.2.80)

>   x   / x   / x   / x   x   / x   /
> For by the dreadful Pluto,   if thou dost not . . . (TC 4.4.127)

4. Some lines have twelve syllables, producing six feet, a **hexameter**. This is also called an **alexandrine**:[15]

> x   /   x   /   x   /   x   / x   / x   /
> Coy looks with heart-sore sighs; one fading moment's mirth
>   (TGV 1.1.30)

Sometimes the fifth strong stress is followed by two weak stresses. This is not strictly speaking a hexameter, but a **triple ending**.

---

[14] US /sih ZOOR uh/; UK /-ZYOOR-/; *also* /-ZHOOR-/ in both countries.
[15] /heck SAM ih tur/; /al ig ZAN drin/ is the oldest pronunciation; /drīn/, /dreen/ are newer and more common.

```
x   / x  /   x    / x / x   / x x
```
And for I know thou'rt full of love and *honesty* (O 3.3.118)

It often occurs in lines ending in a name (*Angelo, Horatio, Octavia, Cassio*) and it may indicate that the two final weak syllables were meant to be reduced to one (/ANJ loh, huh RAY shyoh, ŏk TAYV yuh, KASS yoh/). The same is true of words like *courtier*, which in modern English is usually pronounced with three syllables, but can easily be reduced to two (and must be in many other instances in Shakespeare that occur in the middle of a line):

```
x    / x  /   /   x   x   / x  /  (x)x
```
Oh worthy fool! One that hath been a courtier (AYL 2.7.36)

5. There are also **short lines**, which come in different variations and lengths, including shared lines which together make up a complete line of iambic pentameter:

```
         /    x  x /
```
Cornwall: Bind him, I say.

```
            x    /    x / x   / x
```
Regan: Hard, hard. O filthy traitor! (L 3.7.32)

6. Omission of a syllable including
   a. **headless lines**, which do not contain the first, unstressed syllable. These   are relatively rare in Shakespeare:

```
   /   x  / x  / x / x  / x
```
They were all in lamentable cases (LLL 5.2.273)

Note *lamentable* in its usual UK form.

   b. **broken-backed lines**, which lack an unstressed syllable after a caesura:

```
                      . . . the hour prefix'd . . .
   x    /  x /    /   x  / x   / x
```
Comes fast upon. Good my brother Troilus (TC 4.3.1–3)

7. Verse that is not iambic pentameter is also used, for example, in a long section of Act 3 Scene 1 of *The Comedy of Errors* written with four beats to the line:

```
   x   x    /   x(x)  /    x   /(x)  x  x   /
```
I should kick, being kick'd, and being   at that pass,

```
   x    x    /   x   x  /   x   x /   x x  /
```
You would keep from my heels, and beware of an ass. (CE 3.1.17–18)

8. Shakespeare sometimes includes an **anapest** /AN uh pest/ (two weak stresses followed by a strong one in a single foot) among the iambic feet. This, however, is
rare. Line 55 below could be scanned in two ways: with an anapest in either the
third foot (slightly stressing *with* and *craft*) or in the fourth (stressing *you* and *craft*):

> . . . she purpos'd,
> By watching, weeping, tendance, kissing, to
> O'ercome you with her show, and in time
> *(When she had fitted you with her craft) to work*
> Her son into th' adoption of the crown (Cym 5.5.52–56)

Once in a great while a line begins with two weak syllables:

> I am a subject,
> x   x / x   /   x / x /   x /   x
> And I challenge law. Attorneys are denied me (R2 2.3.133–34)

However, usually lines that seem to contain anapests have extra syllables which
were meant to be compressed to fit the iambic shape (see p. 19).

Shifting the Stress of a Word to Maintain the Iambic Rhythm

Shakespeare stressed some of his words differently than we do today.   If the
words occur in prose passages, there is usually no difficulty in maintaining our modern pronunciation. But if they appear in verse, the meter demands an adjustment
from our current pronunciation. Sometimes in the process the words are transformed
so much that recognition becomes difficult for an audience. Today *revenue* is
stressed on the first syllable, and in North America is pronounced /REV uh noo/ or
in the South /REV uh nyoo/, but in Shakespeare's verse it is sometimes stressed on
the second syllable /ruh VEN yoo/:

> x / x / x   /   x   /   x   /x
> That no revenue hast but thy good spirits (Ham 3.2.58)

A naive audience hearing this pronunciation may not understand the word. To give
another example, some on hearing the line

> And as mine eye doth his /ef FIJ eez/ witness
> Most truly limn'd and living in your face (AYL 2.7.193–4)

might not recognize the word *effigies*, especially since it is not a plural, but an archaic singular form. Another fairly common example is *persever* /pur SEV ur/
(modern *persevere*), but there is a long list of others.
  The most common words which require a stress shift from their modern pronunciation (twenty-eight or more occurrences) are listed among the words on pp. 29–36.

They are not included in the scene-by-scene lists, but all others are. The reader must decide whether to preserve Shakespeare's intended accentuation in these words, following the dictates of the meter, or at times to break with the meter, using the modern pronunciation in order to enhance the listener's understanding. A compromise is often possible. For *revénue*, for example, the reader can emphasize the second syllable slightly more than usual, while lessening the stress on the first. The same is true in phrases like *upon my sécure hour* and *a thousand cómplete courses.*

Marking the stress shifts in the *Guide* is complicated somewhat by regional differences. *Defect, princess, translate* are examples of words that may today be stressed on either the first or second syllable, depending on where the speaker is from. If Shakespeare's meter shows that *translate* must be pronounced with stress on the second syllable, that would be unusual for most Americans and normal for the British. Words of this sort are included in the *Guide* to cue those who would otherwise miss them.   However, if a word can generally be pronounced with varying stress in all varieties of modern English, it is not included in the lists (for example, *perfume, mankind, adverse*, all of which show varying stress in Shakespeare).

Compressing Words

If the following line

And hath given countenance to his speech, my lord (Ham 1.3.113)

is spoken in normal, modern English it is difficult to find the rhythm we expect in Shakespeare. There are twelve syllables rather than the ten found in a normal iambic pentameter line, and it almost seems that there are four major beats, one on each of the syllables *giv-, count-, speech,* and *lord.* To fit the verse into the proper iambic shape it is necessary to delete two syllables. In this case *given* must be reduced to /givn/, and *countenance* to /COWNT nunss/.   The deletion of an entire syllable is known as **syncope** /SINK uh pee/ or **syncopation**. It is very common in Shakespeare, and sometimes, but not always, indicated by an apostrophe. In polysyllabic words it is especially common when the deleted vowel is followed by /l, r, n/: *exc'llent* /EKS lunt/, *gen'ral* /JEN rł/, *rev'rend* /REV rund/, *card'nal* /CARD nł/.

The word may also be compressed when two vowel sounds are next to each other. This occurs in three different ways:

1. The first of two adjacent vowels, each carrying a syllable, becomes a glide:
    chariot /CHĂIR ee ut/ ⇒ /CHĂIR yut/
    glorious /GLOR ee us/⇒ /GLOR yus/
2. Compression of two adjacent vowels across a word boundary:
    many a ⇒ /MEN yuh/
    be unworthy ⇒ /byun WUR thee/
3. The loss of the second of two adjacent vowels, each of which carries a syllable:
    diadem /DĪ uh dem/ ⇒ /DĪ dem/

In this last category some compressed forms have become standard in much of the United States. Three that occur in Shakespeare are

    diamond /DĪ mund/, *violet* /VĪ lit/, *diaper* /DĪ pur/.

The reader should always be alert to the possibility of compression. *Borrower* and *borrowing* should be pronounced with two syllables in verse. The following words are often monosyllabic: *being* /beeng/, *knowing* /noing/, *flower*, which can almost be pronounced as /flar/. Nearly all examples of comparatives and superlatives of words ending in -*ly* and -*y* must be compressed so that *holier, heavier, mightier, prettiest, worthiest,* etc. should be /HOHL yur, HEV yur, MĪT yur, PRIT yist, WURṬH yist/.[16]

Compression may occur in unexpected places, for example, across a word boundary when the second word begins with /h/:

    bury him ⇒ /BĔR yim/
    pity him ⇒ /PIT yim/

It may also occasionally occur in names that otherwise are pronounced fully. It is found at least once for *Priam, Diomed,* and *Hermione,* while *Lewis* almost always calls for a monosyllabic pronunciation in Shakespeare, compressed from /LŌŌ iss/ to /lōōss/ (Cercignani 1981, 282).

Contractions of verbs and pronouns are another sort of compression not always indicated in the text. To avoid introducing an extra unstressed syllable, *I am* should sometimes be read as *I'm; he will* as *he'll; thou hast* as *thou'st; thou art* as *th'art*:

    x   / x / x / x / x   / x
    We are glad the Dolphin is so pleasant with us (H5 1.2.259)

It should be noted that the same word is not always consistently syncopated or compressed. Some words can be pronounced with one or two syllables, depending on where they fall in the verse line: *giv(e)n, heav(e)n, warr(a)nt*; some can have either two or three: *dang(e)rous, prosp(e)rous, temp(o)ral, beck(o)ning, flatt(e)ry, desp(e)rate.*

None of the examples of compression or syncopation given thus far place any particular strain on the modern reader, actor, or audience. More difficult are those instances in which the meter indicates the need for a greater departure from our current pronunciation. For instance, in Shakespeare's time /v/ was sometimes lost between vowels, in a process going back to Middle English (Kökeritz 1953, 324–25; Dobson 1968, 2:965). This is familiar to most readers in the common poetic forms *e'en, o'er, e'er* for *even, over, ever.* But it may give the modern speaker pause when the meter demands a monosyllable for *having, heaven, seven, given, devil,* and also for some words with /ṭh/ and /r/ between vowels, as in the following examples:

---

[16] In Elizabethan English these words were pronounced /HOHL ĭr, HEV ĭr/, etc. or /HOHL ur, HEV ur/ (Dobson, 1968, 2:877; Kökertiz 1953, 288), but the modern reader and audience will probably be more comfortable with the forms given above.

```
x  /  x  /   x   /    x    /  x  /
```
Be absolute for death: *Either* death or life
Shall thereby be the sweeter.   (MM 3.1.5–6)

```
x     /   x   /   x   / x /  x   /
```
Marry, thou dost wrong me, thou dissembler, thou— (MA 5.1.53)

Other examples occur in *whether* (sometimes written *whe'er*), *whither, spirit, Sir-rah*, and *warrant* (Wright 1988, 152). It is possible that in Shakespeare's time all of these words were pronounced with a weakened /th/ or /r/, but in most cases Elizabethan spellings do not indicate that the consonant in question was actually lost.[17]

But the important question is not how Shakespeare pronounced these words, but how we should pronounce them in order to make the meaning clear to a modern audience. Words like *o'er* and *e'er* pose no problem, but to weaken the /r/ of *spirit* or *warrant* to the point of omission might prevent the listener from understanding the line. However there are other ways to maintain the rhythmic integrity of the verse in these cases. *Spirit* can also be pronounced as one syllable by deleting the final vowel, /spĭrt/; *warrant* can be *warr'nt*. *Heaven* and *seven* can be pronounced more or less monosyllabically as /hevn, sevn/, with the /v/ and /n/ spoken almost simultaneously. *Marry* used explosively as an oath could be reduced to one syllable by deemphasizing the /r/, realizing it almost as /may/. In the case of *either, whither, whether*, the best solution is to retain the modern pronunciation or the lines become unintelligible.

The same common sense must govern choices involving syncopation. In the line

Thou hast so wrong'd mine innocent child and me (MA 5.1.63)

innocent should be pronounced /IN sunt/ if the meter is followed strictly. Other examples of words that sometimes demand a radical syncopation are *maj'sty, vag'bond, el'quence, imped'ment, count'feit, rec'mend, lib'tine, carc'sses* (Wright 1988, 152). To completely delete these syllables may make audiences feel too much has been sacrificed in the interest of meter. One alternative is to reduce these syllables to a

---

[17] Elizabethan commentators on pronunciation almost never recorded monosyllabic *heaven*, which may indicate it was a rare variant, perhaps used by poets artificially (Dobson 1968, 2: 911). The same may be true for most of the words with *th* or *r* in this category, many of which have no written forms that show consonantal deletion, but have only the evidence of the meter to indicate something is different. Dobson 1968 and Cercignani 1981 are silent on the subject of an Elizabethan deletion of /th/ and /r/ between vowels. Kökeritz believes /th/ was deleted (1953, 322). Wright speculates that the poets heard /v, th, r/ between vowels as "less than fully formed" (1988, 152). S. Wells states that Shakespeare did not expect these words to be contracted (1979, 23). That full deletion was possible can be demonstrated by looking at some modern dialects. In parts of the southern United States /r/ is lost in this position (*story, Carol*) (Donna Christianson and Walt Wolfram, *Dialects and Education: Issues and Answers*, Englewood Cliffs, NJ: Prentice Hall Regents, 1989, 133); and in the dialect of Belfast, N. Ireland /th/ is deleted between vowels (*feather*) (John Harris, *Phonological variation and change: Studies in Hiberno-English*, Cambridge, UK: Cambridge University Press, 1985, 58).

hint of a vowel when syncopation is demanded, producing a sort of half-syllable (Wright 1988, 158). If a word listed in the scene-by-scene guide contains a syllable which should be syncopated in this way, that syllable is enclosed in parentheses to remind the reader that some sort of reduction is called for. The reader then may choose how far to proceed in each case.

Compression of the word *the* should also be noted. Before a vowel or *h-*, which was more often silent in Shakespeare's time than it is today, *the* can be easily attached to the following word to rid the line of an extra syllable:

> The rugged Pyrrhus, like *th'Hyrcanian* beast (Ham 2.2.450)
> ⇒ /ţh^{y}ur KAYN yun/

Note that these instances are not always marked with an apostrophe:

> A blanket, in *the alarm* of fear caught up (Ham 2.2.509)
> ⇒ /ţh^{y}uh LARM/

Before a consonant, if *the* creates an extra syllable, it is usually attached to a preceding preposition that ends in a vowel. In the following line there are two such instances:

> /   x x /   x /   x   /   x   /
> Even to the court, the heart, *to th'* seat *o'th* brain (Cor 1.1.136)
> ⇒ /tōōţh SEET uţh BRAYN/

A reader's tendency would be to substitute full *the* in both the fourth and fifth feet: *to the seat of the brain*. This may in the end be necessary for clarity but to do so changes the rhythm of the line from what Shakespeare intended (see p. 25). Note again that these instances are not always marked by apostrophes:

> Tweaks me *by the* nose, gives me the lie i'th' throat (Ham 2.2.574)

One final example of reduction from our modern pronunciation needs to be mentioned, the possessive form in words ending in /s/. In Shakespeare's verse words like *Pyrrhus', Phoebus'* would nearly always have two syllables, not three. This form appears relatively often in Shakespeare's works:

> She is sad and passionate at your Highness' tent (J 2.1.544)
> ⇒ /HĪ niss TENT/, not /HĪ niss iz TENT/.

Note also the contraction of *She is* and syncopation of *passionate* to /PASH nut/.

Only those examples of syncopation and compression which otherwise present pronunciation problems are given in the scene-by-scene lists. So, for example, the reader will be expected to find the syncopated form of *enemy* whenever it occurs, but the unfamiliar *hebona* /HEB (uh) nuh/ is listed with syncopation indicated.

Expanding Words

Sometimes a word will not fit the meter unless an extra syllable is added. In some cases this means shifting our modern pronunciation back to what it was a few centuries ago. The most important example is the verb ending *-ed*. In ordinary speech the Elizabethans pronounced this ending much as we do, but in their verse the older, Middle English syllable was sometimes retained (Dobson 1968, 2:885; Wright 1988, 50–51). A word like *saved* is now, as in 1600, /sayvd/, but in the poetry of the day it could sometimes be /SAY vid/. Today the meter demands that we follow the Elizabethan lead or the verse sounds poorly written, and this is the common stage practice.

In some editions of Shakespeare the *-ed* ending is spelled out if it must be expanded to a separate syllable, while an apostrophe is used if it is reduced. *The sea enraged is not half so deaf* (J 2.1.451) would require the pronunciation /en RAY jid/.[18] Modern /en RAYJD/ would be indicated if it were written *enrag'd*. Other editions use an accent over the *e* for a full syllable (either *-èd* or *-éd*) and unmarked *-ed* to indicate our usual pronunciation. The reader should be cautious if using reproductions of the folios and quartos where the apostrophe is used inconsistently to mark elision of the syllable.

Other examples of expansion are found in suffixes like *-tion*. In Shakespeare's time this ending was sometimes pronounced with one syllable (/-syun/ or modern /-shun/) and sometimes with two (/-sih un/) as in Middle English (Dobson 1968, 2:957–58). For example, the meter tells us that in the line

x   /   x / x /   x / x/
Whose power was in the first proportion (1H4 4.4.15)

the suffix was pronounced as two syllables, while in the next example the meter indicates one syllable:

x / x /   x   / x   / x /
I will survey th'inscriptions back again (MV 2.7.14)

Other examples of words that sometimes demand expansion are those that end in *-ial, -ient, -ian, -ious, -iage*:

Too flattering-sweet to be *substantial* (RJ 2.2.141)

I can no longer hold me *patient* (R3 1.3.156)

By'r Lady, he is a good *musician* (1H4 3.1.231)
(with contraction of *he is*)

---

[18] In the *Guide* the *-ed* ending immediately following a stressed syllable will be symbolized /-id/ though it may vary between /-id/ and /-ed/.

Confess yourselves wonderous *malicious* (Cor 1.1.88)
    (with inversion in the third foot and syncopation to *wond'rous*)

To woo a maid in way of *marriage* (MV 2.9.13)

Your mind is tossing on the *ocean*   (MV 1.1.8)

If the meter demands two syllables for *-tion, -tial,* etc., the reader is again faced with the choice of making the verse limp by leaving out the extra syllable, or of sounding odd to an audience by putting it in as /-shee un/. The *-ed* ending may also be somewhat jarring the first time it is heard, but it is such a widely accepted convention that it is soon taken for granted. However, even when the meter demands it, the *-tion* ending is rarely pronounced with two syllables on the stage and to use it may make the reading sound odd or affected. Again a "half-syllable," with a hint of the extra vowel may be a possible solution (Spain 1988, 38).

Monosyllabic words may also occasionally be expanded, especially if /r/ or /l/ are involved:

/   x   x   / x   /   x   / x   /   x
Therefore in *fierce* tempest is he coming (H5 2.4.99)

x /   x   / x   /   x / x   /
This ignorant present, and I *feel* now (M 1.5.57)

Other words of this sort are *weird, more, bear, fourth, gules.* There are also instances of words which are usually two syllables in both Elizabethan and modern English, expanding to three. One of the most common is *business:*

x   /   x   /   x   /   x   / x   /
I must employ you in some *business* (MND 1.1.124)

Some of these expanded words sound distinctly odd today, and the extra syllable should be ignored or pronounced as lightly as possible:

captain /KAP ih tun/, *angry* /ANG gur ee/,
Henry /HEN ur ee/, *children* /CHILL dur un/

This group of "unusual expansions" is listed as each word appears in the scene-by-scene guide to alert the reader that a change is indicated. However other expansions which are not much different than the modern pronunciation are not included, but are left for the reader to discover:

monstrous /MŎN stur us/, *fiddler* /FID ł ur/,
rememberance /ree MEM bur unss/, *prisoners* /PRIZ uh nurz/

Why Follow the Iambic Meter?

With attention to the demands of the iambic meter, seemingly irregular lines can be made regular by expansion, compression, or shifts in syllable stress. But does it really matter if an extra weak syllable is inserted into a line occasionally, or if the rhythm deviates beyond the common variations listed at the beginning of this section? A much debated topic in Shakespearean scholarship has been how strictly the syllables of the verse line should follow the iambic pattern.[19] Some scholars believe that it should be followed as much as possible. Others maintain, and many actors and directors agree with them, judging by the way they pronounce the words on stage, that Shakespeare never intended the meter to be so strictly followed; that the iambic line is not as important as the rhythm of the natural spoken phrase (Wright 1988, 12). This school of thought would claim that it is not the end of the world to break from the iambic pentameter and its permissible variants to produce four-beat lines, or pronounce two weak stresses together in the form of an anapest. If this argument were taken to its logical extreme there would be no need to compress, expand, or shift the stress of any word like *revenue* or *persever* to fit the meter.

To illustrate the difference, the following passage could be spoken with four strong beats and two or more weak stresses in between:

This music mads me, let it sound no more,
  x   / x x / / x x x /
For though it have holp mad men to their wits,
In me it seems it will make wise men mad. (R2 5.5.61–63)

but giving it its iambic reading means lightly stressing *have* and *to*, thereby changing the melody and the emphasis of the line.

If the line already cited from *Coriolanus* were expanded fully to modern English there would be three anapests after an initial inversion:

  / x x x /   x / x x / x x /
Even to the court, the heart, to th' seat o'th brain (Cor 1.1.136)

Obviously there is no loss in meaning in this line when it is expanded in this way, in fact it could be argued that the words are clearer than if an attempt were made to pronounce *to th' seat* as /tōōth SEET/. But the feel of the verse is slightly different.

This difference is even more evident in the following passage. A reading using the accents of modern English would produce

  x / x x / x x / x / x
As many farewells as be stars in heaven,
  x   x /   / x x /   / x / x
With distinct breath and consign'd kisses to them,
He fumbles up into a loose adieu; (TC 4.4.44 – 46)

---

[19] See Wright 1988, 10–12, 151, 154; Kökeritz 1969, 208–12 for a description of that debate.

An iambic reading, however, places first syllable stress on *distinct, consign'd* and *farewells,* producing a very different sort of rhythmic flow.

Proponents of strict iambic readings contend that by following the rhythm more precisely than many contemporary actors do, we find subtle indications of Shakespeare's intentions while at the same time making the line more verse-like; it retains its identity as poetry, rather than drifting into prose (Spain 1988, 22–36; Linklater 1992, 132; Wright 1988, 193–94). Moreover, by following the iambic rhythm generally, the acceptable variations (the inversions, caesuras, alexandrines, etc.) highlight subtle meanings and point to irregularities in the thoughts of the characters, disturbed emotional states, or heightened feelings.[20]   Poets, like composers, set their words to specific rhythms with great deliberation.   Changing iambic feet to anapests is like ignoring the dot on a dotted eighth note or playing in three-quarter time instead of six-eight.   The words may be the same, but the "meaning" of the piece changes.

However there is a danger of going too far. Once the reader understands the scansion of the line, he or she must choose whether or not to carry out any indicated changes.   Should *Lewis* really be pronounced /lo͞oss/ just because the meter demands a monosyllable?   Should *commendable* be pronounced with stress on the first syllable or is the modern pronunciation the best choice?   Kristin Linklater calls these choices "negotiable artistic option over the rule of prosodic law"(1992, 139) and warns of the danger of becoming too pedantic in the pursuit of the perfect rhythm.

In the end, pronunciation decisions should be made by weighing the need to preserve the verse's form against the need to deliver the author's meaning.   Whenever a compression, expansion, or stress shift is demanded, the reader must keep in mind that there will sometimes be a trade-off between audience understanding and strict adherence to the meter.   Any deviation from modern pronunciation must be accompanied by a certain amount of common sense.   It is clear that Shakespeare intended his verse to be spoken iambically, so as a general rule, readers should maintain the iambic rhythm as much as possible by altering their pronunciation in the ways outlined in this section. However, in a line like the following:

Like to a vagabond flag upon a stream (AC 1.4.45)

where *vagabond* must be pronounced /VAG bŏnd/ to maintain the meter, the speaker should pause and ask whether an audience will be more annoyed at the alteration than pleased because it feels the verse. Again, using a half-syllable /VAG [uh] bŏnd/, with a hint of a vowel after the first syllable, may be the best compromise.

---

[20] See for example Wright 1988, 160–73. Wright finds in some syncopations and compressions, ambiguous half-syllables that "crowd the air with meanings only half-spoken" (1988, 158).

A Pronouncing Guide to the Plays

Each play appears in alphabetical order and the words are arranged by scene in the order they appear. The form given in *The Riverside Shakespeare* is listed first, with alternatives from other editions following in boldface type. Some variants from the quartos and folios which were not found in any edition are also listed in italics.

At the beginning of each play are listed the names of people who either appear in or are repeatedly mentioned in that work. This is followed by a list of frequently mentioned places. Only those people and places are listed whose names would pose difficulties for the average native speaker.

Before turning to a play the reader should become familiar with the two lists on pp. 29–36:

1) **The Most Common "Hard" Words in Shakespeare**
2) **The Most Common Reduced Forms**

These words will not appear in the scene-by-scene lists because each occurs so frequently that to include them would have involved considerable repetition.

Special Symbols Used in the Lists

*included on one of the surveys (see pp. 5–6)

( ) meter demands that the enclosed syllable either be deleted or suppressed (see pp. 21–22)

[ ] less common pronunciations

Q and F refer to the quarto and folio versions of Shakespeare's work.

Reminders

1. *Mars' drum, Theseus' love, Proteus' birth.* A possessive after /s/ or /z/ does not create a new syllable: /marz drum/ not /MARZ iz drum/.

2. *Octavius, Antonio, Hortensio.*   Some names ending in *-io, -ius, -ea*, etc. are pronounced with two final unstressed syllables in prose /an TOHN ee oh/, but in verse they often should be compressed:

> Let good Antonio look he keep his day (MV 2.8.25)
> ⇒ /an TOHN yoh/.

However, at the end of a line of verse the two weak syllables may be maintained (a **triple ending**) or compressed to form a **feminine ending**:

> What mercy can you render him, Antonio? (MV 4.1.378)
> ⇒ /an TOHN yoh/ or /-ee oh/.

3. If undecided about a choice of pronunciations, use the older, traditional English forms. The label "older" refers to the form normally used in English until interference from spelling, restored Latin, etc. occurred. It does not refer to ancient Roman or Middle English pronunciations. The "older" form of *huswife* would be /HUZ if/; *liege* would be /leej/; *Actaeon* would be /ak TEE un/.

THE MOST COMMON "HARD" WORDS IN SHAKESPEARE

These words occur over twenty-eight times according to the *Harvard Concordance to Shakespeare* (1973) (the number of occurrences appears in parentheses). Because they occur so often, they will not be listed in the scene-by-scene guide.

Some words are listed because they are stressed differently in Shakespeare's verse than they are in modern English. Words like *offense* /uh FENSS/ present no problems to British speakers, but are included because Americans sometimes use an inappropriate form /AW fenss/, based on sports usage. Note also that some of these words may retain their modern English accentuation if the foot can be inverted (see p. 15). In prose they may also be pronounced as in modern English.

*abhor (-s, -r'd, -r'dst, -red, -ring, all-abhorred) /ab-, ub HOR/ [-OR] to loathe, be horrified by (51).

*adieu (-s) /uh DY$\overline{OO}$, ad Y$\overline{OO}$/ goodbye. Other alternatives not recommended, except in cases where a French character would use the French pronunciation. Some speakers prefer a French pronunciation for this word, but the angl. form has a long history in English and is necessary for some rhymes (107).

afeard /uh FEERD/ afraid. Still used in some dialects of SW England (33).

anon /uh NŎN/ 'soon' or 'at once' (137).

aspect (-s) in verse /ass SPECT/ usually with meaning 'face' (33).

ay /ī/ yes. Note that **aye** 'ever' is /ay/, though a newer pronunciation /ī/ is often used, but not recommended.   Confusion is rampant because in many non-Shakespearean texts the spellings are reversed: **aye** means 'yes' and **ay** is 'ever' (785).

*bade /bad, bayd/ past tense of *bid*, 'ordered, greeted, summoned.' /bayd/ is newer. Both are used equally among scholars in CN, but /bad/ is preferred in the UK and US. Among the general population /bayd/ is the overwhelming choice (47).

　　forbade /for BAD, for BAYD/ did not permit (4).

besiege see **siege**.

business (-es) may be either /BIZ niss/ or /BIZ ih niss/ depending on meter. The latter is virtually unknown in mod. Eng. (253).

*censure (-s, -d, -ing) /SEN shur/; US, CN *also* [-chur] (n) judgement, (v) to find fault with. /-syoor/ is not recommended (34).

ă-bat, ăir-marry, air-pair, ạr-far, ĕr-merry, ĝ-get, ī-high, ĭr-mirror, ł-little, ṇ-listen, ŏ-hot, oh-go, $\overline{oo}$-wood, $\overline{oo}$-moon, oor-tour, ōr-or, ow-how, ţh-that, t̶h̶-thin, ŭ-but, UR-fur, ur-under. ( )- suppress the syllable   [ ]- less common   see p. xi for complete list.

*choler (-s) /CŎL ur/ anger. /COH lur/ is not recommended (28).
   *choleric depending on meter: /CŎL ur ik, CŎL rik/ prone to anger. Never /cuh LĔR ik/ in Shakespeare (10).

contrary /cŏn-, cun TRĔR ee/ or with 1st syllable stress, which in the US is /CŎN trĕr ee/ [-truh ree]; UK /-truh ree/ (49).

*courtier (-s, -'s, -s') in verse /COR tyur/; US, CN *rarely* [COR chur] man of the court. May be /COR tee ur/ in prose or at the end of a line in a triple ending (45).

coz /CUZ/ cousin (44).

cozen (-'d, -s, -er, -ers, -ing, coz'ning, -age, coz'nage) /CUZ in, -ṇ/ deceive (36). *Cozenage, cozening, cozener* may need to be reduced to two syllables (/CUZ nij/, etc.) depending on meter.

*cuckold (-ed, uncuckolded) /CUCK łd, CUCK old/ (n) husband of an adulterous woman, (v) to deceive a husband by committing adultery (44).

defense (UK **defence**) **(-s)**, /dih-, dee FENSS/. US /DEE fenss/ will not fit the meter (46).

Dian (-'s) /DĪ un, -an/ Diana, Roman goddess of the hunt and of chastity (28).

discharge (-'d, -ed, -est, -ing) in verse (n, v) /dis CHĄRJ/ (53).

*discourse (-ed, -er, es) in verse /dis CORSS/ (n) speech, (v) speak (66).

*dispatch (-'d,) (n, v) in verse /dih SPATCH/ often with meaning 'hurry' (97).

dost /DUST/ 2nd person sing. indicative of *do*. /dŏst/ not recommended (451).
   *doth /DU̶T̶H̶/ does. /d̶ŏ̶t̶h̶/ not recommended (1,072).

doublet (-s) /DUB lut/ man's garment worn over a shirt (29).

ducat (-s) /DUCK ut/ gold coin (59).

ere /air/ before (397). **ere't** /airt/ before it (5). **erewhile** /air WHĪL/ hitherto (3).

*err (-s, -ing) to make a mistake. US, UK /ur/ [ĕr]; CN /ĕr/ [ur]. /ĕr/ is the newer form and is non-standard in the UK. Among the general population /ĕr/ is strongly preferred (28).

*exile (-'d) (v, n) 1st or 2nd syllable stress in verse. Today in the US /EGG zīl/ [EK sīl]; CN uses both equally; UK /EK sīl/ [EGG zīl] (33).

farewell (-s) usually with 2nd syllable stress as in mod. Eng., but sometimes stressed on the 1st syllable (380).

feign (-'d, -ed, -ing) /fayn/ 1) to fabricate, 2) to pretend; *feigning* pretending, imaginative (23).
    unfeigned (-ly) /un FAY nid/ honest, true (7).

fie /fī/ expression of disgust or shock (167).

*flourish (-'d, -es, -eth, -ing) US, CN /FLUR ish/, *sometimes newer* [FLo͞oR-, FLŌR-]; UK, E. COAST US /FLUH rish/ (n) embellishment, (v) to thrive (35).

forbade see **bade**.

gallant (-s) (adj) 'brave, full of spirit' is always /GAL unt/. The noun 'man of fashion, ladies' man' is also /GAL unt/ in verse, but in prose may be /guh LĂNT/, a common modern form (71).

hie (-s, -d) /hī/ hurry (61).

import (-s, -ing, -ed, -eth, -less) (n) importance, (v) to mean. Whether noun or verb always /im PORT/ in verse except once at AW 2.3.276 where it is /IM port/ (42).

*Jesu Jesus. US /JAY zo͞o/ [JEE-, JAY so͞o, YAY zo͞o]; UK /JEE zyo͞o/ [-zo͞o], *rarely* [JAY-, YAY-, -so͞o]. The recommended forms are the oldest, /JEE zyo͞o/ in the UK, /JEE zo͞o/ in North America. The others are newer, based on classical and church Latin (28).

levy (-ies, -ied, -ing) /LEV ee/ usually meaning (n) 'army,' (v) 'raise an army or money.' **Levying** may be /LEV ying/ or /LEV ee ing/ depending on meter (30).

*liege (-'s) overlord; **liegeman, -men** vassals, subjects. /leej/ is older and more common in the UK; in North America /leej/ and newer /leezh/ are used equally (145).

madam (-'s, -s) /MAD um/ form of address to a middle- or upper-class woman. Note the difference from Fr. **madame** /mah DAHM, MAH dahm/, found only in H5 3.4, a Fr. language scene (530).

medicine, med'cine (-s) despite the spellings, each of these may be pronounced either /MED ih sin/ or /MED sin/ depending on meter. The latter is the most common UK form, but is unknown in the US (31).

ă-bat, äir-**marry**, air-**pair**, ạr-**far**, ĕr-**merry**, ĝ-**get**, ī-**high**, ĭr-**mirror**, ł-**little**, ṇ-**listen**, ŏ-**hot**, oh-**go**, o͝o-**wood**, o͞o-**moon**, oor-**tour**, ōr-**or**, ow-**how**, ţh-**that**, ᵵh-**thin**, ʊ-**but**, UR-**fur**, ur-**under**. ( )- suppress the syllable [ ]- less common see p. xi for complete list.

*methinks /mee-, mih ~~TH~~INKS/ it seems to me. The former is favored slightly in the US, UK, and strongly in CN (162).
   methought /mee-, mih ~~TH~~AWT/ it seemed to me (53).

monsieur (-s) depending on meter: /muh SYUH, -SYUR/ or with 1st syllable stress /M͞o͞oS-, MUH-/. Fr. form of address to a middle- or upper-class man. The Fr. pronunciation /mö syö/ can also be stressed on either syllable (40).

offense (UK offence) (-'s, -s, -less, -ful) /uh FENSS/. US /AW fenss/ will not fit the meter (150).

princess (-') /PRIN sess/ or /prin SESS/ depending on meter. The most common Standard British pronunciation is /prin SESS/, which is almost unheard of in the US (63).

*prithee /PRIṬH ee/, *sometimes newer* [PRI~~TH~~ ee] I pray thee, please (229).

quoth /kwoh~~th~~/ said (117).

rapier (-s, -'s) /RAY pyur/ type of sword.   /RAY pee ur/ will not usually fit the meter in verse, but may be used in prose (29).

recompense /REK um penss/ (v) to pay back, (n) payment (33).

requite (-s, -ed) /rih-, ree KWĪT/ to return love or repay something. Once stressed on the 1st syllable TmA 4.3.522 (33).
   requital /rih-, ree KWĪT ł/ repayment (7).

seignieur see signior.

*siege (-s) /seej/; US, CN *also newer* [seezh]. Usually 1) military blockade of a town, but also 2) seat, 3) rank, 4) excrement (34).
   besiege (-'d, -ed) US, CN /bee-, bih SEEJ/ [-SEEZH]; UK /bih SEEJ/ to lay
   siege to (16).

signior (-s) /SEEN yor/ form of address to a middle- or upper-class man, based on Italian. Some eds. prefer Ital. signor for the Italian names (pronounced the same way), Fr. seignieur angl. /SEN YUR/; Fr. /sen yör/ for the Fr. names, and Sp. señor /sayn YOR/ for Armado in LLL. In verse they are all stressed on the 1st syllable (139).

*sinew (-s, -ed, -y) /SIN y͞o͞o/; US *also* [SIN ͞o͞o] 1) tendon, 2) nerve, 3) strength (30).
In addition *Riverside* has the archaic variants sinow (-s, -y) /SIN oh/ (7).

sirrah form of address to a servant or inferior (152). /SĬR uh/ is generally used, but if the word had survived into mod. Eng., /SUR uh/ would also have been common in

North America (cf. *syrup, stirrup* with both /UR/ and /ĬR/).

strook *Riverside* uses this archaic form, possibly pronounced /stro͞ok/, or perhaps simply a variant spelling of **struck** (cf. *flood, blood*) (55).
  strooken is usually modernized to **strucken** or **stricken** (6).

*subtle, subtile (-ly, -ties, -ty, -er) /SUT ł/ 1) sly, 2) tricky, 3) delicate. /SUB-/ is not recommended (47). *Subtly, subtilly* are always two syllables /SUT lee/ in verse.

*surfeit (-er, -ed, -ing, -s) /SUR fit/ (n) too much of something, (v) to have too much of something (38).

swounds see **zounds**.

thereas, thereat, etc. see **whereas.**

*thither toward a place. In the US, CN the newer form /T̶H̶IT̶H ur/, with initial *th* as in *thin,* is much more common. In the UK the older form /T̟HIT̟H ur/, with initial *th* as in *then,* is preferred and the newer form is non-standard (98).

toward (-s) (prep.) usually 1 syllable in verse, but sometimes 2 are indicated. If 2 syllables, then /TOH urd/ or /tuh-, toͦo WÂRD/ (as in *war*), depending on meter; if 1, /tōrd, twōrd/. In the UK, CN the usual pronunciation is /tuh-, toͦo WÂRD/; in the US /tōrd, twōrd/ (156). Note the difference from adj., adv. **toward (-ly)** 'about to take place, obedient,' which is usually /TOH wurd, -urd/ (17).

*troth (-s) /troht̶h̶/ truth. Two other common alternatives /trŏt̶h̶/ and US /trawt̶h̶/ will not fit the rhymes (112).

unfeigned see **feign.**

unwonted see **wont.**

*usurp (-ed, -'d, -er(s), -er's, -s, -'st, -ing(ly), -ation) take over unlawfully.
US /yoͦo SURP/ [-ZURP]; CN both /s, z/ forms used equally; UK /yoͦo ZURP/ [-SURP] (69).

vild (-er, -est, -ly) /vīld/ archaic variant of **vile** (57).

*visage /VIZ ij/ face. /VISS ij/ not recommended and is non-standard in the UK (41).

ă-bat, ăir-**marry,** air-**pair,** ą̈r-**far,** ĕr-**merry,** ĝ-**get,** ī-**high,** ĭr-**mirror,** ł-**little,** ṇ-**listen,** ŏ-**hot,** oh-**go,** oͦo-**wood,** oͦo-**moon,** oor-**tour,** ōr-**or,** ow-**how,** t̟h-**that,** t̶h̶-**thin,** ŭ-**but,** UR-**fur,** ur-**under.** ( )- suppress the syllable   [ ]- less common   see p. xi for complete list.

vouchsafe (-'d, -ed, -s, -ing) /vowch SAYF/ to grant. Alternatively, both syllables may be evenly stressed   (62, including 4 instances of the archaic form **voutsafe** /vowt SAYF/).

*wanton (-ly, -ness, -'s, -s) /WŎN tun/; US *also* [WAWN tun] (adj) morally loose, (n) a morally loose person (91).

wherefore why. The usual pronunciation is with 1st syllable stress, even at the beginning of a line where it could have 2nd syllable stress: *Whérefore should I curse him?* It occasionally shows stress shift to the 2nd syllable (144).

   Note that **whereas, whereat, whereby,** etc. as well as **thereat, thereby,** etc. also vary, but usually have 2nd syllable stress. **Therefore**, however, like *wherefore,* is pronounced as it is in mod. Eng. with 1st syllable stress.

whiles /whīlz/; **whilest** /WHĪL ust/; **whil'st** /whīlst/. All 3 forms mean 'while' (122).

*withal /with AWL/; US, CN *also* /with -/ with. In the UK /with -/ is non-standard (151). So also **therewithal** with main stress on either the 1st or last syllable (9).

without usually stressed on the 2nd syllable, as it is today, but 29 times with 1st syllable stress.

wot (-s, -st. -ting) /wŏt/ know (33).

*wont US /wohnt, wawnt, wŏnt/; CN, UK /wohnt/ [wŏnt] custom, **wonted** accustomed, **unwonted** unusual (64). Among the general population /wawnt/ is the most common in the US.

*zounds, swounds /zowndz, zōōndz/ by God's wounds. Both pronunciations were used in Elizabethan English. By the end of the 19th century /zowndz/ alone was recommended, but /zōōndz/ was restored during the 20th century and now predominates in the UK. Both are used equally among scholars in North America and both can be justified on historical grounds (29).

THE MOST COMMON REDUCED FORMS

'a he (183). *'a was a merry man.* Best pronounced as *he* is in modern, informal speech: "He was a merry man." Note in weak position, modern *he* also may lose /h/: "Did 'e go?" /did ee GO/. The unstressed sound spelled *a* could vary between /uh/ and /ih/ in older dialects, hence the spelling variations like *Ursula-Ursley, sirrah-sirry.* Today this final unstressed /ih/ has become /ee/ in most American dialects.

a' /uh/ of, on, in (195). *a' God's name.*

'a' /uh/ have (7). *She might 'a' been.*

e'en /een/ even (36). Note that as an adv. **even** spelled fully (*even till they wink*) should usually be pronounced as 1 syllable, either as /een/ or with the /v/ and /n/ pronounced nearly simultaneously.

e'er /ĕr/ ever (177); so also **howe'er** (9), **howsoe'er** (5), **howsome'er** (2), **soe'er** (6), **some'er** (1), **whatsome'er** (2), **wheresoe'er** (10), **wheresome'er** (1), **whoe'er** (10), **whosoe'er** (3). **Ev'r** is occasionally used, and also indicates that the meter demands 1 syllable.

ha' /hă/ have (25). *I'll ha' thee burnt.* Our normal /hav/ may be substituted for better clarity. **ha't** /hat, havt/ have it (11).

h'as /hʸaz/ he has (24). Our normal modern contraction *he's* /heez/ may also be used.

i' /ih/ in (400). Usually in the combinations:
  i'faith /ih FAYTH/ in faith (a mild oath).
  i'th' in the. *i'th' name of Beelzebub!* Meant to be pronounced /iţh/ in verse to preserve the iambic meter, but in practice *in the* is often substituted (see p. 22).

ne'er /nĕr/ never (234). **Nev'r** also is used which should be pronounced as 1 syllable.

o' /uh/ of (284). *any kind o' thing.* Sometimes with meanings 'on, one.'
  o'th' of the. *the frown o' th' great.* Meant to be pronounced /uţh/ in verse to preserve the iambic meter, but in practice *of the* is often substituted (see p. 22).

o'er /or/ over (219 plus many compounds).

ă-b**a**t, **ä**ir-m**a**rry, **a**ir-p**ai**r, **a̧**r-f**a**r, **ĕ**r-m**e**rry, ĝ-g**e**t, ī-h**i**gh, ĭr-m**i**rror, ł-litt**le**, n̥-list**e**n, ŏ-h**o**t, oh-g**o**, ōō-w**oo**d, ōō-m**oo**n, oor-t**ou**r, ōr-**or**, ow-h**ow**, ţh-**th**at, t̶h̶-**th**in, ŭ-b**u**t, UR-f**ur**, ur-und**er**. ( )- suppress the syllable   [ ]- less common   see p. xi for complete list.

't it. Attached either to the preceding or following word *take't, by't* /taykt , bīt/; *'t may* /tmay/.

t' to. Attached to the following word *t'invite, t'accept;* /tin VĪT, tak SEPT/. It is also possible to use the form /tw-/ to make it clearer that *to* is intended without adding an extra syllable: /twin VĪT, twak SEPT/.
    t'other the other. /TUTH ur/.

ta'en /tayn/ taken (104). So also **mista'en, underta'en, overta'en, o'erta'en**.

th' usually 'the,' sometimes 'thy, thou, they' (1,424). When used as a shortened form of 'the' before a vowel it is attached to the following word. *Th'end* is a single syllable /th^yend/, not 2 distinct syllables /thee END/. Before a consonant it is usually attached to a preceding preposition. Shakespeare probably intended this to be spoken as 1 syllable, but sometimes for clarity it should be spoken as 2 (see p. 22):
    i'th', o'th' (see above under **i', o'**).
    by th' *hung by th' wall* /hung bīth WAWL/ or in reduced form /buth/. This is especially common in oaths like *by th' mass* /buth MASS/.
    to th' *to th' vulgar eye* /tooth-, tuth VUL gur/.

whe'er, whe'r /whĕr/ whether (16). For clarity may also be pronounced /WHETH ur/ (see p. 21).

Some Common Non-spoken Words

dramatis personae cast of characters. /DRAM uh tiss pur SOH nee/; restored Latin /DRAHM ah tiss pĕr SOH nī/.

exeunt stage direction 'they exit.' /EK see unt/.

manet stage direction 'he or she remains' or **manent** 'they remain.' /MAY nut, -nunt/; restored Latin /MAH net/, /MAH nent/.

All's Well That Ends Well

People in the Play

Austringer see **a Stranger.**

Bertram /BUR trum/.

Diana Capilet /dī ANN uh KAP ih let/.

Dumaine (First and Second French Lords) US /dōō MAYN/;
UK, SOUTH. US /dyōō-/; Fr. /dü MEN/.

*Florentine(s) US /FLŌR in teen/ [-tīn]; E. COAST US /FLŎR-/;
UK /FLŎR in tīn/ [-teen] person from Florence.

Gerard de Narbon angl. /juh RAHRD duh NAHR bun/. In the sole verse instance
the foot may be inverted /JĔR ard, -urd/.   Some eds. prefer Fr. **Gérard** /zhay rahr
duh NAHR boh^n/.

Helena /HELL in uh/.

Lafew, Lafeu /luh FYŌŌ/. *Lafeu* in Fr. would be /lah FÖ/.

Lavatch /luh VATCH/.

Mariana /mair ee ANN uh/, or *newer* /-AHN uh/. Her name is not spoken.

*Parolles, Paroles US, CN /puh ROHL iz/ [-iss], *rarely* [-RŎL iss, -iz];
UK /puh ROHL iz, puh RŎL iz/ [-ROHL iss, -RŎL iss]. /puh ROHLZ/ is also used,
but its final syllable would have to be treated as 2 syllables to meet the metrical requirements of the verse.

Rinaldo /rih NAL doh, -NAWL-, -NAHL-/. Some eds. prefer **Reynaldo** /ray-/.

Rossillion 3 or 4 syllables depending on meter /ruh SILL (ee) yun/. Some eds.
prefer **Roussillon** /rōō-, rŏŏ-/. The Fr. /rōō SEE yoh^n/ will not expand to 4 syllables.

a Stranger (F3) mentioned in a stage direction in 5.1. Some eds. prefer F1's
astringer /ASS trin jur/, variant of **austringer** /ŎSS-, AWSS-/ falconer.

ă-bat, ăir-ma**rr**y, air-**pair**, a̱r-**far**, ĕr-me**rr**y, ĝ-get, ī-high, ĭr-mi**rr**or, ł-little, n̩-listen,
ŏ-hot, oh-go, ōō-wood, ōō-moon, oor-**tour**, ōr-**or**, ow-how, t̪h-**that**, t̶h̶-**thin**, ŭ-but,
UR-**fur**, ur-under. ( )- suppress the syllable   [ ]- less common   see p. xi for complete list.

People in the Play (cont.)

Violenta angl. /vī oh LEN tuh/, /vee oh LEN tuh/ is based on Ital. Some eds. do not include her in 3.5, making her the same character as Diana.

Places in the Play

Rossillion see "People in the Play."

St. *Jaques le Grand. The most common angl. forms are US /saynt JAY kweez luh GRAND/; UK /sn̩t-, sint-/. Other forms are [jayks], or *rarely* US [JAY kiz, -keez, -kis]; UK [JAY kwiz, -kwes]. Some eds. prefer Fr. **St. Jacques le Grand**, which would normally be pronounced /sä^n ZHAHK luh GRAH^N/. However in some lines *Jaques / Jacques* should be 2 syllables, which in Shk's time would have been /JAY kis/.

Act 1 Scene 1

34. **fistula** US /FIS chuh luh/; UK *also* /-tyoo luh/ a long, round ulcer.

76. **comfortable** here should be /CUM fur tuh bł/.

88. **collateral** US /cuh LAT rł/; UK *also* [cŏ-] indirect.

91. **hind** /hīnd/ doe.

98. **his reliques, relics** /REL iks/ reminders of him.

113. **barricado** barricade. /băir ih KAY doh/ is older, /-KAH doh/ is newer.

126. **politic** /PŎL ih tik/ good policy.

158. ***brooch** /brohch/ ornament. US [bro͞och] not recommended.

172. **dulcet** /DULL sit/ sweet.

Act 1 Scene 2

1. **The Florentines and *Senoys* are by th' ears** may have been /SEEN oyz/ or /SEEN (oh) eez/, archaic form of **Sienese** which here would have to be /SEE (uh) neez/ or /SYEN eez/. /see uh NEEZ/ is also possible with *the* pronounced fully in a hexameter.

8. **Prejudicates** /prih-, pree JOOD ih kayts/ prejudges.

11. **credence** /CREED ṇss/ trust.

14. **Tuscan** /TŬSS kun/ of Tuscany, a region in Italy.

17. **exploit** here should be /ek SPLOYT/.

53. ***plausive** /PLAW ziv/ [-siv] praiseworthy.

Act 1 Scene 3

25. **barnes** /bạrnz/ dialect word for 'babies.' A more commonly known dialect variant preferred by some eds. is **bairns** /bairnz/, still found in Scotland and North.Eng.

49. ***ergo** /UR go/ is older, /ĔR go/ is newer. The former is more common in the UK, the latter in the US, but both forms appear in all countries.

52. **Charbon** angl. /SHAHR bun/; Fr. /shahr boh^n/. Some eds. prefer Fr. **Chairbonne** /shair bǒn/ good-flesh, i.e., Protestant.

52. **Poysam** /POY sum, -zum/. Some eds. prefer **Poisson** Fr. /pwah soh^n/ fish, i.e., Catholic.

52. **papist** /PAYP ist/ Catholic.

57. **calumnious** /cuh LUM nee us/ slanderous.

73. ***Priam's** King of Troy. US, CN /PRĪ umz/ [-amz]; UK /-amz/, *rarely* [-umz]. Normal development would favor /-um/.

85. **tithe-woman** /TĪṬH-/ 10th woman.

94. **surplice** /SUR pliss/ white priest's garment.

119. **sithence** /SIŦH unss/ since.

144. **enwombed mine** /en WO͞OM id/ born of my womb.

191. **appeach'd** /uh PEECHT/ informed against.

202. **intenible** (F2), **intenable** /in TEN ih bł, -uh bł/ leaky. Some eds. prefer F1's **intemible, inteemible** /in TEEM ih bł/ letting nothing pour out.

ă-bat, ăir-marry, air-pair, ạr-far, ĕr-merry, ĝ-get, ī-high, ĭr-mirror, ł-little, ṇ-listen, ŏ-hot, oh-go, o͞o-wood, o͞o-moon, oor-tour, ōr-or, ow-how, ṭh-that, ŧh-thin, Ŭ-but, UR-fur, ur-under. ( )- suppress the syllable   [ ]- less common   see p. xi for complete list.

202. **sieve** /siv/ strainer.

Act 2 Scene 1

16. **questant** /KWEST unt/ seeker.

35. **I am your accessary, and so farewell** /AK sess ree/ makes the line regular.
/AK sess ĕr ee/ (which in the UK would be /-uh ree/) is possible before an epic
caesura, or, if *I am* is *I'm*, mod. /ak SESS uh ree/ can be used.

42. **Spinii** Ang.Lat. /SPIN ee ī/; Class.Lat. /SPIN ih ee/.

43. **Spurio** /SPUR-, SPOOR ee oh/; Ital. /SPŌOR-/.

43. **cicatrice** /SIK uh triss/ scar.

57. **dilated** /dih-, dī LAYT id/ expansive.

76. **Pippen, Pippin** /PIP in/ father of Charlemagne. Some eds. prefer
Pepin /PEP in/, or Fr. **Pépin** /PAY păⁿ/.

77. ***Charlemain, Charlemagne** US /SHAR luh mayn/, *rarely*
[shar luh MAYN]; CN /SHAR luh mayn/; UK /SHAR luh mayn/
[SHAR luh mīn, shar luh MAYN], *rarely* [shar luh MĪN]. /-mīn/ is
a newer pronunciation, not recommended.   Fr. /sharl mahnʸ/.

97. **Cressid's uncle** /CRESS idz/ Pandar, who brought Troilus and Cressida
together.

122. **empirics** /EM pur iks/ quack doctors.

122. **dissever** /dih SEV ur/ sever.

155. **imposture** archaic variant of F3's **impostor**, both pronounced
/im PŎS tur/ (see App. C).

162. **diurnal** /dī UR nł/ daily.

164. **Hesperus** /HES pur us/ the evening star.

167. ***infirm** /in FURM/ diseased.

170. **venter** /VEN tur/ archaic variant of **venture**.

172. **Traduc'd** slandered. /truh DY$\overline{OO}$ST/; US *also* /-D$\overline{OO}$ST/. /-J$\overline{OO}$ST/ is considered non-standard in the UK.

173. **ne** (F1) /nee/ or when unstressed /nih, nuh/ an old negative. Some eds. prefer F2's **no**.

180. ***estimate** /ES tih mayt/ value. Here rhymes with *rate*. /-mut/ would otherwise be more common in the US.

183. **intimate** /IN tih mayt/ argue.

204. **resolv'd** here should be /REE zŏlvd/ with mind made up.

Act 2 Scene 2

18. **quatch-buttock** /KWŎTCH but uck/ flat buttock.

22. **taffety** /TAF uh tee/ a silk-like cloth worn by whores. Variant of **taffeta** /TAF uh tuh/.

26. **quean** /kween/ ill-behaved woman.

54. **is very sequent** /SEE kwunt/ properly follows.

60. ***huswife** /HUZ if/ is traditional, /HUSS wīf/ is a newer, spelling pronunciation. The former is the most common form in the UK, the latter in the US. In CN both are used equally. In North America /HUSS wif/ is also sometimes used. Some eds. prefer mod. **housewife**.

Act 2 Scene 3

4. **ensconcing** /in SKŎNSS ing/ sheltering.

11. **Galen** /GAY lin/ Gk. doctor.

11. **Paracelsus** /păir uh SEL sus/ famed physician of the 16th century.

29. **facinerious** /fass ih NEER ee us/ wicked. Variant of **facinorous** /fuh SIN ur us/.

ă-bat, ăir-marry, air-pair, ạr-far, ĕr-merry, ĝ-get, ī-high, ĭr-mirror, ł-little, ṇ-listen, ŏ-hot, oh-go, ōō-wood, ōō-moon, oor-tour, ōr-or, ow-how, ţh-that, ŧħ-thin, Ŭ-but, UR-fur, ur-under. ( )- suppress the syllable   [ ]- less common   see p. xi for complete list.

34. ***debile** /DEE bīl, DEB īl/; US *rarely* [DEB ł] weak.

41. **Lustick** /LŬS tik/ merry. Some eds. prefer **Lustig**, pronounced the same way if angl., or as in Germ. /LōōS tik/.

43. ***coranto** courant, a fast dance. US /coh-, cuh RAHN toh/ [-RAN-]; UK /cŏr AHN toh, -AN toh/.

44. **Mort du vinaigre** angl. /mor dōō vin AY gruh/ pseudo-Fr. for 'death of the vinegar.' Fr. /mor dü veen AYG ʳᵘʰ/.

59. **Curtal** /CURT ł/ name of a horse with a short tail.

79. **ames-ace** /AYMZ ayss/ two aces, i.e., ones, lowest throw in dice. Some eds. prefer **ambs-ace** which is sometimes [ĂMZ ayss].

88. **eunuchs** /YŌŌ nuks/ castrated men.

152. **misprision** /mis PRIZH un, -ṇ/ misconduct.

158. ***travails** here should be /TRAV aylz/ labors.

178. **Smile upon this contract.** If /cŏn TRACT/ as elsewhere in Shk, then the 1st foot is inverted with a slight stress on *this*. Mod. /CŎN tract/ works as either a head-less line, or an inverted 1st foot with *smile* considered 2 syllables.

204. **bannerets** /ban ur ETS/, or especially in the UK, /BAN ur ets/ banners.

216. **egregious** /ih GREE jus/ extraordinary.

259. ***pomegranate** US, CN /PŎM uh gran it/; US *also* [PUM-, PŎM gran it, PUM ih gran it]; UK /PŎM uh gran it/ [PŎM gran it].

273. **Tuscan** /TŬSS kun/ of Tuscany, a region in Italy.

282. **curvet** here should be /cur VET/ a leap on horseback.

293. ***capriccio** whim. US /kuh PREE chyoh, -choh/, *rarely* [-PRITCH-]; UK /kuh PREE chyoh, -choh/ [-PRITCH-].

Act 2 Scene 4

41. ***prerogative** /pur RŎG uh tiv/ [prih-, pree-] right. /pree-/ non-standard in the UK.

Act 2 Scene 5

81. **timorous** /TIM (uh) rus/ frightened.

92. **coraggio** /coh RAH joh/ Ital. courage.

Act 3 Scene 2

31. **misprising, misprizing** /mis PRĪZ ing/ undervaluing.

66. **moi'ty, moiety** /MOY tee/ portion, half.

114. **caitiff** /KAYT if/ scoundrel.

117. **ravin, raven, ravine** (F1) all pronounced /RAV in/ ravenous.

Act 3 Scene 3

2. **credence** /CREED n̩ss/ trust.

6. **th' extreme** here should be /T̩H^{Y}EK streem/.

Act 3 Scene 5

24. **lim'd** /līmd/ coated with lime, i.e., paste.

76. **Antonio** /an TOHN yoh/; Ital. /ahn-/.

77. **Escalus** /ES kuh lus/.

85. **jack-an-apes** /JACK uh nayps/ monkey, impertinent fellow.

94. **enjoin'd** here should be /EN joynd/ bound by oath.

Act 3 Scene 6

3. **hilding** /HILL ding/ good-for-nothing.

ă-bat, ăir-marry, air-pair, a̩r-far, ĕr-merry, ĝ-get, ī-high, ĭr-mirror, ł-little, n̩-listen, ŏ-hot, oh-go, o͞o-wood, o͞o-moon, oor-tour, ōr-or, ow-how, t̩h-that, th-thin, ŭ-but, UR-fur, ur-under. ( )- suppress the syllable   [ ]- less common   see p. xi for complete list.

26. **leaguer** /LEEG ur/. Some eds. prefer **laager** /LAH gur/. Both mean 'camp.'

35, 65. **stratagem** /STRAT uh jum/ scheme.

62. ***hic jacet** here lies, i.e., I would die trying. Ang.Lat. /hick JAY sit/; Class.Lat. /heek YAH ket/. Some eds. prefer **hic iacet**, pronounced as in Class.Lat. Occasionally Church Latin /-chet/ is used.

67. **magnanimious** /mag nuh NIM ee us/ archaic variant of **magnanimous** /mag NAN ih mus/.

68. **exploit** /ek SPLOYT/ in verse, but here may be mod. /EK sployt/.

Act 3 Scene 7

37. **persever** /pur SEV ur/ persevere, carry out the plan.

44. **assay** /uh-, ass SAY/. Some eds. prefer **essay** /es SAY/. Both mean 'attempt, test.'

Act 4 Scene 1

11. **linsey-woolsey** /LIN zee WŏŏL zee/ cloth of linen and wool, i.e., mix of words.

19. **choughs', chuffs'** /chufs/ jackdaws'.

21. **politic** /PŎL ih tik/ cunning.

26. ***plausive** /PLAW ziv/ [-siv] plausible.

38. **exploit** /ek SPLOYT/ in verse, but here may be mod. /EK sployt/.

42. **Bajazeth's** some eds. prefer **Bajazet's**, both pronounced /BAJ uh zets/ or more rarely /baj uh ZETS/. A variant with /th/ is also used.

50. **stratagem** /STRAT uh jum/ scheme.

58. **fadom** /FAD um/ archaic variant of **fathom** /FĂṬH um/.

69. **Muskos', Muscos'** /MŬS kohss/.

76. **poniards** /PŎN yurdz/; UK *also newer* [-yardz] daggers.

Act 4 Scene 2

1. Fontibell, Fontybell, Fontibel /FŎNT ih bel/ or / FŎNT ee bel/.

37. **persever** /pur SEV ur/ persevere.

38. **scarre** uncertain meaning, perhaps pronounced /skahr/. Some eds. prefer **snare, surance**.

44, 48. **obloquy** /ŎB luh kwee/ speaking ill of someone.

70. **sate** archaic variant of **sat**. May have been /sayt/ or /sat/.

Act 4 Scene 3

59. **rector** /REK tur/ priest or governor. /-tor/ not recommended.

86. **abstract** /AB stract/ summary.

87. **congied, congeed** /CŎN jeed/ or /cun-, cŏn JEED/ taken formal leave.   Some eds. prefer **congéd** angl. /CŎN-, COHN zhayd/, or with 2nd syllable stress; a Fr. pronunciation is also possible /coh^n zhayd/.

99. **module** /MŎD yo͞ol/; US *also* /MŎJ o͞ol/ image. *Module* was formerly confused with **model**.

100. **prophesier** /PRŎF uh sī ur/ prophet.

101. **sate** archaic variant of **sat**. May have been /sayt/ or /sat/.

123. ***pasty** meat pie. US /PĂSS tee, PAYSS-/; UK /PĂSS tee/ [PAYSS-]. /PAYSS-/ is newer.

141. **militarist** /MIL ih tur ist/ military man.

142. **theoric** /T̶H̶EE uh rik/ theory.

143. **chape** /chayp/ metal tip on the end of a sheath.

161. **Spurio** /SPUR-, SPOOR ee oh/; Ital. /SPO͞OR-/.

ă-bat, ăir-**ma**rry, air-**pa**ir, a̦r-**fa**r, ĕr-**me**rry, ĝ-**g**et, ī-**h**igh, ĭr-**mi**rror, ⱡ-**li**ttle, n̦-**li**sten, ŏ-**h**ot, oh-**g**o, o͞o-**w**ood, o͞o-**m**oon, oor-**tou**r, ōr-**o**r, ow-**h**ow, t̠h-**that**, t̶h̶-**thin**, ŭ-**b**ut, UR-**fu**r, ur-**un**der. ( )- suppress the syllable   [ ]- less common   see p. xi for complete list.

162. **Sebastian** US /suh BĂS chun/; UK /suh BĂST yun/.

162. **Corambus** /koh-, kuh RAM bus/.

163. ***Jaques, Jacques**. Since this is a prose passage it may be pronounced with 1 or 2 syllables and Fr. /zhahk/ may be the best choice. In other instances in Shk it is commonly pronounced /JAY kweez/ (see "Places in the Play"—*St. Jaques le Grand.*)

163. **Guiltian** /ĜIL shun/ is traditional, /-shee un, -tee un/ are also used. Some eds. prefer **Guillaume** Fr. /ĝee yohm/.

163. **Lodowick** /LŎD oh wik, LOHD-, -uh-/.

164. **Gratii** Ang.Lat. /GRAY shee ī/; Class.Lat. /GRAH tih ee/. A mixed form /GRAH tee ī/ is also used.

165. **Chitopher** /CHIT uh fur, KIT uh fur/. *Christopher* may have been intended.

165. **Vaumond** /VOH mund, -mŏnd/; Fr. /voh moh^n/.

165. **Bentii** Ang.Lat. /BEN shee ī/; Class.Lat. /BEN tih ee/. A mixed form /BEN tee ī/ is also used.

169. **cassocks** /KĂSS ucks/ soldiers' long coats.

183. **inter'gatories** questions. US /in TUR guh tor eez/; UK /-tur eez, -treez/.

187. **shrieve's** /shreevz/ archaic variant of **sherrif's**.

213. **advertisement** /ad VURT iss munt, -iz-/ warning. In this prose passage it could be pronounced /AD vur tīz munt/ as in mod. Am. Eng., but since the meanings are so different, the former, older pronunciation is recommended.

220, 300. **lascivious** /luh SIV ee us/ lustful.

236. **armipotent** /ạr MIP uh tunt/ powerful in arms.

251. **Nessus** /NESS us/ centaur who tried to rape Hercules' wife.

254. **volubility** /vŏl yuh BIL ih tee/ quick wit.

267. **tragedians** /truh JEE dee unz/ actors of tragedies.

267. **belie** /bih-, bee LĪ/ slander.

278. **cardecue** /CAR dih kyo͞o/ Fr. coin. Some eds. prefer **quart d'écu**, pronounced the same way if angl., or quasi-Fr. /CAR day kyo͞o, car day KYO͞O/.

306. **pestiferous** /pes TIF ur us/ harmful.

Act 4 Scene 4

3. ***surety** guarantee. Here should be 2 syllables, though in mod. Eng., 3 syllables are more common US /SHUR (ih) tee, SHOOR-/; CN /SHUR-/ [SHOOR-]; UK /SHOR-/ [SHUR-] [SHOOR-].

4. **perfect** here should be /PUR fict/ fully accomplish.

7. **Tartar's** /TAR turz/ people of Central Asia.

9. **Marsellis** /mar SELL iss/ archaic variant of **Marseilles**. The usual mod. pronunciation /mar SAY/ will not fit, but another modern variant from the UK will: [mar SAY łz].

Act 4 Scene 5

1. **snipt-taffata, taffeta** /TAF uh tuh/ type of cloth slashed to show lining beneath.

2. **saffron** /SAFF run/ yellow food coloring used in pastry and in starch for clothes.

6. **humble-bee** pronounced with the same stress as *bumble bee.*

14, 17. **sallets** /SAL its/ herbs or greens for salads. Some eds. prefer **salads**.

16. **marjorom** type of herb. Archaic variant of **marjoram**, both pronounced /MAR jur rum/.

20. **Nebuchadnezzar** US /neb uh kud NEZ ur/; UK /neb yuh-/ king of Babylon.

39. **name** (*maine* F1). Some eds. prefer **mien** /meen/ appearance, manner.

40. **fisnomy** /FIZ nuh mee/ face. Archaic variant of ***physiognomy** /fiz ee ŎG nuh mee/, *rarely older* /fiz ee ŎN uh mee/. Some eds. prefer **phys'nomy** /FIZ nuh mee/ or **phys'namy** (to make clear a pun with *name* in line 39).

ă-bat, ăir-marry, air-pair, ạr-far, ĕr-merry, ĝ-get, ī-high, ĭr-mirror, ł-little, ṇ-listen, ŏ-hot, oh-go, o͝o-wood, o͞o-moon, oor-tour, ōr-or, ow-how, ᶒh-that, t̶h̶-thin, ŭ-but, UR-fur, ur-under. ( )- suppress the syllable [ ]- less common see p. xi for complete list.

66. **patent** US /PAT ṇt/; UK /PAYT ṇt/ [PAT-] license.

80. **Marsellis** /mar SELL iss/ archaic variant of **Marseilles**. In this prose passage the mod. pronunciations may be used /mar SAY/; UK *also* [mar SAY łz].

101. **carbinado'd** slashed. Archaic variant of *carbonado'd, both pronounced /car buh NAH dohd/; UK *rarely older* [-NAY dohd].

Act 5 Scene 2

16. **Foh** indicates an expression of disgust made with the lips /pff/! or /pfuh/! Sometimes rendered as /foh/ or *faugh* /faw/.

17. *close-stool US /CLOHSS sto͞ol, CLOHZ-/; UK /CLOHSS-/, *rarely* [CLOHZ-] chamber pot enclosed in a stool.

33. **cardecue** /CAR dih kyo͞o/ Fr. coin. Some eds. prefer **quart d'écu**, pronounced the same way if angl., or quasi-Fr. /CAR day kyo͞o, car day KYO͞O/.

Act 5 Scene 3

16. **survey** here should be /sur VAY/ sight.

25. **relics** (F3), **reliques** (F1) /REL iks/ remains.

48. **perspective** here should be /PUR spek tiv/.

57. **compt** /cownt/ archaic variant of **count**. Both mean 'account,' and both were pronounced the same way in Elizabethan Eng.

72. **cesse** /sess/ a variant of **cease** which here rhymes with *bless*.

86. **reave** /reev/ bereave, rob.

101. **Plutus** /PLO͞OT us/ god of riches.

108, 297. *surety pledge, guarantee. The 1st instance can be 2 syllables or a triple ending, the 2nd should be 2 syllables, though in mod. Eng. 3 syllables are more common US /SHUR (ih) tee, SHOOR-/; CN /SHUR-/ [SHOOR-]; UK /SHOR-/ [SHUR-] [SHOOR-].

134. **suppliant** /SUP lyunt/ someone who asks humbly for something.

139. ***protestations** US /proh tess-, prŏt ess TAY shunz/;
CN /prŏt ess-/ [proh tess-]; UK /prŏt ess-/.

197. **sequent issue** /SEE kwunt/ subsequent generation.

250. **equivocal** /ih KWIV uh kł/; US *also* /ee-/ arguing both sides of an issue.

254. ***orator** US, CN /OR uh tur/; UK, E. COAST US /ŎR-/. Sometimes /OR ayt ur/ is
used, but it is not recommended. /-tor/ not recommended.

260. **Sathan** archaic form of **Satan**, both pronounced /SAYT n̩, -un/ the devil.

321. **handkercher** /HANK ur chur/ archaic variant of **handkerchief**.

ă-bat, ăir-marry, air-pair, ạr-far, ĕr-merry, ĝ-get, ī-high, ĭr-mirror, ł-little, n̩-listen,
ŏ-hot, oh-go, ōō-wood, ōō-moon, oor-tour, ōr-or, ow-how, t̪h-that, t̶h̶-thin, ŭ-but,
UR-fur, ur-under. ( )- suppress the syllable   [ ]- less common   see p. xi for complete list.

As You Like It

People in the Play

Aliena /ay lee EE nuh/ Celia's pseudonym.

Amiens /AM yenz, -yunz/ are the most common angl. forms. Another angl. variant formerly used was /AYM yenz/. /AM yah^n/ is a more recent semi-angl. form with the wrong Fr. ending; Fr. would be /AHM yă^n/. Used only once.

Celia 2 or 3 syllables depending on meter /SEE l(ee) yuh/.

Corin US /COR in/; E. COAST US, UK /CŎR in/.

Duke Frederick 2 or 3 syllables depending on meter /FRED uh rik, FRED rik/.

Duke Senior /SEEN yur/.

Ganymed /GAN ih med/ or /GAN ee-/ archaic variant of ***Ganymede** /-meed/ Rosalind's pseudonym.

*Jaques /JAY kweez/ [jayks] in all countries. Other endings are only rarely used: US [JAY keez, -kiz, -kis]; UK [JAY kwiz, -kwis]. In some lines it should be 2 syllables, but in others it can be 1 or 2. The normal pronunciation in Shk's time was /jayks/ or if 2 syllables, /JAY kis/.

Le Beau /luh BOH/.

Phebe, Phoebe /FEE bee/.

Rosalind /RŎZ uh lind/ is the traditional form, but for Orlando's rhymes in 3.2 /-līnd/ is indicated.

Rowland de Boys de Bois /ROH lund duh BOYSS, -BOYZ/ Fr: /roh lah^n duh BWAH/.

Silvius 2 or 3 syllables depending on meter /SIL v(ee) yus/.

Places in the Play

Arden, Ardenne /AHR din/; Fr. /ahr den/.

Special Note

Riverside uses the archaic form (still found in some dialects) **wrastle** /RĂSS ł/ 'wrestle,' which occurs throughout the play.

Act 1 Scene 1

13. **manage.** Some eds. prefer **manège** US /mah NEZH, -NAYZH/; UK /man AYZH/ [-EZH, MAN ayzh]; Fr. /mah nezh/. Both words mean 'horsemanship.'

19. **hinds** /hīndz/ menial laborers.

39. **penury** /PEN yur ee/; UK *also* /PEN yoor ee/ poverty.

50. **albeit** /awl BEE it/ although.

55, 56, 59. **villain.** Some eds. prefer to make a contrast in this passage between **villain** and in line 56 **villein** 'a type of serf,' which on historical principles should also be /VIL un/ but which is sometimes /-ayn/ to differentiate it from *villain*.

73. **allotery** /uh LŎT ur ee/ allotment.

87. **Holla** /huh LAH/ a call to attract attention.

92. ***importunes** /im POR chunz/ asks insistently, begs. About half the respondents in the Survey reported a form with 3rd syllable stress in all countries, but that will not fit the meter in verse and is a relatively recent innovation (cf. *fortune*).

102. **revenues** sometimes in verse /ruh VEN yo͞oz/, but in this prose passage may be mod. Eng. US /REV in o͞oz/; UK, SOUTH. US /-yo͞oz/.

146. **as lief** /leef/ as soon.

156. **anatomize** /uh NAT uh mīz/ analyze in detail.

171. **mispris'd, misprized** /mis PRĪZD/ despised.

Act 1 Scene 2

31. ***huswife** /HUZ if/ is traditional, /HUSS wīf/ is a newer, spelling pronunciation.

ă-bat, ăir-marry, air-pair, ạr-far, ĕr-merry, ĝ-get, ī-high, ĭr-mirror, ł-little, ṇ-listen, ŏ-hot, oh-go, o͞o-wood, o͞o-moon, oor-tour, ōr-or, ow-how, ṭh-that, ŧh-thin, ŭ-but, UR-fur, ur-under. ( )- suppress the syllable [ ]- less common   see p. xi for complete list.

The former is the most common form in the UK, the latter in the US. In CN both are used equally. In North America /HUSS wif/ is also sometimes used. Some eds. prefer F1's **housewife**.

42. **lineaments** /LIN ee yuh munts/ distinctive features.

51. ***Peradventure** perhaps. /PUR ad VEN chur/;
US *rarely* [PĔR-, PUR ad ven chur];
UK, CN *also* [PUR-, PĔR ad ven chur, pĕr ad VEN chur].

97. **Bon jour** Fr. /boh^n ZHOOR/ good day.

181. **mispris'd, misprized** /mis PRĪZD/ despised.

251. **quintain** US /KWINT n̩, -in/ wooden target used in tilting.

251. **liveless** /LĪV liss/ archaic variant of **lifeless**.

262. **Albeit** /awl BEE (i)t/ although.

265. **misconsters** /mis CŎN sturz/ misconstrues.

Act 1 Scene 3

74. **eat** /et/ dialect variant of **eaten**.

83. **irrevocable** here should be /ih REV uh kuh bł/; US *also* /ir-/.

120. **martial** /MAR shł/ warlike.

129. **assay'd** /uh-, ass SAYD/. Some eds. prefer **essayed** /es SAYD/. Both mean 'attempted.'

Act 2 Scene 1

19. **translate** transforming. Here should be stressed on the 2nd syllable, the normal UK pronunciation. US /trănss LAYT, trănz-/; UK /trănss LAYT/ [trănz-, trahnz-, trahnss-, trunss-, trunz-].

23. **burghers** /BURG urz/ citizens.

24. **confines** territories. Here should be /cŏn-, cun FĪNZ/.

31. ***antique** (*anticke* F1) ancient. Here /AN teek/, *rarely older* [AN tik]. Some eds. prefer **antic** /AN tik/ grotesquely shaped.

Act 2 Scene 2

10. **Hisperia** Ang.Lat. /hih SPEER ee uh/; Class.Lat. /-SPĔR-/.

14. **sinowy** /SIN (oh) wee/ muscular. Archaic variant of **sinewy**
/SIN y(oo) wee/; US *also* [SIN (oo) wee].

Act 2 Scene 3

8. **priser, prizer** /PRĪZ ur/ prize fighter.

57. ***antique** ancient. Here /AN teek/, *rarely older* [AN tik].

65. **In *lieu of** US, CN /lō͞o, lyō͞o/; UK /lyō͞o/ [lō͞o] in return for.

Act 2 Scene 4

51. **peascod** /PEEZ cŏd/ 'peapod,' but here apparently 'pea plant.'

66. **Holla** /huh LAH/ a call to attract attention.

75. **succor** (UK **succour**) /SUCK ur/ help. /-or/ not recommended.

81. **little reaks, recks** /reks/ takes no care.

Act 2 Scene 5

18, 19. **stanzo(s)** /STANZ oh/ archaic variant of **stanza**. /STAN zuh/ could also be
indicated by the *-o* ending because unstressed /oh/ was often reduced to /uh/.

54. ***Ducdame** US /dō͞ok DAYM/ or /duck-, dō͞ok DAH mee/;
CN /duck DAM ee, dō͞ok DAH mee/; UK /dō͞ok DAH may, duck DAYM/. In the US,
UK many other variants were reported, with 1st syllable /duck-, dō͞ok-/, and final
syllables /-DAH may, -DAY mee/. Probably a nonsense word with 3 syllables to
match *come hither* in the previous stanza. Shk probably intended the latter part of
the word to be /DAY mee/ or /DAM ee/.

62. **banket** /BANK it/ light meal, often of fruit. Archaic variant of **banquet**.

ă-bat, ăir-**marry**, air-**pair**, ạr-**far**, ĕr-**merry**, ĝ-get, ī-high, ĭr-**mirror**, ł-little, ṇ-listen,
ŏ-hot, oh-go, o͝o-**wood**, ō͞o-**moon**, oor-**tour**, ōr-**or**, ow-**how**, ţh-**that**, t̶h̶-**thin**, ŭ-but,
UR-**fur**, ur-**under**. ( )- suppress the syllable   [ ]- less common   see p. xi for complete list.

Act 2 Scene 7

5. **compact** /cum-, cŏm PACT/ composed of.

13–58. **motley** /MŎT lee/ costume of different colored cloth worn by fools.

30. ***chanticleer** a rooster. US /CHĂNT-, SHĂNT ih cleer/; UK /CHĂNT-/, *rarely* [CHAHNT-, SHAHNT-]; *rarely* with 3rd syllable stress in both countries.

31. **contemplative** here should be /cun TEMP luh tiv/ thoughtful.

32. **sans** /sănz/ without.

56. **anatomiz'd** /uh NAT uh mīzd/ examined in detail.

64. **mischievous** here should be /MIS chiv us/. /mis CHEEV us/ is considered non-standard in all countries.

65. ***libertine** /LIB ur teen/, *rarely* [-tīn] person who acts without moral restraint.

88. **eat**. The 2nd *eat* is /et/, a dialect variant of **eaten.**

114, 121. **knoll'd** /nohld/ archaic variant of *knell'd* rung.

115. **sate** archaic variant of **sat**. May have been /sayt/ or /sat/.

144. **Mewling** /MYŌOL ing/ whining.

154. ***capon** US /KAY pŏn, -pun/; CN, UK /KAY pŏn/ [-pun] chicken. /-un/ would be the historically correct form (cf. *canon, poison*).

158. ***pantaloon** foolish old man. US, UK /PANT uh lōōn/ [pant uh LŌŌN]; CN /pant uh LOON/ [PANT uh lōōn].

166. **Sans** /sănz/ without.

180-190. ***Heigh-ho** US /hay ho, hī-/; CN /hī-/, *rarely* [hay-]; UK /hay-/. Shk intended /hay/. In speech the syllables are evenly stressed or spoken as if sighing, with 1st syllable stress.

193. **effigies** /ef FIJ eez/ archaic form of **effigy**, both of which are singular.

194. **limn'd** /limd/ described.

Act 3 Scene 2

44. *parlous /PAR lus/ archaic variant of perilous.

50, 68. *uncleanly /un CLEN lee/, or newer /un CLEEN lee/.

64, 67. civet /SIV it/ a type of perfume.

67. perpend /pur PEND/ consider.

88. *Inde the Indies. Here /īnd/ in keeping with the other rhymes in this
passage.

90. wind here the archaic pronunciation /wīnd/ should be used, in keeping with the
other rhymes.

101. hind /hīnd/ doe.

117. graff US /grăf/; E. NEW ENG., UK /grahf/ archaic variant of graft.

118, 120. medlar /MED lur/ an apple-like fruit.

139. quintessence here should be /KWIN tih senss/ or /kwin tih SENSS/ rather than
mod. /kwin TESS ṇss/.

146. Cleopatra's US /clee oh PAT ruz/; UK also /-PAHT ruz/.

147. Atalanta's /at uh LAN tuz/ the swiftest runner in Gk. myths.

148. Lucretia's /lōō CREE shuz/ Roman who commited suicide after being raped.
At one time many RP speakers in the UK used /lyōō-/ for words beginning lu-, but
today their number is dwindling.

150. *synod US, CN /SIN ud/ [-ŏd]; UK /-ŏd/ [-ud] council of the gods.

176. *Pythagoras' US /pih THAG uh rus/ [pī-]; UK /pī-/ Gk. philosopher.

179. *Trow you US, CN /troh, trow/; UK /trow/ [troh] do you know. Shk's rhymes
elsewhere indicate /-oh/.

ă-bat, ăir-marry, air-pair, ạr-far, ĕr-merry, ĝ-get, ī-high, ĭr-mirror, ł-little, ṇ-listen,
ŏ-hot, oh-go, ōō-wood, ōō-moon, oor-tour, ōr-or, ow-how, ṭh-that, th-thin, ŭ-but,
UR-fur, ur-under. ( )- suppress the syllable   [ ]- less common   see p. xi for complete list.

193. **hooping** /H$\overline{OO}$P ing, H$\overline{oo}$P-/ i.e., power to speak. Variant of ***whooping** /WH$\overline{OO}$P ing/ [H$\overline{oo}$P-, H$\overline{OO}$P-, WH$\overline{oo}$P-].

195. **caparison'd** /kuh PĂIR ih sṇd/ decked out.

225. **Gargantua's** US /gar GAN choo uz/; UK *also* /-tyoo uz/.

228. **catechism** /KAT uh kiz um, -kizm/ series of questions and answers.

232. **atomies** /AT uh meez/ tiny particles.

244. **holla** /HŎL uh/ or /huh LAH/ whoa.

244. **curvets** /cur VETS/; US *also* /CUR vits/ type of leap on horseback.

254. **as lief** /leef/ as soon.

257. **God buy you** good-bye. Some eds. substitute **God b'wi' you** /gŏd BWEE y$\overline{oo}$/ or some other variation of that phrase.

268. **stature** /STATCH ur/ size.

277. **Atalanta's** /at uh LAN tuz/ the swiftest runner in Gk. myths.

308, 309. ***divers** various. US, CN /DĪ vurss, -vurz/ [dī-, dih VURSS]; UK /DĪ vurss/ [-vurz, dī VURSS].

315. **se'nnight** /SEN it, -īt/ week.

324. **penury** /PEN yur ee/; UK *also* /PEN yoor ee/ poverty.

339. ***cony** /KOH nee/, *rarely older* [KUN ee] rabbit.

354. **halfpence** /HAYP ṇss, -unss/.

362. **elegies** /EL uh jeez/ sorrowful poems.

364. ***fancy-monger** love peddler. US /FAN see mŏng gur/ or /-mawng-/, [-mung-]; CN /-mung gur, -mŏng gur/; UK /-mung gur/.

365. **quotidian** /kwoh TID ee un/; UK *also* [kwŏ TID ee un] type of fever.

378. **revenue** sometimes in verse /ruh VEN y$\overline{oo}$/, but in this prose passage may be mod. Eng. US /REV in $\overline{oo}$/; UK, SOUTH. US /-y$\overline{oo}$/.

382. **point-devise, -device** /POYNT dih VĪSS/ fastidious.

383. **accoustrements** /uh CUSS tur munts/ clothes. Archaic variant of
accoutrements /uh C͞OOT ruh munts, uh C͞OOT ur munts/.

Act 3 Scene 3

8. **Ovid** /ŎV id/ Roman poet.

9. **Goths** /gŏths/; US *also* /gawths/ Germanic tribe. Shk pronounced it /gohts/ or
/gŏts/, hence the pun with *goats*.

74. **God 'ild you** God reward you, thank you. /gŏd ILD yo͞o/; US *also* /gawd-/.
Some eds. prefer **God 'ield you** /-EELD-/.

78. **motley** /MŎT lee/ here means 'fool.' See 2.7.13.

79. **bow** /boh/ yoke.

87. ***wainscot** /WAYNZ cŏt, -cut/; US, UK *also newer* [-coht] type of wooden
interior siding.

103. **Wind** /wīnd/ wander.

Act 3 Scene 4

24. **concave** /CŎN-, CŎNG kayv/ or /cŏn-, cun KAYV/.

42. ***traverse** /truh VURSS, TRAV urss/; UK *also* /TRAV URSS/ across.

43. **puisne** /PYO͞O nee/ archaic variant of **puny**.

Act 3 Scene 5

13. **atomies** /AT uh meez/ tiny particles, specks of dust.

17. **swound** archaic variant of **swoon**. In Shk's time the vowel could be either /ow/
or /o͞o/.

23. **cicatrice** /SIK uh triss/ mark.

ă-bat, ăir-marry, air-pair, ạr-far, ĕr-merry, ĝ-get, ī-high, ĭr-mirror, ł-little, ṇ-listen,
ŏ-hot, oh-go, o͞o-wood, o͞o-moon, oor-tour, ōr-or, ow-how, ṭh-that, ŧh-thin, Ŭ-but,
UR-fur, ur-under. ( )- suppress the syllable [ ]- less common   see p. xi for complete list.

56. **lineaments** /LIN yuh munts/ distinctive features.

95. **erst** /urst/ formerly.

105. **yerwhile** may have been /yair-/ variant of **erewhile** /air WH$\overline{\text{I}}$L/ before.

108. **carlot** /CAR lut/ peasant.

123. **damask** /DAM usk/ pink or light red.

Act 4 Scene 1

14. **politic** /PŎL ih tik/ shrewd.

31. **God buy you** good-bye. Some eds. substitute **God b'wi' you**
/gŏd BWEE y$\overline{oo}$/ or some other variation of that phrase.

38. ***gundello** /GUN duh loh, -luh/ boat of Venice. Archaic variant of **gondola**
/GŎN duh luh/.

52. **as lief** /leef/ as soon.

55. **jointure** /JOYN chur/ marriage settlement.

75. ***orators** US, CN /OR uh turz/; UK, E. COAST US /ŎR-/. Sometimes
/OR ayt urz/ is used, but it is not recommended. /-torz/ not recommended.

97. ***videlicet** namely (abbreviated *viz.*). The older, angl. pronunciations are
US /vih DELL ih sit/ [-DEEL-, v$\overline{\text{i}}$-]; UK /vih DEEL ih sit/ [v$\overline{\text{i}}$-, -DELL-]. Newer
pronunciations mix in restored Latin syllables, for example, /-ket/ or /-DAYL-/.
These are not recommended.

100. **Leander** /lee AN dur/ he swam the Hellespont to be with Hero.

103. **Hellespont** /HEL iss pŏnt/ the Dardenelles.

106. ***Sestos** US /SESS tus, -tŏs/; UK /-tŏs/ [-tus]. A newer pronunciation /-ohss/ is
also used, especially in the US. Normal development would favor /-us/.

150. **Barbary** /BAR buh ree/ region in North Africa.

156. **hyen** /H$\overline{\text{I}}$ in/ variant of **hyena**.

Act 4 Scene 3

8, 21. **contents** here should be /cŏn TENTS/.

11. **tenure** archaic variant of **tenor**, both /TEN ur/.

27. ***huswive's** /HUZ ivz/ is traditional, /HUSS wīvz/ is a newer, spelling pronunciation. The former is the most common form in the UK, the latter in the US. In CN both are used equally. In North America /HUSS wivz/ is also sometimes used. Archaic variant of **housewive's**.

35. **Ethiop** /EETH yŏp/ an Ethiopian, i.e., black.

50. **eyne** /īn/ dialect form of *eyes*.

76. **purlieus** US, CN /PUR lo͞oz, -lyo͞oz/; UK /PUR lyo͞oz/, /-lo͞oz/ tract of land on the edge of a forest.

79. ***osiers** US /OH zhurz/ [OH zyurz]; UK /OH zyurz/ willows.

97. **handkercher** /HANK ur chur/ archaic variant of **handkerchief**.

168. ***Heigh-ho!** US /hay ho, hī-/; CN /hī-/, *rarely* [hay-]; UK /hay-/. Shk intended /hay/. Spoken with evenly stressed syllables or as if sighing, with 1st syllable stress.

Act 5 Scene 1

43, 44. **ipse** /IP see/ himself. Restored Latin is /IP say/.

48. ***boorish** US, CN /Bo͞oR ish/, *sometimes* [BOR-]; UK /Bo͞oR ish, BOR-/ peasant (language).

54. ***bastinado** beating with a stick. /bas tih NAH doh/;
UK *rarely older* [bas tih NAY doh].

Act 5 Scene 2

4. **persever** /pur SEV ur/ persevere. Since it is prose, mod. /pur suh VEER/ may be substituted.

ă-bat, ăir-marry, air-pair, ạr-far, ĕr-merry, ĝ-get, ī-high, ĭr-mirror, ł-little, ṇ-listen, ŏ-hot, oh-go, o͞o-wood, o͞o-moon, oor-tour, ŏr-or, ow-how, ṭh-that, t̶h̶-thin, ŭ-but, UR-fur, ur-under. ( )- suppress the syllable   [ ]- less common   see p. xi for complete list.

11. **revenue** sometimes in verse /ruh VEN yo͞o/, but in this prose passage may be mod. Eng. US /REV in o͞o/; UK, SOUTH. US /-yo͞o/.

26. **sound** archaic variant of **swoon**. In Shk's time the vowel could be either /ow/ or /o͞o/.

26. **handkercher** /HANK ur chur/ archaic variant of **handkerchief**.

31. **thrasonical** /t̶h̶ruh SŎN ih k̶l̶/ [t̶h̶ray SŎN ih k̶l̶] boastful.

43. ***nuptial** wedding. US, UK /NUP ch̶l̶/ [-sh̶l̶]; in CN both are used equally.

Act 5 Scene 3

17. **nonino, nonny-no** /NŎN ee NOH/ a nonsense word.

40. **God buy you** good-bye. Some eds. substitute **God b'wi' you** /gŏd BWEE yo͞o/ or some other variation of that phrase.

Act 5 Scene 4

5. **compact** plot. Here should be /cŏm-, cum PACT/.

35. **toward** /TOH wurd, -urd/ about to take place.

41. **motley-minded** /MŎT lee-/ foolish. See 2.7.13.

45. **politic** /PŎL ih tik/ shrewd.

54. **God 'ild you** God reward you, thank you. /gŏd ILD yo͞o/; US *also* /gawd-/. Some eds. prefer **God 'ield you** /-EELD-/.

65. **dulcet** /DULL sit/ sweet.

130. **contents** /cun TENTS/ contentments.

184. **convertites** /CŎN vur tīts/ converts to a religious life.

189. **allies** here with 2nd syllable stress.

192. **victuall'd** /VIT l̶d/ provided with food.

Epilogue

11. **conjure** entreat. US, CN /CŎN jur/, *rarely* [CUN-]; UK /CUN jur/ [CŎN-], *rarely* [cun JOOR]. The older pronunciation for this meaning is /cun JOOR/.

ă-bat, äir-marry, air-pair, ạr-far, ĕr-merry, ĝ-get, ī-high, ĭr-mirror, ł-little, ṇ-listen, ŏ-hot, oh-go, o͞o-wood, o͞o-moon, oor-tour, ōr-or, ow-how, ṭh-that, t̶h̶-thin, ŭ-but, UR-fur, ur-under. ( )- suppress the syllable [ ]- less common see p. xi for complete list.

The Comedy of Errors

People in the Play

Abbess /AB iss/, also called **Aemilia**.

*Adriana US /ay dree AHN uh/ [ad ree AHN uh, ay dree ANN uh];
CN /ay dree ANN uh/ [-AHN-]; UK /ad ree AHN uh/ [-ANN-, ay dree AHN uh].
Recommendation: the oldest angl. form /ay dree ANN uh/.

Aegeon see **Egeon**.

Aemilia, **Emilia** /ee-, ih MEEL ee yuh/. Older /-MILL-/ is now rare. Also called
the **Abbess**.

Angelo /AN juh loh/.

Antipholus /an TIF uh lus/.

*Balthazar, Balthasar /BAL thuh zar/. The scansion is uncertain at 3.1.19 and 22,
but the stress could be on the 1st syllable. A variant form /bal THAZ ur/ is also possible, though rarely used today. Likewise a form with 3rd syllable stress is rare.

*Courtezan, Courtesan US /CORT ih zun, -zan/, *rarely* [cort ih ZAN];
CN /CORT ih zan/ [-zun], *rarely* [cort ih ZAN]; UK /CORT ih zan, cort ih ZAN/.
This word is not spoken in the play.

Dromio 2 or 3 syllables depending on meter /DROH m(ee) yoh/.

Egeon, Aegeon /ih-, ee JEE un/ is usual, but /-ŏn/ is sometimes used.   Traditionally
/-un/ would be the correct form (cf. *Orion*).

Emilia see **Aemilia**.

Luce /looss/. Some eds. call this character **Nell**. At one time many RP speakers in
the UK used /lyoo-/ for words beginning *lu-*, but today their number is dwindling.

*Luciana US /loo see AH nuh, -chee-, -shee-/ [loo see ANN-, loo chee ANN-];
CN /loo see ANN uh/ [-chee AHN-, -chee ANN-]; UK /loo chee AHN uh/
[-see AHN-, -chee ANN-]. Recommendation: the oldest angl. form
/loo shee ANN uh/. /-chee-/ and /-AHN-/ are Ital. forms. At one time many RP
speakers in the UK used /lyoo-/ for words beginning *lu-*, but today their number is
dwindling.

Solinus /soh-, suh LĪ nus/.

Places in the Play

The Centaur /SEN tor/ an inn.

Ephesus /EF ih sus/.

Epidamium (F1) /ep ih DAYM yum/. The usual mod. form of this city is *Epidamnus*. Some eds. prefer the form **Epidamnum** /ep ih DAM num/.

The Porpentine /POR pin tīn/ an inn. Archaic variant of **Porcupine**.

***Syracuse** US /SĬR uh kyo͝oss/; UK /SĪ ruh kyo͝oz/ [SĬR-, -kyo͝oss].
Syracusa angl. US /sĭr uh KYO͞OZ uh/; UK /sī ruh-/ [sĭr uh-];
Ital. /see rah KO͞O zah/.
Syracusian(s) US /sĭr uh KYO͞O zhun(z)/; UK /sī ruh-/ [sĭr uh-].
Syracusan is prefered by some eds. /-sun, -zun, -sn̩, -zn̩/.

Act 1 Scene 1

8. **guilders** /ĜILL durz/ type of money.

11. **intestine** /in TESS tin/; UK *also* [-teen] internal or deadly.

13.***synods** US, CN /SIN udz/ [-ŏdz]; UK /-ŏdz/ [-udz] councils.

20. **confiscate** confiscated. Here should be /cŏn FISS kayt, -ut/.

42. **randon** /RAN dun/ archaic form of **random**.

87–111. **Corinth** US, CN /COR in~~th~~/; UK, E. COAST US /CŎR-/.

92. **amain** /uh MAYN/ with full speed.

93. **Epidaurus** /ep ih DOR us/.

120, 141. **mishap(s)** here /mis HAP(S)/.

122. **dilate** /dih-, dī LAYT/ tell in detail.

ă-bat, ăir-marry, air-pair, ar-far, ĕr-merry, ĝ-get, ī-high, ĭr-mirror, ł-little, n̩-listen, ŏ-hot, oh-go, o͝o-wood, o͞o-moon, oor-tour, ōr-or, ow-how, ţh-that, ~~th~~-thin, ŭ-but, UR-fur, ur-under. ( )- suppress the syllable [ ]- less common see p. xi for complete list.

126. **importun'd** /im POR chund/ asked insistently. About half the respondents in the Survey reported a form with 3rd syllable stress in all countries, but that will not fit the meter in verse and is a relatively recent innovation (cf. *fortune*).

144. **disannul** /dis uh NŬL/ annul.

145. **advocate** /AD vuh kut/ someone who supports a person or cause.

158. **liveless** /LĪV liss/ archaic variant of **lifeless**.

Act 1 Scene 2

2. **confiscate** /CŎN fiss kayt, -ut/ confiscated.

28. **consort** /cun SORT/ keep company with.

44. **capon** US /KAY pŏn, -pun/; CN, UK /KAY pŏn/ [-pun] chicken. /-un/ would be the historically correct form (cf. *canon, poison*).

55. **sixpence** /SIKS punss, -pn̩ss/; US *also* /SIKS penss/.

79. **sconce** /skŏnss/ head.

96. **o'erraught** /or RAWT/ cheated.

101. **mountebanks** /MOWNT uh banks/ quack doctors.

Act 2 Scene 1

16. **situate** US /SITCH (oo) wut/ [-wayt]; UK /-wayt/ situated.

22. **Indu'd** /in DYŌŌD/; US *also* [-DŌŌD] supplied.

38. **unkind** here should be /UN kīnd/.

72. **arrant** /ĂIR unt/ archaic variant of **errand**.

86. **low'reth, loureth** threatens. /LOWR ith/ with the vowel of *how*.

92. **voluble** /VŎL yuh bł/ easily flowing.

104. **homage** /HŎM ij/; US *also* /ŎM ij/ acknowledgement of allegiance.

Act 2 Scene 2

34–7. **sconce** /skŏnss/ double meaning: head, fort.

38. **insconce** /in SKŎNSS/ fortify. Most eds. prefer **ensconce** /en-/.

58–62. **Basting** /BAYST ing/ beating.

75. **periwig** /PĔR ee wig/ *also* /PĔR ih-/ wig.

77. **niggard** /NIG urd/ miser.

109.*****wafts** beckons. US, CN /wŏfts/; SOUTH. US /wăfts/;
UK /wŏfts/ [wăfts, wahfts]. /wăfts/ is newer and considered non-standard by many.

122. **undividable** /un dih VĪ duh bł/.

122. **incorporate** /in COR pur rut, -rayt/ united in body. /-ut / is more usual for an adj.

131. **licentious** here should be /lī SEN chee us/ lustful.

132.*****consecrate** /CŎN suh crut, -crayt/ consecrated.

133.*****contaminate** /cun TAM ih nut, -ayt/ contaminated.

136. **harlot** /HAR lut/ whore.

140. **adulterate** /uh DULL trayt, -trut/ defiled with adultery. /-ut/ is more usual for an adj.

158. **buffet** /BUFF it/ strike.

161. **compact** here should be /cŏm-, cum PACT/ plot.

177. **dross** /drŏss/; US *also* /drawss/ impure matter, rubbish.

193. **prat'st** /praytst/ chatter.

215. **persever** /pur SEV ur/ persevere.

ă-bat, äir-marry, air-pair, ar-far, ĕr-merry, ĝ-get, ī-high, ĭr-mirror, ł-little, n̩-listen, ŏ-hot, oh-go, o͞o-wood, o͞o-moon, oor-tour, ŏr-or, ow-how, t̪h-that, t̪h-thin, ŭ-but, UR-fur, ur-under. ( )- suppress the syllable [ ]- less common   see p. xi for complete list.

Act 3 Scene 1

4. **carcanet** /CAR kuh net/ necklace.

27. **niggardly** /NIG (ur)d lee/ miserly.

28. **cates** /kayts/ food.

31. **Cic'ly, Cicely** /SISS lee/.

31. **Gillian** /JILL yun/.

31. **Ginn** /jin/.

32. *****capon** US /KAY pŏn, -pun/; CN, UK /KAY pŏn/ [-pun] chicken. /-un/ would be the historically correct form (cf. *canon, poison*).

34. *****conjure** here should be /cun JOOR/ summon by magic.

77. **hind** /hīnd/ menial laborer.

101. **rout** /rowt/ crowd.

121. **elsewhere** here with 2nd syllable stress, a form still used in the UK, but unknown in the US.

Act 3 Scene 2

4. **ruinous** /RŌŌ ih nus/. F1 has an archaic variant **ruinate** /RŌŌ ih nut/.

7. **elsewhere** here with 2nd syllable stress, a form still used in the UK, but unknown in the US.

10. *****orator** US, CN /OR uh tur/; UK, E. COAST US /ŎR-/. Sometimes /OR ayt ur/ is used, but it is not recommended. /-tor/ not recommended.

12. **harbinger** /HAR bin jer/ a messenger sent in advance.

22. **compact** /cum-, cŏm PACT/ composed of.

43. *****homage** /HŎM ij/; US *also* /ŎM ij/ acknowledgement of allegiance.

102. **Swart** /swōrt/ black.

114. *****spherical** US, CN /SFEER ih kł/ [SFĔR-]; UK /SFĔR ih kł/.

128. **rheum** /rōōm/ mucus.

137. **armadoes** /arm AY dohz/ archaic form of **armadas** /arm AH duz/ fleets.

137. **carrects** /KĂIR ucts/ large ships. Archaic variant of **carracks** /KĂIR uks/.

137. **ballast** /BĂL ust/ ballasted, loaded with ballast, weight.

138. **Belgia** /BEL juh/ Belgium.

146. **curtal dog** /CURT ł/ dog with tail cut short.

Act 4 Scene 1

1. **Pentecost** /PEN tih cŏst/; US *also* /-cawst/ 7th Sunday after Easter.

2. ***importun'd** /im POR chund/ asked insistently. About half the respondents in the Survey reported a form with 3rd syllable stress in all countries, but that will not fit the meter in verse and is a relatively recent innovation (cf. *fortune*).

4. **guilders** /ĜILL durz/ type of money.

22. **holp** /hohlp/ helped.

28. **charect** /KĂIR uct/ archaic variant of **carat** /KĂIR ut/ a unit of weight.

48, 59. **dalliance** play, frivolity. The 1st instance is /DAL yunss/, the 2nd /DAL ee yunss/.

53. ***importunes** /im POR chunz/ asks insistently. About half the respondents in the Survey reported a form with 3rd syllable stress in all countries, but that will not fit the meter in verse and is a relatively recent innovation (cf. *fortune*).

87. **fraughtage** /FRAWT ij/ cargo.

89. **balsamum** /BAWL suh mum/ balsum or balm, a healing oinment.

89. ***aqua-vitae** distilled liquor, e.g., brandy. US /AHK-, AK wuh VEE tī/, *rarely* [-VĪ tee]; CN /AK wuh VEE tī/ [AHK-]; UK /AK wuh VEE tī/ [-VEE tuh]. /AK wuh VĪ tee/ is the oldest surviving form. /-VEE tay/ not recommended.

ă-bat, ăir-marry, air-pair, ạr-far, ĕr-merry, ĝ-get, ī-high, ĭr-mirror, ł-little, ṇ-listen, ŏ-hot, oh-go, ōō-wood, ōō-moon, oor-tour, ōr-or, ow-how, țh-that, ŧh-thin, ʊ-but, UR-fur, ur-under. ( )- suppress the syllable   [ ]- less common   see p. xi for complete list.

95. ***waftage** passage. US, CN /WŎFT ij/; SOUTH. US /WĂFT-/;
UK /WŎFT-/ [WĂFT-, WAHFT-]. /WĂFT-/ is newer and considered
non-standard by many.

98. **rope's, ropës** here 2 syllables are indicated /ROH piz/.

110. **Dowsabel** /DOW suh bel, -zuh-/ i.e., Luce.

Act 4 Scene 2

19. **sere** /seer/ withered.

32. **Tartar** /TAR tur/ hellish.

37. ***countermands** forbids. /COWNT ur mǎndz/; E. NEW ENG., UK /-mahndz/.
More rarely the stress falls on the last syllable. Here should rhyme with *lands*.

58.***bankrout** /BANK rowt/ [-rut] archaic variant of **bankrupt**.

Act 4 Scene 3

27. **suits of *durance** /DYOOR unss/; US *also* /DŌŌR-/ [DUR-]. Double meaning:
'durable cloth' and 'imprisonment.'

28. **exploits** /ek SPLOYTS/ in verse, but here may be mod. /EK sployts/.

28. **morris-pike.** Some eds. prefer **Moorish pike** /MOOR ish/ [MOR-] a pike of
moorish origin.

48, 49. **Sathan** archaic form of **Satan**, both pronounced /SAYT ṇ, -un/ the devil.

56. ***ergo** /UR go/ is older, /ĚR go/ is newer. The former is more common in the
UK, the latter in the US, but both forms appear in all countries.

69. **diamond** here should be /DĪ uh mund/, the standard UK form.

79. **Avaunt** /uh VAWNT/ begone!

Act 4 Scene 4

41. **respice finem** Ang.Lat. /RESS pih see FĪ nem/;
Class.Lat. /RESS pik ay FEE nem/ look to your end.

54. **Sathan** archaic form of **Satan**, both pronounced /SAYT ṇ, -un/ the devil.

61. **saffron** /SAFF run/ yellow.

71. **Perdie, Perdy** /PUR DEE/ indeed (originally 'by God'). Some eds. prefer the variant **Pardie** /par DEE/.

73. **Sans** /sănz/ without.

75. **Certes** /SUR teez/ certainly.

79. **contraries** /CŎN truh reez/ behavior opposite to what is expected.

82. **suborn'd** /sub ORND/ persuaded someone to do wrong.

101. **harlot** /HAR lut/ whore.

103. **abject** /AB ject/ contemptible.

108. **wan** /wŏn/ pale.

Act 5 Scene 1

20. **controversy** here should be /CŎN truh vur see/, the normal US pronunciation.

37. **priory** /PRĪ (uh) ree/ convent.

97. **assaying** /uh-, ass SAY ing/. Some eds. prefer **essaying** /es SAY ing/. Both mean 'attempting.'

114. ***prostrate** /PRŎS trayt/, US *rarely* [-trut] lying face down.

170. **a-row** /uh ROH/ one after the other.

185.***halberds** US, CN /HAL burdz, HAWL-/; UK /HAL-/ [HAWL-] spears with blades on the end.

192. **bestrid** /bih-, bee STRID/ stood over protectively.

205. **harlots** /HAR luts/ lewd men.

ă-bat, ăir-marry, air-pair, ạr-far, ĕr-merry, ĝ-get, ī-high, ĭr-mirror, ł-little, ṇ-listen, ŏ-hot, oh-go, o͞o-wood, o͞o-moon, oor-tour, ŏr-or, ow-how, ṭh-that, t̶h̶-thin, ŭ-but, UR-fur, ur-under. ( )- suppress the syllable [ ]- less common   see p. xi for complete list.

217. **Albeit** /awl BEE (i)t/ although.

239. **mountebank** /MOWNT uh bank/ quack doctor.

271. **Circe's** /SUR seez/ a sorceress.

311. **untun'd** here stressed on the 1st syllable.

314. ***conduits** blood vessels. Here must be 2 syllables /CŎN dwits/;
UK *also* [CUN dwits, CŎN dywits, CŎN dits, CUN dits].

352–366. **Corinth** US, CN /COR inth/; UK, E. COAST US /CŎR-/.

361. **children** here /CHIL dur in/ is indicated.

369. **Menaphon** /MEN uh fun, -fŏn/. /-ŏn/ is usual in the US and is increasingly
common in the UK, though /-un/ would be the traditional form.

392. **diamond** here should be /DĪ uh mund/, the standard UK form.

401.***travail** here should be /TRAV ayl/ suffering (of childbirth).

Hamlet

People in the Play

Claudius /CLAW dee yus/ his name is never spoken.

Cornelius /cor NEEL yus/.

*****Fortinbras** US /FOR tin brahss/ [-brăss]; UK, CN use both with equal frequency.

Gonzago /gŏn-, gun ZAH goh/ character in the players' piece.

Guildenstern /ĜILL din sturn/.

Horatio /huh RAY shyoh/ [-shoh]; UK *also* [hŏ-].

*****Laertes** /lay AIR teez/ is newer, /lay UR teez/ older. In the US, CN the former is more common, in the UK the latter. /LAY ur teez/ will not fit the meter.

Marcellus /mar SELL us/.

*****Ophelia** US /oh FEEL yuh/ [uh-]; UK /oh-, ŏf-/ [uh-].

*****Osric** /ŎZ rik/ [ŎSS-].

*****The Polack(s)** US /POH lack, -lŏck/; CN, UK /POH lack/; US, CN *rarely* [-luck] Polish soldiers.

Polonius /puh LOHN yus/. In prose it may be /puh LOHN ee yus/.

Reynaldo (Q2) /ray-, rih NAL doh, -NAWL-, -NAHL-/. **Reynoldo** (F1) /-NAWL-; -NŎL-/.

Rosencrantz /ROH zin crănts/.

Voltemand (F1) /VŎL tih mund/. **Valtemand** (Q2) /VŎL-/ or /VAWL-/.

Places in the Play

*****Elsinore** /EL sin or/.

ă-bat, ăir-marry, air-pair, ạr-far, ĕr-merry, ĝ-get, ī-high, ĭr-mirror, ł-little, ņ-listen, ŏ-hot, oh-go, ōō-wood, ōō-moon, oor-tour, ōr-or, ow-how, ţh-that, ŧħ-thin, ŭ-but, UR-fur, ur-under. ( )- suppress the syllable [ ]- less common   see p. xi for complete list.

Act 1 Scene 1

18. **Holla** /huh LAH/ a call to attract attention.

30. **Tush** /tŭsh/ expression of disdain.

57. **avouch** /uh VOWCH/ affirmation.

61. **combated** here should be /CŎM buh tid/.

62. **parle** /pạrl/ conference with an enemy. Some eds. prefer mod. ***parley** /PAR lee/. Newer [-lay] not recommended.

66. **martial** /MAR shł/ warlike.

73. **brazen** /BRAY zun, -zn̩/ brass.

75. **impress** here should be /im PRESS/ forcing into labor.

77. **toward** /TOH wurd, -urd/ about to take place.

83. **emulate** /EM y(uh) lut/ trying to surpass a rival.

86. **compact** here should be /cŏm-, cum PACT/ agreement.

90. **moi'ty, moiety** /MOY tee/ portion.

93. **Had he been vanquisher; as by the same comart** (Q2) /koh MART/ agreement. Some eds. prefer F1's **cov'nant** /KUV nunt/, in which case *by the* should become 1 syllable, *by th'*.

103. **compulsatory** (Q2) by force. /cum PULS uh tree/ in a normal line, or possibly US /-tor ee/; UK /-tur ee/ before a caesura. F1 has **compulsative** /cum PULS uh tiv/.

107. **romage** intense activity. Archaic variant of **rummage**, both pronounced /RUM ij/.

109. **portentous** /por TEN tuss/ prophetic. In Q2 but not F1.

116. ***gibber** /JIB ur/, *rarely* [ĜIB ur] chatter. In Q2 but not F1.

121. **precurse** /pree-, prih CURSS/ indication in advance. In Q2 but not F1.

122. **harbingers** /HAR bin jurz/ advance messengers. In Q2 but not F1.

125. **climatures** /CLĪ muh churz/ regions. Some eds. prefer **climature**. In Q2 but not F1.

140.***partisan** /PART ih zan/ [-san, -zun]; UK *also* /part ih ZAN/ a spear with a blade on the end.

155. **confine** /cŏn-, cun FĪN/ confines, limits of an area.

Act 1 Scene 2

12. **dirge** /durj/ funeral music.

21. **Co-leagued** (Q2) /coh LEEG id/ allied. **Colleagued** (F1) /cuh-, cŏl LEEG id/.

29. **bedred** (Q2) archaic variant of F1's **bedrid** bedridden. Both pronounced /BED rid/.

38. **delated** (Q2) /dih-, dee LAYT id/ described in detail. Variant of F1's **dilated** /dih-, dī LAYT id/.

58. **H'ath** /hʸath/ he hath.

79. **suspiration** /suh spur RAY shun/ sigh.

87. **commendable** here should be /CŎM en duh bł/.

91. **filial obligation** /FIL ył/ a son's obligation.

92. **obsequious** /ŏb-, ub SEEK w(ee) yus/ dutifully mourning.

92. **persever** /pur SEV ur/ persevere.

93. **condolement** /cun DOHL munt/ mourning.

94. **impious** /IM pyus/ lacking in respect, profane.

113–168. **Wittenberg** angl. /WIT n̦ burg/; Germ. /VIT n̦ bĕrk/ city in Germany.

125.***jocund** /JŎCK und/; US, CN *rarely* [JOHK-] merry.

127. **the King's rouse** /rowz/ the King's bumper, deep drinking.

ă-bat, ăir-marry, air-pair, a̦r-far, ĕr-merry, ĝ-get, ī-high, ĭr-mirror, ł-little, n̦-listen, ŏ-hot, oh-go, o͞o-wood, o͞o-moon, oor-tour, ōr-or, ow-how, țh-that, t̶h̶-thin, ŭ-but, UR-fur, ur-under. ( )- suppress the syllable   [ ]- less common   see p. xi for complete list.

127. **bruit** /bro͞ot/ loudly declare.

140.*****Hyperion** /hī PEER yun/ god of the sun. Sometimes newer /-PĔR-/ or
/-ŏn/ are used, but are not recommended.

140. *****satyr** US, CN /SAYT ur/, *rarely* [SAT ur]; UK /SAT ur/ [SAYT-] lecherous,
goat-like creature.

149. **Niobe** /NĪ uh bee, -oh bee/ she wept endlessly when her children were killed.

157. **incestious** (Q2) /in SESS chus/ archaic variant of F1's **incestuous**
/in SESS chwus/; UK *also* /-tywus/.

177. **studient** (Q2) /STO͞OD yunt/; UK, SOUTH. US /STYO͞OD-/. Archaic variant of
F1's **student**.

193. **attent** /uh TENT/ attentive.

200. **cap-a-pe** from head to toe. Archaic variant of *****cap-à-pie**. Traditionally
/kap uh PEE/, still the most common form in the US, CN, and also used in the UK.
A newer form /-PAY/ is preferred in the UK and also used in the US. Stress may also
fall on the 1st syllable. A Frenchified version /kap uh pee AY/ is also increasingly
used. The spelling pronunciation /-PĪ/ is not recommended.

204. **truncheon's** /TRUN chunz/ short staff of office.

239. **grisl'd** (*grissl'd* Q2) graying. Archaic variant of **grizzled**, both pronounced
/GRIZ łd/. F1 has **grisly** (F1) /GRIZ lee/.

247. **tenable** /TEN (uh) bł/ held close. Q1 has **tenible** /TEN (ih) bł/.

Act 1 Scene 3

3. **convey** (*conuay* Q2) /CŎN vay/ transport. Some eds. prefer F1's **convoy.**

9. **suppliance** /suh PLĪ unss/ pastime.

12. *****thews** /t̶h̶yo͞oz/; US, CN *also* [t̶h̶o͞oz] muscles.

15. **cautel** /KAWT ł/ deceit.

21. **The safety and health of this whole state** (Q2) the meter calls for expansion to
/SAYF uh tee/, though some eds. have emmended it to **safety and the health**.
Other eds. prefer **sanity** or F1's **sanctity**.

30. **credent** /CREED ṇt/ trusting.

32. **importunity** /im por-, im pur TYO͞ON ih tee/; US *also* /-TO͞ON-/ insistent requests.

36. **chariest** /CHAIR yist/; E. COAST US *also* [CHĂIR-] most cautious, shyest.

38. **calumnious** /cuh LUM nyus/ slanderous.

49.***libertine** /LIB ur teen/, *rarely* [-tīn] person who acts without moral restraint.

50. **dalliance** /DAL yunss/ frivolity.

51. **reaks** /reks/ pays attention to. Most eds. prefer Q1's **recks**, pronounced the same way.

51. **rede** /reed/ advice.

59. **character** write down. Here with 2nd syllable stress.

65. **courage** (Q2) brave fellow. Some eds. prefer F1's ***comrade**, here showing original 2nd syllable stress US, CN /cŏm RAD/, *rarely* [cum-]; UK /cŏm RAYD/, *rarely* [-RAD, cum-]. Others prefer **comrague** 'fellow rogue,' presumably pronounced /cŏm-, cum RAYG/. *Courage* would require an unusual inversion.

97. **behooves** (Q2) /bih-, bee HO͞OVZ/ is necessary, proper for. UK prefers the F1 spelling **behoves** /bih HOHVZ/.

110. ***importun'd** /im POR chund/ asked insistently. About half the respondents in the Survey reported a form with 3rd syllable stress in all countries, but that will not fit the meter in verse and is a relatively recent innovation (cf. *fortune*).

115. **springes** /SPRIN jiz/ snares.

123. **parle** /pạrl/ conference with an enemy. F1 has ***parley** /PAR lee/. Newer [-lay] not recommended.

125. **teder** (Q3–4) /TED ur/ archaic variant of F1's **tether**.

129. **implorators** (F1) /im PLOR (uh) turz/ those who ask passionately for something. Some eds. prefer **imploratators** (following Q2) /im PLOR uh tay turz/. /-torz/ not recommended.

ă-bat, äir-marry, air-pair, ạr-far, ĕr-merry, ĝ-get, ī-high, ĭr-mirror, ł-little, ṇ-listen, ŏ-hot, oh-go, o͞o-wood, o͞o-moon, oor-tour, ôr-or, ow-how, ţh-that, ᵵh-thin, ŭ-but, UR-fur, ur-under. ( )- suppress the syllable   [ ]- less common   see p. xi for complete list.

Act 1 Scene 4

1. **shrowdly** (Q2) /SHROHD lee/ sharply. Archaic variant of F1's **shrewdly**.

8. **rouse** /rowz/ revels.

9. **Keeps *wassail** (Q1) festivities where much carousing occurs. Here stressed on the 1st syllable US /WŎSS ł, -ayl/, *rarely* [WĂSS ł]; CN /WŎSS ayl/ [WŎSS ł]; UK /WĂSS ayl/ [WŎSS-]. Normal development would favor /WŎSS-/. F1 has the plural form.

10. **draughts** US, CN /drăfts/; UK, EAST. N.ENG. /drahfts/ drinks.

10. **Rhenish** /REN ish/ Rhine wine.

Lines 17–38 are found in Q2 but not in F1.

18. **traduc'd** slandered. /truh DYŌŌST/; US *also* /-DŌŌST/. /-JŌŌST/ is considered non-standard in the UK.

19. **clip** (Q2) call. Variant of Q5's **clepe** /cleep/.

29. **o'er-leavens** /or LEV ņz, -inz/ having too much leaven (sourdough used to make bread rise), i.e., takes over.

30. ***plausive** /PLAW ziv/ [-siv] pleasing.

31. **defect** here should be /dih-, dee FECT/.

36. **ev'l**. Some eds. prefer Q2's **eale** or **evil, e'il, ale**. Q3–4 have **ease**. If *evil*, it could have been pronounced /eel/ in Shk's time, but since the word occurs at the end of the line, it can be pronounced normally /EE vł/ [EE vil], creating a feminine ending.

37. **of a doubt** some eds. prefer **often dout** /dowt/ extinguish, banish. **Over-daub** has also been suggested.

---

47. **canoniz'd** here should be /kan ŎN īzd/ buried according to church rites.

48. ***cerements** waxed grave clothes. /SEER munts/ is older, but virtually extinct. Today the spelling pronunciation /SĔR (uh) munts/ is used, which, if 3 syllables, would force *sepulchre* to be stressed on the 2nd syllable.

48. **sepulchre** /SEP ł kur/ tomb.

50. **op'd** /ohpt/ opened.

52. **complete steel** here should be /CŎM pleet/ full armor.

61, 78. **waves** (Q2). F1 has ***wafts** US, CN /wŏfts/, SOUTH. US /wăfts/;
UK /wŏfts/ [wăfts, wahfts] beckons. /wăfts/ is newer and considered non-standard by
many.

77. **fadoms** /FAD umz/ archaic variant of **fathoms** /FĂTH umz/. Omitted F1.

82.***artere** (*arture* Q2) artery. F1 has **artire**, Q3 has **artyre**. All are pronounced the
same way US /ART ur, -eer/; UK /ART ur/ [-eer]. Some eds. substitute Q5's **artery**,
which here would be /AR tree/.

83. **Nemean lion's** /NEE myun/ lion killed by Hercules.

Act 1 Scene 5

20. **porpentine** /POR pin tīn/ archaic variant of **porcupine**.

21. **blazon** /BLAY zun, -zn̦/ revealing of secrets.

33. **Lethe** /LEE~~TH~~ ee/ river of forgetfulness in Hades.

42. **adulterate** /uh DULL trayt, -trut/ adulterous. /-ut/ is more usual for an adj.

61. **secure** safe, leisure. Here 1st syllable stress is indicated.

62. **hebona** (Q2) /HEB (uh) nuh/ a poison plant, perhaps ebony. Some eds. prefer
F1's **hebonon**, sometimes spelled **hebenon** /HEB (uh) nun/. *H* was often silent in
Shk's time, and with raising of the final vowel to /ee/ (cf. *sirrah-sirry, Ursula-
Ursley*) *hebona* and *ebony* would have been homonyms.

68. **posset** /PŎSS it/ curdle.

72. ***lazar-like** /LAY zur, LAZZ ur/ leper-like.

77. **Unhous'led** /un HOWZ ɫd/ without the eucharist.

77. **unanel'd** /un uh NEELD/ without extreme unction.

89. **matin** /MAT in, -n̦/ morning.

ă-bat, ăir-marry, air-pair, a̞r-far, ĕr-merry, ĝ-get, ī-high, ĭr-mirror, ɫ-little, n̦-listen,
ŏ-hot, oh-go, o͞o-wood, o͞o-moon, oor-tour, ŏr-or, ow-how, t̠h-that, ᵮh-thin, ŭ-but,
UR-fur, ur-under. ( )- suppress the syllable   [ ]- less common   see p. xi for complete list.

90. **gins** /ĝinz/ begins.

94. **sinows** (Q2) /SIN ohz/. Archaic variant of F1's **sinews** /SIN yōōz/;
US *also* [SIN ōōz].

99. **records** here should be /rik-, rek ORDZ/.

102. **commandement** (Q2). Archaic variant of F1's **commandment**, originally
with 4 syllables, /-uh munt/, but here the usual mod. 3-syllable pronunciation is
required.

124. **arrant** /ĂIR unt/ thoroughgoing.

151. **cellarage** /SELL ur ij/ cellar.

156.   **Hic   et ubique**
Ang.Lat.   /HICK et yōō BĪ kwee/
Class.Lat. /HEEK et ōō BEE kway/
          here and everywhere

163. **pioner** soldier who dug trenches and planted mines. It is not certain whether
Shk pronounced this /PĪ uh nur/ or as in mod. **pioneer** /pī uh NEER/.

Act 2 Scene 1

3. **marvell's** (*meruiles* Q2, *maruels* F1) marvellously. Some eds. prefer Q3–4's
marvellous. In any event it should be 2 syllables, either /MARV łss/ or, as indicated
in spellings elsewhere in Shk, /MARV lus/.

42. **converse** /cun VURSS/ conversation.

43. **prenominate** /prih-, pree NŎM (ih) nut, -ayt/ aforementioned. /-ut / is more
usual for an adj.

56. **rouse** /rowz/ carousing.

59. *****Videlicet** namely (abbreviated *viz.*). The older, angl. pronunciations are
US /vih DELL ih sit/ [-DEEL-, vī-]; UK /vih DEEL ih sit/ [vī-, -DELL-]. Newer
pronunciations mix in restored Latin syllables, for example, /-ket/ or /-DAYL-/.
These are not recommended.

59. *****brothel** US, CN /BRŎT̶H̶ ł/ [BRŎT̶H ł, BRAWT̶H̶ ł]; UK /BRŎT̶H̶ ł/ whorehouse.

62. **windlasses** /WIND luss iz/ here means 'roundabout ways.'

62. **assays** /uh-, ass SAYZ/ attempts.

66. **God buy ye** (Q2) /gŏd BĪ yee/; US *also* /gawd-/ good-bye. **God buy you** (F1). Some eds. substitute **God bye ye, God b'wi' ye** or some other variation of that phrase, however it would have to be reduced to something like /gŏd BWEE yee/ to fit the meter.

77. **down-gyved** /down JĪ vid/ hanging down like a prisoner's chains.

100. **fordoes** /for DUZ/ destroys.

110. **beshrow** /bih-, bee SHROH/ curse. Archaic variant of **beshrew** /-SHRO͞O/ which some eds. prefer.

115. **close** /clohss/ secret.

Act 2 Scene 2

13. **voutsafe your rest** (Q2) allow yourself to rest. /vowt SAYF/ archaic variant of F1's **vouchsafe** /vowch SAYF/.

71. **th' assay** /th͏ʸ uh-, th͏ʸ ass SAY/. Some eds. prefer **essay** /es SAY/. Both mean 'test.'

86. **expostulate** /ek SPŎS chuh layt/; UK *also* /-tyoo layt/ discuss, object.

102. **defect** here should be /dih-, dee FECT/.

105. **Perpend** /pur PEND/ consider.

142. **prescripts** (Q2) /PREE scripts/ commands. F1 has **precepts**.

163. **arras** /ĂIR us/ tapestry.

174, 189. ***fishmonger** fish seller. US /FISH mŏng gur/ or /-mawng-/ [-mung-]; CN /-mung gur, -mŏng gur/; UK /-mung gur/.

274. **halfpenny** /HAY puh nee, HAYP nee/.

283. ***conjure** entreat. US, CN /CŎN jur/, *rarely* [CUN-]; UK /CUN jur/ [CŎN-], *rarely* [cun JOOR]. The older pronunciation for this meaning is /cun JOOR/.

ă-bat, ăir-marry, air-pair, ạr-far, ĕr-merry, ĝ-get, ī-high, ĭr-mirror, ł-little, ṇ-listen, ŏ-hot, oh-go, o͞o-wood, o͞o-moon, oor-tour, ŏr-or, ow-how, ṭh-that, t̯h-thin, ŭ-but, UR-fur, ur-under. ( )- suppress the syllable   [ ]- less common   see p. xi for complete list.

284. **consonancy** /CŎN suh nun see/ harmony.

307. ***paragon** US /PĂIR uh gŏn/ [-gun]; CN /-gŏn/; UK /-gun/ [-gn̩] most perfect example.

308. **quintessence** /kwin TESS unss, -n̩ss/ the purest essence.

320. **adventerous** /ad VENT ur us/ archaic variant of **adventurous**.

322. ***gratis** unrewarded. US, UK /GRAHT iss/ [GRAT-], UK *rarely* [GRAYT-]; CN /GRAT-/ [GRAHT-].

324. **sere** archaic variant of **sear** catch of a gunlock. Both pronounced /seer/.

328. **tragedians** /truh JEE dee unz/ actors of tragedies.

339. ***aery, eyrie, aerie** high nest. /AIR ee, EER-/; E. COAST US *also* [ĂIR-]. /ĪR ee/ not recommended. /AIR ee/ is the oldest pronunciation.

339. **eyases** /Ī uh siz/ young hawks.

346. **escoted** /es SKŎT id/ financially supported.

353. **tarre, tar** /tar/ incite.

364. **mouths** (Q2). Some eds. prefer F1's ***mows** grimaces. /mohz/ and /mowz/ were both used in Shk's time and are still used today. Shk's rhymes elsewhere indicate /mohz/.

366. **'Sblood** (Q2) /zblud/ God's (i.e., Jesus') blood. Omitted F1.

383. **swaddling-clouts** (Q2) /SWŎD ling clowts/ swaddling clothes. F1 has **swathing clouts** /SWAYT̩H ing/; US *also* /SWŎT̩H ing/.

386. **prophesy** /PRŎF uh sī/ to predict the future.

391. ***Roscius** famous actor in ancient Rome. Normal development would favor /RŎSH us/. /RŎSH ee yus/ is also used, and restored Latin /RŎS kee yus/ is the most common in all countries.

399. **individable** /in dih VĪ duh bl̩/.

400. **Plautus** /PLAWT us/ Roman writer of comedies.

403–11. **Jephthah** one of the judges of Israel. Following the usual rules, /JEF t̵huh/, but /JEP t̵huh/ has also been used since Elizabethan times. Note /DIP t̵h -/ for *diphth-* is the most common pronunciation today in *diphthong, diphtheria.*

419. **chanson** song. Angl. forms are US /SHAN sun, -sn̥, -sŏn/,
/shahn SAWN, -SOHN/; UK /SHAH^N sah^n/ [SHŎN-, -sŏn]; Fr. /shah^n soh^n/. Normal
development would give /SHAN sn̥, CHAN-/.

423. ***valanced** US /VAYL unst/ [VAL-]; UK /VAL-/ fringed, i.e., bearded. F1 has
valiant.

425. **by' lady** (Q2) /bī-, buh LAY dee/ by Our Lady, a mild oath. F1 has **byrlady**
/bīr-, bur LAY dee/.

427. ***chopine** US /CHŎP in/ [choh PEEN]; UK /choh PEEN/ [CHŎP in] thick-soled
shoe.

437. ***caviary** /kav ee AIR ee/, /kav ee AHR ee/ archaic variant of **caviare, caviar**
/KAV ee ahr/ [kav ee AHR]; the 1st syllable may sometimes also be /kah-/, especially in the US.

441. **sallets** /SAL its/ spicy herbs.

442. **savory** (UK **savoury**) /SAY vur ee/ tasty, spicy.

443. **indict** /in DĪT/ accuse.

446. **Aeneas'** /ih NEE yus/; UK *also* /EE NEE yus/ Prince of Troy.

446. **Dido** /DĪ doh/ Queen of Carthage.

In the recitations by Hamlet and the Player, these names appear several times:

***Priam** King of Troy. US, CN /PRĪ um/ [-am]; UK /-am/, *rarely* [-um]. Normal de-
velopment would favor /-um/.

Pyrrhus /PĬR us/ Achilles' son.

---

450. **th' Hyrcanian** normally /HUR KAYN yun/ of Hyrcania (in the Caucausus).
However, Shk did not pronounce the /h/ in this word, so *th'* can be attached as
/t̥h^yUR KAYN yun/.

457. **gules** red. Here 2 syllables /GYŌŌ łz/ red.

ă-bat, ăir-marry, air-pair, ạr-far, ĕr-merry, ĝ-get, ī-high, ĭr-mirror, ł-little, n̥-listen,
ŏ-hot, oh-go, ōō-wood, ōō-moon, oor-tour, ōr-or, ow-how, t̥h-that, ŧħ-thin, ŭ-but,
UR-fur, ur-under. ( )- suppress the syllable   [ ]- less common   see p. xi for complete list.

459. **impasted** /im PAY stid/ crusted.

462. **coagulate** /coh AG y(uh) lut, -ayt/ coagulated, clotted.

469. ***antique** ancient. Here /AN teek/, *rarely older* [AN tik].

474. **Ilium** (F1) /ILL ee um/; UK *sometimes newer* [Ī lee um] the citadel of Troy. Omitted Q2.

490. **eterne** /ih TURN/; US *also* /ee-/ eternal.

494. ***synod** US, CN /SIN ud/ [-ŏd]; UK /SIN ŏd/ [-ud] council.

501. **Hecuba** /HEK yoo buh/ Queen of Troy.

502–4. **mobled, mobbled** /MŎB ld/ muffled.

506. **bisson** /BISS n̩/ blinding.

506. **rheum** /ro͞om/ tears.

506. **clout** /clowt/ cloth.

507. ***diadem** /DĪ (uh) dem/ [-dum] crown.

509. **the alarm** (Q2). Some eds. prefer F1's **th'Alarum** which however here should be 2 syllables /t͡hʸuh LARM/.

517. **milch** /milch/ milky.

524. **abstract** /AB stract/ summary. F1 has **abstracts**.

549. **God buy to you** (Q2), **God buy'ye** (F1) see 2.1.66.

554. **wann'd** /wŏnd/ paled. F1 has **warm'd**.

558, 559. **Hecuba** /HEK yoo buh/ Queen of Troy.

580. **offal** /ŎF l/; US *also* /AWF l/ animal guts and remains after butchering.

581. **kindless** /KĪND liss/ unnatural.

587. **foh, faugh** indicates an expression of disgust made with the lips /pff/! or /pfuh/! Sometimes vocalized as /foh/ or /faw/.

592. **malefactions** /mal ih FAK shunz/ evil deeds.

599. **May be a dev'l, and the dev'l hath power** (*deale* Q2, *Diuell. . . Diuel* F1) the 1st instance should be 2 syllables /DEV l̵/, the 2nd should be 1 /devl/, with /v/ and /l/ pronounced nearly simultaneously. The Q2 form /deel/ is found in Scotland and some northern Eng. dialects.

Act 3 Scene 1

13. **Niggard** /NIG urd/ miser or miserly.

14. **assay** /uh-, ass SAY/ attempt.

17. **o'erraught** here should be /OR rawt/ passed.

31. **espials** (F1) /ess SPĪ l̵z/ spies. Q2 and *Riverside* omit this word.

50. **harlot's** /HAR luts/ whore's.

70. ***contumely** insolence. Here should be stressed on the 1st syllable /CŎN tyoom lee, -tyum-/; US, CN *also* /-toom-, -tum-/. [-chum-, -choom-] are considered non-standard in the UK. The occasionally used US pronunciation [CŎN tuh mee lee, -too-] is also possible, producing a feminine ending. Often pronounced with 2nd syllable stress in mod. Eng.

71. **despis'd** here should be /DESS pīzd/. F1 has **dispriz'd** /DIS prīzd/ undervalued.

74. ***quietus** final payment on a debt. /kwī EE tus/ is older and in the US more frequently used; /kwī AY tus, kwee AY tus/ are newer and in the UK more frequently used; in CN all 3 are equally used.

75. **fardels** /FAR dl̵z/ burdens.

78. ***bourn** /born, boorn/ boundary. North American [burn] not recommended. Normal development would favor /born/.

86. **awry** (Q2) /uh RĪ/ askew. F1 has **away**.

88. ***orisons** prayers. US, CN /OR ih zunz, -zn̩z/ [-sunz, -sn̩z]; E. COAST US /ŎR-/; UK /ŎR ih zunz, -zn̩z/.

128. **arrant** /ĂIR unt/ thoroughgoing.

ă-bat, ăir-**marry**, air-**pair**, a̧r-far, ĕr-**merry**, ĝ-get, ī-high, ĭr-**mirror**, l̵-little, n̩-listen, ŏ-hot, oh-go, o͞o-wood, o͞o-moon, oor-**tour**, ŏr-or, ow-how, t̥h-that, t̶h-thin, ŭ-but, UR-**fur**, ur-under. ( )- suppress the syllable [ ]- less common   see p. xi for complete list.

136. **calumny** /CAL um nee/ slander.

159. **unmatch'd** here should be /UN matcht/.

159. **stature** (Q2) /STATCH ur/. F1 has **feature**.

188. **unwatch'd** (F1) here with 1st syllable stress. Q2 has **unmatched**.

Act 3 Scene 2

3. **as live** as soon. May have been /liv/ in Shk's time. Variant of **as lief** /leef/. In the US **lieve** /leev/ is still found in some dialects and can also be used here.

9. **robustious** /roh BUS chus/ boisterous.

10. **periwig-pated** /PĚR ih wig PAYT id/; *also* /PĚR ee-/ wig-headed.

12. **inexplicable** /in eks PLICK uh bł/ [in EKS plick uh bł].

12. **dumb shows** /DUM shohz/ pantomime.

13. **Termagant** /TUR muh gunt/ a violent Saracen god.

14. **out-Herods Herod** /HĚR ud/ ranting villain in period plays.

32. **pagan** /PAYG un/ non-Christian.

58. **revenue** here should be /ruh VEN yoo/.

60. **absurd** here should be /AB surd/; US *sometimes* [-zurd], but this is considered non-standard in the UK.

65. **Sh'hath** /sh^{y}ath/. **S'hath** (Q2), **Hath** (F1).

67. **buffets** /BUFF its/ blows.

69. **co-meddled** (Q2) /coh MED łd/ mixed. F1 has **co-mingled** /coh MING głd/ archaic variant of **commingled** US /cuh MING głd/ [coh-], *rarely* [cŏm-]; UK /coh-/ [cŏm-, cuh-].

80. **occulted** /uh CULT id/ [ŏ-] hidden.

84. **stithy** /STIŢH ee/; US *also* /STITH ee/ forge.

94. *capons US /KAY pŏnz, -punz/; CN, UK /KAY pŏnz/ [-punz] chickens.
/-un/ would be the historically correct form (cf. *canon, poison*).

133. by'r lady (F1) /bīr-, bur LAY dee/ by Our Lady, a mild oath.   Q2 has
ber lady, pronounced the same way.

137. this' miching mallecho (miching malicho F1) this is sneaking mischief.
Often rendered as /MITCH ing MAL uh koh/, but the best choice is probably
/MAL uh choh/, following the derivation from Sp. malhecho /mahl AY choh/
'misdeed.' *Mitching,* or *meeching* 'cringing, slinking' (cf. *britches-breeches*) was
still used in New Eng. in the 20th century. Other eds. prefer munching Mallico
(Q2). Note *Riverside* adds an apostrophe to *this* suggesting that *this is* was intended.

155. Phoebus' /FEE bus/ god of the sun.

156. Tellus' /TEL us/ goddess of the earth.

160. comutual /coh MYOOCH wool/; UK *also* [-MYOOT yool, -chł].   Archaic variant of commutual US /cum-/ [coh-], *rarely* [cŏm-]; UK /coh-/ [cŏm-, cum-].

174. operant /ŎP (ur) runt/ vital, active.

197. enactures /en AK churz/ fulfillments.

200. for aye /ay/ forever.   /ī/ is often used, but not recommended.

228. *mischance in verse normally with 2nd syllable stress.

240. Baptista angl. /bap TISS tuh/, but is sometimes given the continental pronunciation /bahp TEES tah/, or a mix of the 2 /bap TEES tuh/, etc.

244. Lucianus /loo shee AYN us/, /loo see-/, are the oldest angl. forms. Normal
development would favor the former. Another anglicization is /-ANN-/. Other
choices based on Ital. and restored Latin are /-chee-, -AHN-/. At one time many RP
speakers in the UK used /lyoo-/ for words beginning *lu-,* but today their number is
dwindling.

252. mistake here /mis TAYK/ to take wrongfully. The spelling mis-take, which
some eds. prefer, reflects this pronunciation.

258. Hecat's /HEK uts/ goddess of witchcraft. /HEK uh tee/ is the usual non-
Shakespearean pronunciation.

ă-bat, ăir-marry, air-pair, ạr-far, ĕr-merry, ĝ-get, ī-high, ĭr-mirror, ł-little, ņ-listen,
ŏ-hot, oh-go, ōō-wood, ōō-moon, oor-tour, ōr-or, ow-how, ţh-that, t̶h̶-thin, ŭ-but,
UR-fur, ur-under. ( )- suppress the syllable   [ ]- less common   see p. xi for complete list.

262. ***extant** still in existence. US /EK stunt/ [ek STĂNT]; UK /ek STĂNT/, *rarely* [EK stunt]; in CN both are used equally.

271. **strooken** (Q2) /STRŏŏK in/ or perhaps simply a variant spelling of F1's **strucken**. Some eds. prefer **stricken**.

276. **Provincial** /pruh VIN shł, -chł/. Some eds. substitute **Provencial** /proh VEN shł, -chł/. Both are archaic forms of **Provençal** /prŏv un SAHL, -ahⁿ-, -ŏn-/; US *also* /proh-/ of Provence, southern France.

281. **Damon** /DAY mun/. Sometimes newer /-ŏn/ is used. /-un/ would be the historically correct form (cf. *canon, poison*).

284. **pajock** some eds. believe this is a misprint for or variant of **peacock** still pronounced /PAY cŏck/ in some dialects. Others believe it is related to **patchock** /PATCH ŏck, -uck/ 'scoundrel,' which here would be pronounced /PAJ ŏck, -uck/.

294. **perdy, perdie** /PUR DEE/ by God, indeed. Some eds. prefer the variant **pardie** /par DEE/.

296. **voutsafe** (Q2) /vowt SAYF/ grant. Archaic variant of F1's **vouchsafe** /vowch SAYF/.

316. **commandement**. Archaic variant of **commandment**, originally with 4 syllables, /-uh munt/, but in this prose passage the usual mod. 3-syllable pronunciation may be used.

328. **stonish** (Q2) /STŎN ish/ short form of F1's **astonish**.

369. **'Sblood** /zblud/ God's (i.e., Jesus') blood. F1 has **why**.

Act 3 Scene 3

14. **weal** /weel/ welfare.

20. **mortis'd** /MORT ist/ joined.

24. **viage** (Q2) /VĪ ij/ archaic variant of F1's **voyage**.

28. **arras** /ĂIR us/ tapestry.

37. **primal** /PRĪ mł/ original.

68. **limed** /LĪ mid/ caught in a trap made of lime paste.

69. **assay** /uh-, ass SAY/ attempt.

90. **th'incestious** (Q2) /t͓hʸin SESS chus/ archaic variant of F1's **th'incestuous** /t͓hʸin SESS chwus/; UK *also* /-tywus/.

Act 3 Scene 4

14. **rood** /rōōd/ cross.

18. **boudge** /BUJ/, or possibly /bōōj/. Archaic variant of **budge**.

38. ***bulwark** structure for defense. US, CN /BULL wurk/ [BŬL wurk]; UK /BULL WURK, -wurk/. The vowels /or/, /ahr/ not recommended in the final syllable, and are non-standard in the UK.

54. **presentment** /pree-, prih ZENT munt/ likeness.

56. ***Hyperion's** /hī PEER yunz/ god of the sun. Sometimes newer /-PĔR-/ or /-ŏn/ are used, but are not recommended.

67. ***moor** /moor/ [mor] swamp.

73. **apoplex'd** (Q2) /AP uh plekst/ paralyzed. Omitted F1.

79. **sans** (Q2) /sănz/ without. Omitted F1.

83. **mutine** /MYŌŌT in, -ṇ/ to rebel.

86. **ardure** warm emotion. Archaic variant of **ardor** (UK **ardour**), all pronounced /ARD ur/.

97. **tithe** /tīt͓h/ 10th part.

98. **precedent** /prih-, pree SEED unt, -ṇt/ preceding.

100. ***diadem** /DĪ (uh) dem/ [-dum] crown.

144. **gambol** /GAM bł/ frolic.

153. **pursy** /PUR see/ fat, short-winded.

ă-bat, ăir-**marry**, air-**pair**, ạr-**far**, ĕr-**merry**, ĝ-**get**, ī-**high**, ĭr-**mirror**, ł-**little**, ṇ-**listen**, ŏ-**hot**, oh-**go**, ōō-**wood**, ōō-**moon**, oor-**tour**, ōr-**or**, ow-**how**, t͓h-**that**, t̶h̶-**thin**, ŭ-**but**, UR-**fur**, ur-**under**. ( )- suppress the syllable   [ ]- less common   see p. xi for complete list.

168. **use** (Q2) /yo͞oss/ habit. Omitted F1.

175. **scourge** /SKURJ/ instrument of punishment.

184. **reechy** /REECH ee/ filthy.

190. **paddock** /PAD uk/ toad.

190. **gib** /ĝib/ a male cat.

Lines 202–210 are found in Q2 but not in F1.

206. **enginer** archaic variant of **engineer**. In Shk's time it may have been /EN jih nur/ or mod. /en jih NEER/.

207. **petar** /puh TAR/ archaic variant of **petard** /puh TARD/ bomb.

Act 4 Scene 1

1. **profound** here should be /PROH fownd/ deep.

2. **translate** here should be stressed on the 2nd syllable, the normal UK pronunciation US /trănss LAYT, trănz-/; UK /trănss LAYT/ [trănz-, trahnz-, trahnss-, trunss-, trunz-].

9. **arras** /ĂIR us/ tapestry.

Act 4 Scene 3

6. **scourge** /SKURJ/ severe punishment.

20. **politic** (Q2) /PŎL ih tik/ shrewd. Omitted F1.

27. **hath eat** /et/ dialect variant of **eaten**.

60. **cicatrice** /SIK uh triss/ scar.

62. ***homage** /HŎM ij/; US *also* /ŎM ij/ acknowledgement of allegiance.

64. **congruing** (Q2) here should be /CŎN groo ing/ in agreement with. F1 has ***conjuring** solemnly charging. Here should be US, CN /CŎN jur ing/, *rarely* [CUN-]; UK /CUN-/ [CŎN-]. However the older pronunciation for this meaning is /cun JOOR ing/.

Act 4 Scene 4

Lines 9–66 are found in Q2 but not in F1.

16. **frontier** here should be /FRUN teer/ [FRŎN-].

27. **th'imposthume** /t̠hʸim PŎS choͦom/; UK *also* /-tyoͦom, -tyoͦom/ abcess.

30. **God buy you** see 2.1.66.

40. ***Bestial** beastlike. /BEST yl̠/; US *also* [-chl̠].   US, CN /BEES-/ not recommended.

40. **craven** /CRAY vin, -vn̠/ cowardly.

Act 4 Scene 5

2. **importunate** /im POR chuh nut/; UK *also* /-tyoo nut/ insistant.

26. **shoon** /shoͦon/ Scottish and Northern English dialect form of *shoes*.

42. **God dild you** /gŏd ILD yoͦo/; US *also* /gawd/ God reward you, thank you. Some eds. prefer **God 'ield you** /-EELD-, -ILD-/.

52. **clo'es** /clohz/ a pronunciation of *clothes* which is still the most common in the US.

58. **Gis** /jiss/ Jesus.

119. **harlot** /HAR lut/ whore.

137. **throughly** archaic variant of *thoroughly*. /T̶H̶ROͦO lee/ is the normal pronunciation on stage, but to enhance clarity a syncopated form of the modern pronunciation may be used: *thor'ghly*.

165. **bier** /beer/ coffin.

181. **columbines** /CŎL um bīnz/ a flower.

196. **pole** archaic spelling of **poll** /pohl/ head.

ă-bat, ăir-**marry**, air-**pair**, ạr-**far**, ĕr-**merry**, ĝ-**get**, ī-**high**, ĭr-**mirror**, l̠-**little**, n̠-**listen**, ŏ-**hot**, oh-**go**, oͦo-**wood**, oͦo-**moon**, oor-**tour**, ōr-**or**, ow-**how**, t̠h-**that**, t̶h̶-**thin**, ŭ-**but**, UR-**fur**, ur-**under**. ( )- suppress the syllable   [ ]- less common   see p. xi for complete list.

199. **God 'a' mercy** (Q2) /uh/ God have mercy. F1 has **Gramercy** /gruh MUR see/ God grant mercy.

201. **God buy you** see 2.1.66. **God buy ye** (F1).

203. **commune** here should be /CŎM yōōn/ share.

207. **collateral** US /cuh LAT rł/; UK *also* [cŏ-] indirect.

214. **obscure** here should be /ŎB skyoor/; US *also* [-skyur].

Act 4 Scene 7

10. **unsinow'd** /un SIN ohd/ weak. Archaic variant of **unsinewed** which many eds. prefer /un SIN yōōd/; US *also* [-ōōd].

11. **th'are** (*tha'r* Q2), **they are** (F1). Should be 1 syllable /thair/ they're.

21. **gyves** /jīvz/ chains, fetters. Some eds. substitute **guilts**.

40. **Claudio** /CLAW dyoh/.

64. **exploit** here should be /ek SPLOYT/.

77. **riband** (Q3) /RIB und/. Archaic variant of **ribbon**. Omitted F1.

87. ***demi-natur'd** /DEM ee-/ i.e., become half-man, half-beast.

92. **Lamord** /luh MORD/. Some eds. prefer **Lamond** /luh MŎND/.

93. ***brooch** /brohch/ ornament. US [brōōch] not recommended.

100. **scrimers** (Q2) /SKREEM urz/ fencers. Omitted F1.

117. **plurisy** archaic variant of **pleurisy** excess. Both pronounced /PLŌŌR ih see/; US *also* /PLUR-/.

127. **sanctuarize** /SANK chwuh rīz/; UK *also* [-ty(oo)uh-] provide asylum to.

129. **close** /clohss/ confined.

141. **mountebank** /MOWNT uh bank/ quack doctor.

143. **cataplasm** /KAT uh plazm/ poultice.

152. **assay'd** /uh-, ass SAYD/. Some eds. prefer **essayed** /es SAYD/. Both mean 'attempted.'

160. **chalice** /CHAL iss/ goblet.

160. ***nonce** /nŏnss/ occasion. US, CN [nunss] not recommended.

166. **askaunt** (*ascaunt* Q2) at a sideways angle. Archaic variant of **askant** US /uh SKĂNT/; UK, E. NEW ENG. /uh SKAHNT/ [uh SKĂNT]. The archaic vowel was pronounced /-AW-/ and gave rise to RP /-AH-/. *Some eds.* prefer F1's **aslant** /uh SLĂNT/.

172. **crownet** (*cronet* Q2) /CROWN it/. F1 has **coronet** which here should be US /COR (uh) net, -nit/; E. COAST US, UK /CŎR-/. Both mean 'small crown.'

177. **chaunted** archaic variant of **chanted** US, CN /CHĂNT id/; E. NEW ENG, UK /CHAHNT id/. The archaic vowel was pronounced /-AW-/, and gave rise to RP /-AH-/.

179. ***indued** /in DYOOD/; US *also* [-DOOD] accustomed to. Some eds. prefer **endued** /en-/.

191. **drowns** (Q2). Some eds. prefer **douts** (following F1's *doubts*) /dowts/ extinguishes.

Act 5 Scene 1

4. **sate** archaic variant of **sat**. May have been /sayt/ or /sat/.

9. **se offendendo** (F1) gravedigger's mistake for *se defendendo* 'in self-defense.' The older anglicized form would be /see ŏff in DEN doh/; US *also* /-awf-/. The more common restored Latin form is /say-/. Q2 has **so offended**.

> 12–48. **argal** /ĄRG ł/ the gravedigger's mistake for ***ergo** /UR go/ is older, /ĔR go/ is newer. The former is more common in the UK, the latter in the US, CN.

14. **goodman** (F1) /GooD mun/ title of a man under the rank of gentleman. Q2 has **good man**.

23. **an't, on't** /unt/ of it.

> ă-bat, äir-marry, air-pair, ąr-far, ĕr-merry, ĝ-get, ī-high, ĭr-mirror, ł-little, n̨-listen, ŏ-hot, oh-go, oō-wood, oō-moon, oor-tour, ŏr-or, ow-how, t̨h-that, th̶-thin, Ŭ-but, UR-fur, ur-under. ( )- suppress the syllable   [ ]- less common   see p. xi for complete list.

28. **even-Christen** (Q2) /CRISS ņ/ fellow-Christian. Archaic variant of F1's **Christian**.

60. **get thee in** (Q2). F1 has **get thee to Yaughan** /YAWN, YAW un/. Some eds. substitute **Johan**, /YOH hahn/ referring to a local innkeeper.

60. **sup** (*soope* Q2) mouthful. F1 has **stoup** /sto͞op/ tankard.

63. **contract** /cun TRACT/ shorten.

63. **behove** /bih-, bee HOHV/ advantage.

89. **mazzard, mazard** /MAZ urd/ head.

92. **loggats** /LŎG uts/; US *also* /LAWG uts/ a game where blocks of wood are thrown at a stake.

102. **sconce** /skŏnss/ head.

105. ***recognizances** /rih CŎG nih zun siz/; *rarely older* [rih CŎN ih-] pledges before a court to perform specific acts.

138. **equivocation** /ih kwiv uh KAY shun/; US *also* /ee-/ using vague or deceptive answers in an argument.

173. **lien** (*lyen* Q2) /līn/ past participle of *lie* in some dialects. F1 has **lain**.

180. **flagon** /FLAG un/ drinking vessel.

180. **Rhenish** /REN ish/ Rhine wine.

181, 184. **Yorick('s)** /YOR ik/; E. COAST US, UK /YŎR ik/.

189. **gibes** /jībz/ sarcastic comments.

189. **gambols** /GAM błz/ leaps, frolics.

213. **Imperious** (Q2) /im PEER yus/ imperial. **Imperiall** (F1) /im PEER ył/.

221. **Foredo** /for DO͞O/ destroy.

226. **obsequies** /ŎB suh kweez/ burial services.

227. **warranty** (Q2) authorization. Some eds. prefer **warrantise, -ize** (*warrantis* F1) US /WŌR un tīz/; UK, E. COAST US /WŎR un tīz/.

232. **crants** (Q2) /crănts/ garland. F1 has **rites**.

237. *****requiem** /REK w(ee) yum/ funeral music.

253. **Pelion** /PEE lee un/ mountain in NE Greece. Sometimes newer /-ŏn/ is used, but is not recommended.

261. **splenitive, splenative** /SPLEN uh tiv/ impetuous, quick-tempered.

274. **thou't** (*th'owt* Q2) /ţhowt/ archaic variant of F1's **thou'lt** /ţhowlt/.

275–6. **Woo't** /wo͞ot/ variant of **wilt** in the sense 'wilt thou.'

276. *****eisel** US, CN /EE zł/ [AY zł]; UK /AY zł, EE zł/ vinegar. /ĪZ ł/ not recommended.

278. **outface** here should be /OWT fayss/ outdo.

283. **Ossa** /ŎSS uh/ Greek mountain.

Act 5 Scene 2

6. **mutines** /MY͞OOT inz, -ṇz/ mutineers.

6. **bilboes** (F1) /BIL bohz/ shackles attached to a heavy iron bar. **bilbo** (Q2).

29. **benetted** /bih-, bee NET id/ caught in a net.

33. **statists** /STAYT ists/ statesmen.

36. **yeman's service** (Q2) /YEE munz/ solid service. Archaic variant of F1's **yeoman's** /YOH munz/.

42. **amities** /AM ih teez/ friendships.

44. **That on the view and knowing of these contents**. Usually /cŏn TENTS/ in Shk, but if *knowing* is pronounced with 2 syllables, mod. /CŎN tents/ may be used.

48. **ordinant** (Q2) /OR dih nunt/ guiding. F1 has **ordinate** /OR dih nut/ orderly, ordered.

ă-bat, ăir-marry, air-pair, ạr-far, ĕr-merry, ĝ-get, ī-high, ĭr-mirror, ł-little, ṇ-listen, ŏ-hot, oh-go, o͞o-wood, o͞o-moon, oor-tour, ōr-or, ow-how, ţh-that, t̶h̶-thin, ŭ-but, UR-fur, ur-under. ( )- suppress the syllable   [ ]- less common   see p. xi for complete list.

sequent /SEE kwunt/ referring to what followed.

78. **portraiture** /POR truh chur/ picture.

87. **chough, chuff** /chuf/ jackdaw.

Lines 106–143 are found in Q2 but not in F1.

112. **perdition** /pur DISH un/; UK *also* [PUR DISH un] loss.

116. ***extolment** praise. /ek STOHL munt/; UK *sometimes* and US *rarely* [-STŎL-].

118. **semblable** /SEM bluh bł/ likeness, equal.

119. **umbrage** /UM brij/ shadow.

---

147. **Barbary, Barb'ry** /BAR buh ree, BAR bree/ region in North Africa.

148. **impawn'd** (Q2) /im PAWND/. F1 has **impon'd** /im POHND/. Both mean 'wagered.'

149. **poniards** /PŎN yurdz/; UK *also newer* [-yardz] daggers.

155. **margent** /MAR junt/ archaic variant of **margin**. Omitted F1.

158. **germane** US /jur MAYN/; UK /JUR MAYN/ [JUR mayn] pertinent.

189. **breed** (Q2). F1 has **bevy** /BEV ee/ company.

189. **drossy** /DRŎSS ee/; US *also* /DRAWSS ee/ worthless.

219. ***augury** /AWG yur ee/ [AWG ur ee]; UK *also* /AWG yoor ree/ prediction of the future.

249. **president** archaic variant of ***precedent**, both /PRESS ih dunt/. It is not clear whether /PREZ-/ was used in Shk's time.

267. **stoups** /sto͞ops/ tankards.

272, 326. **union** (F1) pearl. Q2c, Q3–4 have **onyx** /ŎN iks/, *rarely* [OHN iks].

306. **springe** /sprinj/ snare.

308. **sounds** archaic variant **of swoons**. In Shk's time the vowel could be either /ow/ or /o͞o/.

325. **incestious** (Q2) /in SESS chus/ archaic variant of F1's **incestuous** /in SESS chwus/; UK *also* /-tywus/.

341. ***antique** ancient. Here /AN teek/, *rarely older* [AN tik].

347. **Absent** /ub-, ab SENT/ keep away from.

355. **prophesy** /PRŎF uh sī/ predict the future.

365. **toward** here should be 1 syllable /tord/ about to take place.

374. **commandement**. Archaic variant of **commandment**, originally with 4 syllables, /-uh munt/, but here the usual mod. 3-syllable pronunciation is required.

394. ***mischance** in verse normally with 2nd syllable stress.

ă-bat, ăir-marry, air-pair, ạr-far, ĕr-merry, ĝ-get, ī-high, ĭr-mirror, ł-little, ṇ-listen, ŏ-hot, oh-go, ōō-wood, o͞o-moon, oor-tour, ōr-or, ow-how, ṭh-that, t̶h̶-thin, ŭ-but, UR-fur, ur-under. ( )- suppress the syllable   [ ]- less common   see p. xi for complete list.

Henry IV part one

People in the Play

Bardolph /BAR dŏlf/; US *also* /-dawlf/. Some eds. prefer **Russell**.

Bullingbrook Shk also spelled this name **Bullinbrook, Bullingbrooke, Bullinbrooke**, and pronounced it /BULL in brŏōk/. Pope was the first to change it to **Bolingbroke** in the early 18th century. Today pronounced US, CN /BOHL ing brŏōk/ [BULL-, BŎL-]; UK /BŎL-/, *rarely* [BULL-].

Drawer /DRAW ur/ tapster, the person who draws the liquor at a tavern.

Falstaff US /FAWL stăff/; E. NEW ENG., UK /-stahff/. Some eds. prefer **Oldcastle**.

Gadshill /GADZ hill/.

Glendower, Owen /GLEN dowr, GLEN dow ur/ or /glen DOWR, -DOW ur/ depending on meter. Some eds. prefer Welsh **Owain Glyndûr**, normally /OH īn/ or /OH in glin DŌŌR/, but with stress shifts as needed in verse.

Lancaster US /LANG kăst ur, -kᵘss tur/; UK /LANG kᵘss tur/ [-kahst ur, -kăst ur].

Northumberland /north UM bur lund/.

Ostler /ŎSS lur/.

Peto /PEET oh/. Some eds. prefer **Harvey**.

Poins /poynz/.

Scroop /skrŏōp/. Some eds. prefer mod. **Scrope**, pronounced the same way.

Westmerland archaic variant of **Westmor(e)land**, all pronounced /WEST mur lund/ in the UK. US is usually /west MOR lund/ which will not fit the meter.

Worcester /WŏōS tur/.

Places in the Play

Gadshill /GADZ hill/.

*Ravenspurgh here should be 3 syllables /RAV in SPURG, -SPUR/ or /RAY vin-/.
Sometimes spelled **Ravenspur** /-SPUR/.

Shrewsbury 3 syllables in verse US /SHR͞OOZ bĕr ee/ [SHROHZ-];
UK /SHROHZ bur ee/ [SHR͞OOZ-], or in prose /-bree/.

A Recurring Word in the Play

'sblood (Q1) /zblud/ God's (i.e., Jesus') blood. Omitted F1.

Act 1 Scene 1

1. **wan** /wŏn/ pale.

4. **stronds** /strŏndz/ shores. Archaic variant of **strands**.

12. **intestine** /in TESS tin/; UK *also* [-teen] internal.

13. **close** /clohz/ hand-to-hand combat.

16. **allies** here with 2nd syllable stress.

19. **sepulchre** /SEP ł kur/ tomb.

24. **pagans** /PAY gunz/ non-Christians.

39. **Herfordshire, Herefordshire.** In the US both would be /HUR furd shur/.
In the UK the county is normally /HĔR ih furd shur/ [-sheer] which here should
be 3 syllables /HĔR furd shur, -sheer/.

55–70. **Holmedon('s)** /HOHM dun/ mod. *Homildon, Humbleton.*

67. **discomfited** /dis CUM fit id/ defeated.

71, 95. **Mordake** /MOR dayk, -duk/. Some eds. prefer **Murdoch** /MUR dŏck/.

72. **Athol, Atholl** /A̶T̶H̶ ł/.

ă-bat, ăir-**marry**, air-**pair**, ạr-**far**, ĕr-**merry**, ĝ-**get**, ī-**high**, ĭr-**mirror**, ł-**little**, ṇ-**listen**,
ŏ-**hot**, oh-**go**, o͞o-**wood**, o͞o-**moon**, oor-**tour**, ŏr-**or**, ow-**how**, ţh-**that**, t̶h̶-**thin**, ŭ-**but**,
UR-**fur**, ur-**under**. ( )- suppress the syllable   [ ]- less common   see p. xi for complete list.

73. **Murray** US /MUR ee/; E. COAST US, UK /MUH ree/. Some eds. prefer **Moray** which in this case is pronounced the same way.

73. **Menteith** /men TEE~~TH~~/.

89. **Plantagenet** /plan TAJ ih nit/.

97. **Malevolent** /muh LEV uh lunt/ hostile.

Act 1 Scene 2

7. ***capons** US /KAY pŏnz, -punz/; CN, UK /KAY pŏnz/ [-punz] chickens.
/-un/ would be the historically correct form (cf. *canon, poison*).

10. **taffata, taffeta** /TAF uh tuh/ a silk-like cloth.

15. **Phoebus** /FEE bus/ god of the sun.

34. **dissolutely** /DIS uh lo͞ot lee/ riotously.   At one time many RP speakers in the UK
used /lyo͞o-/ for syllables beginning with *lu-*, but today their number is dwindling.

41. **Hybla** /HĪ bluh/ region of Sicily.

43. ***durance** /DYOOR unss/; US *also* /Do͞oR-/ [DUR-] double meaning: durability,
prison clothes.

74. **gib** /ĝib/ male cat.

76. **Lincolnshire** /LINK un shur/ [sheer].

78. **Moor-ditch** /MOOR ditch/ [MOR-].

90. **iteration** /it ur AY shun/ repetition (of scriptures).

109. **omnipotent** /ŏm NIP uh tunt/ all-powerful.

116. **Madeira** /muh DEER uh/ type of wine.

116. ***capon's** US /KAY pŏnz, -punz/; CN, UK /KAY pŏnz/ [-punz] chicken's.
/-un/ would be the historically correct form (cf. *canon, poison*).

128, 178. ***vizards** /VIZ urdz/ masks. /-ạrdz/ not recommended. Some eds. prefer
visors.

158. **All-hallown summer** /awl HAL ohn, -un/; US *also* /HŎL-/ Indian summer.

172. **exploit** /ek SPLOYT/ in verse, but here may be mod. /EK sployt/.

179. **buckrom, buckram** /BUCK rum/ coarse linen cloth stiffened with paste.

180. ***nonce** /nŏnss/ occasion. US, CN [nunss] not recommended.

196. **unyok'd** here should be /UN yohkt/ undisciplined.

Act 1 Scene 3

11. **scourge** /SKURJ/ instrument of punishment.

13. **holp** /hohlp/ helped.

17. **peremptory** overbearing. Here stressed on the 1st syllable, either /PĔR um tur ee/; US *also* /-tor ee/ or /PĔR um tree/.

19. **frontier** here should be /FRUN teer/ [FRŎN-] i.e., forehead.

24. **Holmedon** /HOHM dun/ mod. *Homildon, Humbleton.*

27. **misprision** here expanded to /mis PRIZH ee un/ misunderstanding.

31. **extreme** here should be /EK streem/.

36. **milliner** /MILL ih nur/ seller of fancy goods.

38. **pouncet-box** /POWN sit-/ perfume box.

43. **untaught** here should be /UN tawt/.

44. **slovenly** /SLUV un lee/ messy.

50. **popingay** /PŎP in gay/ parrot. Archaic variant of **popinjay**.

58. **parmaciti** fatty substance in whales, used as an ointment. A variant of **parmacity**, both pronounced /par muh SIT ee/. Other eds. prefer **parmaceti, parmacety** /par muh SET ee, -SEE tee/, mod. ***spermaceti** /SPURM uh SET ee, -SEE tee/.

ă-bat, ăir-marry, air-pair, ạr-far, ĕr-merry, ĝ-get, ī-high, ĭr-mirror, ł-little, ṇ-listen, ŏ-hot, oh-go, ōō-wood, ōō-moon, oor-tour, ōr-or, ow-how, ţh-that, ᵵh-thin, Ŭ-but, UR-fur, ur-under. ( )- suppress the syllable   [ ]- less common   see p. xi for complete list.

60. ***saltpetre, -peter** a component of gunpowder. Here should be /sawlt PEET ur/, a pronunciation used with /SAWLT peet ur/ in all countries.

78. **proviso** /pruh VĪ zoh/ stipulation.

98, 103. **Severn's** /SEV urnz/.

107. **combatants** here should be stressed on the 1st syllable as is usual in the UK /CŎM buh tunts/ [CUM-].

113. **belie him** /bih-, bee LĪ/ not tell the truth about him.

128. **Albeit** /awl BEE (i)t/ although.

137. **ingrate** here should be /in GRAYT/ ungrateful.

191. **adventerous** /ad VENT rus/ archaic variant of **adventurous**.

199. **exploit** here should be /ek SPLOYT/.

204. **fadom-line** /FAD um-/ archaic variant of **fathom-** /FĂTH um-/ rope used for measuring depth.

207. **corrival** /coh-, cuh RĪ vł/ rival.

222. **hollow, hollo** /HŎL uh, -oh/ call.

232. ***mischance** in verse normally with 2nd syllable stress.

234. **Farewell** /FAIR ee wel/ (from *Fare thee well*) may have been intended, though our usual pronunciation is possible in a headless line.

239. **scourg'd** /SKURJD/ harshly punished.

240. ***pismires** /PISS mīrz/; US *also* [PIZ mīrz] ants.

243. **Gloucestershire** /GLŎSS tur shur/ [-sheer]; US *also* /GLAWSS-/.

249. **Berkeley** US /BURK lee/; UK /BARK lee/.

262. ***divers** various. Here should be stressed on the 1st syllable US, CN /DĪ vurss, -vurz/; UK /DĪ vurss/ [-vurz].

267. **prelate** /PREL ut/ high-ranking churchman.

268. The Archbishop here should be /ARCH bish up/ if *the* is pronounced fully, or if compressed /thᵞarch BISH up/ as in mod. Eng.

271. Bristow /BRIST oh/ archaic variant of **Bristol** /BRIST ł/.

Act 2 Scene 1

1. ***Heigh-ho!** US /hay ho, hī-/; CN /hī-/, *rarely* [hay-]; UK /hay-/. Shk intended /hay/. Spoken with evenly stressed syllables or as if sighing, with 1st syllable stress.

17. **christen** /CRISS ņ/ archaic variant of **christian**.

24. **gammon of bacon** /GAM un/ ham.

25. **Charing Cross** US /chăir ing CRAWSS/; UK /-CRŎSS/ [chair-].

26. **pannier** /PAN ee ur, PAN yur/ large basket.

55. **Wild.** Some eds. prefer **Weald** /weeld/ a forest in SE Eng.

75. **mustachio** moustache. US /muh STASH ee oh/ [muh STASH oh, -STAHSH-]; UK /muh STAHSH ee yoh/ [-STASH-].

76. **burgomasters** US /BUR guh măss turz/; UK /-mahss turz/ mayors.

76. **great oney'rs** /WUN yurz/ great ones. Other suggestions include ***oyez-ers** /OH yez urz/ [OH yay urz] court officials, **moneyers** /MUN ee urz/ rich men, **owners, mynheers** /mīn HEERZ, -HAIRZ/ gentlemen, **wonners** /WUN urz/ or /WOHN urz/ dwellers, **younkers** /YŬNG kurz/ young lords.

Act 2 Scene 2

3–97. Stand close /clohss/ keep hidden.

12. **squier** /skwīrᵞ/ archaic variant of **square** carpenter's square.

24. **veriest** /VĚR ee ist/ most exceeding.

36, 55. ***exchequer** /eks CHEK ur/; US *rarely* [EKS chek ur] treasury.

ă-bat, ăir-marry, air-pair, ąr-far, ĕr-merry, ĝ-get, ī-high, ĭr-mirror, ł-little, ņ-listen, ŏ-hot, oh-go, ōō-wood, ōō-moon, oor-tour, ōr-or, ow-how, ţh-that, ŧħ-thin, Ŭ-but, UR-fur, ur-under. ( )- suppress the syllable   [ ]- less common   see p. xi for complete list.

42. **ostler** /ŎSS lur/ person who tends the horses.

53. ***vizards** /VIZ urdz/ masks. /-ạrdz/ not recommended. Some eds. prefer **visors**.

67. **Gaunt** /gawnt/ Hal's grandfather.

The Complete Oxford begins 2.3 here—line nos. in parentheses.

---

100. (2.3.8) **arrant** /ĂIR unt/ thoroughgoing.

Act 2 Scene 3 (*The Complete Oxford* 2.4)

stage direction: solus /SOH lŭss/ alone.

15. **hind** /hīnd/ menial laborer.

29. **pagan** /PAYG un/ non-Christian.

38. **fortnight** /FORT nīt/; US *also* [FORT nit] two weeks. Virtually obsolete in the US.

49. **manage**. Some eds. prefer **manège** US /mah NEZH, -NAYZH/; UK /man AYZH/ [-EZH, MAN ayzh]; Fr. /mah nezh/. Both words mean 'horsemanship.'

52. **palisadoes** defences made of stakes. /pal ih SAY dohz/ is older, but a newer, spelling pronunciation /-SAH-/ is also used.

52. **frontiers** here with 1st syllable stress /FRUN teerz/ [FRŎN-] fortifications.

52. **parapets** /PĂIR uh pets, -pits/ walls of a fortification.

53. ***basilisks** canons. US /BĂSS ih lisks/ [BAZ ih lisks]; UK /BAZ-/ [BĂSS-]; CN both used equally.

53. **culverin** /CŬL vur in/ an early type of canon.

62. **portents** here should be /por TENTS/ omens.

65. **Gilliams** /ĜILL yumz/.

71. **Esperance** angl. /ES pur unss/; Fr. /es pĕr ah^{n}ss/ hope.

85. **paraquito** /păir uh KEE toh/ parakeet.

92. **mammets** /MAM its/ dolls. Variant of **maumets** /MAW mits/.

Act 2 Scene 4 (*The Complete Oxford* 2.5)

7–91. **drawer(s)** /DRAW ur/ tapster, the person who draws the liquor at a tavern.

8. **christen** /CRISS ṇ/ archaic variant of **Christian**.

23, 59. **pennyworth** the older form is /PEN urth/, but in these prose passages the newer, spelling pronunciation /PEN ee wurth, -WURTH/ may be used.

25. **sixpence** /SIKS punss, -pṇs/; US *also* /SIKS penss/.

33. **president** (F1) example. Archaic variant of ***precedent**, both /PRESS ih dunt/. It is not clear whether /PREZ-/ was used in Shk's time.

38. **Pomgarnet** /PUM-, PŎM gar nit/ room in the tavern. Archaic variant of ***Pomegranate** US, CN /PŎM uh gran it/; US *also* [PUM-, PŎM gran it, PUM ih gran it]; UK /PŎM uh gran it/ [PŎM gran it].

45–424. **by'r lady** /bīr-, bur LAY dee/ by Our Lady (i.e., Mary).

54. **Michaelmas** /MIK ł mus/ Sept. 29.

70. **agate-ring** /AG ut/ a jewel.

70. **caddis-garter** /KAD iss/ worsted-taped garters.

75. **Barbary** /BAR buh ree/ region in North Africa.

93. **goodman** /GŏŏD mun/ title of a man under the rank of gentleman.

111. **Rivo!** /REE voh/ drink up!

119. ***extant** in existence. US /EK stunt/ [ek STĂNT]; UK /ek STĂNT/, *rarely* [EK stunt]; in CN both are used equally.

137. **lath** US /lăth/; UK, E. NEW ENG. /lahth/ [lăth] narrow strip of wood.

ă-bat, ăir-marry, air-pair, ạr-far, ĕr-merry, ĝ-get, ī-high, ĭr-mirror, ł-little, ṇ-listen, ŏ-hot, oh-go, ŏŏ-wood, ōō-moon, oor-tour, ōr-or, ow-how, țh-that, ᵮh-thin, ʊ-but, UR-fur, ur-under. ( )- suppress the syllable   [ ]- less common   see p. xi for complete list.

169. **ecce signum** Ang.Lat. /EK see SIG num/; Class.Lat. /EK ay SIG nōōm/ behold the proof (or sign).

193–219. **buckrom, buckram** /BUCK rum/ coarse linen cloth stiffened with paste.

222–232. **Kendal green** /KEN dł/ named after a town in Westmoreland.

237. ***strappado** a type of torture. /struh PAH doh/; UK *rarely older* [struh PAY doh].

242. **sanguine** /SANG gwin/ red-faced.

280, 316. **extempore** /ek STEM pur ree/ on the spur of the moment.

320. **exhalations** /eks huh LAY shunz, eks uh-/ [egz uh-] meteors.

327. **bumbast** /BUM băst/ cotton stuffing. Variant of **bombast** formerly pronounced the same way, though now /BŎM băst/ is the only pronunciation used.

330. **talent** /TAL unt/ archaic variant of **talon**.

336. **Amamon** /uh MAY mun/ a devil. Sometimes newer /-mŏn/ is used. /-un/ would be the historically correct form (cf. *Orion, Jason*).

337. ***bastinado** beating with a stick. /bas tih NAH doh/; UK *rarely older* [bas tih NAY doh].

357. **Mordake** /MOR dayk, -duk/. Some eds. prefer **Murdoch** /MUR dŏck/.

362. **buffeting** /BUFF it ing/ fighting.

380. **join'd stool** /JOYND stōōl/ a well-crafted stool. Some eds. prefer **joint stool**.

387. **in King Cambyses' vein** /kam BĪ seez/ ranting. A newer pronunciation /-zeez/ is also used.

395. **harlotry** /HAR luh tree/ scoundrely.

400. ***camomile** /KAM uh mīl/; US, CN *also* /-meel/. /-īl/ is older.

408. **micher** /MITCH ur/ truant.

429. **peremptorily** /pur EM tur ih lee/ decisively.

437. **poulter's** /POHL turz/ seller of poultry.

451. **bombard** /BŎM bard/ leather bottle. /BUM burd/ is an archaic variant.

456–535. ***capon** US /KAY pŏn, -pun/; CN, UK /KAY pŏn/ [-pun] chicken.
/-un/ would be the historically correct form (cf. *canon, poison*).

463. **Sathan** archaic form of **Satan**, both pronounced /SAYT n̥, -un/ the devil.

487. ***Heigh!** US /hay, hī/; CN /hī/, *rarely* [hay]; UK /hay/. Shk intended /hay/.

500–528. **arras** /ĂIR us/ tapestry.

535–9. Falstaff's bill reads:
2s. 2d. *two shillings and tuppence* /TUP unss, -n̥ss/
4d. *fourpence* /FOR punss, -pn̥ss/
5s. 8d. *five shillings and eightpence* /AYT punss, -pn̥ss/
2s. 6d. *two shillings and sixpence* /SIKS punss, -pn̥ss/
ob. (*obulus* /ŎB uh lus/) stands for *ha'pence* /HAYP n̥ss, -unss/.
2s. 2d., etc. could also be read *two shillings tuppence* or *two and tuppence.*

538. **anchoves** archaic variant of ***anchovies**. Shk probably said
/AN chuh veez/, a pronunciation used today along with /AN choh veez/
or /an CHOH veez/ in all countries.

540. **half-pennyworth** /HAYP nee WUR~~TH~~/.

542. **keep close** /clohss/ keep secret.

Act 3 Scene 1

28. **colic** /CŎL ik/ stomachache.

31. ***beldame** grandmother. Some eds. prefer **beldam**, both pronounced the same
US /BEL dam, -dum/; UK /BEL dam/, *rarely* [-dum]. /-daym/ is also used, but
normal development would probably favor /-dam, -dum/.

33. ***grandam** /GRAN dam/; US *rarely* [-dum] grandmother. Informally
/GRAN um/.

40. **extraordinary** here main stress should fall on the 3rd syllable
US /ek struh OR dih nĕr ee/; UK /-dih nuh ree/ or reduced to /-dn̥ ree/.

ă-bat, ăir-marry, air-pair, ạr-far, ĕr-merry, ĝ-get, ī-high, ĭr-mirror, ł-little, n̥-listen,
ŏ-hot, oh-go, o͝o-wood, o͞o-moon, oor-tour, ōr-or, ow-how, ţh-that, ŧħ-thin, ŭ-but,
UR-fur, ur-under. ( )- suppress the syllable   [ ]- less common   see p. xi for complete list.

64. **Wye** /wī/ river in Wales.

65–75. **Severn** /SEV urn/.

68. **agues** /AY gyo͞oz/ malarial fevers.

79. **tripartite** here should be /TRĪ par tīt/ in 3 parts.

95. **moi'ty, moiety** /MOY tee/ portion.

128. **ballet-mongers** sellers of songs. US /BAL ut mŏng gurz/ or /-mawng-/ [-mung-]; CN /-mung gurz, -mŏng gurz/; UK /-mung gurz/. *Ballet* is an archaic variant of **ballad**.

129. **brazen** /BRAY zun, -zṇ/ brass.

138. **cavil** /KAV ł/; UK *also* /KAV il/ quibble.

161. **cates** /kayts/ delicacies.

182. **Defect** here may be /DEE fect/ or /dih FECT/; US *also* /dee-/.

196. **harlotry** /HAR luh tree/ hussy.

201. *****parley** /PAR lee/ conference with an enemy. Newer [-lay] not recommended.

231. **By'r lady** /bīr-, bur LAY dee/ by Our Lady (i.e., Mary).

235. **brach** /bratch/ female dog.

248. **comfit-maker's** /CUM fit/ [CŎM fit] candy maker's.

251. **sarcenet, sarsenet** /SAR snit/ fine silk, hence 'flimsy.'

251. *****surety** guarantee. Here should be 2 syllables, though in mod. Eng., 3 syllables are more common US /SHUR (ih) tee, SHOOR-/; CN /SHUR-/ [SHOOR-]; UK /SHOR-/ [SHUR-] [SHOOR-].

252. **Finsbury** US /FINZ b(ĕ)r ee/; UK /-b(u)r ee/ North of London.

255. **protest** here 2nd syllable stress is indicated.

Act 3 Scene 2

7. **scourge** /SKURJ/ punishment.

25. **newsmongers** newspeddlers. US /-mŏng gurz/ or /-mawng-/ [-mung-]; CN /-mung gurz, -mŏng gurz/; UK /-mung gurz/.

59. **wan** possibly /wŏn/, archaic variant of **won**.

61. **bavin** /BAV in/ bundle of brushwood, kindling.

66. **gibing** /JĪ bing/ sarcastic.

69. ***Enfeoff'd** put a person in possession of lands, i.e., surrendered. /en FEEFT/, UK *rarely older* [en FEFT].

78. **extraordinary** here main stress should fall on the 3rd syllable US /ek struh OR dih nĕr ee/; UK /-dih nuh ree/.

107. **renowmed** /rih-, ree NOW mid/ archaic variant of **renowned** /rih-, ree NOWN id/.

112. **swathling** /SWŎ***T***H ling/ or /SWAY***T***H ling/ archaic variant of **swaddling** /SWŎD ling/.

114. **Discomfited** /dis CUM fit id/ defeated.

145. **northren** /NOR***T***H run/ archaic variant of **northern**.

155. ***salve** heal. US /salv/ [sav]; NEW ENG. *also* [sahv]; CN /salv/ [sahlv, sav, sahv]; UK /salv/. Normal development would favor the *l*-less form (cf. *halve, calve*).

172. **advertisement** here should be /ad VURT iss munt, -iz-/ news.

175, 178. **Bridgenorth, Bridgnorth** /BRIJ north/.

176. **Gloucestershire** /GLŎSS tur shur/ [-sheer]; US *also* /GLAWSS-/.

Act 3 Scene 3

30. **memento mori** Ang.Lat. /muh MEN toh MOR ī/; Class.Lat. /mem EN toh MOR ee/ reminder of death.

32. **Dives** /DĪ veez/ rich man in the Bible.

ă-bat, ăir-**marry**, air-**pair**, ạr-**far**, ĕr-**merry**, ĝ-**get**, ī-**high**, ĭr-**mirror**, ł-**little**, ṇ-**listen**, ŏ-**hot**, oh-**go**, o͞o-**wood**, o͞o-**moon**, oor-**tour**, ōr-**or**, ow-**how**, ṭh-**that**, t̶h-**thin**, ŭ-**but**, UR-**fur**, ur-**under**. ( )- suppress the syllable   [ ]- less common   see p. xi for complete list.

39. **ignis fatuus** US /IG niss FATCH oo us/; UK /FAT yoo us/ will o' the wisp.

57. **tithe** /tīṭh/ 10th part.

69. **Dowlas** /DOW lus/ coarse linen.

79. **denier** coin of little value. /duh NEER, DEN yur/ are older;
/DEN yay, den YAY/ are newer, based on Fr.

80. **younker** /YŬNG kur/ fashionable young man.

90. **Newgate** a London prison. /NYŌO gut/ is older and rarer, especially in North
America. The US variant is /NŌO-/. /-gayt/ is newer and more common.

98. **arras** /ĂIR us/ tapestry.

134. **ought** /awt/ archaic variant of **owed**.

159. **pennyworth** the older form is /PEN urth/, but in this prose passage the newer,
spelling pronunciation /PEN ee wurth, -WURTH/ may be used.

172. **guesse** /ĜESS/ (*ghesse* Q1) archaic variant of F1's **guests**.

183. ***exchequer** /eks CHEK ur/; US *rarely* [EKS chek ur] treasury.

189. ***heinously** /HAYN us lee/ terribly. /HEEN us lee/ is non-standard though
common in the UK.

Act 4 Scene 1

18. **justling** /JUSS ling/ turbulent. Archaic variant of **jostling** /JŎS ling/.

36. **advertisement** here should be /ad VURT iss munt, -iz-/ advice.

46. **exact** here should be /EG zact/.

58. ***mischance** in verse normally with 2nd syllable stress.

70. **arbitrement, arbitrament** /ạr BIT ruh munt/ inspection.

96.***comrades** here with 2nd syllable stress US, CN /cŏm RADZ/, *rarely* [cum-];
UK /cŏm RAYDZ/, *rarely* [-RADZ, cum-].

96. **daff'd** /dăft/ thrust aside. Archaic variant of **doffed** /dŏft/; US *also* /dawft/.

102. **midsummer** here should be /MID sum ur/.

105. **cushes** perhaps /Kōō SH iz/ armor for thighs. Variant of **cuisses** /KWISS iz/ which some eds prefer. Others prefer **cuishes** /KWISH iz/.

105. **gallantly** is in an inverted foot, pronounced as in mod. Eng. /GAL unt lee/.

109. **wind** /wīnd/ turn a horse.

112. **agues** /AY gyōōz/ malarial fevers.

125. **Worcester** /Wōō S tur/.

Act 4 Scene 2

1, 39. **Coventry** US /KUV ṇ tree/; UK /KŎV ṇ tree/ [KUV-].

---

3. **Sutton Co'fil', Cophill** /SUT ṇ COH fil/ or /COH feel/ archaic variant of mod. **Sutton Coldfield** /COHLD feeld/.

12. **sous'd** /sowst/ pickled.

12. **gurnet** /GUR nit/ type of fish.

15. **yeomen's** /YOH minz/ freemen who own small farms.

17. **banes** /baynz/ proclamation in church of an intended marriage. Archaic variant of **banns** /banz/.

18. **as lieve** /leev/ 'as soon,' still used in some US dialects. Some eds. prefer **lief** /leef/.

19. **caliver** /KAL ih vur/ light musket.

24, 31. **ancient(s)** /AYN chunt/ archaic variant of the rank **ensign** US /EN sṇ/; UK /-sīn/.

---

25. **Lazarus** /LAZ uh russ/ beggar in Jesus' parable.

29. **ostlers** /ŎSS lurz/ innkeepers.

ă-bat, ăir-marry, air-pair, ạr-far, ĕr-merry, ĝ-get, ī-high, ĭr-mirror, ł-little, ṇ-listen, ŏ-hot, oh-go, ōō-wood, ōō-moon, oor-tour, ōr-or, ow-how, ţh-that, th-thin, ŭ-but, UR-fur, ur-under. ( )- suppress the syllable   [ ]- less common   see p. xi for complete list.

31. **feaz'd** /feezd/ frayed.   Some eds. prefer **faced**.

35. **draff** /drăf/ pig swill.

37. **gibbets** /JIB its/ posts from which they hung corpses after hanging.

41. **gyves** /jīvz/ chains, fetters.

46. **Saint Albons** archaic variant of **St. Albans**.   Both pronounced
US /saynt AWL bunz/; UK /sint-, sņt-/.

47. **Daventry** /DAV in tree/, pronounced /DAYN tree/ locally.

51. **Warwickshire** US /WŌR ik shur/ [-sheer]; E. COAST US, UK /WŎR-/.   Place
names in the US often have /-wik-/ but this is not recommended for Shk.

67. **Tush** /tŭsh/ expression of disdain.

Act 4 Scene 3

69. **boroughs** towns.   US /BUR ohz/ [-uz]; E. COAST US /BUH rohz/ [-ruz];
UK /BUH ruz/.

79. **edicts** /EE dicts/ decrees.

109. ***surety** guarantee.   Here should be 2 syllables, though in mod. Eng., 3 syllables
are more common US /SHUR (ih) tee, SHOOR-/; CN /SHUR-/ [SHOOR-];
UK /SHOR-/ [SHUR-] [SHOOR-].

Act 4 Scene 4

2. **Marshal** here an archaic form /MAR uh shł/ is indicated.

24. **Mordake** /MOR dayk, -duk/.   Some eds. prefer **Murdoch** /MUR dŏck/.

31. **corrivals** (F1), **corivals** (Q1–6) /coh-, cuh RĪ vłz/ associates.

Act 5 Scene 1

3. **southren** /SUŢH run/ archaic variant of **southern**.

19. **exhal'd** here with 1st syllable stress, /EKS hayld/, the normal US form.

20. **portent** here should be /por TENT/ omen.

21. **unborn** here should be /UN born/.

29. **chewet** /CH$\overline{OO}$ it/ jackdaw.

42, 58. **Doncaster** US /DŎNG kăss tur/ [DŎNG kᵘss tur];
UK /DŎNG kᵘss tur/ [-kahss tur, -kăss tur].

45. **Gaunt** /gawnt/ Hal's grandfather.

69. **unkind** here should be /UN kīnd/.

72. **articulate** /ạr TIK yuh layt, -lut/ articulated, i.e, stated in articles.

102. **Albeit** /awl BEE (i)t/ although.

123. **Colossus** /kuh LŎS us/ giant.

140. **scutcheon** /SKUTCH un/ escutcheon, heraldic device often shown at funerals.

141. **catechism** /KAT uh kiz um, -kizm/ series of questions and answers.

Act 5 Scene 2

39. **scourge** /SKURJ/ punish harshly.

49. **Monmouth** /MŎN muth/; UK *also* [MUN-].

61. **cital** /SĪT ł/ recital.

68. **misconstrued** here should be /mis CŎN str$\overline{oo}$d/.

96. **Esperance** angl. /ES pur unss/; Fr. /es pĕr ahⁿss/ hope. The final *e* may have been sounded /uh/ to make the line scan correctly.

Act 5 Scene 3

14. **Holmedon** /HOHM dun/ mod. *Homildon, Humbleton.*

ă-bat, ăir-marry, air-pair, ạr-far, ĕr-merry, ĝ-get, ī-high, ĭr-mirror, ł-little, ṇ-listen, ŏ-hot, oh-go, $\overline{oo}$-wood, $\overline{oo}$-moon, oor-tour, ōr-or, ow-how, ṭh-that, ŧh-thin, ŭ-but, UR-fur, ur-under. ( )- suppress the syllable   [ ]- less common   see p. xi for complete list.

21. **Semblably** /SEM bluh blee/ similarly.

27. **wardrop** /WŌR drup/ or perhaps /-drŏp/, archaic variant of **wardrobe** which some eds. prefer.

stage direction after 28: **solus** /SOH lŭss/ alone.

58. ***carbonado** slashed meat. /car buh NAH doh/; UK *rarely older* [-NAY doh].

Act 5 Scene 4

23. **ungrown** here should be /UN grohn/.

34. **assay thee** /uh-, ass SAY/ make trial of thee.

45, 58. **Gawsey** /GAW zee, -see/.

45. **succor** (UK **succour**) /SUCK ur/ help. /-or/ not recommended.

59. **Monmouth** /MŎN muth/; UK *also* [MUN-].

82. **survey** here should be /sur VAY/.

83. **prophesy** /PRŎF uh sī/ to predict the future.

100. **ignominy** /IG nuh min ee/ disgrace.

114. **termagant** /TUR muh gunt/ violent.

159. **retrait** /rih-, ree TRAYT/ archaic variant of **retreat**.

Act 5 Scene 5

37. **prelate** /PREL ut/ high-ranking churchman.

Henry V

People in the Play

Aunchient, Ancient (Pistol) both spellings pronounced /AYN chunt/. Archaic variant of the rank **ensign** US /EN sṇ/; UK /-sīn/.

Bardolph /BAR dŏlf/; US *also* /-dawlf/.

Beaumont /BOH mŏnt, -munt/. The latter is more common in the UK; Fr. /BOH mohⁿ/.

Berri, Berry /BĔR ee/.

Bourbon /BOOR bun/; *newer* /-bŏn/; Fr. /BOOR bohⁿ/. /-un/ would be the normal angl. form (cf. *Simon*).

Dolphin (Lewis) /DŎL fin/; US *also* /DAWL-/ angl. form of **Dauphin** 'the French heir to the throne' which here would be Fr. /DOH făⁿ/. In Shk's time /l/ in this position was often silent, so *dolphin* and *dauphin* were probably both /DAW fin/.

Ely /EE lee/ his name is not spoken.

Erpingham /UR ping um/, though in the US /UR ping ham/ would be usual.

Exeter /EK sih tur/.

Fluellen /floo-, floo WEL un/. Some eds. prefer **Llewellyn** /loo-, loo WEL in/.

Gloucester /GLŎS tur/; US *also* /GLAWSS-/.

Gower /GOW ur/.

Grandpré angl. /grand PRAY/; Fr. /grahⁿ PRAY/. An older angl. form /-PREE/ was used by Shk.

Jamy /JAY mee/.

Katherine /KATH rin/ or /KATH ur rin/ but should be 2 syllables in verse.

Lewis, Louis the meter calls for 1 syllable /LOO (i)ss/.

ă-bat, ăir-**marry**, air-**pair**, ạr-**far**, ĕr-**merry**, ĝ-**get**, ī-**high**, ĭr-**mirror**, ł-**little**, ṇ-**listen**, ŏ-**hot**, oh-**go**, ōō-**wood**, ōō-**moon**, oor-**tour**, ōr-**or**, ow-**how**, ţh-**that**, t̶h̶-**thin**, ŭ-**but**, UR-**fur**, ur-**under**. ( )- suppress the syllable   [ ]- less common   see p. xi for complete list.

People in the Play (cont.)

Monmouth (Henry) /MŎN muth/; UK *also* [MUN-].

Montjoy /MŎNT joy/ or /mŏnt JOY/ depending on meter. Some eds. prefer F1's **Mountjoy** /MOWNT-/.

Northumberland /north UM bur lund/.

Nym, Nim /nim/.

Orleance here should be /OR l(ee) yunss, OR leenss, or LEENSS/ depending on meter. Archaic variant of **Orleans** /OR l(ee) yunz, OR leenz, or LEENZ/. Other eds. prefer Fr. **Orléans** /or lay ahⁿ/.

Pistol, Aunchient see **Auncient.**

Rambures /ram BYOORZ/; Fr. /rahⁿ bür/.

Salisbury 2 or 3 syllables, depending on meter US /SAWLZ b(ĕ)r ee/; UK /SAWLZ b(u)r ee/ [SĂLZ-].

Scroop /skrōōp/. Some eds. prefer mod. **Scrope**, pronounced the same way.

Suffolk /SUFF ᵘk/.

Warwick US /WŌR ik/; E. COAST US, UK /WŎR-/. Place names in the US often have /-wik/ but this is not recommended for Shk.

Westmerland archaic variant of **Westmor(e)land**, all variants are pronounced /WEST mur lund/ in the UK. US is usually /west MOR lund/ which will not fit the meter.

Places in the Play

***Agincourt** /AZH in cor/ [AJ-, -cort]. Sometimes Fr. /ah zhaⁿ coor/ is used.

Callice, Callis /KAL iss/ city on northern coast of France. Both are archaic variants of **Calais** which here should be /KAL ay/, the normal UK form; Fr. /KAH lay/.

Harflew /HAR flōō/ archaic variant of **Harfleur** /HAR flur/; Fr. /AHR flör/.

Special Note on the French Scenes

Henry V is unique in Shakespeare in that it contains several sections of extended French dialogue. No attempt is made to include a guide to the pronunciation of these scenes. A native speaker should be consulted for assistance wherever French is used.

Notes on Fluellen's Welsh Accent

Shk indicates the Welsh accent with the following spelling substitutions: *k* becomes *g (knock* becomes *knog), d* becomes *t (God* becomes *Got), b* becomes *p (by* becomes *py), v* becomes *f (valorous* becomes *falorous).* The reader should bear in mind that these substitutions are in no way sufficient to represent a true Welsh accent, which is best learned by listening to a native speaker. Seeing *by* spelled *py* does not mean the reader should simply use the English sound in *pie.* In Welsh /b, d, g/ may some-times sound somewhat like /p, t, k/, but without the accompanying puff of air that characterizes /p, t, k/ in both Welsh and English. One way to think of it is, that in Welsh /b, d, g/ are half-way between the sounds of Eng. /p, t, k/ and Eng. /b, d, g/.

The *f -v* confusion should be ignored. It is not a characteristic of Welsh, but many English speakers believe it is because the Welsh spell /v/ with *f (Dafydd* /DAH viţh/ 'David').

Shk's omission of the initial *w* in *woman, world,* and *work,* is a widespread Welsh feature. Also a feature of North Wales is the lack of /z/ and /zh/ which are pro-nounced /ss/ and /sh/.

Prologue

13. **casques** /kăsks/; UK *also* [kahsks] helmets.

17. **accompt** /uh COWNT/ archaic variant of **account**, pronounced the same way.

25. ***puissance** power (i.e., an army). Here must be 3 syllables, traditionally /PYOO ih sŋss/. In all countries one of several Frenchified pronunciations is most common: US /PWEE sŋss/; CN /-sahnss/; UK /-sahⁿss/ but these will not fit the meter.

Act 1 Scene 1

14. **esquires** here should be /ess KWĪRZ/, the usual UK form.

15. ***lazars** /LAY zurz, LAZZ urz/ lepers.

ă-bat, ăir-marry, air-pair, ạr-far, ĕr-merry, ĝ-get, ī-high, ĭr-mirror, ł-little, ņ-listen, ŏ-hot, oh-go, ōō-wood, ōō-moon, oor-tour, ōr-or, ow-how, ţh-that, ŧh-thin, ŭ-but, UR-fur, ur-under. ( )- suppress the syllable   [ ]- less common   see p. xi for complete list.

16. **indigent** /IN dih jint/ poor, needy.

17. **almshouses** poorhouses. /AHMZ-/ is older; /AHLMZ-, AWLMZ-/ are newer. In the UK the latter are non-standard.

40. **prelate** /PREL ut/ high-ranking churchman.

48. **charter'd *libertine** /LIB ur teen/, *rarely* [-tīn] licensed freeman.

52. **theoric** /~~THEE~~ uh rik/ theory.

58. **sequestration** /see kwih STRAY shun/ [sek wih-] separation.

66. **crescive** /CRESS iv/ growing.

69. **perfected** here should be /PUR fikt id/ fully accomplished.

Act 1 Scene 2

14. **bow** /boh/ distort.

16. **miscreate** /MIS cree ut, -ayt/ miscreated, i.e., spurious.

In lines 37–91 these names appear several times:

*Capet first king of the French dynasty. Here should have 1st syllable stress. The most common pronunciations are /KAH pay, KAP et/; US *also* [KAY pet]. /KAY pet, KAP et/ are older, angl. forms, /KAH pay/ is based on Fr.   Mixed forms like /KAP ay/ are also used.

Elbe /ELB/ German river.

Lewis, Louis the meter calls for 1 syllable /L$\overline{OO}$ (i)ss/.

Lorraine region on the French-German border. Here with 1st syllable stress US /L$\overline{OR}$ ayn/; E. COAST US, UK *also* /LŎR-/.

Pepin /PEP in/; Fr. **Pépin** /PAY pă^n/ father of Charlemagne.

Pharamond /FĂIR uh mund, -mŏnd/ legendary Frankish king.

Sala angl. /SAY luh/ one of the rivers at the mouth of the Rhine. Some eds. prefer Germ. **Saale** angl. /SAH luh/; Germ. /ZAH leh/. Others prefer **Saal**, however it should be 2 syllables.
  Salique, Salic /SAL ik/ [SAY lik].

---

38.   **In terram Salicam   mulieres   ne succedant**
Ang.Lat. /in TĔR um SAL ih kum   myōō LĪ uh reez nee suk SEE dṇt/
Class.Lat. /in TĔR ahm SAHL ih kahm Mōō LEE ĕr ayss nay sōōk KAY dahnt/
No woman shall succeed in Salique land.

40. **gloze, glose** /glohz/ interpret. Some eds. prefer **gloss**.

53. **Meisen** /MĪ sṇ, -sun/ archaic variant of **Meissen**, pronounced the same way.

65. **Childeric** /CHIL dur ik/. Some eds. prefer Fr. **Childéric** /sheel day reek/.

67. **Blithild** /BLIṬH ild, BLIŦH ild/.

67. **Clothair** /CLOH ŧhair, -tair/ a Frankish king. Some eds. prefer **Clotaire** /CLOH tair/.

74. **Lingare** /LING gar/ the mod. form is **Lingard** /LING gard/.

75. ***Charlemain, Charlemagne** US, CN /SHAR luh mayn/,
rarely [shar luh MAYN]; UK /SHAR luh mayn/ [shar luh MAYN].
/-mīn/ is a newer pronunciation, not recommended. Fr. /sharl mahn^y/.

82. **Ermengare** /UR min gar/. The mod. form is **Ermengard** or **Ermingarde** /UR min gard/.

91. **Howbeit** here should be /how BEE (i)t/ nevertheless.

95. **progenitors** /proh-, pruh JEN ih turz/ ancestors. /-torz/ not recommended.

116, 119. ***puissant** powerful. The traditional forms are /PWISS ṇt/, /PYŌŌ sṇt/, but these are now rare. In all countries one of several Frenchified pronunciations is the most common: /PWEE sṇt/ in the US, /-sahnt/ in CN, and /-sah^{n}t/ in the UK, but all 3 may be found in each country.

121. **exploits** here should be /ek SPLOYTS/.

132. **spiritualty** /SPĬR (ih) chōōl tee/ clergy.

143. **coursing** /COR sing/ hunting, running.

151. **assays** /uh-, ass SAYZ/ attacks.

ă-bat, äir-**marry**, air-**pair**, ạr-**far**, ĕr-**merry**, ĝ-**get**, ī-**high**, ĭr-**mirror**, ł-**little**, ṇ-**listen**, ŏ-**hot**, oh-**go**, ōō-**wood**, ōō-**moon**, oor-**tour**, ōr-**or**, ow-**how**, ṭh-**that**, ŧh-**thin**, ʋ-**but**, UR-**fur**, ur-**under**. ( )- suppress the syllable   [ ]- less common   see p. xi for complete list.

154. th'ill neighborhood (F1). Some eds. prefer **the bruit thereof** (following Q1–3) /bro͞ot/ report.

157. chevalry /SHEV ł ree/ body of knights. Archaic variant of **chivalry** /SHIV ł ree/.

182. Congreeing /cun-, cŏn GREE ing/ agreeing.

182. close /clohz/ cadence.

184. *divers various. US, CN /DĪ vurss, -vurz/; UK /DĪ vurss/ [-vurz]. Some eds. prefer **diverse**, which however should be stressed on the 1st syllable.

191. *magistrates /MAJ ih strayts/; US *also* [-struts].

192. venter /VEN tur/ archaic variant of **venture**.

203. executors here should be /EK suh kyo͞ot urz/ executioners.   /-orz/ not recommended.

213. defeat (F1). Some eds prefer **defect** (Q1–3). Here stress should fall on the 2nd syllable.

216. Gallia /GAL yuh/ France.

226. empery /EM pur ee/ imperial power.

248. *predecessor US /PRED ih sess ur/; UK /PREE dih sess ur/; in CN both /PREE-/ and /PRED-/ are used equally. Rarely with stress on the 3rd syllable. /-or/ not recommended.

250, 295. savor (UK **savour**) /SAY vur/ have the characteristic of.

252. galliard /GAL yurd/; UK *also newer* /GAL yard/ a lively dance.

255. in *lieu of US, CN /lo͞o, lyoo/; UK /lyo͞o/ [lo͞o] in return for.

Act 2 prologue

2. dalliance /DAL yunss/ sportiveness.

10. coronets small crowns. US /COR uh nets, -nits/, /cor uh NETS/; E. COAST US /CŎR-, cŏr-/; UK /CŎR uh nits/ [-nets, cŏr uh NETS].

24. Masham /MASS um, MASH um/.

30–42. **Southampton** /sow~~th~~ HAMP tun/ [-AMP-, su~~th~~-, suʈh-].

Act 2 Scene 1

30. **Gadslugs** (Q1–3) /gadz LUGZ/ God's ears. **This hand** (F1).

45–51. **solus** /SOH lus/ double meaning: unmarried, alone.

46. **egregious** /ih GREE jus/ notorious.

47. **mervailous** /mar VAY lus/ archaic variant of **marvellous** which here would be /mar VEL us/. -er- was often pronounced /-ar-/ in Shk's time. Some eds. make this a prose passage which would allow 1st syllable stress.

49. **perdy, perdie** /PUR DEE/ by God, indeed. Some eds. prefer the variant **pardie** /par DEE/.

54. **Barbason** /BAR buh sŏn, -sun, -sṇ/ a devil. /-ŏn/ is usual in the US and is increasingly common in the UK. /-un/ would be the traditional form (cf. *Solomon*).

62. **exhale** draw your sword. Here with 2nd syllable stress, /eks HAYL/, the normal UK form.

71. **Couple a gorge** in Pistol's bad Fr. it might be /CŌOP ł ah GORJ/, or Fr. /gorzh/, his mistake for *couper à gorge* or *coupez la gorge* /cōo pay/ cut the throat.

74. **spittle, Spital** /SPIT ł/ hospital in Spitalfields.

76. *****lazar** /LAY zur, LAZZ ur/ leper.

76. **Cressid's** /CRESS idz/ Cressida, a false lover.

77. **Tearsheet** /TAIR sheet/.

78. *****quondam** former. US /KWŎN dum/, *rarely* [-dam]; UK /-dam/, *rarely* [-dum].

79. **pauca** shortened form of *pauca verba* 'few words,' i.e., 'enough said.' Ang.Lat. /PAW kuh VUR buh/; Class.Lat. /POW kah WĔR bah/.

119. **quotidian** /kwoh TID ee un/; UK *also* [kwŏ TID ee un] type of fever.

ă-bat, ăir-marry, air-pair, ạr-far, ĕr-merry, ĝ-get, ī-high, ĭr-mirror, ł-little, ṇ-listen, ŏ-hot, oh-go, ōō-wood, ōō-moon, oor-tour, ōr-or, ow-how, ʈh-that, ~~th~~-thin, ŭ-but, UR-fur, ur-under. ( )- suppress the syllable   [ ]- less common   see p. xi for complete list.

119. **tertian** /TUR shun/ type of fever returning every 48 hours.

119. ***lamentable** US /luh MEN tuh bł/ [LAM en tuh bł];
CN, UK /LAM un tuh bł/ [luh MEN-].

124. **corroborate** /kuh RŎB ur ut/ Pistol's mistake for *corrupted*.

127. **condole** /cun DOHL/ grieve with.

Act 2 Scene 2

4. **sate** archaic variant of **sat**. May have been /sayt/ or /sat/.

13–148. **Masham** /MASS um, MASH um/.

42. **excess** here should be /ek SESS/, the most common UK form.

53. ***orisons** prayers. US, CN /OR ih zunz, -zn̩z/ [-sunz, -sn̩z]; E. COAST US /ŎR-/;
UK /ŎR ih zunz, -zn̩z/.

87. **appertinents, appurtenants** /uh PURT ih nunts/ fittings.

108. **hoop** /ho͞op, ho͝op/ variant of ***whoop** /who͞op/ [ho͞op, ho͝op, who͝op].

117. **glist'ring** /GLIS tring/ glistening.

123. **Tartar** /TAR tur/ Tartarus, hell.

127. **affiance** /uh FĪ unss/ trust.

139. ***indued** /in DYo͞oD/; US *also* [-Do͞oD] **endowed**.

190. ***puissance** power (i.e., army). Here must be 3 syllables, traditionally
/PYo͞o ih sn̩ss/. In all countries one of several Frenchified pronunciations is now
the most common: /PWEE sn̩ss/ in the US, /-sahnss/ in CN, and /-sah[n]ss/ in the UK,
but none of these will fit the meter here.

Act 2 Scene 3

2. **Staines** /staynz/ town west of London.

3, 6. **ern, erne** (F1) /urn/ mourn. Some eds. make the 1st instance **yearn** and
the 2nd **earn**.

4. **blithe** /blīṭh/; US *also* /blīt̶h̶/ merry.

5. **Falstaff** US /FAWL stăff/; E. NEW ENG., UK /-stahff/.

12. **christom** /CRISS um/ archaic variant of **chrisom** /CRIZ um/ child in its chrisom-cloth, i.e., newly christened.

25. **up'ard** /UP urd/. Some eds. prefer Q1–3's **upward**, or F1's **up-peer'd**.

32. **incarnate** /in CAR nit/ [-nayt] in the flesh. /-ut/ is usual for adjs.

38. **rheumatic** suffering from a cold. Usually /rōō MAT ik/ today, but elsewhere in Shk /RŌŌM uh tik/ which fits better here since the hostess means *lunatic*.

46. **Southampton** /sowt̶h̶ HAMP tun/ [-AMP-, sut̶h̶-, suṭh-].

48. **chattels** /CHAT łz/ property.

53. **Caveto** /kah VET oh/ beware. Pistol may mean *cavete*, Ital. be careful.

62. ***huswifery** /HUZ if ree/ is traditional, /-wīf ree, -wiff ree/ are newer, based on spelling. Some eds. prefer **housewifery** /HOWSS-/.

62. **Keep close, I thee command** (F1) /clohss/ keep hidden. **Keepe fast thy buggle boe** (Q1–3) /BUG ł boh/ keep your hobgoblin secure, i.e., your privates.

Act 2 Scene 4

5. **Brabant** angl. /BRAB unt/; Dutch /BRAH bahnt/; Fr. /BRAH bah[n]/ former duchy where Belgium is today.

25. **Whitsun** /WHIT sṇ/ Pentecost, the 7th Sunday after Easter.

39. ***ordure** manure. US /OR dyoor/ [-dyur, -joor, -jur]; CN /-dyur/ [-dyoor, -jur]; UK /OR dyoor/, *rarely* [-jur]. Normal development in the US would result in /-jur/.

46. **niggardly** /NIG urd lee/ miserly.

54. **Cressy** /CRESS ee/ angl. variant of Fr. **Crécy** /CRAY see/.

ă-bat, äir-marry, air-pair, aṛ-far, ĕr-merry, ĝ-get, ī-high, ĭr-mirror, ł-little, ṇ-listen, ŏ-hot, oh-go, ōō-wood, ōō-moon, oor-tour, ōr-or, ow-how, ṭh-that, t̶h̶-thin, ŭ-but, UR-fur, ur-under. ( )- suppress the syllable   [ ]- less common   see p. xi for complete list.

57. **mountain** (F1). Some eds. prefer **mountant** /MOWNT unt, -ṇt/ gaining the ascendency, or **mounting**.

85. **sinister** illegitimate. Here should be /sin ISS tur/.

89. **demonstrative** /duh MŎN struh tiv/.

108. **betrothed** /bih-, bee TROHṬH id/ engaged to be married.

109. **That shall be swallowed in this controversy**. Despite the spelling with *-ed, swallowed* is 2 syllables /SWŎL ohd/, followed by /CŎN truh vur see/, the normal US pronunciation.

124. **womby** /WŌŌM ee/ hollow.

126. **ordinance** artillery. Archaic spelling of **ordnance**. Both would have to be 3 syllables in this line /OR dih nunss/.

132. **Louvre** palace of the Fr. kings. Here should be 2 syllables, angl. /LŌŌV ruh/ or /LŌŌV ur/. The former is common in the UK.

Act 3 Chorus

2. **celerity** /suh LĔR ih tee/ speed.

6. **Phoebus** /FEE bus/ god of the sun.

14. ***rivage** /RIV ij/ shore. [riv AHZH] is a new pronunciation based on Fr. and will not fit the meter. /RĪ vij/, mentioned in some dictionaries., is now obsolete.

21. ***puissance** power. Here the line allows a double or triple ending. The traditional forms are /PWISS ṇss/, /PYŌŌ (ih) sṇss/, but these are now rare. In all countries one of several Frenchified pronunciations is the most common: /PWEE sṇss/ in the US, /-sahnss/ in CN, and /-sah[n]ss/ in the UK, but all 3 may be found in each country.

26. **ordinance** artillery. Archaic spelling of **ordnance**. Both should be 3 syllables in this line /OR dih nunss/.

35. ***eche out** US /eech/ [etch]; UK /etch/ [eech]. Elsewhere rhymes with *speech*. Some eds. prefer **eke out** /eek/. Both mean 'increase.'

Act 3 Scene 1

25. **yeomen** /YOH mun/ freemen who own small farms.

Act 3 Scene 2

20. **Avaunt** /uh VAWNT/ be off!

20. **cullions** /CŬL yunz/ scoundrels, literally 'testicles.'

25. **lenity** /LEN ih tee/ leniency.

44. **half-pence** (F1), **hapence** (Q1–2) /HAYP n̥ss, -unss/.

48. **handkerchers** /HANK ur churz/ archaic variant of **handkerchiefs**.

Note on dialects: Shk's spellings are not a reliable guide to the correct reproduction of the Scots, Irish, and Welsh dialects of Jamy, Macmorris, and Fluellen in this scene. The notation of this guide is also ill-suited to help the reader understand the phonetic nuances of dialect speech. Jamy's *gud* 'good' for example represents a Scots sound that in some dialects is pronounced with the tongue forward from the usual English /ōō/, somewhat like German *ü*; in other dialects it is /uh/. These accents are best learned by listening to native speakers.

The Complete Oxford begins 3.3 here—line nos. in parentheses.

---

81. (3.3.26) *__pristine__ US /priss TEEN/ [PRISS teen]; in the UK, CN both are used equally.

84. (3.3.29) **God-den** /gud-, gōōd EN/ good evening. Some eds. prefer **Good e'en**.

87. (3.3.31) **pioners** soldiers who dug trenches and planted mines. It is not certain whether Shk pronounced this /PĪ uh nurz/ or as in mod. **pioneers** /pī uh NEERZ/.

95. (3.3.39) **voutsafe** /vowt SAYF/ grant. Archaic variant of **vouchsafe** /vowch SAYF/.

110, 113. (3.3.54, 57) **God sa' me** /say/ God save me.

ă-bat, ăir-marry, air-pair, a̯r-far, ĕr-merry, ĝ-get, ī-high, ĭr-mirror, l̯-little, n̯-listen, ŏ-hot, oh-go, ōō-wood, ōō-moon, oor-tour, ōr-or, ow-how, ţh-that, th-thin, Ŭ-but, UR-fur, ur-under. ( )- suppress the syllable   [ ]- less common   see p. xi for complete list.

119. (3.3.63) **tway, twae** /tway/ Scots 'two.'

126. (3.3.70) ***peradventure** perhaps. /PUR ad VEN chur/;
US *rarely* [PĔR-, PUR ad ven chur];
UK, CN *also* [PUR-, PĔR ad ven chur, pĕr ad VEN chur].

137. ***parley** (3.3.79) /PAR lee/ conference with an enemy. Newer [-lay] not recommended.

Act 3 Scene 3 (*Complete Oxford* continues this as 3.3—line nos. in parentheses)

2. (3.3.85) **parle** /pạrl/ conference with an enemy.

15. (3.3.98) **impious** /IM pyus/ lacking in respect, profane.

22. (3.3.105) **licentious** /lī SEN chus/ lustful.

26. (3.3.109) **precepts** here should be /prih-, pree SEPTS/.

26. (3.3.109) **leviathan** /luh VĪ uh ~~th~~un/ sea monster.

41. (3.3.124) **Herod's** /HĔR udz/ King in Judea in Jesus' lifetime.

45. (3.3.128) **succors** (UK **succours**) /SUCK urz/ help. /-orz/ not recommended.

Act 3 Scene 4

56. **Foh** indicates an expression of disgust made with the lips /pff/! or /pfuh/!
Sometimes vocalized as /foh/ or **faugh** /faw/.

Act 3 Scene 5

1. **Somme** /sŏm/; US *also* /sum/.

7. **scions** /SĪ unz/ living plants grafted onto root stock.

8. **Spirt up, Spurt up** /spurt/ sprout up.

14. **Albion** /AL bee un/ Britain.

33. **lavoltas** bounding dances. /luh VOHLT uz/ or older /luh VŎLT uz/.

33. ***corantos** courants, a type of dance. US /cuh-, coh RAHN tohz/ [-RAN-];
UK /-RAHN-, -RAN-/.

Some of the names in the list in lines 40–5 appear under "People in the Play."

---

40. **Charles Delabreth** /del uh BRET, -BRETH/. Some eds. prefer **Delabret**. 1st
syllable stress is also possible.

42. **Alanson** angl. /AL un sun, -sn̩/ or /uh LAN sun/; Fr. **Alençon** /ah lah^n soh^n/. At
4.8.96 it has 1st syllable stress.

42. **Brabant** angl. /BRAB unt/; Dutch /BRAH bahnt/; Fr. /BRAH bah^n/ former
duchy where Belgium is today.

43. **Jacques Chatillion, Rambures, Vaudemont** there are 2 possibilities for this
line. *Jacques* should be 2 syllables, usually /JAY kweez/ (see *As You Like It* "People
in the Play"), followed by /shuh TILL yun, RAM byoorz, VOH duh mŏnt/ or /shuh
TILL ee yun, ram BYOORZ, vohd MŎNT/. Some eds. prefer **Chatillon** or
Châtillon; Fr. /shah tee yoh^n, rah^n bür, voh duh moh^n/.

44. **Roussi** /R$\overline{OO}$ see, r$\overline{oo}$ SEE/ are both possible.

44. **Faulconbridge** /FAWL kun brij/ or the older pronunciation [FAW kun-], still
used by some in the UK. Some eds. prefer **Falconbridge** which may also be /FAL-/;
UK *also* [FŎL-]. Others prefer **Fauconbridge** /FAW kun-/, **Fauconberg**
angl. /-burg/; Fr. /-bĕrg/.

45. **Foix** angl. /foyz/; Fr. /fwah/.

45. **Lestrake** /LESS strayk/. Some eds. prefer F1's **Lestrale** /LESS strahl/ or
Lestrelles /LESS strel/.

45. **Bouciqualt, Boucicault** /B$\overline{OO}$ see koh/ which is also the Fr. pronunciation;
US *also* /B$\overline{OO}$ see kawlt/.

45. **Charolois** /SHĂIR uh loiz/ archaic variant of **Charolais** /shăir uh LAY/;
US *also* /shahr-/; Fr. /shahr oh lay/.

49. **pennons** /PEN unz/ banners.

52. **rheum** /r$\overline{oo}$m/ spit, i.e., waters.

ă-bat, ăir-**marry**, air-**pair**, a̩r-**far**, ĕr-**merry**, ĝ-**get**, ī-**high**, ĭr-**mirror**, ł-**little**, n̩-**listen**,
ŏ-**hot**, oh-**go**, $\overline{oo}$-**wood**, $\overline{oo}$-**moon**, oor-**tour**, ōr-**or**, ow-**how**, t̪h-**that**, ŧħ-**thin**, ʊ-**but**,
UR-**fur**, ur-**under**. ( )- suppress the syllable [ ]- less common   see p. xi for complete list.

54, 64. **Roan** /rohn, ROH un/ archaic angl. variant of **Rouen** which here would be Fr. /rwah^n/ or /RŌŌ ah^n/.

Act 3 Scene 6

7. *****Agamemnon** chief king of the Greeks at Troy. US, CN /ag uh MEM nŏn/; UK /-nŏn/ [-nun].

14. **Antony** /AN tuh nee/. Some eds. prefer F1's **Anthony** which in the UK is also usually pronounced with /t/.

36. *****spherical** US, CN /SFEER ih kł/ [SFĔR-]; UK /SFĔR ih kł/.

57. *****figo** /FEE goh/, /FIG oh/ an obscene gesture, also called the *fig of Spain*. Some eds. prefer the variant **fico** /FEE koh/.

61. **arrant** /ĂIR unt/ thoroughgoing.

70, 75. **perfit(ly)** /PUR fit (lee)/ archaic variant of **perfect(ly)**. Also /PAR fit/ in Shk's time.

72. **sconce** /skŏnss/ fortification.

98. **perdition** /pur DISH un/; UK *also* [PUR DISH un] losses.

102. **bubukles, bubuckles** /BYŌŌ buck łz/ pimples. Some eds. prefer **bubuncles** /BYŌŌ bunk łz/.

112. **lenity** /LEN ih tee/ leniency.

130. *****exchequer** /eks CHEK ur/; US *rarely* [EKS chek ur] treasury.

Act 3 Scene 7

12. **pasterns** /PĂSS turnz/ part of a horse's foot.

13. *****entrails** /EN traylz/; US *also* [-trłz] guts.

18. **Hermes** /HUR meez/ messenger of the gods.

21. *****Perseus** he rode the winged horse, Pegasus. /PUR see us/ [-syŌŌss], US *rarely* [-sŌŌss]. The traditional pronunciation is /PUR see us/, the restored pronunciation is /-s(y)ŌŌss/.

27, 33. **palfrey(s)** /PAWL free(z)/; UK *also* [PŎL-] saddle horse.

29. ***homage** /HŎM ij/; US *also* /ŎM ij/ acknowledgement of allegiance.

44. **courser** /COR sur/ warhorse.

53. **kern** /kurn/ Irish foot soldier.

54. **strossers** /STRŎSS urz/; US *also* /STRAWSS-/ archaic variant of *trousers*.

59. **as live** as soon. May have been /liv/ in Shk's time. Variant of **as lief** /leef/. In the US **lieve** /leev/ is still found in some dialects and can also be used here.

141, 148. **mastiffs** /MĂST ifs/; UK *sometimes* [MAHST-] powerful watchdogs.

148. **robustious** /roh BUS chus/ boisterous.

152. **shrowdly** /SHROHD lee/ badly. Archaic variant of **shrewdly**.

Act 4 Chorus

9. **umber'd** /UM burd/ darkened.

43. ***largess, largesse** generous gift. Here should have 1st syllable stress US /LAR jess/ [-zhess]; CN, UK /LAR zhess/ [-jess]. Forms with /j/ are older.

Act 4 Scene 1

23. **slough** /sluff/ skin.

23. **legerity** /luh JĔR ih tee/ nimbleness.

40. ***puissant** powerful. The traditional forms are /PWISS n̩t/, /PYŌŌ sn̩t/, but these are now rare. In all countries one of several Frenchified pronunciations is the most common: /PWEE snt/ in the US, /-sahnt/ in CN, and /-sah^{n}t/ in the UK, but all 3 may be found in each country.

60. ***figo** /FEE goh/, /FIG oh/ an obscene gesture, also called the *fig of Spain*. Some eds. prefer the variant **fico** /FEE koh/.

ă-bat, ăir-marry, air-pair, ạr-far, ĕr-merry, ĝ-get, ī-high, ĭr-mirror, ł-little, n̩-listen, ŏ-hot, oh-go, ōō-wood, ōō-moon, oor-tour, ōr-or, ow-how, t̠h-that, t̶h̶-thin, Ŭ-but, UR-fur, ur-under. ( )- suppress the syllable   [ ]- less common   see p. xi for complete list.

67. **prerogatifes, prerogatifs.** Fluellen's version of **prerogatives** rights /pur RŎG uh tivz/ [prih-, pree-]. /pree-/ non-standard in the UK.

69, 71. **Pompey('s)** /PŎMP ee/ Roman general.

115. **Thames** /temz/ the major river of London.

160. **arbitrement, arbitrament** /ạr BIT ruh munt/ settlement.

161. ***peradventure** perhaps. /PUR ad VEN chur/;
US *rarely* [PĔR-, PUR ad ven chur];
UK, CN *also* [PUR-, PĔR ad ven chur, pĕr ad VEN chur].

164. ***bulwark** structure for defense. US, CN /BỤLL wurk/ [BŬL wurk];
UK /BỤLL WURK, -wurk/. The vowels /or/, /ahr/ not recommended in the final
syllable and are non-standard in the UK.

169. **beadle** /BEE dł/ local official in charge of whippings.

223. **enow** /ih NOW/; US *also* /ee-/ archaic variant of **enough**.

250. ***homage** /HŎM ij/; US *also* /ŎM ij/ acknowledgement of allegiance.

255. **flexure** /FLEK shur/; UK *also* [-syoor] bowing.

273. **Phoebus** /FEE bus/ god of the sun.

274. ***Elysium** the realm of the blessed in the afterlife. US /ih LEEZH yum/
[-LIZ-, -LIZH-, -LEESS-, -LISS-]; UK /-LIZ-/; *also* /ee-/ in all countries. The oldest
forms still in use are /-LIZ-/, /-LIZH-/. The historic form is /ih LIZH um/.

275. ***Hyperion** /hī PEER yun/ god of the sun. Sometimes newer /-PĔR-/ or
/-ŏn/ are used, but are not recommended.

296. **contrite** here should be /CŎN trīt/ remorseful.

301. **chauntries** archaic variant of **chantries** US /CHĂNT reez/;
UK, E. NEW ENG. /CHAHN treez/ chapels. The archaic vowel was pronounced
/-AW-/ and gave rise to RP /-AH-/.

Act 4 Scene 2

2. **varlot** attendant.   Archaic variant of **varlet**, both pronounced /VAR lut/.

11. **dout** /dowt/ extinguish.

18. **shales** /shaylz/ archaic variant of **shells.**

28. **enow** /ih NOW/; US *also* /ee-/ archaic variant of **enough.**

29. **hilding** /HILL ding/ base.

35. **sonance** /SOH nunss/ sound.

43. ***bankrout** /BANK rowt/ [-rut] archaic variant of **bankrupt.**

46. **torch-staves** /stayvz/ staffs.

49. ***gimmal'd** hinged. US /ĜIM łd/; UK /JIM łd/, the latter is the older form, the former a spelling pronunciation. Some eds. prefer **gimmal** or **gemmelled** /JEM łd/ having double rings.

55. **liveless** /LĪV liss/ archaic variant of **lifeless.**

58. **provender** /PRŎV n̩ dur/ dry food for animals.

60. ***guidon** US /ĜĪ dn̩, -dun/ [-dŏn]; UK /-dŏn/ [-dn̩, -dun] standard. The normal pronunciation would be /-dun/ (cf. *canon, poison).*

Act 4 Scene 3

6. **God buy you.** Some eds. substitute **God bye ye, God be wi' ye** or some other variation of that phrase, however it would have to be reduced to something like /gŏd BWEE yuh/ to fit the meter.

20. **enow** /ih NOW/; US *also* /ee-/ archaic variant of **enough.**

40–57. **Crispian** /CRISP ee un/.

54. **Talbot** US /TAL but/ [TAWL-]; UK /TAWL but/ [TŎL-, TAL-].

105. **bullet's crasing** (F1, Q1–3) variant of **crazing**, both pronounced /CRAY zing/ meaning 'breaking into pieces,' or 'ricocheting.' Some eds. prefer F2's **grasing**, variant of **grazing**, both pronounced /GRAY zing/ ricocheting.

107. **relapse** here should be /REE laps/, the normal US form. The usual UK form is /rih LAPS/.

ă-bat, ăir-**marry**, air-**pair**, a̩r-**far**, ĕr-**merry**, ĝ-**get**, ī-**high**, ĭr-**mirror**, ł-**little**, n̩-**listen**, ŏ-**hot**, oh-**go**, o͞o-**wood**, o͞o-**moon**, oor-**tour**, ōr-**or**, ow-**how**, t̩h-**that**, ŧħ-**thin**, ŭ-**but**, UR-**fur**, ur-**under**. ( )- suppress the syllable   [ ]- less common   see p. xi for complete list.

114. **slovenry** /SLUV un ree/ untidiness.

131. ***vaward** US /VAW wurd, VAY-/ [VOW-]; UK /VAW wurd/
[VAY-, VOW-, VAW WURD]. The vowel of *war* not recommended in the
2nd syllable. Archaic variant of **vanguard**.

Act 4 Scene 4

In this scene Pistol's prisoner speaks a dialect, or archaic form of French which is in
some cases different from present-day standard French. *Moi* is /moy/ which Pistol
repeats. *Bras* is /brahss/.

8. **Perpend** /pur PEND/ consider.

8. **Dew** the soldier says *Dieu* /dyö/ which Pistol interprets as *dew*, which was
/dih-o͞o/ in Shk's Eng.

11. **Egregious** /ih GREE jus/ extraordinary.

26–28. **Le Fer** /luh FAIR/.

28, 31. **firk** /furk/ beat.

37. **Owy, cuppele gorge, permafoy** Pistol is trying to say *Oui, couper la gorge,
par ma foi* 'Yes, cut (your) throat, by my faith.' In French: /wee, ko͞o pay lah
GORZH, par mah FWAH/. -er- sometimes represented /ahr/ in Shk's Eng.

Act 4 Scene 5

7. ***perdurable** (F1) here should be /PUR dyur uh bł/; US *also* [-dur-] lasting.
Omitted Q1–2.

14. **pander** (F1) /PAN dur/ pimp. Q1–2 have **leno** Latin 'pimp.'
Ang.Lat. /LEE noh/; Class.Lat. /LAY noh/.

19. **enow** (F1) /ih NOW/; US *also* /ee-/ archaic variant of Q1–2's **enough**.

Act 4 Scene 6

21. **raught** /rawt/ reached.

35. ***alarum** US, CN /uh LAHR um/ [-LĂIR-]; UK /uh LĂIR um, uh LAHR um/
a call to arms.

Act 4 Scene 7

2. **arrant** /ĂIR unt/ thoroughgoing.

11–100. **Monmouth** /MŎN mu~~th~~/; UK *also* [MUN-].

20–27. **Macedon** /MĂSS uh dun, -dŏn/. /-ŏn/ is usual in the US and is increasingly common in the UK. /-un/ would be the traditional form (cf. *Solomon*).

28, 106. **Wye** /wī/ river in Wales.

39–45. **Clytus** some eds. prefer **Cleitus** both pronounced /CLĪ tuss/ Alexander's friend.

49. **gipes** some eds. prefer **gypes**. Fluellen's version of **gibes** /jībz/ 'sarcastic comments' with the /b/ slightly *p*-like.

51. **Falstaff** US /FAWL stăff/; E. NEW ENG., UK /-stahff/.

61. **skirr** /skur/ scurry.

62. **Assyrian** /uh SĬR yun/.

80. **Yerk** /yurk/ kick.

91. **Crispin Crispianus** /CRISP in crisp ee AY nuss/; Class.Lat. /-AHN ōōs/.

103. **Saint Tavy's** Fluellen's version of **St. Davy's**. The use of the letter *T* is deceptive. The Welsh would use a /d/ more or less like that in Eng.

111. **Jeshu** (Q1–2) Fluellen's Welsh version of Q3's **Iesu** /JEE zōō, -zyōō/ (see p. 31, *Jesu*).

133. **craven** /CRAY vin, -vṇ/ coward.

138. **Belzebub** /BEL zih bub/ archaic variant of **Beelzebub** /bee EL zih bub/ a devil.

141. **arrant** /ĂIR unt/ thoroughgoing.

154, 157. **Alanson** angl. /AL un sun, -sṇ/, /uh LAN sun/; Fr. **Alençon** /ah lah^n soh^n/. At 4.8.96 with 1st syllable stress.

ă-bat, äir-marry, air-pair, ạr-far, ĕr-merry, ĝ-get, ī-high, ĭr-mirror, ł-little, ṇ-listen, ŏ-hot, oh-go, ōō-wood, ōō-moon, oor-tour, ōr-or, ow-how, ţh-that, ~~th~~-thin, ŭ-but, UR-fur, ur-under. ( )- suppress the syllable   [ ]- less common   see p. xi for complete list.

Act 4 Scene 8

4. **peradventure** perhaps. /PUR ad VEN chur/;
US *rarely* [PĔR-, PUR ad ven chur];
UK, CN *also* [PUR-, PĔR ad ven chur, pĕr ad VEN chur].

9. **'Sblud, 'Sblood** /zblud/ God's (i.e., Jesus') blood. Some eds. prefer **God's plood**
(following Q1).

9, 34. **arrant** /ĂIR unt/ thoroughgoing.

Some of the names listed in this scene appear in "People in the Play."

18–96. **Alanson ('s)** angl. /AL un sun/, /uh LAN sun, -sn̥/; Fr. **Alençon**
/ah lah^n soh^n/. Line 96 must have 1st syllable stress (or possibly 3rd, if the Fr.
pronunciation is used).

36. **avouchment** /uh VOWCH munt/ affirmation.

44. **martial law** /MAR shł/ laws of war.

63. **twelvepence** /TWELV punss, -pn̥ss/; US *also* /TWELV penss/.

77. **Bouciqualt, Boucicault** /BOO see koh/ which is also the Fr. pronunciation;
US *also* /BOO see kawlt/.

84, 104. **esquire(s)** here should be /ess KWĪR(Z)/, the usual UK form.

92. **Charles Delabreth** /del uh BRET, -BRETH/. Some eds. prefer **Delabret**.
1st syllable stress is also possible.

93. **Jacques of Chatillion** there are 2 possibilities: *Jacques* can be 2 syllables,
usually /JAY kweez/ (see AYL "People in the Play") and *Chatillion*
angl. /SHAT ł yun, SHAT il yun/. Or *Jacques* can be 1 syllable /jayks/,
followed by /shuh TIL yun/. Some eds. prefer **Chatillon** or Fr. **Châtillon**
/shah tee yoh^n/. *Jacques* in Fr. is /zhahk/.

95. **Sir Guichard Dolphin** in Shk's time /GWITCH-, ĜITCH urd DŎL fin/
which in the US today would have become /DAWL-/ in some areas; Fr. /ĜEE shar/.
Some eds. prefer **Guischard** /ĜISH urd/ or Fr. **Guiscard Dauphin**
angl. /ĜIS card DAW fin/; Fr. /ĜEES car DOH fã^n/.

96. **Anthony** US /AN thuh nee/; UK /AN tuh nee/ [-thuh nee]. Some eds. prefer
Antony.

96. **Brabant** angl. /BRAB unt/; Dutch /BRAH bahnt/; Fr. /BRAH bah^n/ former duchy where Belgium is today.

98. **Edward** some eds. prefer Fr. **Édouard** /AY dwahr/.

99. **Roussi** /R$\overline{OO}$ see/.

99. **Faulconbridge** /FAWL kun brij/ or the older pronunciation [FAW kun-], still used by some in the UK. Some eds. prefer **Falconbridge** which may also be /FAL-/; UK *also* [FŎL-]. Others prefer **Fauconbridge** /FAW kun-/, **Fauconberg** angl. /-burg/; Fr. /-bĕrg/.

99. **Foix** angl. /foyz/; Fr. /fwah/.

100. **Marle** /marl/.

100. **Vaudemont** here should be 3 syllables /VOH duh mŏnt/; Fr. /voh duh moh^n/.

100. **Lestrake** /LESS strayk/. Some eds. prefer **Lestrale** /LESS strahl/, **Lestrelles** /LESS strel/.

104. **Ketley** (F1) /KET lee/ archaic variant of **Keighley** /KEE~~TH~~ lee, KEE lee/. Some eds. prefer **Kikely** /KĪK lee/.

104. **esquire** here should be /ess KWĪR/, the usual UK form.

108. **stratagem** /STRAT uh jum/ plan.

123. **Non nobis** Ang.Lat. /NŎN NOH bis/; Church Latin /NOHN NOH beess/ Psalm 115.

123. **Te Deum** Ang.Lat. /TEE DEE um/; Church Latin /TAY DAY $\overline{oo}$m/ hymn of thanksgiving.

Act 5 Chorus

16. **Blackheath** /black HEE~~TH~~/, or with evenly stressed syllables.

21. **ostent** here should be /ŏ STENT/ display.

26. **th'*antique** ancient. Here /TH ^{y}AN teek/, *rarely older* [AN tik].

ă-bat, äir-**marry**, air-**pair**, ạr-**far**, ĕr-**merry**, ĝ-**get**, ī-**high**, ĭr-**mir**ror, ł-**little**, ṇ-**listen**, ŏ-**hot**, oh-**go**, $\overline{oo}$-**wood**, $\overline{oo}$-**moon**, oor-**tour**, ōr-**or**, ow-**how**, ţh-**that**, ~~th~~-**thin**, ʊ-**but**, UR-**fur**, ur-**und**er. ( )- suppress the syllable   [ ]- less common   see p. xi for complete list.

27. **plebeians** /plih BEE unz/ common people.

Act 5 Scene 1

5–53. **scald** /skawld/ scabby.

---

19. **bedlam** /BED lum/ crazy.

20. **Parca's** /PAR kuz/ one of the Fates.

21. **qualmish** nauseated. /KWAHM ish/ is older; /KWAHL mish, KWAWL mish/ are newer. In UK the latter are non-standard.

28. **Cadwallader** /KAD wawl uh dur/ last of the Welsh kings.

34. **victuals** /VIT łz/ food.

65. **woodmonger** woodseller. US /WŏŏD mŏng gur/ or /-mawng-/ [-mung-]; CN /-mung gur, -mŏng gur/; UK /-mung gur/.

66. **God buy you** (F1) good-bye. Some eds. substitute **God b'wi' you** /gŏd BWEE yŏŏ/ or some other variation of that phrase.

73. **avouch** /uh VOWCH/ uphold.

80. ***huswife** /HUZ if/ is traditional, /HUSS wīf/ is a newer, spelling pronunciation. The former is the most common form in the UK, the latter in the US. In CN both are used equally. In North America /HUSS wif/ is also sometimes used. Some eds. prefer mod. **housewife**. Here means **hussy**.

81. **spittle, Spital** /SPIT ł/ hospital in Spitalfields.

89. **Gallia** /GAL yuh/ France.

Act 5 Scene 2

17. ***basilisks** canons. US /BĂSS ih lisks/ [BAZ ih lisks]; UK /BAZ-/ [BĂSS-]; CN both used equally.

31. **congreeted** /cun-, cŏn GREET id/ greeted each other.

44. **leas** /leez/ fields.

45. **darnel** /DAR nł/ a weed.

45. **femetary** a weed. Probably /FEM ih tuh ree, -tree/, variant of **fumitory**
US /FY$\overline{OO}$M ih tor ee/; UK /-tuh ree, -tree/.

46. **coulter** /KOHL tur/ cutting edge of a plow.

47. **deracinate** /dih-, dee RĂSS ih nayt/ wipe out.

48, 54. **mead(s)** /meedz/ meadows.

48. **erst** /urst/ formerly.

49. **cowslip** /COW slip/ a yellow flower.

49. **burnet** /BUR nit/ a flower. US *also* /bur NET/ which does not fit the meter.

72. **tenures** archaic variant of **tenors** 'general principles,' both /TEN urz/.

81. **re-survey** here should be /ree sur VAY/.

82. **peremptory** here should be /PĔR um tur ee/; US *also* /-tor ee/ final.

137. **vauting** (*vawting* F1) /VAWT ing/ archaic variant of **vaulting**.

140. **buffet** /BUFF it/ box.

142. **jack-an-apes** /JACK uh nayps/ monkey.

144. ***protestation** expressions of love. US /proh tess-, prŏt ess TAY shun/;
CN /prŏt ess-/ [proh tess-]; UK /prŏt ess-/.

158. **prater** /PRAY tur/ chatterer.

183, 207. **Saint Denis** US /saynt DEN iss/; UK /sint-, sn̩t-/ patron saint of France.

208. **Constantinople** /cŏn stan tih NOH pł/.

210. **flower-de-luce** /FLOWR duh l$\overline{oo}$ss/ lily flower, the national emblem of France.
Main stress may also fall on the 3rd syllable, the usual US form. At one time many
RP speakers in the UK used /ly$\overline{oo}$-/ for words beginning *lu-,* but today their number is
dwindling.

215. **moi'ty, moiety** /MOY tee, MOY uh tee/ portion.

ă-bat, ăir-marry, air-pair, ạr-far, ĕr-merry, ĝ-get, ī-high, ĭr-mirror, ł-little, n̩-listen,
ŏ-hot, oh-go, $\overline{oo}$-wood, $\overline{oo}$-moon, oor-tour, ōr-or, ow-how, ţh-that, t̶h-thin, ŭ-but,
UR-fur, ur-under. ( )- suppress the syllable   [ ]- less common   see p. xi for complete list.

235. **avouch** /uh VOWCH/ affirm.

240. **Plantagenet** /plan TAJ ih nit/.

341–42.   **Praeclarissimus**   **filius**   **noster**   **Henricus,**
Ang.Lat.   /pree clair ISS ih muss   FIL ee us   NŎST ur   hen RĪ kuss/
Class.Lat.   /prī clah RISS ih mōōs   FEE lee ōōs   NŎST ĕr   hen REE kōōs/
          Our most famous son, Henry,

          Rex   Angliae,   **et   Heres**   **Franciae**
Ang.Lat.   /reks   ANG lih ee   et   HEER eez   FRAN shih ee/
Class.Lat.   /rayks   AHNG glih ī   et   HAY rayss   FRAHN kih ī/
          King of England and heir of France.
Praeclarissimus is an error for **Praecarissimus** most dear:
Ang.Lat. /pree kair-/; Class.Lat. /prī kahr-/. Some eds. prefer the Latin variant
Haeres instead of *Heres* which would be the same in Ang.Lat. and /HĪR ayss/ in
Class.Lat.

362. **spousal** /SPOW zł/ union.

366. **incorporate** /in CORP rut, -rayt/ united. /-ut / is more usual for an adj.

372. ***surety** guarantee. Here should be 2 syllables, though in mod. Eng., 3 syllables
are more common US /SHUR (ih) tee, SHOOR-/; CN /SHUR-/ [SHOOR-];
UK /SHOR-/ [SHUR-] [SHOOR-].

Julius Caesar

People in the Play

Antony, Mark 2 or 3 syllables depending on meter /ANT (uh) nee/.
  Antonio 3 or 4 syllables depending on meter /an TOHN (ee) yoh/.
  Some eds. prefer **Antonius** /-yus/.

Artemidorus of Cnidos /art ih mih DOR us/; US /NĪ dus, -dŏs/; UK /-dŏs/ [-dus].
A newer pronunciation /-ohss/ is also used, especially in the US. Normal development would favor /-us/. Class.Lat. /K-NEE dŏs/.

Brutus /BRO͞OT us/.

*Caius (Cassius, Ligarius) US, CN /KĪ us/, *rarely* [KAY us];
UK /KĪ us, KAY us/. Ang.Lat. /KAY us/; Class.Lat. /KĪ o͞os/. Another angl. form /keez/ is sometimes used, but doesn't fit the meter.

Calphurnia usually 3 syllables /cal FUR n(ee) yuh/. Some eds. prefer
Calpurnia /-PUR-/.

Casca /CĂSS kuh/.

*Cassius 2 or 3 syllables depending on meter /CĂSS (ee) yus/; US *also*
/CASH us/, /CASH ee yus/. Normal development would favor /CASH us/.

Cato /KAYT oh/.

Cicero 2 or 3 syllables depending on meter /SISS (uh) roh/.

Cinna /SIN uh/.

Claudio (F1) /CLAW dyoh/. Some eds. prefer **Claudius** /CLAW dyus/.

Clitus /CLĪ tus/.

Cnidos see **Artemidorus**.

Dardanius /dar DAYN yus/.

Decius Brutus /DEE shus BRO͞OT us/; sometimes newer /-syus/ is used.

ă-bat, ăir-marry, air-pair, ạr-far, ĕr-merry, ĝ-get, ī-high, ĭr-mirror, l̩-little, n̩-listen,
ŏ-hot, oh-go, o͞o-wood, o͞o-moon, oor-tour, ōr-or, ow-how, ţh-that, th-thin, ŭ-but,
UR-fur, ur-under. ( )- suppress the syllable   [ ]- less common   see p. xi for complete list.

People in the Play (cont.)

Flavius /FLAY vee yus/. Sometimes called **Flavio** /FLAY vee yoh/.

Lepidus, M. Aemilius /LEP ih dus/. *Aemilius* /ih MIL ee us/ is not spoken. At 3.2.264 /lep ID us/ is indicated.

Ligarius /lih GAIR yus/.

Lucilius, Lucillius 3 or 4 syllables depending on meter /loo SILL (ee) yus/. At one time many RP speakers in the UK used /lyoo-/ for words beginning *lu-,* but today their number is dwindling.

Lucius /LOO shus, -syus/. The former is nearly universal in the US, the latter is most common in the UK. Normal development would favor /LOO shus/. At one time many RP speakers in the UK used /lyoo-/ for words beginning *lu-,* but today their number is dwindling.

Murellus (F1) /muh RELL us/. Some eds. prefer **Marullus** /muh RŬL us/.

Messala /muh SAY luh/; restored pronunciation /mess AH lah/.

Metellus Cimber /muh TEL us SIM bur/.

Octavius /ŏk TAY vyus/.

Pindarus /PIN dur us/.

Plebeians /plih BEE unz/ common people. This word is not spoken.

Pompey /PŎMP ee/.

Popilius Lena, Popillius Laena both pronounced /puh PILL yus LEE nuh/.

Portia /POR shuh/.

Publius 2 or 3 syllables depending on meter /PUB l(ee) yus/.

Strato /STRAYT oh/

Titinius /tī-, tih TIN yus/.

Trebonius /trih BOHN yus/.

Varrus (F1) /VĂIR us/. Some eds. prefer **Varro** /VĂIR oh/.

People in the Play (cont.)

Volumnius 3 or 4 syllables depending on meter /vuh LUM n(ee) yus/.

Places in the Play

Philippi /fih LIP ī/. Occasionally the Gk. form with 1st syllable stress is used in mod. Eng., but it will not fit the meter in Shk.

Sardis /SĄR diss/.

Tiber /TĪ bur/.

A Frequently Used Phrase

the ides of March /īdz/ March 15.

Act 1 Scene 1

40. **sate** archaic variant of **sat**. May have been /sayt/ or /sat/.

41. *****livelong** US /LIV lŏng, -lawng/, *rarely* [LĪV-]; UK /LIV lŏng/ [LĪV-].

47. **concave** here should be /CŎN-, CŎNG kayv/.

67. *****Lupercal** the Roman protector of flocks. /LOOP ur kal/, *rarely* [-kł]. At one time many RP speakers in the UK used /lyoo-/ for words beginning *lu-,* but today their number is dwindling.

75. *****servile** /SUR vīl/, *rarely* [SUR vł] slave-like.

Act 1 Scene 2

45. **construe** here should be /CŎN stroo/.

50. **cogitations** /cŏj ih TAY shunz/ thoughts.

78. **rout** /rowt/ mob.

95. **as lief** /leef/ as soon.

ă-bat, ăir-ma**rry**, air-**pair**, ąr-**far**, ĕr-**merry**, ĝ-**get**, ī-**high**, ĭr-**mirror**, ł-**little**, ņ-**listen**, ŏ-**hot**, oh-**go**, oo-**wood**, ōo-**moon**, oor-**tour**, ōr-**or**, ow-**how**, th-**that**, th-**thin**, ŭ-**but**, UR-**fur**, ur-un**der.** ( )- suppress the syllable   [ ]- less common   see p. xi for complete list.

101. chafing /CHAY fing/ raging.

105. Accoutred /uh CŌOT urd/ clothed.

107. buffet /BUFF it/ fight.

109. controversy here should be /CŎN truh vur see/, the normal US pronunciation.

112. Aeneas /ih NEE yus/; UK *also* /EE NEE yus/ Prince of Troy.

114. *Anchises /an-, ang KĪ seez/; US *also newer* [-zeez] Aeneas's father.

136. Colossus /kuh LŎS us/ giant.

238. coronets small crowns. US /COR uh nets, -nits/, /cor uh NETS/;
E. COAST US /CŎR-, cŏr-/; UK /CŎR uh nits/ [-nets, cŏr uh NETS].

244. howted /HOWT id/ archaic variant of **hooted**.

248, 251. swound (ed) archaic variant of **swoon**. In Shk's time the vowel could be
either /ow/ or /ōo/.

Act 1 Scene 3

6. riv'd /rīvd/ split.

28. Howting /HOWT ing/ archaic variant of **Hooting**.

31. portentous /por TEN tuss/ prophetic.

34. construe here should be /CŎN strōo/.

81. *thews /t̶h̶yōoz/; US, CN *also* [t̶h̶ōoz] muscles.

106. hinds /hīndz/ double meaning: female deer, menial laborers.

109. offal /ŎF ł/; US *also* /AWF ł/ animal guts and remains after butchering.

131. Stand close /clohss/ keep hidden.

135. incorporate /in COR pur rut, -rayt/ a part of. /-ut / is more usual for an adj.

143. praetor's /PREE turz/ Roman official. /-torz/ not recommended.

159. **alchymy** /AL kuh mee/ the study of the transformation of base metals to gold. Archaic variant of **alchemy,** pronounced the same way.

Act 2 Scene 1

7, 35. **taper** /TAY pur/ slender candle.

33. **mischievous** here should be /MIS chiv us/. /mis CHEEV us/ is considered non-standard in all countries.

44. **exhalations** /eks huh LAY shunz, eks uh-/ [egz uh-] meteors.

54. **Tarquin** /TAR kwin/ king of Rome who raped Lucretia.

65. **phantasma** /fan TAZ muh/ evil vision.

84. **Erebus** /ĔR ih bus/ hell.

126. **palter** /PAWL tur/ shift position in an argument.

129. **cautelous** /KAWT uh lus/ deceitful.

200. *****augurers** /AWG yur urz/ [AWG ur urz]; UK *also* /-yoor-/ prophets.

227. **untir'd** here should be /UN tīrd/.

246.*****wafter** waving. US, CN /WŎFT ur/; SOUTH. US /WĂFT-/; UK /WŎFT-/ [WĂFT-, WAHFT-]. Variant of **wafture** /-chur/; UK *also* /-tyoor/. /WĂFT-/ is newer and considered non-standard by many.

266. **rheumy** /RŌŌM ee/ dank.

287. **harlot** /HAR lut/ whore.

307. **construe** here should be /CŎN strŌŌ/ explain for legal purposes.

308. **charactery** /kuh RAK tur ee/ secret writing.

317, 318. **exploit** here should be /ek SPLOYT/.

ă-bat, ăir-marry, air-pair, ạr-far, ĕr-merry, ĝ-get, ī-high, ĭr-mirror, ł-little, ṇ-listen, ŏ-hot, oh-go, ōō-wood, ōō-moon, oor-tour, ōr-or, ow-how, ṭh-that, t̶h̶-thin, Ŭ-but, UR-fur, ur-under. ( )- suppress the syllable   [ ]- less common   see p. xi for complete list.

Act 2 Scene 2

37. ***augurers** /AWG yur urz/ [AWG ur urz]; UK *also* /-yoor-/ prophets.

39. ***entrails** /EN traylz/; US *also* [-trĭz] guts.

76. **statuë, statua** here should be 3 syllables /STATCH oo uh/;
UK *also* /STAT yoo uh/.

80. **portents** here should be /por TENTS/ omens.

89. **relics, reliques** /REL iks/.

89. ***cognizance** /CŎG nih zunss, -zṇss/; *rarely older* [CŎN ih-] sign.

113. **ague** /AY gyo͞o/ malarial fever.

Act 2 Scene 4

35. **praetors** /PREE turz/ Roman officials. /-torz/ not recommended.

Act 3 Scene 1

33. ***puissant** powerful. The traditional forms are /PWISS ṇt/, /PYO͞O sṇt/, but
these are now rare. In all countries one of several Frenchified pronunciations is the
most common: /PWEE sṇt/ in the US, /-sahnt/ in CN, and /-sah^{n}t/ in the UK, but all 3
may be found in each country.

57, 81. **enfranchisement** /en FRAN chiz munt/ liberty.

77. **Et tu, Brute** and you, Brutus. Ang.Lat. /et to͞o BRO͞O tee/, but now universally
Class.Lat. /BRO͞O tay/.

125. ***prostrate** /PRŎS trayt/, US *rarely* [-trut] lying face down.

136. **Thorough** archaic variant of *through*, used when the meter demands 2
syllables. It is often pronounced as *thorough* on stage, but using /-o͞o/ in the
final syllable will bring it closer to mod. *through*.

136. **untrod** here should be /UN trŏd/.

202. **close** /clohz/ come to terms with.

206. **lethe** /LEE~~TH~~ ee/ stream of death.

209. **strooken** (*stroken* F1) /STRo͞oK in/ or perhaps simply a variant spelling of **strucken**.   Some eds. prefer **stricken** (F2).

215. **compact** here /cŏm-, cum PACT/ agreement.

259. **prophesy** /PRŎF uh sī/ to predict the future.

271. ***Ate** goddess of discord. /AYT ee/ is the older, angl. form; /AHT ay/ is the newer, restored form and much more common; /AHT ee/ is a mixed form, heard occasionally.

Act 3 Scene 2

95. ***Lupercal** the feast honoring the Roman protector of flocks. /LO͞OP ur kal/, *rarely* [-kł]. At one time many RP speakers in the UK used /lyo͞o-/ for words beginning *lu-,* but today their number is dwindling.

173. **Nervii** /NURV ee ī/ a Belgian tribe. Restored Latin /NĚRV-/.

188. **statuë, statua** here should be 3 syllables /STATCH oo uh/;
UK *also* /STAT yoo uh/.

196. **vesture** /VES chur/ clothing, covering.

217. ***orator** US, CN /OR uh tur/; UK, E. COAST US /ŎR-/. Sometimes /OR ayt ur/ is used, but it is not recommended.   /-tor/ not recommended.

242. **drachmaes** Gk. coins. Archaic pl. form /DRAK meez/. Some eds. prefer **drachmas** /DRAK muz/.

251. **recreate yourselves** /REK ree ayt/ refresh yourselves, amuse yourselves.

Act 4 Scene 1

20. ***divers** various. Here should be stressed on the 1st syllable
US, CN /DĪ vurss, -vurz/; UK /DĪ vurss/ [-vurz].

30. **provender** /PRŎV ṇ dur/ dry food for animals.

32. **to wind** /wīnd/ turn a horse.

ă-bat, ăir-marry, air-pair, ạr-far, ĕr-merry, ĝ-get, ī-high, ĭr-mirror, ł-little, ṇ-listen,
ŏ-hot, oh-go, o͝o-wood, o͞o-moon, oor-tour, ōr-or, ow-how, ţh-that, ᵺ-thin, ŭ-but,
UR-fur, ur-under. ( )- suppress the syllable   [ ]- less common   see p. xi for complete list.

46. ***covert** secret . Here should be stressed on the 1st syllable
US, CN /KOHV urt/ [KUV-]; UK /KUV-/ [KOHV-], *rarely* [KŎV-].

Act 4 Scene 3 (*The Complete Oxford* continues this as 4.2—line nos. in parentheses)

2. (4.2.57) **Lucius Pella** US /LOO shus PELL uh/, /-syus/. The former is nearly
universal in the US, the latter is most common in the UK. Normal development
would favor /LOO shus/. At one time many RP speakers in the UK used /lyoo-/ for
words beginning *lu-,* but today their number is dwindling.

3. (4.2.58) **Sardians** /SAR dee unz/.

16, 17 (4.2.70) ***chastisement** punishment. Here stress should be on 1st syllable
/CHĂSS tiz munt/; US *also* /-tīz-/.

44. (4.2.100) **bouge** /BUJ/, or possibly /booj/. Archaic variant of **budge**.

73. (4.2.130) **drachmaes** Gk. coins. Archaic pl. form /DRAK meez/. Some eds.
prefer **drachmas** /DRAK muz/.

85. (4.2.141) **riv'd** /rīvd/ split.

164. (4.2.218) **close** /clohss/ secretly.

164, 275. (4.2.218, 328) **taper** /TAY pur/ slender candle.

171. (4.2.225) **tenure** archaic variant of **tenor**, both /TEN ur/.

228. (4.2.282) **niggard** /NIG urd/ give a small amount to.

Act 5 Scene 1

19. **exigent** /EK sih junt, EG zih junt/ emergency.

21. ***parley** /PAR lee/ conference with an enemy. Newer [-lay] not recommended.

34. **Hybla** /HĪ bluh/ region of Sicily.

76. **Epicurus** /ep ih KYOOR us/; US *also* /-KYUR-/ Gk. philosopher.

78. ***presage** here should be /pree-, prih SAYJ/ foretell.

79. ***ensign** flag. US, CN /EN sn̩/, US *rarely* [-sīn]; UK /-sn̩, -sīn/.

82. **consorted** /cun SORT id/ accompanied.

109. **Thorough** archaic variant of *through*, used when the meter demands 2 syllables. It is often pronounced as *thorough* on stage, but using /-o͞o/ in the final syllable will bring it closer to mod. *through*.

Act 5 Scene 3

3. *****ensign** standard-bearer. US, CN /EN sn̩/, US *rarely* [-sīn]; UK /-sn̩, -sīn/.

37. **Parthia** /PAR t͟hyuh/ in NW Iran.

84. **misconstrued** here should be /mis CŎN stro͞od/.

96. *****entrails** /EN traylz/; US *also* [-trl̵z] guts.

104. *****Thasos, Thassos** island near Philippi. US /T͞HASS ŏss, -us/ [T͞HAHSS-, T͞HAYSS-]; UK /T͞HAYSS-, T͞HASS ŏss/ [-us]. A newer pronunciation /-ohss/ is also used, especially in the US. /T͞HAYSS us/ is the traditional anglicization. Some eds. prefer F1's **Tharsus** /TAR sus/,

108. **Labio** /LAY bee oh/ (F1) some eds. prefer **Labeo**, pronounced the same way.

Act 5 Scene 5

2. **Statilius** /stuh TIL yus/.

ă-bat, ăir-**marry**, air-**pair**, a̩r-**far**, ĕr-**merry**, ĝ-**get**, ī-**high**, ĭr-**mirror**, l̵-**little**, n̩-**listen**, ŏ-**hot**, oh-**go**, o͞o-**wood**, o͞o-**moon**, oor-**tour**, ōr-**or**, ow-**how**, t͟h-**that**, t͟h-**thin**, ŭ-**but**, UR-**fur**, ur-**under**. ( )- suppress the syllable   [ ]- less common   see p. xi for complete list.

King Lear

The Complete Oxford line nos. are based on what it calls *The Tragedy of King Lear*, the folio text.

People in the Play

*Albany US /AWL buh nee/, *rarely* [AL-]; CN, UK /AWL-/ [AL-].

Burgundy /BUR gun dee/.

Cordelia /cor DEEL yuh/.

Cornwall /CORN wawl/; UK *also* [-wł].

Curan US /CUR un/; UK, E. COAST US /CUH run/.

Gloucester /GLŎS tur/; US *also* /GLAWSS-/.

Goneril, Gonerill /GŎN ur il, -ł/.

Lear /leer/.

Oswald US /ŎZ wawld/; UK /-włd/.

Regan /REE gun/.

Act 1 Scene 1

7. **moi'ty** /MOY tee/ or **moiety** /MOY uh tee/ portion.

47. **amorous *sojourn** a temporary stay. If *amorous* is reduced to /AM russ/, then *sojourn* is stressed on the 1st syllable, the more usual pronunciation in all countries US, CN /SOH jurn/; UK /SŎJ urn/ [-URN, SOH jurn, SUJ urn]. If *amorous* is /AM ur us/, then *sojourn* is stressed on the 2nd syllable.

64. ***champains** (F1), **champaigns** open country. Here should have 1st syllable stress /SHAM paynz/; US *sometimes older* [CHAM paynz]. Omitted Q1.

65. **meads** /meedz/ meadows.

75. **felicitate** /fuh LISS ih tayt, -tut/ made happy. /-ut/ would be the usual adj. form.

85. **be interess'd** (F1) /IN tur est/ establish a claim, be closely connected. Omitted Q1.

110. **Hecat, Hecate** /HEK ut/ goddess of witchcraft. /HEK uh tee/ is the usual non-Shakespearean pronunciation.

114. **Propinquity** /proh PINK wih tee/ kinship.

116. ***Scythian** /SI̶T̶H̶ yun/ [SIṮH yun] *Scythia* was north of the Black Sea. Some scholars prefer restored Latin /SK-/.

137. **revenue** here should be /ruh VEN yo͞o/.

139. **coronet** here should be US /COR (uh) net, -nit/; E. COAST US, UK /CŎR-/. Some eds. prefer **crownet** /CROWN it/. Both mean 'small crown.'

161. **miscreant** (F1) /MIS cree unt/ scoundrel. Q1 has **recreant** /REK ree yunt/ coward.

166. **recreant** may be a triple or double ending /REK r(ee) yunt/ traitor. Omitted Q1.

173. **allot** /uh LŎT/ grant.

228. **unchaste** (F1) here should be /UN chayst/. Q1 has **unclear** /UN cleer/.

240. **th' entire** may either be /T̶H̶ᵞEN tīr/, forming a 5-foot line, or /t̶hee en TĪ ur/ in a hexameter.

259. **unpriz'd** here should be /UN prīzd/.

265. ***benison** US, CN /BEN ih sun, -sṇ/ [-zun, -zṇ]; UK /-z-/ [-s-] blessing.

278. **alms** charity for the poor. /ahmz/ is older; /ahlmz, awlmz/ are newer. In the UK the latter are non-standard.

281. **covers**. Some eds. prefer ***covert** 'hidden,' here stressed on the 1st syllable US, CN /KOHV urt/ [KUV-]; UK /KUV-/ [KOHV-], *rarely* [KŎV-].

298. ***infirm** /in FURM/ sick.

Act 1 Scene 2

7. **compact** /cum-, cŏm PACT/ composed.

ă-bat, ăir-marry, air-**pair**, ạr-**far**, ĕr-**merry**, ĝ-**get**, ī-high, ĭr-mirror, ł-little, ṇ-listen, ŏ-hot, oh-go, o͞o-**wood**, o͞o-**moon**, oor-**tour**, ōr-**or**, ow-how, t̶h-that, t̶h̶-thin, ŭ-but, UR-**fur**, ur-under. ( )- suppress the syllable   [ ]- less common   see p. xi for complete list.

53–74. **revenue** sometimes in verse /ruh VEN yōō/, but in this prose passage may be mod. Eng. US /REV in ōō/; UK, SOUTH. US /-yōō/.

72. **perfect** (F1). Q1 has the archaic variant **perfit** /PUR fit/. Also /PAR fit/ in Shk's time.

92. **auricular assurance** /aw-, uh-, or RIK yuh lur/ proof one can hear.

98. **wind me** /wīnd/ worm your way in, insinuate yourself.

106. **scourg'd** /SKURJD/ harshly punished.

106. **sequent** /SEE kwunt/ following.

112. ***Machinations** (F1) plots. /mack ih NAY shunz/ is older, /mash-/ is a newer, spelling pronunciation. The former is more common in the US, the latter in the UK, while in CN both are used equally. Omitted Q1.

123. **treachers** /TRETCH urz/ traitors.

123. ***spherical** (F1) US, CN /SFEER ih kł/ [SFĔR-]; UK /SFĔR ih kł/. Q1 has **spiritual**.

130. **Ursa Major** /UR suh MAY jur/ the Great Bear constellation.

131. **Fut** /fŏŏt/ God's foot!

132. **maidenl'est** /MAYD n̦ list/ in Shk's time, but in this prose passage **maidenliest** /-lee ist/ may be substituted.

136. **Tom o' Bedlam** (F1) /tŏm uh BED lum/ crazy beggar. Q1 has **them of Bedlam**.

Lines 144–152 are in Q1, but omitted in F1.

146. **maledictions** /mal uh DIK shunz/ curses.

147. **diffidences** /DIFF ih dunss iz/ suspicions.

148. ***nuptial** wedding. US, UK /NUP chł/ [-shł]; in CN both are used equally.

150. **sectary** /SEK tuh ree/; US *also* /SEK tair ee/ devotee.

---

164. **allay** /uh LAY/ diminish.

Act 1 Scene 4

49. **mungrel** /MUNG grł/ variant of **mongrel**, pronounced the same in the UK; US, CN *also* /MŎNG grł, MAWNG-/.

112. **Brach** /bratch/ female dog.

122. **thou *trowest** you believe. Here the rhymes demand /TROH ist/, though /TROW ist/ is also used in all countries and is the dominant form in the UK.

---

lines 140–155 are in Q1, but omitted in F1.

146. **motley** /MŎT lee/ the costume of different colored cloth worn by fools.

153. **an't, on't** /unt/ of it.

---

159. **eat** /et/ dialect variant of **ate** which is also commonly /et/ in the UK.

174. ***breeches** /BRITCH iz/ is traditional, /BREECH iz/ is newer. The former pronunciation is more common in the UK and the latter in the US, CN.

200. **sheal'd** /sheeld, shayld/ archaic variants of **shelled**.

200. **peascod** /PEEZ cŏd/ peapod.

202. **insolent *retinue** band of followers. Here archaic /ruh TIN yo͞o/ seems called for, however if *insolent* is syncopated to *ins'lent*, then as in mod. Eng. US /RET ih no͞o/, /RET n̩ o͞o/; UK, SOUTH. US /-nyo͞o/.

211. **weal** /weel/ commonwealth.

214. **know** (F1). Q1 has ***trow** US, CN /troh, trow/; UK /trow/ [troh] know. Shk's rhymes elsewhere indicate /-oh/.

225. ***Whoop!** /who͞op/ [ho͞op, hŏŏp, who͝op].

237. **savor** (UK **savour**) /SAY vur/ character, style.

244. **Epicurism** riotous living. Here should be /ep IK yoor izm/, /-yur-/; 1st syllable stress is usual in mod. Eng.

ă-bat, ăir-**marry**, air-**pair**, ạr-**far**, ĕr-**merry**, ĝ-**get**, ī-**high**, ĭr-**mirror**, ł-**little**, n̩-**listen**, ŏ-**hot**, oh-**go**, o͞o-**wood**, o͞o-**moon**, oor-**tour**, ōr-**or**, ow-**how**, ţh-**that**, t̶h̶-**thin**, ŭ-**but**, UR-**fur**, ur-**under**. ( )- suppress the syllable   [ ]- less common   see p. xi for complete list.

245. ***brothel** US, CN /BRŎT̶H̶ ł/ [BRŎT̠H ł, BRAWT̶H̶ ł]; UK /BRŎT̶H̶ ł/ whorehouse.

251. **besort** /bih-, bee SORT/ befit.

279. **organs of increase** here /in CREESS/ reproductive organs.

280. **derogate** degraded. /DĔR (uh) gut/; UK *also newer* [DEER-].

285. **cadent** /KAY dunt, -dṇt/ falling.

293, 326. **dotage** /DOHT ij/ senility.

295. **fortnight** /FORT nīt/; US *also* [FORT nit] 2 weeks. Virtually obsolete in the US.

306. **comfortable** here may be 3 or 4 syllables /CUMF tur bł/, /CUM fur tuh bł/.

308. **flea** /flee/ archaic and dialect variant of **flay** /flay/ to skin.

323. **politic** (F1) /PŎL ih tik/ cunning. Omitted Q1.

339. **compact** /cum PACT/ confirm.

343. **attax'd, ataxed** /uh TAKST/. Others prefer F1's **at task** or Q1c's **attask'd** US /uh TĂSKT/; E. NEW ENG., UK /uh TAHSKT/ all mean 'blamed.'

Act 2 Scene 1

8. **ear-bussing** (Q1) /BŬS ing/ ear-kissing. F1 has **ear-kissing**.

10. **toward** /TOH wurd, -urd/ about to take place.

17. **queasy question** /KWEE zee/ i.e., delicate nature.

45. **revengive** (Q1) /ree-, rih VEN jiv/. F1 has **revenging**.

46. **parricides** /PĂIR ih sīdz/ father-killers.

53. ***alarum'd** US, CN /uh LAHR umd/ [-LĂIR-]; UK /uh LĂIR umd, uh LAHR umd/ called to arms.

55. **gasted, ghasted** US /GĂS tid/; UK, E. NEW ENG. /GAHSS tid/ frightened.

62. **coward** (F1). Q1 has **caitiff** /KAYT if/ scoundrel.

65. **pight** /pīt/ **pitched**.

74. **dullard** /DULL urd/ stupid person.

97. **consort** (F1) /CŎN sort/ group. Omitted Q1.

100. **revenues** here should be /ruh VEN yo͞oz/.

103. ***sojourn** reside temporarily. Here with 1st syllable stress
US, CN /SOH jurn/; UK /SŎJ urn/ [-URN, SOH-, SUJ-].

107. **bewray** (F1) /bih-, bee RAY/ reveal. Q1 has **betray**.

Act 2 Scene 2

19. **finical** /FIN ih kł/ finicky.

22. **pandar, pander** /PAN dur/ pimp.

22. **mungril** /MUNG grł/ variant of **mongrel**, pronounced the same in the UK;
US, CN *also* /MŎNG grł, MAWNG-/.

28. **brazen-faced** /BRAY zun-, -zṇ-/ shameless.

33. **cullionly** /CŬL yun lee/ rascally.

33. ***barber-monger** a fop, someone who constantly goes to the barber.
US /BAR bur mŏng gur/ or /-mawng-/ [-mung-]; CN /-mung-, -mŏng-/;
UK /-mung-/.

38. ***carbonado** slash. /car buh NAH doh/; UK *rarely older* [-NAY doh].

45. **goodman** /Go͞oD mun/ title of a man under the rank of gentleman.

75. **t'intrinse** /twin TRINSS, -TRINZ/ too intricate. Some eds. prefer **intrince**
/in TRINSS/.

78. ***Renege** (Q1) deny. US /ree-, rih NEG, -NIG/ [-NEEG, -NAYG];
CN /-NEG, -NAYG/; UK /rih NAYG/ [-NEEG, -NEG, -NIG]. **Revenge** (F1).

ă-bat, ăir-**marry**, air-**pair**, ạr-**far**, ĕr-**merry**, ĝ-**get**, ī-**high**, ĭr-**mirror**, ł-**little**, ṇ-**listen**,
ŏ-**hot**, oh-**go**, o͞o-**wood**, o͞o-**moon**, oor-**tour**, ōr-**or**, ow-**how**, ţh-**that**, t̶h̶-**thin**, ŭ-**but**,
UR-**fur**, ur-**under**. ( )- suppress the syllable   [ ]- less common   see p. xi for complete list.

78. **halcyon beaks** US /HAL see ŏn/ [-un]; UK /-un/ [-ŏn] kingfisher, i.e., weathervane.

83. **Sarum** /SAIR um/.

87. **contraries** /CŎN truh reez/ opposites.

103. **observants** /ŎB zur vunts/ attendants.

105. **sincere** here should be /SIN seer/.

108. **Phoebus'** /FEE bus/ god of the sun.

118. **compact** (F1) /cum-, cŏm PACT/ leagued with. Q1 has **conjunct** /cun JUNCT/ with the same meaning.

123. **exploit** here should be /ek SPLOYT/.

126. **ancient** (F1). Q1c, Q2 have **miscreant** /MIS cr(ee) yunt/ scoundrel.

164. **comfortable** here should be /CUM fur tuh bł/.

Act 2 Scene 3 (*The Complete Oxford* continues this as 2.2—line nos. in parentheses)

8. (2.2.171) **penury** /PEN yur ee/; UK *also* /PEN yoor ee/ poverty.

13. (2.2.176) **president** example. Archaic variant of ***precedent**, both /PRESS ih dunt/. It is not clear whether /PREZ-/ was used in Shk's time.

14. (2.2.177) **Bedlam** /BED lum/ crazy.

20. (2.2.183) **Turlygod** (F1, Q1c, Q2) /TUR lee gŏd/; US *also* /-gawd/, or **Tuelygod** (Q1u) perhaps US /TOO lee-/; UK, SOUTH. US /TYOO lee-/ unexplained.

Act 2 Scene 4 (*The Complete Oxford* continues this as 2.2—line nos. in parentheses)

34. (2.2.210) **contents** here /cŏn TENTS/.

35. (2.2.211) **meiny, meinie** (F1) /MAYN ee/ household servants.   Q1 has **men**.

52. (2.2.227) **arrant** (F1) /ĂIR unt/ thoroughgoing. Omitted Q1.

54. (2.2.229) **dolors** (F1) (UK **dolours**) /DOH lurz/; UK *also* /DŎL urz/ pains. /-lorz/ not recommended. Omitted Q1.

57. (2.2.232) **Hysterica passio, Histerica passio** Ang.Lat. /hih STĔR ih kuh PĂSH oh/, /PĂSS ee yoh/, /PASH ee yoh/; Class.Lat. /hih STĔR ih kah PAH see yoh/. Some eds. prefer **hysteria** /hih STEER ee uh/; US *also* /-STĔR-/.

85. (2.2.258) **perdie, perdy** by God, indeed. Usually US /pur DEE/; UK /PUR DEE/, but here rhymes with *fly*. Some eds. prefer the variant **pardie** /par DEE/.

132. (2.2.304) **Sepulchring** entombing. Here /suh-, sep PŬL cring/ is indicated.

148. (2.2.321) **confine** confines, limits of an area. Here /cŏn-, cun FĪN/.

197. (2.2.370) **dotage** /DOHT ij/ senility.

203. (2.2. 376) ***sojourn** reside temporarily. Here with 1st syllable stress US, CN /SOH jurn/; UK /SŎJ urn/ [-URN, SOH-, SUJ-].

208. (2.2.381) **abjure** /ab-, ub JOOR/; US *also* /-JUR/ renounce.

210. (2.2.383) ***comrade** US, CN /CŎM rad/, *rarely* [CUM-, CŎM rayd]; UK /CŎM rayd/, *rarely* [-rad, CUM-].

237. (2.2.410) **avouch** /uh VOWCH/ affirm.

Act 3 Scene 1

55. (33) **Holla** /huh LAH/ or /HŎL uh/ a call.

Act 3 Scene 2

2. ***hurricanoes** waterspouts. US /hur ih KAH nohz, -KAY-/;
E. COAST US /huh rih-/; CN /hur ih KAH nohz/ [-KAY nohz];
UK /huh rih KAY nohz/ [-KAH nohz]. The older pronunciation is /-KAY-/.

5. **Vaunt-*couriers** US /VAWNT CUR yurz/ [COOR-];
E. COAST US /CŬR-/ [COOR-]; UK /COOR-/ [CŬR-] forerunners. Main stress
may also fall on the 2nd syllable. A variant form is *vancouriers*.

ă-bat,	äir-marry,	air-pair,	ɑ̞r-far,	ĕr-merry,	ĝ-get,	ī-high,	ĭr-mirror,	ł-little,	n̩-listen,
ŏ-hot,	oh-go,	ōō-wood,	ōō-moon,	oor-tour,	ōr-or,	ow-how,	ҭh-that,	~~th~~-thin,	ʊ-but,
UR-fur,	ur-under.	( )- suppress the syllable		[ ]- less common			see p. xi for complete list.		

8. **germains, germens** /JUR munz/ seeds.

20. ***infirm** /in FURM/ sick.

21. ***servile** /SUR vīl/, *rarely* [SUR vł] slave-like.

27. **house** /howz/ find a house.

29. **louse** /lowz/ become infested with lice.

50. **pudder** (F1) /PUD ur/ commotion. Archaic variant of **pother** /PŎṬH ur/. Q1's **powther** is meant to indicate /PUṬH ur/. Q2 has **thundering**.

54. **simular** /SIM juh lur/ counterfeiter.

55. **incestuous** (F1) /in SESS chwus/; UK *also* /-tywus/. Q1 has an archaic variant **incestious** /in SESS chus/.

55. **Caitiff** /KAYT if/ scoundrel.

56. ***covert** secret. Here stressed on the 1st syllable
US, CN /KOHV urt/ [KUV-]; UK /KUV-/ [KOHV-], *rarely* [KŎV-].

57. **Close** /clohss/ hidden.

61–78. ***hovel** poor cottage or shed. US /HUV ł/, *rarely* [HŎV ł];
CN /HUV-/ [HŎV-/; UK /HŎV-/ [HUV-].

75. ***heigh-ho!** (F1) US /hay ho, hī-/; CN /hī-/, *rarely* [hay-]; UK /hay-/. Shk intended /hay/. Spoken with evenly stressed syllables or as if sighing, with 1st syllable stress. Q1 has **hey ho.**

79. ***courtezan, courtesan** (F1) a rich man's whore. US /CORT ih zun, -zan/, *rarely* [cort ih ZAN]; CN /CORT ih zan/ [-zun], *rarely* [cort ih ZAN]; UK /CORT ih zan, cort ih ZAN/. Omitted in Q1.

84. **heretics** (F1) /HĔR (ih) tiks/ dissenters. Omitted in Q1.

85. **Albion** (F1) /AL bee un/ Britain. Here rhymes with *confusion* (4 syllables in this instance). Omitted in Q1.

91. **usurers** (F1) /Y$\overline{OO}$ zh(u)r urz/; UK *also* [-zh(yoo)r urz, -zh(oo)r urz] those who lend money for interest. Omitted in Q1.

Act 3 Scene 3

14. **privily** /PRĬV ih lee/ privately.

19. **toward** /TOH wurd, -urd/ about to take place.

Act 3 Scene 4

14. **filial ingratitude** /FĬL yⱡ/ a child's ingratitude.

30. **unfed** here should be /UN fed/.

46. **Through** (Q2, F1). Some eds. make this a verse passage which calls for **Thorough** (Q1), used when the meter demands 2 syllables. It is often pronounced as *thorough* on stage, but using /-ōō/ in the final syllable will bring it closer to mod. *through*.

53. *****quagmire** bog. US, CN /KWĂG mīr/, US *rarely* [KWŎG-]; UK /KWŎG-/ [KWĂG-]. Normal development would favor /KWĂG-/.

70. **subdu'd** here with 1st syllable stress.

71. **unkind** here should be /UN kīnd/.

76. **alow** (F1), **a lo** (Q1) /uh LOH/ 'below,' or perhaps a call like *halloo!* or the crow of a rooster.

91. *****out-paramour'd** US, CN /owt PĂIR uh moord/ [-mord]; UK /-mord/ [-moord] had more mistresses than.

93. *****sloth** US, CN /slawth/ [slohth]; UK /slohth/ [slŏth] laziness.

96. *****brothels** US, CN /BRŎTH ⱡz/ [BRŎTH ⱡz, BRAWTH ⱡz]; UK /BRŎTH ⱡz/ whorehouses.

99. **Dolphin** (F1) /DŎL fin/; US *also* /DAWL-/. Meaning unclear, but *Dolphin* is the angl. form for the French heir to the throne. The mod. form is **Dauphin** angl. /DAW fin/; Fr. /doh fã^n/.

99. **suum mun nonny** (F1) the noise of the wind. Q1 has *hay no on ny* which some eds. have as **hay no nony**.

ă-bat, äir-**marry**, air-**pair**, ạr-far, ĕr-**merry**, ĝ-get, ī-high, ĭr-**mirror**, ⱡ-little, ṇ-listen, ŏ-hot, oh-go, ōō-wood, ōō-moon, oor-tour, ōr-or, ow-how, ţh-that, <s>th</s>-thin, ŭ-but, UR-fur, ur-under.   ( )- suppress the syllable   [ ]- less common   see p. xi for complete list.

100. **sessa** /SESS uh/ uncertain meaning, perhaps 'let it go!' or 'be quiet.' F1 has **sesey** /SESS ee/. Q2 has **cease**. Some eds. prefer Fr. **cessez** /sess ay/ stop.

115. **Flibbertigibbet** (F1) /FLIB urt ee jib it/ a devil.

117. **squinies** /SKWIN eez/ archaic form of F1's **squints**.

120. **Swithold** /SWIŢH ld, SWIŦH ld/ St. Withold. Some eds. prefer **Swithin, Swithune**, both pronounced /SWIŢH in, -un/ or /SWIŦH -/.

120. **'old** /ohld/ an upland plain. Dialect variant of **wold** /wohld/.

124. **aroint, aroynt** /uh ROYNT/ begone.

132. **sallets** /SAL its/ 'spicy herbs,' or in other words, 'spicy jokes.' Some eds. prefer **salads**.

134. **tithing** /TĪ ţhing/ district.

140. **Smulkin** (F1) /SMŬL kin/ a devil. Some eds. prefer **Smolking** based on *Smolkin* from Q1's *snulbug*. /SMŬL kin/ or /SMŎL kin/ is probably indicated in this case (i.e., *Smolkin* is the same as *Smolkin'*, alternative form of *Smolking*).

143. **Modo** /MOH doh/ a devil.

144. **Mahu** /MAH hoo/ a devil. May have been /MAY-/ for Shk.

152. **ventured** (F1). Q1 has the archaic variant **ventered** /VEN turd/.

157. **learned Theban** /LURN id ŦHEE bun/ scholar.

161. ***Importune** /im POR chun/ ask insistently. About half the respondents in the Survey reported a form with 3rd syllable stress in all countries, but that will not fit the meter in verse and is a relatively recent innovation (cf. *fortune*).

174. ***hovel** poor cottage or shed. US /HUV l/, *rarely* [HŎV l]; CN /HUV-/ [HŎV-]; UK /HŎV-/ [HUV-].

180. **Athenian** /uh ŦHEEN yun/.

182. **Rowland, Roland** /ROH lund/ in a line from a lost ballad.

Act 3 Scene 5

21. **persever** (F1), **persevere** (Q1) /pur SEV ur/ is normal in Shk's verse, but in this prose passage mod. /pur suh VEER/ may be used.

Act 3 Scene 6 (*The Complete Oxford* line nos. in parentheses where they differ)

6. **Frateretto** /frat ur RET oh/ a devil.

10–13. **yeoman** /YOH mun/ freeman who owns a small farm.

Lines 17-56 are contained in Q1, but omitted in F1.

21, 56. **justicer** /JUST ih sur/ judge. Q1 has **justice**.

22. **sapient** /SAY pyunt/ wise.

25. **bourn** /born/ southern England form of *burn* /burn/ stream. A more recent, spelling pronunciation is /boorn/. Q has *broome*.

30. **Hoppedance, Hopdance** US /HŎP dănss/; UK /-dahnss/.

43. **minikin** /MIN ih kin/ dainty.

---

63. (21) **Trey, Tray** /tray/ name of a dog.

64. (22) **Avaunt** /uh VAWNT/ begone!

68. (26) **Mastiff** /MĂST tiff/; UK *sometimes* [MAHST-] powerful watchdog.

69. (27) **brach** /bratch/ female dog.

69. (27) **lym** bloodhound. Here the rhyme indicates /lim/. Some eds. prefer F1's, Q1's **him** male dog. The more usual term for *bloodhound* was **lyam** /LĪ um/ or **lyme** /līm/.

74. (32) **Sessa** /SESS uh/ uncertain meaning, perhaps 'off you go.' F1's **sese** may indicate **cease** /seess/, **seize** /seez/, **cess** /sess/ (an archaic variant of *cease* and *seize*), or **sessey** /SESS ee/ stop. Some eds. prefer Fr. **cessez** /sess ay/ stop. Omitted Q1.

76. (34) **anatomize** /uh NAT uh mīz/ dissect.

ă-bat, ăir-marry, air-pair, ạr-far, ĕr-merry, ĝ-get, ī-high, ĭr-mirror, ł-little, ṇ-listen, ŏ-hot, oh-go, ōō-wood, o͞o-moon, oor-tour, ōr-or, ow-how, ṭh-that, ᵵh-thin, ŭ-but, UR-fur, ur-under. ( )- suppress the syllable   [ ]- less common   see p. xi for complete list.

111. **bewray** (Q1) /bih-, bee RAY/ reveal. Omitted F1.

Act 3 Scene 7

10. **festinate** /FESS tih nayt, -nut/ hasty. /-ut/ would be the usual form for an adj.

40. **hospitable** here should be /HŎS pih tuh bł/ welcoming.

62. **holp** /hohlp/ helped.

63. ***dearn** (Q1), **dern** dread. Both pronounced /durn/. Some eds. prefer F1's **stern**.

103. **Bedlam** (Q1) /BED lum/ lunatic. Omitted F1.

Act 4 Scene 1

4. **esperance** (F1) /ES pur unss/ hope. Q1 has *experience*.

5. ***lamentable** here should be /LAM un tuh bł/ the usual UK pronunciation.

10. **parti-ey'd** (Q1c) /PAR tee-/ i.e., bleeding from the eyes. Some eds. prefer Q1u, F1's **poorly led** or **poorly eyed**.

20. **defects** here should be /dih-, dee FECTS/.

49. **'parel** /PĂIR ł/ apparel.

---

lines 58–63 are in Q1, but omitted in F1.

59. **Obidicut** /oh BID ih kut/ a devil.

60. **Hobbididence** /hŏb ih DID nss/ a devil. Some eds. prefer **Hoberdidance** /hŏb ur-/.

60. **Mahu** /MAH hoo/ a devil. May have been /MAY-/ for Shk.

61. **Modo** /MOH doh/ a devil.

61. **Flibbertigibbet** /FLIB urt ee jib it/ a devil.

62. ***mowing** /MOH ing/ [MOW ing] grimacing. Both were used in Shk's time but his rhymes elsewhere indicate /moh/.

---

70. **excess** here should be /ek SESS/, the most common UK form.

Act 4 Scene 2 (*The Complete Oxford* line nos. in parentheses where they differ)

17. **distaff** cleft staff used in spinning thread. US /DIS stăf/;
E. NEW ENG., UK /DIS stahf/.

Lines 31–50, 62–8 are in Q1, but omitted in F1.

39. **savor** (UK **savour**) /SAY vur/ smell.

63. **Bemonster** /bih-, bee MŎN stur/ make monsterous.

68. **mew** /myo͞o/ either means 'lock up' or indicates a derisive comment.

---

79. (47) **justicers** (Q1c) /JUST ih surz/, **justices** (Q1u, F1).

Act 4 Scene 3 (This scene contained in Q1 and *Riverside* is omitted in F1)

22. **diamonds** here should be /DĪ mundz/, the most common pronunciation in the US.

Act 4 Scene 4 (*The Complete Oxford* 4.3)

3. **femiter** (Q1) /FEM ih tur/ a weed. F1 has **fenitar** /FEN ih tur/ which may be a misprint or an alternative form. Both are variants of **fumitory** which here would be /FYO͞OM ih tree/. Some eds. prefer **fumitor, fumiter**, both pronounced /FYO͞OM ih tur/.

4. **hardocks** /HARD ŏks/ another name for **burdocks**.

5. **Darnel** /DAR nl̷/ a weed.

17. **aidant** /AYD ṇt/ helpful.

17. **remediate** /ree-, rih MEED ee ut/ medicinal.

26. ***importun'd** /im POR chund/ importunate, asking insistently. About half the respondents in the Survey reported a form with 3rd syllable stress in all countries, but that will not fit the meter in verse and is a recent innovation (cf. *fortune*).

ă-bat, ăir-marry, air-pair, ạr-far, ĕr-merry, ĝ-get, ī-high, ĭr-mirror, l̷-little, ṇ-listen, ŏ-hot, oh-go, o͞o-wood, o͞o-moon, oor-tour, ŏr-or, ow-how, ţh-that, th-thin, ŭ-but, UR-fur, ur-under. ( )- suppress the syllable   [ ]- less common   see p. xi for complete list.

Act 4 Scene 5 (*The Complete Oxford* 4.4)

13. **descry** /dih SKRĪ/ see.

25. **eliads** /ELL yudz/ flirting looks. Variant of ***oeillades** US, CN /ILL yudz/,
CN *also* /AYL yudz/; UK *rarely* [ILL yudz]. The pronunciation based on
Fr. /uh YAHDZ/, prefered in the UK, would have to have 1st syllable stress here.

Act 4 Scene 6 (*The Complete Oxford* 4.5)

13. **choughs, chuffs** /chufs/ jackdaws.

15. **sampire** /SAM pīr/ an aromatic plant, eaten pickled. Archaic variant of
samphire /SAM fīr/.

21. **chafes** /chayfs/ rages.

26. **th' extreme** here should be /ṬHᵞEK streem/.

49. **goss'mer** /GŎSS mur/ spider's thread.

57. ***bourn** /born, boorn/ boundary. North American [burn] not recommended.
Normal development would favor /born/.

71. **welk'd** (Q1), **wealk'd** (F1) /welkt/ twisted. Some eds. prefer **whelked**.

88. **clothier's** /CLOH ṭhyurz, -ṭhee urz/ one engaged in the cloth trade.

92. **clout** (F1) /clowt/ center of target. Q1 has **air**.

92. **hewgh** (F1), **hagh** (Q1) sound imitating an arrow in flight or whistling.
Some eds. prefer **whew**.

93. **marjorum** type of herb. Archaic variant of **marjoram**. Both pronounced
/MAR jur rum/.

105. **ague-proof** (F1) /AY gyōo/ malarial fever. Q1 has *argue-proofe*.

119. ***presages** (F1) here should be /pree-, prih SAY jiz/ foretells. Q1 has
presageth.

122. **fitchew** /FITCH ōo/ polecat, i.e., whore.

124. **Centaurs** /SEN torz/.

130. **civet** /SIV it/ a type of perfume.

130. **apothecary** US /uh PŎ̵T̵H̵ uh kĕr ee/; UK /-kuh ree/ druggist.

137. **squiny** /SKWIN ee/ archaic variant of **squint**.

160. **beadle** /BEE dł/ local officer in charge of whippings.

163. **usurer** /YO͞O zh(u)r ur/; UK *also* [-zh(yoo)r ur, -zh(oo)r ur] someone who lends money for interest.

164. **Thorough** (F1) archaic variant of Q1's **Through** which is often pronounced as mod. *thorough* in Shk, but here it should be 1 syllable, making *Through* the better choice.

180. **wawl, waul** (F1) /wawl/ yowl. Q1 has **wail**.

184. **stratagem** /STRAT uh jum/ scheme.

206. **redeems** here with 1st syllable stress.

209. **toward** /TOH wurd, -urd/ about to take place.

213. **descry** /dih SKRĪ/ sight.

225. ***benison** US, CN /BEN ih sun, -sn̩/ [-zun, -zn̩]; UK /-z-/ [-s-] blessing.

226. **proclaim'd** here should be /PROH claymd/.

Note on the dialect of southwest England: Shk's spellings are not a reliable guide to the correct reproduction of the dialect in this scene. The notation of this guide is also ill-suited to help the reader understand the phonetic nuances of dialect speech. The correct representation of the dialect is best learned by listening to a native speaker and imitating his or her speech. There are however some general guidelines. At the beginnings of words and in the middle of words:
/s/ becomes /z/
/f/ becomes /v/
/t̵h̵/ becomes /t̠h/
/sh/ becomes /zh/.
Further, /r/ is pronounced wherever it occurs with the sound of North American English.

ă-bat, ăir-**marry**, air-**pair**, a̠r-**far**, ĕr-**merry**, ĝ-**get**, ī-**high**, ĭr-**mirror**, ł-**little**, n̩-**listen**, ŏ-**hot**, oh-**go**, o͞o-**wood**, o͞o-**moon**, oor-**tour**, ōr-**or**, ow-**how**, t̠h-**that**, t̵h̵-**thin**, ŭ-**but**, UR-**fur**, ur-**under**. ( )- suppress the syllable   [ ]- less common   see p. xi for complete list.

235–244. **Chill** /chill, chɫ/ Somerset dialect for *ich will,* 'I will.'

235. **cagion** (Q1) /KAY jun/ occasion. Some eds. prefer F1's **'casion** /KAY zhun/.

238. **chud** /chud/ If I could.

239. **vortnight** SW England dialect for **fortnight** /FORT nīt/; US *also* [FORT nit] 2 weeks. Virtually obsolete in the US.

240. **che vor'ye** /chuh VOR yih/ I warrant you.

241. **Ice** (F1), **I's, Ise** /īss/ dialect form for 'I'll,' today found only in NW England.

241. **costard** /CŎST urd/ head.

241. **ballow** (F1) /BAL oh/ cudgel. Some eds. prefer **baton** /BAT ṇ/.

275. **mature** here 1st syllable stress is indicated.

Act 4 Scene 7 (*The Complete Oxford* 4.6)

34. ***perdu** (Q1) sentry. Here stress should fall on the 1st syllable. US /PĔR do͞o/ [PĔR dyo͞o, PUR do͞o, PUR dyo͞o]; UK /PUR dyo͞o, PĔR dyo͞o/ or /PUR DYO͞O/ with equal stress. The traditional form is /PUR-/. Omitted F1.

38. ***hovel** stay in a poor cottage. US /HUV ɫ/, *rarely* [HŎV-]; CN /HUV-/ [HŎV-]; UK /HŎV-/ [HUV-].

93. **arbiterment** (Q1) /ạr BIT ur munt/ decisive encounter. Archaic variant of **arbitrement, arbitrament** /ạr BIT ruh munt/. Omitted F1.

Act 5 Scene 1

12. **conjunct** (Q1) /cun JUNCT/ in league with. Omitted F1.

44. **avouched** /uh VOWCH id/ affirmed.

46. ***machination** plotting. US /mack ih NAY shun/ is older, /mash-/ is a newer, spelling pronunciation. The former is more common in the US, the latter in the UK, while in CN both are used equally. Omitted Q1.

Act 5 Scene 3

50. **impress'd lances** here should be /IM prest/ drafted soldiers.

69. **compeers** /cum PEERZ/ equals.

71. **Holla** /huh LAH/ a call to attract attention.

87. **banes** /baynz/ proclamation in church of an intended marriage. Archaic variant of **banns** /banz/.

92. ***heinous** /HAYN us/ hateful. /HEEN us/ is non-standard though common in the UK.

132. **Maugre** /MAW gur/ in spite of.

136. **Conspirant** (F1) /cun SPĪ runt/ conspirator. Q1 has *Conspicuate*.

154. **unknown** here should be /UN nohn/.

156. **stopple** (Q1), **stople** /STŎP ł/ plug. F1 has **stop**.

176. **prophesy** /PRŎF uh sī/ predict the future.

217. ***puissant** powerful. The traditional forms are /PWISS ṇt/, /PYŌŌ sṇt/, but these are now rare. In all countries one of several Frenchified pronunciations is the most common: /PWEE sṇt/ in the US, /-sahnt/ in CN, and /-sahⁿt/ in the UK, but all 3 may be found in each country.

236. **aye** /ay/ ever. /ī/ is often used, but not recommended.

277. ***falchion** type of sword. /FĂL chun/ [-shun]; *older* [FAWL chun].

284. ***Caius** US, CN /KĪ us/, *rarely* [KAY us]; UK /KĪ us, KAY us/.
Ang.Lat. /KAY us/; Class.Lat. /KĪ ōōs/. Another angl. form /keez/ is also sometimes used, but not recommended.

ă-bat, ăir-**marry**, air-**pair**, ạr-**far**, ĕr-**merry**, ĝ-**get**, ī-**high**, ĭr-**mirror**, ł-**little**, ṇ-**listen**, ŏ-**hot**, oh-**go**, ōō-**wood**, ōō-**moon**, oor-**tour**, ōr-**or**, ow-**how**, ţh-**that**, t͟h-**thin**, ŭ-**but**, UR-**fur**, ur-**under**. ( )- suppress the syllable   [ ]- less common   see p. xi for complete list.

Macbeth

People in the Play

Banquo /BANG kwoh/.

Cathness, Caithness /KAY~~TH~~ ness, -niss/.

Donalbain /DŎN ł bayn/.

***Fleance** US /FLEE ahnss/ [FLAY unss, FLEE-], *rarely* [FLAY ahnss];
CN /FLEE ahnss, FLAY unss/; UK /FLEE unss, FLAY-/ [FLEE ahnss],
rarely [FLAY ahnss]. Normal development would favor /FLEE unss/.

Hecat, Hecate /HEK ut/ goddess of witchcraft. /HEK uh tee/ is the usual
non-Shakespearean pronunciation.

Malcolm /MAL kum/.

Menteth, Menteith /men TEE~~TH~~/.

Rosse, Ross US /rawss/; UK /rŏss/. In CN /ŏ, aw/ are pronounced the same way.

Seyton /SEE tun, SEET ṇ/.

***Siward** US /SOO̅ wurd, SEE wurd/; CN /SEE wurd/; UK /SEE wurd/, *rarely*
[SYOO̅-, SOO̅-]. The older form is /S(Y)OO̅-/. /SEE-/ is a newer spelling
pronunciation. Some eds. prefer F1's **Seyward**, pronounced the same way.

Places in the Play

Birnan Wood /BURN un/. Some eds. prefer **Birnam** /BURN um/.

Cawdor /KAW dur/. Sometimes a spelling pronunciation /-dor/ is used.

***Dunsinane** /DUN sih nayn/, *rarely* [dun sih NAYN]. At 4.1.93 2nd syllable
stress is indicated. Some eds. prefer mod. **Dunsinnan** /DUN sih nun/.

Glamis the 2-syllable pronunciation /GLAHM iss/ can be used in all instances.
Sometimes the meter also permits the mod., 1-syllable pronunciation /glahmz/.

Special Words

thane /t̶hayn/ Scottish lord.

weïrd, weird having power to control men's fate. In verse it should be 2 syllables /WEE urd/, /WIH urd/. F1 spells it *wey(w)ard,* influenced by *wayward.*

Act 1 Scene 1

8. ***Graymalkin** gray cat. US /gray MAWL kin/, *rarely* [-MĂL-];
UK /-MĂL-/ [-MAWL-], *rarely* [-MAW kin-, -MŎL-]. Some eds. prefer **Grimalkin**
/grih-/. The Survey revealed a significant difference between this word and ***malkin**
'wench' in the UK : /MAW kin/ [MAWL-, MŎL-].

9. **Paddock** /PAD uk/ toad.

Act 1 Scene 2

9. **Macdonwald, Macdonald** both are /muk-, mack DŎN ɫd/.

13, 30. **kerns** /kurnz/ Irish foot soldiers.

25. **gins** /ĝinz/ begins.

31, 49. **Norweyan** /nor WAY un/ variant of **Norwegian**.

34. **captans** here /CAP ih tunz/ is indicated.

40. **Golgotha** here should be /GŎL guh t̶huh/; US *also* /GAWL-/ hill where Jesus
died.

54. **Bellona's** /buh LOHN uz/ goddess of war.

59. **Sweno** /SWEE noh/.

60. **deign** /dayn/ grant.

61. **Saint Colme's** /saynt KOHL meez/; UK /sint-, sṇt-/. Some eds. prefer **Saint Co-lum's** /KŎL umz/.

ă-bat, ăir-**ma**rry, air-**pa**ir, ạr-**fa**r, ĕr-**me**rry, ĝ-**ge**t, ī-**hi**gh, ĭr-**mi**rror, ɫ-**li**ttle, ṇ-**li**sten,
ŏ-**ho**t, oh-go, o͞o-**wo**od, o͞o-**mo**on, oor-**to**ur, ōr-**o**r, ow-**ho**w, t̶h-**tha**t, t̶h-**thi**n, ŭ-**bu**t,
UR-**fu**r, ur-**un**der. ( )- suppress the syllable   [ ]- less common   see p. xi for complete list.

Act 1 Scene 3

4. **mounch'd** archaic variant of **munch'd**, both pronounced /muncht/.

6. **Aroint thee, Aroynt thee** /uh ROYNT/ begone.

6. **ronyon, runnion** /RUN yun/ scabby creature.

7. **Aleppo** /uh LEP oh/ city in present-day Syria.

8. **sieve** /siv/ strainer.

22. **sev'nnights** variant of **se'nnights** /SEN nits, -nīts/ weeks.

39. **Forres** US /FŌR iss/; UK, E. COAST US /FŎR-/.

71. **Sinel's, Sinell's** /SĪN łz, SIN łz/ Macbeth's father.

84. **insane** here /IN sayn/ is indicated.

95. **Norweyan** /nor WAY un/ variant of **Norwegian**.

Act 1 Scene 4

42. **Enverness** /en vur NESS/ archaic variant of **Inverness** /in-/.

45. **harbinger** /HAR bin jur/ advance messenger.

Act 1 Scene 5

27. ***chastise** punish. Here should be /CHĂSS tīz/, the usual US pronunciation, also used in CN; in the UK 2nd syllable stress is usual.

39. **entrance** here /ENT ur unss/ is indicated.

44. **th' access** here should be /ţh^y ak SESS/.

Act 1 Scene 6

6. **frieze** /freez/ area between a door lintel and the cornice.

7. **coign** /koyn/ corner.

8. **procreant cradle** /PROH cr(ee) yunt/ bed for reproduction.

13. **God 'ield** /gŏd-, gud EELD us, -ILD-/; US *also* /gawd-/ thanks.

20. **ermites** /UR mits/ archaic variant of **hermits**, i.e., who will pray for you.

22. **purveyor** here should be /PUR vay ur/ someone who prepares the way for a king.

23. **holp** /hohlp/ helped.

26. **compt** /cownt/ archaic variant of **count** 'account,' pronounced the same way.

Act 1 Scene 7

3. **trammel up** /TRAM ł/ catch (in a net).

4. **surcease** /sur SEESS/ end, death.

11. **chalice** /CHAL iss/ goblet.

22. ***cherubin** angel. US, CN /CHĔR uh bin/ [-yuh-]; UK uses both equally. /KĔR-/ not recommended. Some eds. prefer **cherubins, cherubim**.

23. ***couriers** US /CUR yurz/ [COOR-]; E. COAST US /CŬR-/ [COOR-]; UK /COOR-/ [CŬR-].

54. **unmake** here with 1st syllable stress.

64. ***wassail** carousing. Here stressed on the 1st syllable US /WŎSS łz, -aylz/, *rarely* [WĂSS łz]; CN /WŎSS aylz/ [WŎSS łz]; UK /WĂSS aylz/ [WŎSS-]. Normal development would favor /WŎSS-/.

67. **limbeck** /LIM bek, -bik/ archaic variant of *alembic*, part of a distillery.

71. **spungy** archaic variant of **spongy**, both pronounced /SPUN jee/.

ă-bat, äir-**marry**, air-**pair**, ạr-**far**, ĕr-**merry**, ĝ-**get**, ī-**high**, ĭr-**mirror**, ł-**little**, ṇ-**listen**, ŏ-**hot**, oh-**go**, o͞o-**wood**, o͞o-**moon**, oor-**tour**, ōr-**or**, ow-**how**, ţh-**that**, ~~th~~-**thin**, ŭ-**but**, UR-**fur**, ur-**under**. ( )- suppress the syllable   [ ]- less common   see p. xi for complete list.

Act 2 Scene 1

14. **largess, largesse** generous gifts. Here should have 1st syllable stress US /LAR jess/ [-zhess]; CN, UK /LAR zhess/ [-jess]. Forms with /j/ are older.

15. **diamond** here should be /DĪ uh mund/, the standard UK form.

18. **defect** here should be /dih-, dee FEKT/.

46. **dudgeon** /DUJ un/ dagger handle.

46. **gouts** /gowts/ drops.

53. ***Alarum'd** US, CN /uh LAHR umd/ [-LĂIR-]; UK /uh LĂIR umd, uh LAHR umd/ called to arms.

55. **Tarquin's** /TAR kwinz/ king of Rome who raped Lucretia.

Act 2 Scene 2

6. **possets** /PŎSS its/ spiced milk drinks.

49. ***Infirm** /in FURM/ irresolute.

59. **multitudinous** US /mŭl tih TOOD (ih) nus/; UK, SOUTH. US /-TYOOD-/ vast.

59. ***incarnadine** /in CAR nuh dīn/ [-deen] make red. The latter is newer and non-standard in UK.

Act 2 Scene 3

4. **Belzebub** /BEL zih bub/ a devil. Archaic variant of **Beelzebub** /bee EL zih bub/.

6. **enow** /ih NOW/; US *also* /ee-/ archaic variant of **enough**.

8–35. **equivocator, equivocates** /ih KWIV uh kay tur/; US *also* /ee-/ an *equivocator* is someone who uses vague or deceptive answers in an argument. /-tor/ not recommended.

57. **prophesying** /PRŎF uh sī ing/ predicting the future.

59. **obscure** here should be /ŎB skyoor/; US *also* [-skyur].

60. ***livelong** US /LIV lŏng, -lawng/, *rarely* [LĪV-]; UK /LIV lŏng/ [LĪV-].

72. **Gorgon** /GOR gun/ Medusa, whose sight could kill.

74. ***alarum-bell** US, CN /uh LAHR um/ [-LĂIR-]; UK /uh LĂIR um, uh LAHR um/ a bell that calls men to arms.

82. ***parley** /PAR lee/ conference with an enemy. Newer [-lay] not recommended.

116. ***breech'd** covered. /britcht/ is traditional, /breecht/ is newer. The former pronunciation is more common in the UK and the latter in the US, CN.

131. **pretense** (UK **pretence**) intention, design. Here should be /prih TENSS/, the normal UK pronunciation, or /pree TENSS/ based on the most common US pronunciation /PREE tenss/.

135. **consort** /cun SORT/ keep company.

136. **unfelt** here should be /UN felt/.

Act 2 Scene 4

7. **travelling** (F3) /TRAV ling/. F1 has ***travailing** 'laboring,' which in Shk's time was also pronounced /TRAV ling/. Mod. pronunciations /truh VAYL ing, TRAV ayl ing/ will not fit the meter and cannot be compressed.

18. **eat** /et/ dialect variant of **ate** which is also commonly /et/ in the UK.

24. **suborned** /sub ORND/ bribed.

28. **ravin up** /RAV in/ devour. Some eds. prefer F1's **raven** pronounced the same way.

31, 35. ***Scone**. At 5.9.41 rhymes with *one* which in Shk's time was pronounced /ohn/. Today the Scots say /sko͞on/, also used by a minority in England, but unknown in the US. In both the US and England /skohn/ is the usual pronunciation. US /skŏn, skun/ are not recommended.

33. **Colmekill** /KOHM kill/ Iona Island in W. Scotland.

34. ***predecessors** US /PRED ih sess urz/; UK /PREE dih sess urz/; in CN both /PREE-/ and /PRED-/ are used equally. Rarely with stress on the 3rd syllable. /-orz/ not recommended.

ă-bat, ăir-m**arr**y, air-p**air**, ar-f**ar**, ĕr-m**err**y, ĝ-**g**et, ī-h**igh**, ĭr-m**irr**or, ł-lit**tle**, ņ-lis**ten**, ŏ-h**o**t, oh-go, o͝o-w**oo**d, o͞o-m**oo**n, oor-t**our**, ōr-**or**, ow-h**ow**, ţh-**th**at, ~~th~~-**th**in, ʊ̆-b**u**t, UR-f**ur**, ur-und**er**. ( )- suppress the syllable [ ]- less common see p. xi for complete list.

*benison US, CN /BEN ih sun, -sn̩/ [-zun, -zn̩]; UK /-z-/ [-s-] blessing.

Act 3 Scene 1

17. **indissoluble** that cannot be dissolved. Here should be /in DIS sŏl yuh bł/.

31. **parricide** /PĂIR ih sīd/ killing of a father.

56. **Mark Antony's** /ANT (uh) neez/. F1's *Anthony's* which in the UK is also usually pronounced with /t/.

66. **rancors** (UK **rancours**) /RANK urz/ ill will. /-orz/ not recommended.

92. **mungrels** /MUNG grłz/ variant of **mongrels**, pronounced the same in the UK; US, CN *also* /MŎNG grłz, MAWNG-/.

93. **Shoughs** shaggy lap dogs. /shufs/, *rarely older* [shŏks]. Sometimes spelled **Shocks**.

93. ***demi-wolves** /DEM ee-/ half-dog, half-wolf.

108. **buffets** /BUFF its/ knocks.

119. **avouch** /uh VOWCH/ justify.

Act 3 Scene 2

14. **close** /clohz/ heal.

33. **lave** /layv/ wash.

34. ***vizards** /VIZ urdz/ masks. /-ardz/ not recommended.

38. **eterne** /ih TURN/; US *also* /ee-/ eternal.

40. ***jocund** /JŎCK und/; US, CN *rarely* [JOHK-] merry.

Act 3 Scene 4

18. ***nonpareil** one without equal. /nŏn puh RELL/ is the oldest form, still common in the US, but now vanished from the UK and CN, where it has been replaced with /nŏn puh RAYL/ [-RAY], based on mod. Fr. /-RAY/ is also common in the US.

/-RĪ, -RĪL/ are occasionally heard, but not recommended. Sometimes 1st syllable stress is used.

42. **mischance** in verse normally with 2nd syllable stress.

65. **Authoriz'd** /aw ~~THOR~~ īzd/ is the older pronunciation, but here an inverted foot will allow the mod. pronunciation /AW ~~thur~~ īzd/.

65. **grandam** /GRAN dam/; US *rarely* [-dum] grandmother. Informally /GRAN um/.

75. **humane** here should be /HY$\overline{OO}$ mayn/; US *sometimes* [Y$\overline{OO}$ mayn].

75. **weal** /weel/ commonwealth.

92. **Avaunt** /uh VAWNT/ begone!

100. **th' Hyrcan** normally /HUR kun/ of Hyrcania (in the Caucausus). However, Shk did not pronounce the /h/ in this word, but attached *th'* as /ṬH^{Y}UR kun/.

123. **Augures, Augurs** /AWG yurz/ [-urz]; UK *also* /-yoorz/ auguries, prophecies.

124. **choughs, chuffs** /chufs/ jackdaws.

142. **initiate fear** /ih NISH yut, -yayt/ fear of a beginner. /-ut/ is more usual for an adj.

Act 3 Scene 5

2. **beldams** hags. US /BEL damz, -dumz/; UK /BEL damz/, *rarely* [-dumz].

7. **close** /clohss/ hidden.

15. **Acheron** /AK ur ŏn, -un/ a river in Hades. /-ŏn/ is usual in the US and is increasingly common in the UK. /-un/ would be the traditional form (cf. *Solomon*).

26. **sleights** /slīts/ tricks.

ă-bat, ăir-marry, air-**pair**, ạr-**far**, ĕr-**merry**, ĝ-**get**, ī-**high**, ĭr-**mirror**, ł-**little**, ṇ-**listen**, ŏ-**hot**, oh-**go**, $\overline{oo}$-**wood**, $\overline{oo}$-**moon**, oor-**tour**, ōr-**or**, ow-**how**, ṭh-**that**, ~~th~~-**thin**, ŭ-**but**, UR-**fur**, ur-und**er**. ( )- suppress the syllable   [ ]- less common   see p. xi for complete list.

Act 3 Scene 6

28. **malevolence** /muh LEV uh lunss/ ill will.

31. **Northumberland** /no̶r̶t̶h̶ UM bur lund/.

36. *****homage** /HŎM ij/; US *also* /ŎM ij/ acknowledgement of allegiance.

38. **exasperate** exasperated. /eg ZĂSS pur ayt, -ut/; UK *also* /-ZAHSS-/.

Act 4 Scene 1

1. **brinded** /BRIN did/ archaic variant of **brindled** /BRIND łd/ tawny with dark streaks.

5. *****entrails** /EN traylz/; US *also* [-trłz] guts.

12. **Fillet** /FILL it/ slice. This is the usual form in the UK; US /fill AY/ will not fit the meter.

17. **howlet's** /HOW lits/ young owl's. Variant of **owlet's**.

24. **ravin'd** /RAV ind/ glutted.

26. **blaspheming** here should be /blăss FEEM ing/; UK, E. NEW ENG. *also* [blahss-] speaking irreverently.

29. **Tartar's** /TAR turz/ people of Central Asia.

33. **chawdron, chaudron** /CHAW drun/ entrails.

34. **cau'dron** (*Cawdron* F1) /KAW drun/ archaic variant of **cauldron** /KAWL drun/.

37. **baboon's** here should be /BAB o͞onz/.

After line 43 some eds. add a song from another source, which contains lines with the words

Liard /LĪ urd/ gray. In some cases it was written *Lyer* or *Liand* which are probably errors.

younker /YŬNG kur/ young lord.

---

59. **germains, germens** /JUR munz/; **germain** (F1), **germen** 'seed' in the collective sense.

65. **sweaten** /SWET n̩/ sweated. In Shk's time *sweat* had the vowel of *sea*, hence the rhyme with *eaten*.

66. **gibbet** /JIB it/ post from which they hung corpses after hanging.

69. **unknown** here should be /UN nohn/.

91. **chafes** /chayfs/ is angry.

96. **bodements** /BOHD munts/ omens.

stage direction after 106: **Hoboys, Hautboys** /HOH boyz/ or /OH boyz/ archaic variant of *oboes*.

123. **blood-boltered** /BOHL turd/ matted with blood. Some eds. prefer **blood-balter'd** /BAWL turd/.

134. **aye** /ay/ ever. /ī/ is often used, but not recommended.

144. **exploits** here should be /ek SPLOYTS/.

Act 4 Scene 2

35. **gin** /jin/ snare.

57. **enow** /ih NOW/; US *also* /ee-/ archaic variant of **enough**.

Act 4 Scene 3

8. **dolor** (UK **dolour**) /DOH lur/; UK *also* /DŎL ur/ pain. /-or/ not recommended.

34. **affeer'd** /uh FEERD/ confirmed.

58. **avaricious** /av uh RISH us/ greedy.

63. **cestern** /SESS turn/ archaic variant of **cistern** /SISS turn/.

78. ***stanchless** insatiable. Variant of **staunchless** /STAWNCH liss/. The *stanch*-variant was pronounced with the vowel of *tan* in Elizabethan Eng. The *staunch*-variant in words of this sort (*graunt, chaunt*) gave rise to RP /-AH-/.

ă-bat, ăir-marry, air-pair, ạr-far, ĕr-merry, ĝ-get, ī-high, ĭr-mirror, ł-little, n̩-listen, ŏ-hot, oh-go, ŏŏ-wood, ōō-moon, oor-tour, ōr-or, ow-how, ţh-that, t̶h̶-thin, ʊ-but, UR-fur, ur-under. ( )- suppress the syllable   [ ]- less common   see p. xi for complete list.

78, 84. **avarice** /AV uh riss/ greed.

88. **foisons** /FOY zunz, -zn̦z/ harvests, plenty.

93. **perseverance** here should be /pur SEV (uh) runss/.

108. **blaspheme** here should be /blăss FEEM/; UK, E. NEW ENG. *also* [blạhss-] speak irreverently.

123. **abjure** /ab-, ub JOOR/; US *also* /-JUR/ renounce.

143. **assay** /uh-, ass SAY/. Some eds. Prefer **essay** /es SAY/. Both mean 'attempt, test.'

180. **niggard** /NIG urd/ miser.

187. **create** here should be /CREE ayt/.

Act 5 Scene 1

20. **stand close** /clohss/ keep hidden.

39. **accompt** /uh COWNT/ archaic variant of **account**, pronounced the same way.

Act 5 Scene 2

10. **unrough** here should be /UN ruff/ beardless.

18. **minutely** /MIN it lee/ occurring every minute.

27. **weal** /weel/ commonwealth.

Act 5 Scene 3

8. **epicures** /EP ih kyoorz/; US *also* /-kyurz/ pleasure-seekers, those leading riotous lives.

21. **disseat** (F1) /dis SEET/ dethrone.   F2 has **disease**.

35. **skirr** /skur/ scour.

52. ***pristine** here should be /PRISS teen/ perfect, as in its original state.

55. **cyme** (F1) /sīm/ tops of the colewort used as a purgative. Some eds. prefer F4's **senna** /SEN uh/ a type of tree whose leaves are a purgative.

55. **What rhubarb, *cyme*, or what purgative drug** some eds. prefer **senna** because it improves the meter, but *cyme* could also be considered 2 syllables, extended to /SAH eem/, (see MND 2.1.249). *Purgative* in either case is reduced to 2 syllables /PURG (uh) tiv/.

Act 5 Scene 4

19. **unsure** here with 1st syllable stress. Note 3 syllables are indicated for *speculative*.

Act 5 Scene 5

4. **ague** /AY gyo͞o/ malarial fever.

12. ***treatise** story. US /TREET iss/, *rarely* [-iz]; CN /-iss/; UK both /s/ and /z/ forms used equally.

42. **th'equivocation** /t̹hʸih kwiv uh KAY shun/; US *also* /ee-/ using vague or deceptive answers in an argument.

46. **avouches** /uh VOWCH iz/ affirms.

48. **gin** /ĝin/ begin.

50. ***alarum-bell** US, CN /uh LAHR um/ [-LĂIR-]; UK /uh LĂIR um, uh LAHR um/ bell calling men to arms.

Act 5 Scene 6

1. **leavy** /LEEV ee/ archaic variant of **leafy**.

10. **harbingers** /HAR bin jurz/ advance messengers.

ă-bat, ăir-marry, air-pair, ạr-far, ĕr-merry, ĝ-get, ī-high, ĭr-mirror, ł-little, ṇ-listen, ŏ-hot, oh-go, o͞o-wood, o͞o-moon, oor-tour, ōr-or, ow-how, t̹h-that, th-thin, ʊ-but, UR-fur, ur-under. ( )- suppress the syllable   [ ]- less common   see p. xi for complete list.

Act 5 Scene 7 (*The Complete Oxford* 5.8—line nos. in parentheses)

17. (5.8.4) **kerns** /kurnz/ Irish foot soldiers.

18. (5.8.5) **staves** /stayvz/ staffs.

22. (5.8.9) **bruited** /BR$\overline{OO}$T id/ announced.

Act 5 Scene 8 (*The Complete Oxford* 5.10)

20. **palter** /PAWL tur/ use vague or deceptive arguments.

Act 5 Scene 9 (*The Complete Oxford* 5.11)

7. **prowess** here 1 syllable is indicated /PROW (i)ss/.

16. **knoll'd** /nohld/ rung. Archaic variant of **knell'd**.

41. ***Scone** here meant to rhyme with *one* which in Shk's time was pronounced /ohn/. Today the Scots say /sk$\overline{oo}$n/, also used by a minority in England, but unknown in the US. In both the US and England /skohn/ is the usual pronunciation. US /skŏn, skun/ are not recommended.

Measure for Measure

People in the Play

Abhorson /ub HOR sun, -sṇ/ [ub OR sun].

Angelo 2 or 3 syllables depending on meter /AN j(uh) loh/.

Barnardine /BAR nur deen/.

Claudio 2 or 3 syllables depending on meter /CLAW d(ee) yoh/.

Escalus /ES kuh lus/.

Francisca /fran SIS kuh/.

Juliet /J͞O͞OL yit, -yet/ or a triple ending /J͞O͞OL ee yit, -yet/. If the meter allows it, the mod. variant /jo͞o lee ET/ may also be used.
  Julietta /jo͞ol YET uh/.

Lodowick 2 or 3 syllables depending on meter /LŎD (oh) wik, LOHD-, (-uh-)/.

*Lucio 2 or 3 syllables depending on meter /L͞O͞OCH (ee) yoh/ is newer and more common, based on Ital. Older and less common are [L͞O͞OS (ee) yoh], US *rarely* [L͞O͞OSH (ee) yoh].   At one time many RP speakers in the UK used /lyo͞o-/ for words beginning *lu-*, but today their number is dwindling.

Mariana /mair ee ANN uh/ is older, /-AHN uh/ is newer.

Pompey /PŎM pee/.

*Provost US /PROH vohst/, *rarely* [PRŎV ohst, -ust]; UK /PRŎV ust/ [-ŏst].

Varrius /VĂIR yus/.

Vincentio (the Duke) /vin SEN shee yoh/; Ital.: /veen CHEN tsee oh/. His name is not spoken.

Act 1 Scene 1

41. **advertise** here should be /ad VUR tiss, -tīz/ make publicly known.

ă-b**a**t, ăir-m**a**rry, air-p**ai**r, ạr-f**a**r, ĕr-m**e**rry, ĝ-g**e**t, ī-h**i**gh, ĭr-m**i**rror, ł-litt**le**, ṇ-list**en**, ŏ-h**o**t, oh-g**o**, o͞o-w**oo**d, o͞o-m**oo**n, oor-t**ou**r, ōr-**or**, ow-h**ow**, t̪h-t**h**at, t̶h̶-t**h**in, ŭ-b**u**t, UR-f**ur**, ur-und**er**. ( )- suppress the syllable   [ ]- less common   see p. xi for complete list.

51. **leaven'd** /LEV ṇd, -ind/ referring to the gradual rising of dough, i.e., thoughtful.

56. ***importune** /im POR chun/ urge. About half the respondents in the Survey reported a form with 3rd syllable stress in all countries, but that will not fit the meter in verse and is a relatively recent innovation (cf. *fortune*).

67. **privily** /PRIV ih lee/ privately.

70. **aves** hails. /AY veez/ is the older, angl. form. The newer /AH vayz/ is much more common and based on classical and church Latin.

Act 1 Scene 2

8, 12. **Commandement(s)**. Archaic variant of **commandment(s)**, originally with 4 syllables, /-uh munt/, but in this prose passage the usual mod. 3-syllable pronunciation may be used.

33. **as lief** /leef/ as soon.

33. **kersey** /KUR zee/ coarse woolen cloth.

50. **dolors** (UK **dolours**) /DOH lurz/; UK *also* /DŎL urz/ pains, with pun on *dollars*. /-orz/ not recommended.

59. **sciatica** /sī AT ih kuh/ pain in the lower back.

100. **burgher** /BURG ur/ citizen.

120. ***demigod** half-god. /DEM ee gŏd, DEM ih-/; US *also* /-gawd/.

129. **ravin down, raven down** /RAV in/ devour.

133. **as lief** /leef/ as soon.

145. **contract** here should be /cŏn TRACT/.

150. **propagation**. Some eds. prefer **procuration** /prŏck yur AY shun/ 'obtaining,' or **prorogation** /proh ruh GAY shun/; UK *also* [prŏ-] delay.

167. **unscour'd** here should be /UN skowrd/.

181. **assay** /uh-, ass SAY/ attempt, test.

Act 1 Scene 3

3. **complete** here should be /CŎM pleet/ fully defended.

26. **use** here is the noun /yōoss/.

Act 1 Scene 4

5. **votarists** /VOHT (uh) rists/ those bound by vows to religious life.

11. **prioress** /PRĪ ur ess, -iss/ nun who is 2nd in rank at a convent.

34. **enskied** /en SKĪD/ placed in the sky.

38. **blaspheme** here should be /blăss FEEM/; UK, E. NEW ENG. *also* [blahss-] speak
irreverently.

43. **foison** /FOY zun, -zņ/ harvest.

44. **tilth** /tilth/ plowing.

60. **rebate** blunt. Here should be /rih-, ree BAYT/.

62. **use** /yōoss/ custom.

76. **Assay** /uh-, ass SAY/ try, test.

Act 2 Scene 1

11. **coher'd** /koh HEERD/ agreed with.

35. **confessor** here should be /CŎN fess ur/. /-or/ not recommended.

42. **commonweal** /CŎM un weel/ commonwealth.

52. ***malefactors** /MAL ih fak turz/, *rarely* [mal ih FAK turz] evil doers. /-torz/ not
recommended.

55. **profanation** /prŏf uh NAY shun/ desecration.

ă-bat, äir-**marry**, air-**pair**, ạr-**far**, ĕr-**merry**, ĝ-**get**, ī-**high**, ĭr-**mirror**, ł-**little**, ņ-**listen**,
ŏ-**hot**, oh-**go**, ōō-**wood**, ōō-**moon**, oor-**tour**, ōr-**or**, ow-**how**, ţh-**that**, th-**thin**, Ŭ-**but**,
UR-**fur**, ur-**under**. ( )- suppress the syllable   [ ]- less common   see p. xi for complete list.

90–107. **pruins** in Shk's time probably /PR$\overline{OO}$ inz/, archaic and dialect variant of **prunes.**

93–242. **threepence** /~~THR~~EP unss, -ṇss/ [~~THRUP-~~, ~~THRIP-~~, ~~THR$\overline{oo}$P-~~]. Some eds. prefer **three pence** which should be pronounced the same way.

---

124. ***Hallowmas** US /HŎL-, HAL oh muss/ [-mass]; UK /HAL oh mass/ [-muss]. All Saints Day, Nov. 1. The older form is /-muss/.

126. ***All-hallond eve** /awl HAL und/; US *also* /-HŎL-/ archaic variant of **All-Hallows eve** /awl HAL ohz/; US *also* /-HŎL-/. Some eds. prefer **All Hallow Eve.**

174, 184. **caitiff** /KAYT if/ scoundrel.

255. **carman** /CAR mun/ driver of a cart.

Act 2 Scene 2

19. **access** here should be /ak SESS/.

39. **cipher** /S$\overline{I}$ fur/ zero.

40. **record** here should be /rek-, rik ORD/.

41. **severe** here should be /SEV eer/.

60. **deputed** /duh PY$\overline{OO}$T id/ appointed.

61. **truncheon** /TRUN chun/ staff of office.

92. **th' edict** decree. Here should be /ţhee DICT/ in a headless line.

98. **successive** here should be /SUCK sess iv/.

128. **profanation** /prŏf uh NAY shun/ desecration.

131. **blasphemy** /BLĂSS fuh mee/; UK, E. NEW ENG. *also* /BLAHSS-/ irreverent speech.

132. **avis'd** /uh V$\overline{I}$ZD/ archaic variant of **advised.**

149. **sicles** /SIK łz/ type of coins. Archaic variant of **shekels** /SHEK łz/.

154. **dedicate** /DED ih kayt, -ut/ dedicated.

Act 2 Scene 3

39. **Benedicite** Ang.Lat. /ben uh DISS ih tee/;
Church Lat. /bay nay DEE chee tay/ bless you.

41. ***respites** reprieves. Here should be US /RESP its/, *rarely* [-īts];
CN /RESP its/ [-īts]; UK /RESP īts/ [-its]. /RESP it/ is older, but /-īt/ has
been in use since the 17th century.

Act 2 Scene 4

9. **sere** /seer/ dry. Some eds. prefer **seared** /seerd/.

18. **access** here should be /ak SESS/.

24. **swounds** archaic variant of **swoons**. In Shk's time the vowel could be either
/ow/ or /ōō/.

28. **obsequious** /ub-, ŏb SEE kw(ee) yus/ fawning.

29. **untaught** here should be /UN tawt/ ignorant.

57. **compell'd** here should be /CŎM peld/.

58. **accompt** /uh COWNT/ archaic variant of **account**, pronounced the same way.

80. **enshield** /EN sheeld/ concealed, guarded. Some eds. prefer **enshell'd,
enshielded**.

111. **Ignomy** /IG nuh mee/ disgrace. Some eds. prefer **Ignominy** /IG nuh min ee/
which will not fit the meter.

122. **fedary, feodary** (F2) /FED uh ree/ confederate. *Feodary* is usually a variant of
feudary /FYŌŌD uh ree/ 'vassal,' which is incorrect here.

155. **unsoil'd** here should be /UN soyld/.

159. **calumny** /CAL um nee/ slander.

162. **prolixious** /proh LIK shus/ excessive.

ă-bat, ăir-marry, air-pair, ạr-far, ĕr-merry, ĝ-get, ī-high, ĭr-mirror, ł-little, ņ-listen,
ŏ-hot, oh-go, ōō-wood, ōō-moon, oor-tour, ōr-or, ow-how, ţh-that, ŧħ-thin, ŭ-but,
UR-fur, ur-under. ( )- suppress the syllable   [ ]- less common   see p. xi for complete list.

Act 3 Scene 1

9. ***Servile** /SUR vīl/, *rarely* [SUR vĭl] slave-like.

26. **ingots** /ING guts/; UK *also* [-gŏts] gold or silver cast in bars.

31. **sapego** /suh PEE goh/ creeping skin disease. Variant of **serpigo**
/sur PEE goh, -PĪ-/ which some eds. prefer.

31. **the rheum** /rōōm/ disease of the lungs.

35. ***alms** charity for the poor. /ahmz/ is older; /ahlmz, awlmz/ are newer.
In the UK the latter are non-standard.

36. **palsied** /PAWL zeed/; UK *also* [PŎL-].

58. **leiger** resident ambassador. Also written **leaguer, ledger, leger, legier, lieger**
and pronounced as /LEE gur, LEJ ur, LEE jur/.

66, 67. ***durance** /DYOOR unss/; US *also* /DŌŌR-/ [DUR-] imprisonment.

90. **enew** US /ih NŌŌ/, SOUTH. US, UK /ih NYŌŌ/ drive prey into the water during a
hunt.

93, 96. **prenzie** (F1) /PREN zee/ uncertain meaning. Some eds. prefer **precise**
which here should be /PREE sĭss/, **puny, precious** or F2's **princely**.

114. **perdurably** here should be /PUR dyur uh blee/; US *also* [-dur-] eternally.

120. **delighted.** Some eds. prefer **dilated** /dih-, dī LAYT id/ expansive.

129. **penury** /PEN yur ee/; UK *also* /PEN yoor ee/ poverty.

162. **assay** test. Usually /uh-, ass SAY/ in Shk, but as a noun in this prose passage,
may be mod. /ASS ay/.

203. ***peradventure** perhaps. /PUR ad VEN chur/;
US *rarely* [PĔR-, PUR ad ven chur];
UK, CN *also* [PUR-, PĔR ad ven chur, pĕr ad VEN chur].

214. ***nuptial** wedding. US, UK /NUP chĭl/ [-shĭl]; in CN both are used equally.

214. **affianc'd** /uh FĪ unst/ engaged to be married.

222. **combinate-husband** /CŎM bih nut, -ayt/ the man sworn by oath to be her
husband. /-ut / is more usual for an adj.

Act 3 Scene 2 (*The Complete Oxford* continues this as 3.1—line nos. in parentheses)

6. (3.1.275) **usuries** /Y$\overline{OO}$ zhur eez/; UK *also* [-zhyoor eez, -zhoor eez] lending money for interest.

36. (3.1.304) ***whoremonger** pimp. US /HOR mŏng gur/, /-mawng-/ [-mung-]; CN /-mung gur, -mŏng gur/; UK /-mung gur/.

97. (3.1.363) **lenity** /LEN ih tee/ leniency.

99. (3.1.365) **severity** /suh VĔR ih tee/.

174. (3.1.433) **ungenitur'd** /un JEN ih churd/; UK *also* /-tyoord/ sexless.

175. (3.1.434) **continency** /CŎN tih nun see/ sexual self-restrained.

186. (3.1.445) **calumny** /CAL um nee/ slander.

279. (3.1.535) **betrothed** /bih-, bee TROHṬH id/ fiancée.

Act 4 Scene 1

28. **circummur'd** /sur kum MY$\overline{OO}$RD/ surrounded by a wall.

30. **planched** made of boards. US /PLĂN chid/; E. NEW ENG., UK /PLAHN chid/. Some eds. prefer **plancked** /PLANK id/.

71. **pre-contract** /PREE cŏn TRACT/ a contract made in the past.

75. **tithe's** /tīṭhz/ 10th part due to the church. Some eds. prefer **tilth's**.

Act 4 Scene 2

11. **gyves** /jīvz/ chains, fetters.

58. ***yare** /yair/; US *also* /yạr/ ready.

67. **traveller's**. Some eds. prefer **travailer's** 'laborer's' which here should have 1st syllable stress /TRAV ayl urz/. In Shk's time both words were /TRAV ł urz/, and here should be compressed to 2 syllables.

ă-bat, ăir-**marry**, air-**pair**, ạr-**far**, ĕr-**merry**, ĝ-**get**, ī-**high**, ĭr-**mirror**, ł-**little**, ṇ-**listen**, ŏ-**hot**, oh-**go**, ōō-**wood**, ōō-**moon**, oor-**tour**, ōr-**or**, ow-**how**, ṭh-**that**, t̶h̶-**thin**, ŭ-**but**, UR-**fur**, ur-**under**. ( )- suppress the syllable   [ ]- less common   see p. xi for complete list.

89. *postern small back or side gate. US, CN /PŎST urn/ [POHST urn];
UK /PŎST urn/, *rarely* [POHST urn].

92, 97. *countermand US, CN /COWNT ur mănd/; UK /-mahnd/ the revoking of a
command.

110. celerity /suh LĔR ih tee/ speed.

130. Bohemian /boh HEEM ee yun/ Czech.

143. reakless, reckless /REK liss/ heedless.

160. *respite reprieve. US /RESP it/, *rarely* [rih-, ree SPĪT];
CN /RESP it/ [RESP īt], [ree-, rih SPĪT]; UK /RESP īt/ [-it, rih SPĪT].
/RESP it/ is older, but /-īt/ has been in use since the 17th century.

186. avouch /uh VOWCH/ affirm.

Act 4 Scene 3

55. billets /BILL its/ clubs.

71, 76. Ragozine /RAG uh zeen, -zin/.

74. reprobate /REP ruh bayt/ a depraved person.

79. Prefix'd appointed. Here may be /prih-, pree FIKST/ or with inverted foot,
newer /PREE fikst/

94. contents here should be /cŏn TENTS/.

100. weal-balanc'd /weel-/ balanced with regard to public welfare. Most eds. prefer
well-balanced.

104. commune here should be /CŎM yo͞on/ speak intimately.

118. close /clohss/ silent.

128. *covent religious order. US /KUV ṇt/ [KŎV-]; UK /KŎV ṇt/ [KUV-].
US /KOHV-/ not recommended. Archaic variant of convent.

128. confessor here should be /CŎN fess ur/. /-or/ not recommended.

141. perfect here should be /PUR fikt/ inform.

174. **medlar** /MED lur/ an apple-like fruit.

Act 4 Scene 4

26. **credent bulk** /CREED ṇt/ massive trust.

Act 4 Scene 5

6, **Flavio's** /FLAY vyohz/.

8. **Valentius** (F1 *Valencius*) /vuh LEN shus/ does not fit the meter. Most eds. prefer **Valentinus** /val en TĪ nus/.

8. **Rowland** /ROH lund/.

8. **Crassus** /CRĂSS us/.

10. **Flavius'** /FLAY vyus/.

Act 4 Scene 6

5. *****peradventure** perhaps. /PUR ad VEN chur/;
US *rarely* [PĔR-, PUR ad ven chur];
UK, CN *also* [PUR-, PĔR ad ven chur, pĕr ad VEN chur].

Act 5 Scene 1

10. *****covert** here should be stressed on the 1st syllable US, CN /KOHV urt/ [KUV-];
UK /KUV-/ [KOHV-], *rarely* [KŎV-] secret.

13. *****razure, rasure** erasure, obliteration. US, CN /RAY shur/, US *rarely* [-zhur];
UK /-zhur/, *rarely* [shur]. /zh/ is more likely to used if the z spelling is used.

53, 88. **caitiff** /KAYT if/ scoundrel.

56. **caracts, characts** /KĂIR ukts/ symbols of office.

98. **concupiscible** /cŏn KYŌŌP (ih) sih bł/ moved by strong sexual desire.

ă-bat, ăir-marry, air-pair, ạr-far, ĕr-merry, ĝ-get, ī-high, ĭr-mirror, ł-little, ṇ-listen,
ŏ-hot, oh-go, ōō-wood, ōō-moon, oor-tour, ōr-or, ow-how, ţh-that, ŧħ-thin, ŭ-but,
UR-fur, ur-under. ( )- suppress the syllable   [ ]- less common   see p. xi for complete list.

106, 306. **suborn'd** /sub ORND/ persuaded someone to do something wrong.

125–143. **Lodowick** /LŎD (oh) wick, LOHD-, (uh-)/.

130. **swing'd** /swinjd/ beat.

158. **convented** /cun VENT tid/ summoned.

209. **contract** here should be /cŏn TRACT/.

227. **affianc'd** /uh FĪ unst/ engaged to be married.

242. **Compact** /cum-, cŏm PACT/ in league with.

257. *****chastisement** punishment. Here stress should be on 1st syllable /CHĂSS tiz munt/; US *also* /- tīz-/.

259. **throughly** archaic variant of *thoroughly*. /T̶H̶ROO lee/ is the normal pronunciation on stage, but to enhance clarity a syncopated form of the modern pronunciation may be used: *thor'ghly.*

262.   **Cucullus   non   facit   monachum**
Ang.Lat.   /kyoo KŬL us   nŏn   FAY sit   MŎN uh kum/
Class.Lat. /koo KooL oos nŏn   FAH kit   MŎN ah koom/.
        the hood does not make the monk.

311. **touze, touse** /towz/ pull roughly.

333. *****fleshmonger** fish-seller, pimp. US /FLESH mŏng gur/ or /-mawng-/ [-mung-]; CN /-mung gur, -mŏng gur/; UK /-mung gur/.

342. **close** /clohz/ come to terms, finish.

347. **giglets** /ĜIG lits/ loose women.

351. **foh** indicates an expression of disgust made with the lips /pff/! or /pfuh/! Sometimes rendered as /foh/ or **faugh** /faw/.

373. **sequent** /SEE kwunt/ subsequent.

378. **consummate** /CŎN suh mut, -ayt/ completed.

383. *****Advertising** attentive. Here should be /ad VUR tih sing, -zing/.

387. **unknown** here should be /UN nohn/.

392. **remonstrance** /rih-, ree MŎN strunss/ grievance.

394. **celerity** /suh LĔR (ih) tee/ speed.

433. ***importune** /im POR chun/ ask insistently. About half the respondents in the Survey reported a form with 3rd syllable stress in all countries, but that will not fit the meter in verse and is a relatively recent innovation (cf. *fortune*).

503. ***extol** praise. /ek STOHL/; UK *sometimes* and US *rarely* [-STŎL].

512. ***nuptial** wedding. US, UK /NUP chł/ [-shł]; in CN both are used equally.

529. **gratulate** gratifying. /GRACH oo layt, -lut/; UK *also* /GRAT yoo-/. /-ut / is more usual for an adj.

533. **Ragozine** /RAG uh zeen, -zin/.

ă-bat, ăir-ma**rry**, air-p**air**, ạr-f**ar**, ĕr-me**rry**, ĝ-g**et**, ī-h**igh**, ĭr-m**irror**, ł-li**ttle**, ņ-li**sten**,
ŏ-h**ot**, oh-g**o**, ōō-w**ood**, ōō-m**oon**, oor-t**our**, ōr-**or**, ow-h**ow**, țh-t**hat**, ŧħ-t**hin**, ʊ-b**ut**,
UR-f**ur**, ur-und**er**. ( )- suppress the syllable   [ ]- less common   see p. xi for complete list.

The Merchant of Venice

People in the Play

Sometimes some of these names can be given an Italian (or, for *Arragon*, a Spanish) accent in performance. These pronunciations are indicated here as accurately as possible within the limits of this notation. Shakespeare, however, probably intended them to be anglicized.

Antonio 3 or 4 syllables depending on meter /an TOHN (ee) yoh/; Ital. /ahn-/.

*Arragon, Aragon US /ĂIR uh gŏn/, *rarely* [-gun]; UK /-gŏn/ [-gun]. Sp. /ah rah GOHN/. /-un/ would be the traditional form (cf. *Solomon*).

*Balthazar, Balthasar by far the most common pronunciation is /BAL thuh zar/. It is rarely /bal ~~thuh~~ ZAR/ which will also fit the verse, but another rare pronunciation /bal ~~THAZ~~ ur/ will not.

Bassanio 3 syllables in verse /buh SAH nyoh/; Ital. /bah-/. In prose it may be /-nee yoh/.

Bellario 3 or 4 syllables depending on meter /buh LAH r(ee) yoh/ Portia's assumed name.

Gobbo /GŎB oh/.

*Gratiano 3 or 4 syllables depending on meter US /grahsh (ee) YAH noh/ [grash-], *rarely* [graysh-]; CN /grahsh-/ [grash-]; UK /grash-/ [grahsh-]. Ital. **Graziano** /grah ts(ee) YAH noh/.

Launcelot 2 or 3 syllables depending on meter. US /LAWNSS (uh) lŏt/ [LAHNSS-, LĂNSS-]; CN /LAWNSS-/ [LĂNSS]; UK /LAWNSS (uh) lut/ [LAHNSS-]. Archaic variant of **Lancelot**. Note that in CN and some parts of the US /LAWNSS-/ and /LAHNSS-/ are pronounced the same, and that in E. New Eng. and Standard British, /LAHNSS-/ corresponds to US /LĂNSS-/ (cf. *dance, chance*). The usual UK pronunciation of *Lancelot* is with 2 syllables /LAHNSS lut/; the North American with 3 /LĂNSS uh lŏt/. In Elizabethan Eng. words of this sort (*graunt-grant, chaunt-chant*) showed a dialect difference with the *-aun-* spelling reflecting /AW/ (the ancestor of RP /AH/) and the *-an-* spelling reflecting the vowel of *land*, the forerunner of the pronunciation found in North America.

Leonardo always 3 syllables /l(ee) yuh NAHR doh, l(ee) yoh-/; Ital. /lay oh-/.

Nerissa /nuh RISS uh/; Ital. /nay REESS ah/.

People in the Play (cont.)

Portia /POR shuh/ is the normal pronunciation, sometimes expanded to /POR shee uh/ to fit the meter.

Salarino /sal uh REE noh/; Ital. /sah lah REE noh/. In many editions, including *Riverside,* this character is left out, presumed to be the same as **Salerio.** In any case his name is not spoken.

Salerio always 3 syllables in verse. US, CN /suh LĔR yoh/, US *rarely* [-LEER-]; UK /-LĔR-/ [-LEER-]. /suh LEER yoh/ is the older angl. form, /suh LĔR yoh/ is newer, based on Ital. /sah LĔR yoh/.

Solanio /soh-, suh LAHN ee oh/. His name is not spoken.

Stephano the messenger in 5.1. /stef AH noh/ fits best, though in *The Tempest* stress is on the 1st syllable.

Tubal US /TŌŌ bł/; UK, SOUTH. US /TYŌŌ-/.

Places in the Play

*Padua 2 or 3 syllables depending on meter /PAD y(oo) wuh/ [PAJ (oo) wuh]. An Ital. vowel /PAHD-/ is not recommended, since the Ital. form is *Padova.*

Tripolis /TRIP uh lis, -uh-/.

Act 1 Scene 1

9. **argosies** /ĄRG uh seez/ large merchant ships.

10. **burghers** /BURG urz/ citizens.

19. **Piring** /PĪ ring/ means **peering**.

23. **ague** /AY gyōō/ malarial fever.

50. **Janus** /JAY nus/ Roman 2-faced god.

56. **Nestor** /NEST ur/ oldest of the Greeks at Troy. /-or/ not recommended.

ă-bat, ăir-marry, air-pair, ạr-far, ĕr-merry, ĝ-get, ī-high, ĭr-mirror, ł-little, ṇ-listen, ŏ-hot, oh-go, ōō-wood, ōō-moon, oor-tour, ōr-or, ow-how, ţh-that, ₮ħ-thin, ʊ-but, UR-fur, ur-under. ( )- suppress the syllable   [ ]- less common   see p. xi for complete list.

84. **alablaster** a type of white rock. US /AL uh blăss tur/;
E. NEW ENG., UK /-blahss-/ [-blăss-]. Archaic variant of **alabaster**
/-băss-, -bahss-/.

85. **jaundies** /JAWN deez/ yellowing of the skin. Archaic variant of **jaundice**
/JAWN diss/.

102. **gudgeon** /GUJ in/ bait fish.

111. A non-iambic line, with **commendable** pronounced as in mod. Eng. with stress
on 2nd syllable to rhyme with *vendible,* though elsewhere in Shk stress falls on the
1st syllable.

166. **Cato's** /KAYT ohz/.

171. ***Colchis'** country where Jason won the Golden Fleece. US /KOHL kiss/
[KŎL-]; UK /KŎL kiss/. Normal development would favor /KŎL kiss/,
/KOHL chiss/ not recommended.

171. **strond** /strŏnd/ archaic variant of **strand** shore.

175. ***presages** here should be /pree-, prih SAY jiz/ foretells.

Act 1 Scene 2

39, 58. **Neapolitan('s)** /nee uh PŎL ih tun/ of Naples.

45, 60. **Palentine** (Q1) /PAL in tīn/ archaic variant of Q2's **Palatine**
/PAL uh tīn/ region in Germany.

55. **le Bon** angl. /luh BŎN/; Fr. /luh BOH^N/.

60. **throstle** /T̶H̶RŎSS ł/ thrush.

66. **Falconbridge** /FAWL-, FAL kun brij/; UK *also* [FŎL-],
rarely older [FAW kun-].

71. **pennyworth** the older form is /PEN ur̶t̶h̶/, but in this prose passage the newer,
spelling pronunciation /PEN ee wurt̶h̶, -WURT̶H̶/ may be used.

73. **dumb show** /DUM shoh/ pantomime.

82. ***surety** pledge to repay something. Here may be 2 or 3 syllables
US /SHUR (ih) tee, SHOOR-/, CN /SHUR-/ [SHOOR-],
UK /SHOR-/ [SHUR-] [SHOOR-].

96. **Rhenish** /REN ish/ Rhine wine.

106. **Sibylla** /sih BIL uh/ she was promised long life by Apollo.

114. **Marquis** angl. /MAR kwiss/; Fr. /MAR kee, mar KEE/.

114. **Montferrat** (Q1) angl. /mŏnt fuh RAT/; Fr. /moh^n fĕr AH/;
Mount- (F1) /mownt-/.

Act 1 Scene 3

18. **argosy** /ĄRG uh see/ large merchant ship.

19–107. **Rialto** /ree AL toh/ is older, /ree AHL toh/ is newer based on Ital.

34. **Nazarite** /NAZ uh rīt/ Jesus.

44. ***gratis** without cost. US, UK /GRAHT iss/ [GRAT-], UK *rarely* [GRAYT-];
CN /GRAT-/ [GRAHT-].

45–141. **usance(s)** /YŌŌ zṇss, -zunss/ interest on money.

61. **albeit** /awl BEE (i)t/ although.

62. **excess** here should be /ek SESS/, the most common UK form.

71–8. **Laban('s)** /LAY bun(z)/, but sometimes newer [-banz] is used.

72, 160. **Abram** /AY brum/ Abraham.

78. **compremis'd** agreed. Variant of **compromised**, both /CŎM pruh mīzd/.

79. **eanlings** /EEN lingz/ newborn lambs.

79. **pied** /pīd/ 2 or more colors in splotches.

86. ***fulsome** lustful. /FỤLL sum/; US *rarely* [FŬL-].

88. **parti-color'd** /PAR tee-/ with splotches of different colors.

ă-bat, ăir-marry, air-pair, ạr-far, ĕr-merry, ĝ-get, ī-high, ĭr-mirror, ł-little, ṇ-listen,
ŏ-hot, oh-go, ōō-wood, ōō-moon, oor-tour, ōr-or, ow-how, ṭh-that, t̶h̶-thin, ṳ-but,
UR-fur, ur-under. ( )- suppress the syllable   [ ]- less common   see p. xi for complete list.

112. ***gaberdine** loose garment of coarse cloth. US /GAB ur deen/, *rarely* [gab ur DEEN]; UK /gab ur DEEN/ [GAB ur deen]; in CN both are used equally.

117. **rheum** /r$\overline{oo}$m/ spit.

Act 2 Scene 1

5. **Phoebus'** /FEE bus/ god of the sun.

21. **comer** /KUM ur/ visitor.

24. ***scimitar** US /SIM ih tar/ [-tur]; CN /-tar/; UK /-tur/ [-tar] a curved sword.

25. **Sophy** /SOH fee/ Shah of Persia.

26. **Solyman** Turkish ruler. /SŎL-, SŬL ih mun/ or /SŎL ee-, SŬL ee-/. Archaic variant of ***Suleiman** /S$\overline{OO}$ lay mahn, S$\overline{OO}$ lih mahn/. Sometimes also with final syllable stress.

32. **Lichas** US /LĪ kus/ [-kăss]; UK, CN /-kăss/ [-kus] Hercules' servant. Normal development would favor /-kus/.

35. **Alcides** /al SĪ deez/ Hercules.

Act 2 Scene 2

11. **Fia!** /FĪ uh/ Launce's version of **Via** /VĪ uh/ onward! /VEE uh/ is newer.

19–20. **bouge** /BUJ/, or possibly /b$\overline{oo}$j/. Archaic variant of **budge**.

32. **commandement**. Archaic variant of **commandment**, originally with 4 syllables, /-uh munt/, but in this prose passage the usual mod. 3-syllable pronunciation may be used.

45. **Be God's sonties** /SŎNT eez/ 'By God's saints' or 'sancitities.' Some eds. prefer **By** but the spelling *Be* indicates it was the unstressed form of *by* /buh, bih/.

57, 60. ***ergo** therefore. /UR go/ is older, /ĔR go/ is newer. The former is more common in the UK, the latter in the US, CN, but both forms appear in all countries.

68. ***hovel-post** post supporting a shed. US /HUV ł/, *rarely* [HŎV ł]; CN /HUV-/ [HŎV-]; UK /HŎV-/ [HUV-].

89, 91. **Margery** /MARJ ur ee/.

121. **Gramercy** /gruh MUR see/ thanks.

131. **cater-cousins** /KAY tur KUZ inz/ intimate friends.

186. **To allay** /twuh LAY/ relieve.

188. **misconst'red** /mis CŎN sturd/ misconstrued.

196. **ostent** here should be /ŏ STENT/ appearance.

197. ***grandam** /GRAN dam/; US *rarely* [-dum] grandmother. Informally /GRAN um/.

Act 2 Scene 3

11. **pagan** /PAYG un/ non-Christian.

16. ***heinous** /HAYN us/ hateful. /HEEN us/ is non-standard though common in the UK.

Act 2 Scene 4

22. **masque** US /măsk/; UK, E. NEW ENG. /mahsk/ [măsk] masked dancing and pantomime.

Act 2 Scene 5

3. **gurmandize** /GUR-, GOOR mun dīz/ to eat like a glutton. Archaic variant of **gormandize** /GOR-/.

23–8. **masque(s)** US /măsk/; UK, E. NEW ENG. /mahsk/ [măsk] masked dancing and pantomime.

43. **Jewess' eye.** Some eds. prefer **Jewĕs eye** 'Jew's eye' indicating an older genitive form /JŌŌ iz/.

44. **Hagar's** /HAY garz, -gurz/ Abraham's non-Jewish wife.

ă-bat, ăir-marry, air-pair, ȧr-far, ĕr-merry, ĝ-get, ī-high, ĭr-mirror, ł-little, ṇ-listen, ŏ-hot, oh-go, ōō-wood, ōō-moon, oor-tour, ōr-or, ow-how, ṭh-that, t̶h̶-thin, ŭ-but, UR-fur, ur-under. ( )- suppress the syllable   [ ]- less common   see p. xi for complete list.

Act 2 Scene 6

14. **younger.** Some eds. prefer **younker** /YŬNG kur/ young lord.

27. **Albeit** /awl BEE (i)t/ although.

47. **close night** /clohss/ secret night.

52. ***Beshrow me** /bih-, bee SHROH/ damn me. Archaic variant of **Beshrew** /-SHR͞OO/.

59, 64. **masque(-ing)** US /măsk/; UK, E. NEW ENG. /mahsk/ [măsk] masked dancing and pantomime.

Act 2 Scene 7

20. **dross** /drŏss/; US *also* /drawss/ impure matter, rubbish.

41. **The Hyrcanian** normally /HUR KAYN yun/ of Hyrcania (in the Caucausus). However, Shk did not pronounce the /h/ in this word, so *the* can be attached as /t̪hʸUR KAYN yun/.

51. **cerecloth** /SEER-/ shroud.

51. **obscure** here should be /ŎB skyoor/; US *also* [-skyur].

52. **immur'd** /ih MYOORD/ imprisoned.

65. **glisters** /GLIS turz/ glistens.

Act 2 Scene 8

8. **gondilo** Venetian boat. Archaic variant of **gondola**, both pronounced /GŎN duh luh/ (final *-o* could be /-uh/- or /-oh/).

44. **ostents** here should be /ŏ STENTS/ shows.

Act 2 Scene 9

6. ***nuptial** wedding. US, UK /NUP chł/ [-shł]; in CN both are used equally.

28. **martlet** /MART lit/ a bird, the martin.

61. **distinct** here 1st syllable stress is indicated.

68. ***iwis** /ih WISS/; US, CN *also* /ee WISS/ indeed.

78. ***wroth** anger. US /rawth/; CN /rawth/ [rohth]; UK /rŏth/ [rohth], *rarely* [rawth].

82. **heresy** /HĔR ih see/ dissent from the dominant thinking.

Act 3 Scene 1

1, 46. **Rialto** /ree AL toh/ is older, /ree AHL toh/ is newer based on Ital.

3. **lading** /LAYD ing/ cargo.

11. **prolixity** /proh LIK sih tee/ long-windedness.

42. **Rhenish** /REN ish/ Rhine wine.

44 ***bankrout** /BANK rowt/ [-rut] archaic variant of **bankrupt**.

48. **usurer** /YOO zhur ur/; UK *also* [-zhyoor ur, -zhoor ur] someone who lends money for interest.

79–108. **Genoa** /JEN oh uh/.

83. **diamond** in this prose passage may be either /DĪ uh mund/ or US *also* /DĪ mund/.

84. **Frankford** /FRANK furd/ archaic variant of **Frankfurt** /FRANK furt/.

100. **argosy** /ARG uh see/ large merchant ship.

113. ***divers** various. US, CN /DĪ vurss, -vurz/ [dī-, dih VURSS]; UK /DĪ vurss/ [-vurz, dī VURSS].

121. **turkis** (*Turkies* Q1, Q2, F1) /TUR kiss/ archaic variant of **turquoise** US /TUR kwoyz/ [-koyz]; UK /TUR kwoyz/ [-kwahz].

121. **Leah** /LEE uh/.

ă-bat, ăir-marry, air-pair, ạr-far, ĕr-merry, ĝ-get, ī-high, ĭr-mirror, ł-little, ṇ-listen, ŏ-hot, oh-go, ōō-wood, ōō-moon, oor-tour, ōr-or, ow-how, ṭh-that, ŧh-thin, ŭ-but, UR-fur, ur-under. ( )- suppress the syllable   [ ]- less common   see p. xi for complete list.

126. **fortnight** /FORT nīt/; US *also* [FORT nit] 2 weeks. Virtually obsolete in the US.

Act 3 Scene 2

14. ***Beshrow** /bih-, bee SHROH/ curse. Archaic variant of **beshrew** /-SHRŌŌ/.

22. ***peize, peise** weigh down. US /peez/, *sometimes* [payz]; UK /peez, payz/.
Dialect evidence shows that /ee/ was the form found in southern England, and /ay/ in the north. Some eds. prefer **piece** 'extend.'

23. ***eche** US /eech/ [etch]; UK /etch/ [eech]. Elsewhere it rhymes with *speech*.
Some eds. prefer **eke** /eek/. Both mean 'increase.'

51. **dulcet** /DULL sit/ sweet.

55. **Alcides** /al SĪ deez/ Hercules.

58. **Dardanian** /dar DAYN yun/ Trojan.

60. **th' exploit** here should be /th^y ek SPLOYT/.

93. **gambols** /GAM bɫz/ frolics.

96. **sepulchre** /SEP ɫ kur/ tomb.

111. **allay** /uh LAY/ diminish.

112. **excess** here should be /ek SESS/, the most common UK form.

115. ***demigod** half-god. /DEM ee gŏd, DEM ih-/; US *also* /-gawd/.

173. ***presage** here should be /pree-, prih SAYJ/ foretell.

243. ***shrowd** /shrohd/ harsh, wicked. Archaic variant of **shrewd**.

243. **contents** here should be /cŏn TENTS/.

269. **Barbary** /BAR buh ree/ region in North Africa.

280. **magnificoes** /mag NIF ih kohz/ important people.

285. **Chus** /kŭss, kōōss, chōōz, kōōz/ have all been suggested. Recommendation:
/kōōss/ or **Cush** /kŭsh/, in order to avoid a homonym with *cuss*.

302. **through** here should be 2 syllables /th^uh roo/. Some eds. prefer **thorough**, often used when the meter demands 2 syllables, pronounced as *thorough*.

Act 3 Scene 3

2. **gratis** at no cost. US, UK /GRAHT iss/ [GRAT-], UK *rarely* [GRAYT-]; CN /GRAT-/ [GRAHT-].

Act 3 Scene 4

13. **egall** /EE gł/ archaic variant of **equal**.

15. **lineaments** /LIN yuh munts/ distinctive features.

53. **traject** (*tranect* Q1,2, F1) /TRAJ ikt, -ekt/ ferry crossing.

63. **accoutered** /uh COOT urd/ clothed.

Act 3 Scene 5

16. **Scylla** /SILL uh/, restored Lat. [SKILL uh] a sea monster.

17. **Charybdis** /kuh RIB dis/ a whirlpool.

22. **enow** /ih NOW/; US *also* /ee-/ enough.

29. **jealious** (Q1) /JEL yus/ archaic variant of Q2's, F1's **jealous**.

39, 40. **Moor** /moor/ [mor] black woman.

Act 4 Scene 1

8. **obdurate** unmoveable. Here should be /ŏb-, ub DYOOR it/; US *also* /-DYUR-/ [-DUR-]. 1st syllable stress is more usual today.

25. **humane** here should be /HYOO mayn/; US *sometimes* [YOO mayn]. Some eds. prefer **human**.

ă-bat, ăir-marry, air-pair, ạr-far, ĕr-merry, ĝ-get, ī-high, ĭr-mirror, ł-little, ņ-listen,
ŏ-hot, oh-go, ŏŏ-wood, ōō-moon, oor-tour, ōr-or, ow-how, ţh-that, th-thin, Ʊ-but,
UR-fur, ur-under. ( )- suppress the syllable   [ ]- less common   see p. xi for complete list.

26. **moi'ty, moiety** /MOY tee/ portion.

29. **Enow** /ih NOW/; US *also* /ee-/ enough.

30. **commiseration** /kuh miz ur RAY shun/ pity.

32. **Tartars** /TAR turz/ fierce people of Central Asia.

36. **Sabaoth** (Q1) 'armies' commonly confused with Q2's, F1's **Sabbath**. In any case it should be pronounced with 2 syllables /SAB ~~uth~~/.

46. **ban'd** /baynd/ poisoned.

92. **abject** /AB jekt/ contemptible.

92. **slavish** /SLAY vish/ like a slave.

97. **viands** /VĪ undz/ food.   /VEE undz/ not recommended.

122. *****bankrout** /BANK rowt/ [-rut] archaic variant of **bankrupt**.

128. **inexecrable** (Q1, F1) /in EKS uh cruh bł/ something that cannot be cursed enough. Some eds. prefer F3's **inexorable** /in EK sur uh bł/; US *also* /-EG zur-/ unyielding.

131. *****Pythagoras** US /pih ~~TH~~AG uh rus/ [pī-]; UK /pī-/ Gk. philosopher.

160. *****importunity** /im por-, im pur TYO͞ON ih tee/; US *also* /-TO͞ON-/ asking insistently.

173. **throughly** archaic variant of *thoroughly*. /~~THR~~O͞O lee/ is the normal pronunciation on stage, but to enhance clarity a syncopated form of the modern pronunciation may be used: *thor'ghly*.

179. **impugn** /im PYO͞ON/ oppose.

220. *****precedent** /PRESS ih dunt/.

235. **tenure** archaic variant of **tenor**, both /TEN ur/.

296. **Barrabas** (F1) here should be /BĂIR uh bus/. The mod. form is **Barabbas** /buh RAB us/. Criminal at the time of Jesus' crucifixion.

298. **pursue** here with 1st syllable stress.

311, 332. **confiscate** /CŎN fiss kayt, -ut/ confiscated.

379. ***gratis** at no cost. US, UK /GRAHT iss/ [GRAT-], UK *rarely* [GRAYT-]; CN /GRAT-/ [GRAHT-].

410 ***lieu** US, CN /lo͞o, lyo͞o/; UK /lyo͞o/ [lo͞o] return.

444. **'scuse** /skyo͞oss/ excuse.

451. **commandement, commandment** here an archaic form in 4 syllables is indicated /-uh munt/.

Act 5 Scene 1

7. **Thisby, Thisbe** /~~TH~~IZ bee/ she secretly met with her lover, Pyramus.

10. **Dido** /DĪ doh/ Queen of Carthage.

11. ***waft** beckoned. US, CN /wŏft/; SOUTH. US /wăft/; UK /wŏft/ [wăft, wahft]. /wăft/ is newer and considered non-standard by many.

12. **Carthage** /CAR thij/ ancient city in N. Africa.

13. **Medea** /mih DEE uh/ enchantress who helped Jason.

14. **Aeson** Jason's father. /EE sun, -sn̩/, but /-ŏn/ is becoming more common. /-un/ would be the historically correct form (cf. *canon, poison*).

16. **unthrift** here should be /UN ~~thr~~ift/ wasteful.

21. ***shrow** /shroh/ archaic variant of **shrew** which here should rhyme with *so*.

39–44. **Sola!** /soh LAH/ a call to attract attention.

43. **hollowing** /HŎL uh wing/, /huh LOH ing/ calling. Variant of **hollering** which some eds. prefer.

59. **patens** /PAT n̩z, -inz/ plates, i.e., the stars.

62. **quiring** archaic variant of **choiring**, both pronounced /KWĪR ing/.

62. ***cherubins** angels. US, CN /CHĔR uh binz/ [-yuh-]; UK uses both equally. /KĔR-/ not recommended.

ă-bat, ăir-marry, air-pair, ąr-far, ĕr-merry, ĝ-get, ī-high, ĭr-mirror, ł-little, n̩-listen, ŏ-hot, oh-go, o͞o-wood, o͞o-moon, oor-tour, ōr-or, ow-how, ţh-that, ~~th~~-thin, ŭ-but, UR-fur, ur-under. ( )- suppress the syllable   [ ]- less common   see p. xi for complete list.

64. **vesture** /VES chur/ covering.

80. ***Orpheus** here should be 2 syllables /OR fyus/ [-fyo͞oss].   The former is the traditional pronunciation /OR fee us/, here compressed to 2 syllables; the latter is a restored pronunciation.

85. **stratagems** /STRAT uh jumz/ schemes.

87. **Erebus** /ĔR ih bus/ hell.

109. **Endymion** /en DIM ee un/ a shepherd loved by the moon. Sometimes newer /-ŏn/ is used, but it is not recommended.

127. **Antipodes** /an TIP uh deez/ the opposite side of the world.

147. **paltry** /PAWL tree/ worthless.

175. **too unkind** here should be /twun KĪND/.

230. **Argus** /A̧RG us/ 100-eyed monster of Gk. mythology.

254. ***surety** guarantee, bail. Here should be 2 syllables, though in mod. Eng. 3 syllables are more common US /SHUR (ih) tee, SHOOR-/; CN /SHUR-/ [SHOOR-]; UK /SHOR-/ [SHUR-] [SHOOR-].

262. **In *lieu of** US, CN /lo͞o, lyo͞o/; UK /lyo͞o/ [lo͞o] in return for.

276. **argosies** /A̧RG uh seez/ large merchant ships.

298, 300. **inter'gatories, -y** /in TUR guh tree(z)/ questions under oath.

A Midsummer Night's Dream

People in the Play

Demetrius 3 or 4 syllables depending on meter /dih MEE tr(ee) yus/.

Egeus /ee-, ih JEE yus/.

Helena /HELL in uh/.

Hermia 2 or 3 syllables depending on meter /HUR m(ee) yuh/.

Hippolyta /hih PŎL ih tuh/.

Lysander /lī SAN dur/.

*Oberon /OH bur un/, /-ŏn/. The former is preferred in the UK, and the latter in the US. /-un/ would be the traditional form (cf. *Solomon*).

Philostrate /FILL uh strayt/.

Pyramus /PĬR uh mus/. In the play performed by Quince and company.

*Theseus 2 or 3 syllables depending on meter /~~TH~~EE s(ee) yus/ [-syōōss],
US *rarely* [-sōōss]. The traditional pronunciation is /~~TH~~EE s(ee) yus/, the restored
pronunciation is /-s(y)ōōss/.

Thisby, Thisbe /~~TH~~IZ bee/. In the play performed by Quince and company.

*Titania 3 or 4 syllables depending on meter. Virtually all combinations of
/tī-, tih-, -TAN-, -TAYN-, -TAHN-/ are found in all countries. The most common
variants are US /tih TAHN (ee) yuh, tī TAYN-/; CN /tih TAN (ee) yuh/;
UK /tih TAHN (ee) yuh/. On historical principles the best choices are
/tih-, tī TAYN ee yuh/.

Places in the Play

Athens /A~~TH~~ inz/.
  Athenian /uh ~~TH~~EEN (ee) yun/. In verse it is always 3 syllables.

ă-bat, ăir-**marry**, air-**pair**, a̧r-**far**, ĕr-**merry**, ĝ-**get**, ī-**high**, ĭr-**mirror**, ł-**little**, ņ-**listen**,
ŏ-**hot**, oh-**go**, ōō-**wood**, ōō-**moon**, oor-**tour**, ōr-**or**, ow-**how**, ţh-**that**, ŧh-**thin**, ŭ-**but**,
UR-**fur**, ur-**under**. ( )- suppress the syllable   [ ]- less common   see p. xi for complete list.

Act 1 Scene 1

1, 125. ***nuptial** wedding. US, UK /NUP chł/ [-shł]; in CN both are used equally.

---

5. **dowager** /DOW uh jur/ widow.

6. **revenue** sometimes in verse /ruh VEN yōō/, but here as in mod. Eng.
US /REV in ōō/; UK, SOUTH. US /-yōō/.

33. **gawds, gauds** /gawdz/ trinkets, toys.

65. **abjure** /ab-, ub JOOR/; US *also* /-JUR/ renounce.

71, 90. **aye** /ay/ ever.   /ī/ is often used, but not recommended.

---

71. **mew'd** /myōōd/ caged.

73. **Chaunting** archaic variant of **chanting** US /CHĂNT ing/;
E. NEW ENG, UK /CHAHNT ing/.   The archaic vowel was pronounced /-AW-/,
and gave rise to RP /-AH-/.

80. **patent** US /PAT ņt/; UK /PAYT ņt/ [PAT-] privilege.

106. **avouch** /uh VOWCH/ affirm.

107. **Nedar's** /NEE durz/.

137. **misgraffed** mismatched. US /mis GRĂF id/;
E. NEW ENG., UK /mis GRAHF id/ archaic variant of **misgrafted.**

143. **momentany** (Q1) /MOH men tay nee, -tuh nee/ archaic variant of
momentary (F1).

145. **collied** /CŎL eed/ darkened.

151. **edict** decree.   Here should be /ee DIKT/.

157. **dowager** /DOW uh jur/ widow.

158. **revenue** here should be /ruh VEN yōō/.

173. **Carthage queen** /CAR thij/ Dido, ruler of Carthage in N. Africa.

183. **lodestars** /LOHD starz/ guiding stars.

191. **translated** here should be stressed on the 2nd syllable, the normal
UK pronunciation. US /trănss LAYT id, trănz-/;
UK /trănss-/ [trănz-, trahnz-, trahnss-, trunss-, trunz-].

209. **Phoebe** /FEE bee/ the moon.

212. **flights**. Some eds. prefer **sleights** /slīts/ tricks.

223. **midnight** here with 2nd syllable stress.

242. **eyne** /īn/ dialect form of *eyes*.

Act 1 Scene 2

11. ***lamentable** US /luh MEN tuh bł/ [LAM un tuh bł]; CN, UK /LAM un tuh bł/
[luh MEN-].

27. **condole** /cun DOHL/ grieve.

29, 40. **Ercles', 'erk'les** /URK leez/ archaic variant of **Hercules'**.

35. **Phibbus'** /FIB us/ Bottom's pronunciation of **Phoebus'** /FEE bus/ the sun.

41. **condoling** /cun DOHL ing/ pathetic.

52. **Thisne** /T̶H̶I̶Z̶ nee/ Bottom's mistake for **Thisbe** /T̶H̶I̶Z̶ bee/.

68. **extempore** /ek STEM pur ree/ composed on the spur of the moment.

96, 109. **perfit** /PUR fit/ archaic variant of **perfect**. Also /PAR fit/ in Shk's time.

Act 2 Scene 1

3, 5. **Thorough** archaic variant of *through*, used when the meter demands 2
syllables. It is often pronounced as *thorough* on stage, but using /-o͞o/ in the final
syllable will bring it closer to mod. *through*.

7. **moon's, moonës** here the older genitive /MO͞ON iz/ is indicated.

10, 15. **cowslips** /COW slips/ a yellow flower.

ă-bat, ăir-marry, air-pair, ạr-far, ĕr-merry, ĝ-get, ī-high, ĭr-mirror, ł-little, ṇ-listen,
ŏ-hot, oh-go, o͝o-wood, o͞o-moon, oor-tour, ōr-or, ow-how, ţh-that, t̶h̶-thin, ŭ-but,
UR-fur, ur-under. ( )- suppress the syllable   [ ]- less common   see p. xi for complete list.

13. **savors** (UK **savours**) /SAY vurz/ smells, perfumes.

20. **wrath.** Some eds. prefer ***wroth** US /rawth/; CN /rawth/ [rohth]; UK /rŏth/ [rohth], *rarely* [rawth]. Both mean 'angry' here.

23. **changeling** here /CHAYNJ uh ling/ is indicated.

36. **quern** /kwurn/ a type of primitive grinder.

37. ***huswife** /HUZ if/ is traditional, /HUSS wīf/ is a newer, spelling pronunciation. The former is the most common form in the UK, the latter in the US. In CN both are used equally. In North America /HUSS wif/ is also sometimes used. Some eds. prefer mod. **housewife.**

50. **dewlop** US /DŌŌ lŏp/, UK /DYŌŌ-/ archaic variant of **dewlap** /-lap/ loose skin of the throat.

55. **quire** /kwīr/ archaic variant of **choir.**

55. **loff** /lŏf/ archaic variant of **laugh.**

66. **Corin** US /COR in/; E. COAST US, UK /CŎR in/ a shepherd.

68. **Phillida** /FILL ih duh/ a shepherdess.

71. **buskin'd** /BUSK ind/ wearing knee-length boots.

78. **Perigenia** (Q1), **Peregenia** (F1) /pĕr ih JEEN yuh/. Some eds. substitute ***Perigouna** /pĕr ih GŌŌ nuh/ [-GOW-].

79. **Aegles** /EEG leez/. Some eds. substitute **Aegle** /EEG lee/, the correct form in Greek.

80. **Ariadne** /air ee AD nee/, E. COAST US *also* /ăir-/. /ăir ee AHD nee/ is a newer, partially restored Gk. pronunciation.

80. **Antiopa** /an TĪ oh puh, -uh puh/.

83. **mead** /meed/ meadow.

85. **margent** /MAR junt/ archaic variant of **margin.**

97. **murrion flock** flock dead of plague. Archaic spelling which may have had the ending /-yun/ or /-un/, but in any case was a variant of **murrain** US, CN /MUR in/; E. COAST US, UK /MUH rin/.

105. **rheumatic diseases** here should be /RŌŌM uh tik/ referring to colds, co
etc.

106. **thorough** archaic variant of *through*, used when the meter demands 2
syllables. It is often pronounced as *thorough* on stage, but using /-ōō/ in the final
syllable will bring it closer to mod. *through*.

109. **Hiems'** winter's. Ang.Lat. /HĪ umz/; Class.Lat. /HIH emss/.

110. **chaplet** /CHAP lit/ garland.

112. **childing** /CHĪLD ing/ fruitful.

114. **By their increase** here should be /in CREESS/ by what they produce.

115. **progeny** children. /PRŎJ ih nee/; UK *also* [PROH-], a newer form.

123, 163. **vot'ress** /VOHT riss/ female member of a religious group.

151. **dulcet** /DULL sit/ sweet.

174. **leviathan** /luh VĪ uh ~~th~~un/ sea monster.

192. **wode within this wood.** *Wode* is a variant of **wood** /wŏŏd/ 'furious, mad'
which some eds. prefer. It was also /wōōd, wohd/ in the dialects of northern England, and there may be a pun on *wooed within this wood.*

195. **adamant** /AD uh munt/ double meaning: magnet, the hardest substance.
/-ant/ not recommended.

231. **Daphne** /DAFF nee/ nymph changed to a laurel tree.

232. **hind** /hīnd/ doe.

249. **I know a bank where the wild *thyme* blows.** Normally /tīm/, but here perhaps
scanned as 2 syllables, /TAH eem/. Alternatively, *where* may be scanned as 2 syllables in an inverted foot.

251. **woodbine** here 2nd syllable stress is indicated.

252. ***eglantine** sweet-briar. Here should be /EGG lun tīn/ for the rhyme, though
/-teen/ is the most common form in the US and is also used in the UK.

ă-bat, ăir-marry, air-**pair**, ạr-far, ĕr-**merry**, ĝ-get, ī-high, ĭr-mirror, ł-little, ṇ-listen,
ŏ-hot, oh-go, ōō-**wood**, ōō-**moon**, oor-**tour**, ōr-**or**, ow-how, ţh-that, ~~th~~-thin, ŭ-but,
UR-**fur**, ur-under. ( )- suppress the syllable   [ ]- less common   see p. xi for complete list.

...OWN dł/ circle dance.

4. **rere-mice** /REER-/ bats.

13, 24. **Philomele** /FILL uh meel, -oh-/ the nightingale. Variant of **Philomel** /-mel/.

30. **ounce** /ownss/ lynx.

57. **humane** courteous. Here should be /HY$\overline{OO}$ mayn/; US *sometimes* [Y$\overline{OO}$ mayn].

99. **sphery** /SFEER ee/ like a sphere.

99. **eyne** /īn/ dialect form of *eyes*.

139–41. **heresies (-sy)** /HĔR ih seez/ dissent from the dominant thinking.

149. **eat** /et/ dialect variant of **ate** which is also commonly /et/ in the UK.

150. **sate** archaic variant of **sat**. May have been /sayt/ or /sat/.

Act 3 Scene 1

2. **marvail's** (*maruailes* Q1; *maruailous* Q2, F1) archaic forms of **marvellous** marvellously. Short forms are /MARV łss/ or /MARV luss/, but in this prose section mod. /MARV ł us/ can be used.

13. **By'r lakin** /bīr-, bur LAY kin/ by Our Lady (i.e., Mary).

13. **parlous** /PAR lus/ archaic variant of **perilous** which here would have to be /PĔR (ih) lus/.

79. **toward** /TOH wurd, -urd/ about to take place.

82, 84. **savors** (UK **savours**) /SAY vurz/ smells.

95. **juvenal** /J$\overline{OO}$ vin ł/ youth. Some eds. substitute **juvenile** US /J$\overline{OO}$ vin ł, -īl/; UK /-īl/.

95. **eke** /eek/ also.

98. **Ninus'** /NĪ nus/ founder of Ninevah. Given the pun with *ninny*, Quince and company probably pronounce it /NIN us/.

125. **woosel** /WŌŌZ ł/ blackbird. Variant of **ouzel, ousel** both pronounced /ŌŌZ ł/.

127. **throstle** /~~THR~~ŎSS ł/ thrush.

161. **aery** /AIR ee/ of the air. Some eds. prefer **airy**, pronounced the same way.

165. **gambol** /GAM bł/ frolic.

166. **apricocks** /AYP rih cŏcks/; US, CN *also* /AP-/ dialect variant of **apricots**.

168. **humble-bees** pronounced with the same stress as *bumble bees*.

169. **night-tapers** /TAY purz/ slender candles.

187. **Peascod** /PEEZ cŏd/ peapod.

Act 3 Scene 2

7. **close** /clohss/ hidden.

12. ***nuptial** wedding. US, UK /NUP chł/ [-shł]; in CN both are used equally.

21. **russet-pated** /RŬSS it PAY tid/ red-headed.

21. **choughs, chuffs** /chufs/ jackdaws.

32. **translated** transformed. Here should be stressed on the 2nd syllable, the normal UK pronunciation. US /trănss LAYT id, trănz-/; UK /trănss-/ [trănz-, trahnz-, trahnss-, trunss-, trunz-].

41. **Stand close** /clohss/ keep hidden.

55. **th'Antipodes** /ţhʸan TIP uh deez/ the opposite side of the world.

74. **mispris'd** here should be /MIS prīzd/ mistaken.

85. ***bankrout** /BANK rowt/ [-rut] archaic variant of **bankrupt.**

ă-bat, ăir-marry, air-pair, ar-far, ĕr-merry, ĝ-get, ī-high, ĭr-mirror, ł-little, ṇ-listen, ŏ-hot, oh-go, ōō-wood, ōō-moon, oor-tour, ōr-or, ow-how, ţh-that, ŧh-thin, ŭ-but, UR-fur, ur-under. ( )- suppress the syllable   [ ]- less common   see p. xi for complete list.

90. **misprision** /mis PRIZH un, -ŋ/ mistake.

101. **Tartar's** /TAR turz/ people of Central Asia.

105. **espy** /ess SPĪ/ see.

137. **perfect** here may be given its normal pronunciation in an inverted foot /PUR fikt/.

138. **eyne** /īn/ dialect form of *eyes*.

141. **Taurus'** /TOR us/ mountain range in Turkey.

157. **exploit** here should be /ek SPLOYT/.

171. ***sojourn'd** resided temporarily. Here stress should fall on the 2nd syllable. US, CN /soh JURND/; US *rarely* [sŏ-]; UK /sŏ JURND/ [soh-], *rarely* [suh-].

175 (Q1), 335. **aby** /uh BĪ/ to pay for an offence. F1 has *abide*.

187. **engilds** /en ĜILDZ/ covers with gold.

188. **oes** variant spelling of **ohs, O's**.

208. **incorporate** /in COR pur rut, -rayt/ united in body. /-ut / is more usual for an adj.

234. **miserable** here should be /MIZ ur uh bł/.

237. **persever** /pur SEV ur/ persevere.

257. **Ethiop** /EETH yŏp/ Ethiopian.

263. **Tartar** /TAR tur/ member of a Central Asian tribe.

291. **statures** /STATCH urz/ sizes.

329. **minimus** /MIN ih mus/ small creature.

357. **Acheron** /AK ur ŏn, -un/ a river in Hades. /-ŏn/ is usual in the US and is increasingly common in the UK. /-un/ would be the traditional form (cf. *Solomon*).

380. **Aurora's** /uh ROR uz/, UK *also* [aw-] goddess of dawn.

380. **harbinger** /HAR bin jur/ advance messenger.

387. **aye** /ay/ ever. /ī/ is often used, but not recommended.

387. **consort** /cun SORT/ keep company.

409. **recreant** /REK r(ee) yunt/ coward.

433. **daylight** here with 2nd syllable stress.

Act 4 Scene 1

8–24. **Mounsieur** /mown SEER, MOWN seer/ lower-class variant of **Monsieur**.

---

12. **humble-bee** pronounced with the same stress as *bumble bee*.

19. **neaf** /neef/ fist.

23. **Cavalery, Cavaliery** /kav uh LEER ee/ cavalier, form of address to a fashionable gentleman.

24. **marvail's** (*Maruailes* Q1) archaic forms of F1's **marvellous** marvellously. Short forms are /MARV łss/ or /MARV luss/, but in this prose section mod. /MARV ł us/ can be used.

31. **provender** /PRŎV n̩ dur/ dry food for animals.

47. **dotage** /DOHT ij/ blind love for someone.

52. **coronet** small crown. US /COR uh net, -nit/, /cor uh NET/; E. COAST US /CŎR-, cŏr-/; UK /CŎR uh nit/ [-net, cŏr uh NET].

55. **flouriets'** may have been /FLOWR yits/, but *iet* could also be pronounced /-it/ in Shk's day, making it the same as **flow'rets'** /FLOWR its/ (cf. *Daniel, Dan'el*).

96. **night's** (Q1), **nightës** here the older genitive /NĪT iz/ is indicated. F1 has **the night's**.

105. ***vaward** US /VAW wurd, VAY-/ [VOW-]; UK /VAW wurd/ [VAY-, VOW-,VAW WURD]. The vowel of *war* not recommended in the 2nd syllable. Archaic variant of **vanguard**.

122. **Thessalian** /th̶huh SAYL yun/ from Thessaly, a region in Greece.

ă-bat, ăir-marry, air-pair, a̩r-far, ĕr-merry, ĝ-get, ī-high, ĭr-mirror, ł-little, n̩-listen, ŏ-hot, oh-go, o͞o-wood, o͞o-moon, oor-tour, ōr-or, ow-how, t̩h-that, t̶h-thin, ŭ-but, UR-fur, ur-under. ( )- suppress the syllable [ ]- less common   see p. xi for complete list.

125. **hollow'd, holla'd, holloed** /HŎL ud, -ohd/ given a hunting cry.

126. **Thessaly** /~~THESS~~ uh lee/ region in Greece.

130. **Nedar's** /NEE durz/.

167. **gaud** /gawd/ trinket, toy.

172. **betrothed** /bih-, bee TROHŢH id/ engaged to be married.

202. ***Heigh-ho!*** US /hay ho, hī-/; CN /hī-/, *rarely* [hay-]; UK /hay-/. Shk intended /hay/. Spoken with evenly stressed syllables or as if sighing, with 1st syllable stress.

215. **ballet** /BAL ut/ archaic variant of **ballad.**

218. ***Peradventure*** perhaps. /PUR ad VEN chur/;
US *rarely* [PĔR-, PUR ad ven chur];
UK, CN *also* [PUR-, PĔR ad ven chur, pĕr ad VEN chur].

Act 4 Scene 2

12, 13. ***paramour*** US, CN /PĂIR uh moor/ [-mor]; UK /-mor/ [-moor] lover.

13. ***paragon*** US /PĂIR uh gŏn/ [-gun]; CN /-gŏn/; UK /-gun/ [-gṇ] most perfect example.

20–23. **sixpence** /SIKS punss, -pṇss/; US *also* /SIKS penss/.

36. **ribands** /RIB undz/ archaic variant of **ribbons.**

Act 5 Scene 1

8. **compact** /cum-, cŏm PACT/ composed of.

16. **aery, airy** /AIR ee/ of the air.

32, 39. **masque(s)** US /măsk/; UK, E. NEW ENG. /mahsk/ [măsk] masked dancing and pantomime.

44. **Centaurs** /SEN torz/.

45. **eunuch** /Y$\overline{OO}$ nuk/ castrated man.

48. ***Bacchanals** orgiasitic followers of Bacchus. US /bahk uh NAHLZ/
[back uh NALZ, BACK uh nlz]; UK /BACK uh nalz/ [back uh NALZ,
bahk uh NAHLZ]. The /ah/ vowel is newer.

49. **Thracian singer** /T̶H̶RAY shun/ Orpheus.

51. **Thebes** /t̶heebz/ city in Greece.

55. ***nuptial** wedding. Here should be 2 syllables US, UK /NUP chł/ [-shł]; in CN
both are used equally.

75. ***nuptial** wedding. Here should be 3 syllables. Shk probably intended
/NUP shee ł/, but today /NUP chuh wł, NUP shuh wł/ are common, though
considered non-standard in the UK.

130. **certain** here should be /sur TAYN/ to rhyme with *plain*, however final syllable
stress was not usual for this word in Shk's time.

138. **Ninus'** /NĪ nus/ founder of Ninevah. Given the pun with *ninny* at 3.1.98 they
probably pronounce it /NIN us/.

177. **eyne** /īn/ dialect form of *eyes*.

196. **Limander, Lemander** /lee MAN dur/ mistake for *Leander* /lee AN dur/.

198–9. **Shafalus, Shaphalus** /SHAF uh lus/ mistake for *Cephalus* /SEF uh lus/.

198–9. **Procrus** /PROHK rus, PRŎCK-/ mistake for *Procris* /PROH cris/.

239–60. **lanthorn** archaic variant of **lantern**. Probably pronounced /LAN turn/, but
possibly /LANT horn/ or /LAN t̶hurn, -t̶horn/.

323. ***videlicet** namely (abbreviated *viz.*). The older, angl. pronunciations are
US /vih DELL ih sit/ [-DEEL-, vī-]; UK /vih DEEL ih sit/ [vī-, -DELL-]. Newer pronunciations mix in restored Latin syllables, for example, /-ket/ or /-DAYL-/. These
are not recommended.

332. **cowslip** /COW slip/ a yellow flower.

353–61. **Bergomask, bergamask** US /BUR guh măsk/; UK, E. NEW ENG. /-mahsk/
[-măsk] country dance.

ă-bat, ăir-**marry**, air-**pair**, ạr-**far**, ĕr-**merry**, ĝ-**get**, ī-**high**, ĭr-**mirror**, ł-**little**, ṇ-**listen**,
ŏ-**hot**, oh-**go**, o͞o-**wood**, o͞o-**moon**, oor-**tour**, ŏr-**or**, ow-**how**, t̪h-**that**, t̶h-**thin**, ŭ-**but**,
UR-**fur**, ur-**under**.   ( )- suppress the syllable   [ ]- less common   see p. xi for complete list.

369. **fortnight** /FORT nīt/; US *also* [FORT nit] 2 weeks. Virtually obsolete in the US.

384. **Hecat's, Hecate's** /HEK uts/ goddess of witchcraft. /HEK uh tee/ is the usual non-Shakespearean pronunciation.

Much Ado About Nothing

People in the Play

Sometimes some of these names can be given an Italian pronunciation in performance. These pronunciations are indicated here as accurately as possible within the
limits of this notation. Shakespeare, however, probably intended them to be
anglicized.

Antonio /an TOHN ee yoh/; Ital. /ahn-/. Occurs only once, in prose.
  Anthony US /AN ~~thuh~~ nee/; UK /AN tuh nee/ [-~~thuh~~ nee].

***Balthasar** by far the most common pronunciation is /BAL thuh zar/. It is rarely
/bal ~~thuh~~ ZAR/ which will also fit the verse, but another rare pronunciation
/bal ~~THAZ~~ ur/ will not.

Beatrice 2 or 3 syllables depending on meter /BEE (uh) triss/.

Benedick /BEN ih dick/.

***Borachio** US /bor AH chee yoh/ [bor AH kee oh]. In CN, UK the latter is rarely
used. Shk. intended /ch/.

Claudio 2 or 3 syllables depending on meter /CLAW d(ee) yoh/.

Conrade, Conrad both pronounced /CŎN rad/.

Leonato /lee uh-, lee oh NAH toh/.

Margaret /MAR guh rit/ or /MAR grit/ depending on meter.

Don Pedro /dŏn PAY droh, PED-/. In the US the former is more common, in the
UK the latter. /PEED-/ is an older, angl. form, now rare.

Seacole /SEE kohl/ one of the watch in 3.3, 3.5. Some eds. prefer **Seacoal**, pronounced the same way. This was the older name for what we now call simply *coal*.

Ursula US /UR suh luh/; UK /UR syoo luh, -syuh luh/. 3 syllables in verse, but in 1
instance may be 2 or 3. Occurs once as **Ursley** /URS lee/.

Verges /VUR jiss, VUR jeez/. Like *Jaques* the former is recommended by historians, but the latter is often used today (See AYL "People in the Play").

ă-bat, ăir-**marry**, air-**pair**, ạr-**far**, ĕr-**merry**, ĝ-get, ī-high, ĭr-**mirror**, ł-little, ṇ-listen,
ŏ-hot, oh-go, ōō-**wood**, ōō-**moon**, oor-**tour**, ōr-**or**, ow-**how**, ţh-**that**, ₮ħ-**thin**, ŭ-but,
UR-**fur**, ur-under. ( )- suppress the syllable   [ ]- less common   see p. xi for complete list.

Places in the Play

Messina /muh SEE nuh/.

Act 1 Scene 1

2. ***Arragon, Aragon** US /ĂIR uh gŏn/, *rarely* [-gun]; UK /-gŏn/ [-gun].
Sp. /ah rah GOHN/ region of Spain. /-un/ would be the traditional form
(cf. *Solomon*).

11. ***Florentine** US /FLŌR in teen/ [-tīn]; E. COAST US /FLŎR-/;
UK /FLŎR in tīn/ [-teen].

30. **Mountanto** /mown TAN toh, -TAHN-/. Some eds. prefer **Montanto** /mŏn-/
a sarcastic comment based on the word for an upward thrust in fencing.

36. ***Padua** /PAD y(oo) wuh/ [PAJ (oo) wuh/. An Ital. vowel /PAHD-/ is not
recommended, since the Ital. form is *Padova*.

50. **victual** /VIT ł/ food.

50. **holp** /hohlp/ helped.

134. **predestinate** /pree-, prih DESS tih nayt, -nut/ inevitable. /-ut/ would be more
usual for an adj.

234. **heretic** /HĔR ih tik/ dissenter.

240. **rechate** /rih-, ree CHAYT/ notes on a horn to call hounds. Variant of **recheat**
/rih-, ree CHEET/.

241. **winded** /WIN did/ blown.

242. **baldrick** /BAWL drik/ shoulder strap for a horn.

253. ***brothel-house** whorehouse. US, CN /BRŎ͞TH ł/ [BRŎ͞TH ł, BRAW͞TH ł];
UK /BRŎ͞TH ł/.

280. **embassage** /EM buh sij/ ambassador's message.

287. **basted** /BAY stid/ loosely stitched.

315. ***salv'd** softened. US /salvd/ [savd]; E. NEW ENG. [sahvd];
CN /salvd/ [sahlvd, savd, sahvd]; UK /salvd/. Normal development would favor
the *l*-less form (cf. *halve, calve*).

315. **treatise** narrative. US /TREET iss/, *rarely* [-iz]; CN /-iss/; UK both /s/ and /z/
forms used equally.

Act 1 Scene 2

23. **peradventure** perhaps. /PUR ad VEN chur/;
US *rarely* [PĔR-, PUR ad ven chur];
UK, CN *also* [PUR-, PĔR ad ven chur, pĕr ad VEN chur].

Act 1 Scene 3

47. **betroths** /bih-, bee TROHṬHZ/ engages to be married.

61. **arras** /ĂIR us/ tapestry.

Act 2 Scene 1

40. **sixpence** /SIKS punss, -pṇss/; US *also* /SIKS penss/.

40. **berrord** bear keeper. Archaic variant of **bearward** or **bearherd**. All were
pronounced /BAIR urd/, but recent, spelling pronunciations /BAIR wârd/ (as in *war*),
/-hurd/ are also used today.

74, 79. **cinquepace** /SINK uh payss/, /SINK payss/ lively dance.

77. **ancientry** /AYN shun tree, -chun-/ ancient tradition.

96. **Philemon's** /fih LEE munz/ [fĭ-] he entertained Jupiter in his cottage.
Sometimes newer /-ŏn/ is used. /-un/ would be the traditional form (cf. *Simon*).

139. **libertines** /LIB ur teenz/, *rarely* [-tīnz] people who act without moral restraint.

147. **peradventure** perhaps. /PUR ad VEN chur/;
US *rarely* [PĔR-, PUR ad ven chur];
UK, CN *also* [PUR-, PĔR ad ven chur, pĕr ad VEN chur].

189. **usurer's** /YO͞O zhur urz; UK *also* [-zhyoor urz, -zhoor urz] someone who lends
money for interest.

ă-bat, ăir-**marry**, air-**pair**, ạr-**far**, ĕr-**merry**, ĝ-**get**, ī-**high**, ĭr-**mirror**, ł-**little**, ṇ-**listen**,
ŏ-**hot**, oh-**go**, o͞o-**wood**, o͞o-**moon**, oor-**tour**, ŏr-**or**, ow-**how**, ṭh-**that**, t̶h̶-**thin**, ŭ-**but**,
UR-**fur**, ur-**under**. ( )- suppress the syllable   [ ]- less common   see p. xi for complete list.

194. **drovier** /DROHV ee ur/ archaic variant of **drover** livestock dealer. *-ier* could also be /-ur/ in Shk's day.

195. **bullocks** /BULL uks/ bulls or oxen. /-ŏks/ not recommended.

247. **poniards** /PŎN yurdz/; UK *also newer* [-yardz] daggers.

256. ***Ate** goddess of discord. /AYT ee/ is the older, angl. form; /AHT ay/ is the newer, restored form and much more common; /AHT ee/ is a mixed form, heard occasionally.

264. **arrand** /ĂIR und/ archaic variant of **errand**.

265. **Antipodes** /an TIP uh deez/ the opposite side of the world.

269. **Cham's** /kamz/ ruler of China. Archaic variant of **Khan's** /kahnz/.

269. **embassage** /EM buh sij/ ambassador's message.

306. **heralt** /HĔR ɫt/ archaic variant of **herald**.

320. ***Heigh-ho!** US /hay ho, hī-/; CN /hī-/, *rarely* [hay-]; UK /hay-/. Shk intended /hay/. Spoken with evenly stressed syllables or as if sighing, with 1st syllable stress.

Act 2 Scene 2

5. **med'cinable** medicinal. Elsewhere in Shk's verse /MED sin uh bɫ/. Some eds. prefer **medicinable** which in this prose passage may be /muh DISS nuh bɫ/.

9. ***covertly** secretly. US /koh VURT lee/ [KOH vurt lee, KUV urt lee], *rarely* [kuh VURT lee]; CN /koh VURT lee/ [KOH vurt lee]; UK / koh VURT lee/ [KUV urt lee, KOH vurt lee, kuh VURT lee], *rarely* [KŎV urt lee].

Act 2 Scene 3

14. **tabor** /TAY bur/ small drum. /-bor/ not recommended.

20. **ortography** /or TŎG ruh fee/ correct spelling. Archaic variant of **orthography** /or T̶H̶ŎG-/. Probably an error for *orthographer* /or T̶H̶ŎG ruh fur/ someone who is a stickler for the correct use of words.

42. **with a pennyworth, penn'worth** with more than he bargained form. Both pronounced /PEN ur̶t̶h̶/.

73. **leavy** /LEEV ee/ archaic variant of **leafy**. Here supposed to rhyme with **heavy**. In Shk's time the rhyme could have been /LEE vee : HEE vee/ or /LEV ee : HEV ee/.

82. **as live** as soon. May have been /liv/ in Shk's time. Variant of **as lief** /leef/. In the US **lieve** /leev/ is still found in some dialects and can also be used here.

140. **halfpence** /HAYP ṇss, -unss/ here 'small bits.'

158.***alms** good deed. /ahmz/ is older; /ahlmz, awlmz/ are newer. In the UK the latter are non-standard.

168, 216. **dotage** /DOHT ij/ love-sickness.

169. **daff'd** /dăft/ discarded. Archaic variant of **doffed** /dŏft/; US *also* /dawft/.

189. **Hector** /HEK tur/ Trojan hero. /-tor/ not recommended.

218. **dumb show** /DUM shoh/ pantomime.

Act 3 Scene 1

36. **haggards** /HAG urdz/ wild hawks.

38. **new-trothed** /-TROH ţhid/ newly engaged.

42. **wrastle** /RĂSS ł/ archaic variant of **wrestle**.

52. **Misprising, Misprizing** /mis PRĪZ ing/ undervaluing.

65. **agot** a type of jewel. Archaic variant of **agate**, both pronounced /AG ut/.

71. **Sure, sure, such carping is not commendable** here, as elsewhere in Shk, /CŎM en duh bł/. However, if *is* is contracted (*carping's*) then the mod. form /cuh MEN duh bł/ can be used.

73. **As Beatrice is, cannot be commendable.** *Beatrice* should be 2 syllables with /CŎM en duh bł/ in a regular line, or mod. /cuh MEN duh bł/ in a broken-backed line.

104. **limed** here should be 1 syllable /līmd/ caught in a trap made of lime paste.

ă-bat, ăir-marry, air-pair, ąr-far, ĕr-merry, ĝ-get, ī-high, ĭr-mirror, ł-little, ṇ-listen, ŏ-hot, oh-go, ŏŏ-wood, ōō-moon, oor-tour, ōr-or, ow-how, ţh-that, ~~th~~-thin, Ŭ-but, UR-fur, ur-under. ( )- suppress the syllable   [ ]- less common   see p. xi for complete list.

Act 3 Scene 2

2. **consummate** /CŎN suh mayt, -mut/ consummated.

2. ***Arragon, Aragon** US /ĂIR uh gŏn/, *rarely* [-gun]; UK /-gŏn/ [-gun];
Sp. /ah rah GOHN/ region in Spain. /-un/ would be the traditional form
(cf. *Solomon*).

50. **civet** /SIV it/ a type of perfume.

98. **holp** /hohlp/ helped.

131. ***untowardly** unluckily. US /un TORD lee, un tuh WÂRD lee/ (as in *war*);
CN /un tuh WÂRD lee /; UK /un tuh WÂRD lee/ [un TWÂRD lee, -TORD-]. 1st
syllable stress is also possible.

Act 3 Scene 3

9. **desartless** /dih ZART liss/ archaic variant of **desertless** /dih ZURT liss/
undeserving.

24. **lanthorn** archaic variant of **lantern**. Probably pronounced /LAN turn/, but
possibly /LANT horn/ or /LAN ~~th~~urn, -~~th~~orn/.

25. **vagrom** /VAY grum/ Dogberry's mistake for **vagrant**.

77, 83. ***by'r lady** /bīr-, bur LAY dee/ by Our Lady (i.e., Mary).

94. **vigitant** /VIJ ih tunt/ Dogberry's mistake for *vigilant*.

103. **close** /clohss/ hidden.

123. **Tush** /tŭsh/ expression of disdain.

134. **reechy** /REE chee/ grimy.

Act 3 Scene 4

6. ***rebato** a stiff ornamental collar. /ruh BAHT oh/; US *rarely older*
[ruh BAYT oh].

16. **Milan's** elsewhere in verse always /MILL unz/, but in this prose passage it could
be mod. /mih LAHNZ/.

54. ***Heigh-ho!** US /hay ho, hī-/; CN /hī-/, *rarely* [hay-]; UK /hay-/. Shk intended /hay/. Spoken with evenly stressed syllables or as if sighing, with 1st syllable stress.

59. ***trow** US, CN /troh, trow/; UK /trow/ [troh] I wonder. Shk's rhymes elsewhere indicate /-oh/.

73–8. **carduus benedictus** /CAR dyoo us ben uh DIK tus/; US *also* /CAR joo us/ blessed thistle, a medicinal herb.

82. ***by'r Lady** /bĭr-, bur LAY dee/ by Our Lady (i.e., Mary).

Act 3 Scene 5

9. **Goodman** /Go͞oD mun/ title of a man under the rank of gentleman.

16. **palabras** angl. /puh LAB ruz/; Sp. /pah LAHB rahss/ from *pocas palabras* few words,' i.e., 'best to keep quiet.'

32. **arrant** /ĂIR unt/ thoroughgoing.

46. **aspicious** /uh SPISH us/ Dogberry's error for *suspicious*. Some eds. prefer **auspicious**.

52. **suffigance** /suh FIJ unss/ Dogberry means *sufficient*.

Act 4 Scene 1

53. **show'd.** Q, F1 have the archaic variant **shew'd** which could be either /sho͞od/ or /shohd/.

68. ***nuptial** wedding. US, UK /NUP chł/ [-shł]; in CN both are used equally.

78. **catechizing** /KAT uh kīz ing/ series of questions and answers.

104. **impious** /IM pyus/ profane.

135. **unknown** here should be /UN nohn/.

146. **belied** /bih-, bee LĪD/ slandered.

ă-bat, ăir-marry, air-**pair**, ạr-**far**, ĕr-**merry**, ĝ-**get**, ī-**high**, ĭr-**mirror**, ł-**little**, ṇ-**listen**, ŏ-**hot**, oh-**go**, o͞o-**wood**, o͞o-**moon**, oor-**tour**, ōr-**or**, ow-**how**, ţh-**that**, ŧh-**thin**, ŭ-**but**, UR-**fur**, ur-**under**.   ( )- suppress the syllable   [ ]- less common   see p. xi for complete list.

167. **tenure** archaic variant of **tenor**, both /TEN ur/.

185. **misprision** /mis PRIZH un, -n̩/ misunderstanding.

194. **eat** /et/ dialect variant of **eaten**.

200. **thoroughly** archaic variant of *thoroughly*. /THROO lee/ is the normal pronunciation on stage, but to enhance clarity a syncopated form of the modern pronunciation may be used: *thor'ghly*.

213. ***travail** here should be /TRAV ayl/ double meaning: hard work, labor of childbirth.

306. **rancor** (UK **rancour**) /RANK ur/ ill-will. /-or/ not recommended.

316. **Comfect** /CUM fekt/ [CŎM fekt] variant of **Comfit** /CUM fit/ [CŎM fit] a candy.

Act 4 Scene 2

3. ***malefactors** /MAL ih fak turz/, *rarely* [mal ih FAK turz] evildoers. /-torz/ not recommended.

Act 5 Scene 1

5. **sieve** /siv/ strainer.

14. **lineament** /LIN yuh munt/ distinctive feature.

32. **advertisement** here should be /ad VURT iss munt, -iz-/ advice.

42–218. **belied** /bih-, bee LĪD/ slandered.

46. **Good den** /good-, guh DEN/ good evening. Some eds. prefer **Good e'en**.

58. **Tush** /tŭsh/ expression of disdain.

59. **dotard** /DOHT urd/ senile old man.

78. **daff** /dăf/ thrust aside. Archaic variant of **doff** /dŏf/; US *also* /dawf/.

94. **fashion-monging** foppish. US /FASH un mŏng ging, -ing/ or /-mawng-/ [-mung-]; CN /-mung-, -mŏng-/; UK /-mung-/.

125. **scabbard** /SKAB urd/ sword sheath.

262. **your wronger** US /RAWNG ur/; UK /RŎNG-/ someone who has done you wrong.

321. **arrant** /ĂIR unt/ thoroughgoing.

Act 5 Scene 2

30. **Leander** /lee AN dur/ he swam the Hellespont to be with Hero.

31. **pandars** /PAN durz/ pimps. Some eds. prefer **panders**, pronounced the same way.

32. ***quondam** US /KWŎN dum/, *rarely* [-dam]; UK /-dam/, *rarely* [-dum] former.

32. ***carpet-mongers** ladies' men. US /CAR pit mŏng gurz/ or /-mawng-/ [-mung-]; CN /-mung-, -mŏng-/; UK /-mung-/.

53. **noisome** /NOY sum/ disgusting.

63. **politic** /PŎL ih tik/ shrewdly managed.

66. **epithite** /EP ih ~~th~~it/ expression. Archaic variant of **epithet** /EP ih ~~th~~et/, /EP ih ~~th~~it/.

83. **rheum** /rōōm/ tears.

Act 5 Scene 3

5. ***guerdon** /GURD ṇ/ reward.

26. **Phoebus** /FEE bus/ god of the sun.

Act 5 Scene 4

17. **confirm'd** here should be /CŎN furmd/.

38. **Ethiope** /EE ~~th~~ee ohp/ person from Ethiopia.

ă-bat, ăir-marry, air-pair, ạr-far, ĕr-merry, ĝ-get, ī-high, ĭr-mirror, ł-little, ṇ-listen, ŏ-hot, oh-go, ōō-wood, ōō-moon, oor-tour, ŏr-or, ow-how, ṭh-that, ~~th~~-thin, Ŭ-but, UR-fur, ur-under. ( )- suppress the syllable [ ]- less common   see p. xi for complete list.

44. **Tush** /tŭsh/ expression of disdain.

45, 46. **Europa** /yoor ROH puh/; US *also* /yur-/ the 1st instance is 'Europe,' the second refers to one of Jupiter's loves.

48. **low** soft mooing sound. Today /LOH/, but here an archaic variant rhyming with *cow* is indicated.

Othello

People in the Play

Sometimes some of these names are given an Italian pronunciation in performance. These pronunciations are indicated here as accurately as possible within the limits of this notation. Shakespeare, however, probably intended them to be anglicized.

*Bianca US /bee AHNG kuh/ [bee ANG kuh]; UK /bee ANG kuh/, *rarely* [bee AHNG kuh]; CN both are used equally. Ital. /bee AHNG kah/.

Brabantio usually 3 syllables /bruh BAN sh(ee) yoh/, /-BAHN-/. Some eds. prefer Ital. **Brabanzio** /brah BAHN ts(ee) yoh/.

*Cassio 2 or 3 syllables depending on meter /KĂSS (ee) yoh/.

Desdemona /dez dih MOH nuh/.
 *Desdemon /DEZ dih mohn/ [-mŏn, -mun].

Emilia usually 3 syllables /ih MEEL (ee) yuh/.   An older pronunciation /-MILL-/ is now rare.

*Gratiano 3 or 4 syllables depending on meter. US /grahsh (ee) YAH noh/ [grash-], *rarely* [graysh-]; CN /grahsh-/ [grash-]; UK /grash-/ [grahsh-]. Some eds. prefer Ital. **Graziano** /grah ts(ee) YAH noh/.

Iago /ee AH goh/, except at at 5.2.154 where it is 2 syllables, /YAH goh/.

Lodovico /lohd-, lŏd uh VEE koh/; Ital. /loh doh VEE koh/.

Montano (F1) /mŏn TAN oh, -TAHN-/. **Mountanio** (Q1) /mown TAN yoh, -TAYN-, -TAHN-/.

*Othello /uh ~~THEL~~ oh/ [oh-]; UK *also* /ŏ-/.

Roderigo 3 or 4 syllables depending on meter /rŏd ur REE goh/.

ă-bat, ăir-ma**rry**, air-pa**ir**, a̱r-fa**r**, ĕr-me**rry**, ĝ-**get**, ī-**high**, ĭr-mi**rror**, ł-li**ttle**, ṇ-li**sten**, ŏ-**hot**, oh-**go**, o͞o-**wood**, o̅o̅-**moon**, oor-**tour**, ŏr-**or**, ow-**how**, t̠h-**that**, ~~th~~-**thin**, ŭ-**but**, UR-**fur**, ur-un**der**. ( )- suppress the syllable   [ ]- less common   see p. xi for complete list.

Recurring Words in the Play

ancient /AYN chunt/ archaic variant of the rank ensign US /EN sṇ/; UK /-sīn/.

*moor, -ship /moor/ [mor] black man.

Act 1 Scene 1

1. Tush (Q1) /tŭsh/ expression of disdain. Omitted F1.

4. 'Sblood /zblud/ God's (i.e., Jesus') blood. Omitted F1.

13. bumbast circumstance /BUM băst/ inflated style. Variant of bombast which formerly was pronounced the same way, though now /BŎM băst/ is the only pronunciation used.

14. epithites /EP ih thits/ expressions. Archaic variant of epithets /EP ih thets, -its/.

16. Certes /SUR teez/ certainly.

19. arithmetician /ăir-, uh rith muh TISH un/ one skilled in arithmetic.

20. *Florentine US /FLŌR in teen/ [-tīn]; E. COAST US /FLŎR-/; UK /FLŎR in tīn/ [-teen] person from Florence.

24. theoric /THEE uh rik/ theory.

25. toged, togaed /TOH gud/ wearing togas.

25. consuls /CŎN słz/ Roman officials.

30. Christen'd /CRISS ṇd/. Some eds. prefer Christian.

31. debitor /DEB ih tur/ archaic variant of *debtor*. /-tor/ not recommended.

39. affin'd (F1) /uh FĪND/ bound. Q1 *assign'd*.

46. obsequious /ub-, ŏb SEE kw(ee) yus/ fawning.

48. provender /PRŎV ṇ dur/ dry food for animals.

54. *homage /HŎM ij/; US *also* /ŎM ij/ acknowledgement of allegiance.

61. demonstrate here should be /dem ŎN strayt/.

63. extern /ek STURN/ external.

75. **timorous** /TIM (uh) rus/ terrifying.

99. **draughts** US, CN /drăfts/; UK, E. NEW ENG. /drahfts/ drinks.

111. **Barbary** /BAR buh ree/ region in North Africa.

113. **coursers** /COR surz/ warhorses.

113. **gennets, jennets** /JEN its/ Spanish horses.

114. **profane** if this line is iambic, /PROH fayn/ is indicated.

125. **gundolier** /gun duh LEER/ Venetian boatman. Archaic variant of **gondolier** /gŏn-/.

126. **lascivious** /luh SIV yus/ lustful.

141, 166. **taper('s)** /TAY pur/ slender candle.

152. **fadom** /FAD um/ depth, ability. Archaic variant of **fathom** /FĂṬH um/.

158. **Sagittary** here should be /SAJ ih tree/ an inn.

Act 1 Scene 2

3. **contriv'd** here should be /CŎN trīvd/ premeditated.

5. **yerk'd** /yurkt/ stabbed.

12. **magnifico** /mag NIF ih koh/ important person.

18. **signiory, signory**, /SEEN yur ee/ the Venetian government.

21. **provulgate** (Q1) /proh VŬL gayt/ make public. Some eds. prefer F1's
*promulgate** which here should be /prŏ MŬL gayt/ [proh-] rather than the
usual /PRŎM ul gayt/.

33. **Janus** /JAY nus/ Roman 2-faced god.

41. **sequent** (F1) /SEE kwunt/ successive. Q1 has **frequent**.

ă-bat, ăir-marry, air-pair, ạr-far, ĕr-merry, ĝ-get, ī-high, ĭr-mirror, ł-little, ņ-listen,
ŏ-hot, oh-go, o͝o-wood, o͞o-moon, oor-tour, ōr-or, ow-how, ṭh-that, ŧh-thin, ŭ-but,
UR-fur, ur-under. ( )- suppress the syllable   [ ]- less common   see p. xi for complete list.

43. **consuls** /CŎN słz/ senators.

50. **carract** /KĂIR ukt/ a type of large merchant ship.   Archaic variant of **carrack** /KĂIR uk/.

56. **Holla** /huh LAH/ a call to attract attention.

70. **guardage** /GARD ij/ guardianship.

86. **direct** here should be /DĪ rekt/ regular.

99. **pagans** /PAY gunz/ non-Christians.

Act 1 Scene 3

5. **accompt** (F1) /uh COWNT/ archaic variant of Q1's **account**, pronounced the same way.

18. **assay** /uh-, ass SAY/ attempt.

23. ***facile** US /FASS ł/ [-īl]; CN /-īl/ [-ł]; UK /-īl/ easy.

33, 234. **the Ottomites** /ŎT uh mīts/ the Turks.

37. **restem** /ree-, rih STEM/ to retrace their passage.

40. **servitor** /SURV ih tur/ servant. /-tor/ not recommended.

44. **Marcus Luccicos** /loō CHEE kohss/.

49. **Ottoman** /ŎT uh mun/ Turkish.

61. **mountebanks** /MOWNT uh banks/ quack doctors.

64. **Sans** /sănz/ without.

105. ***conjur'd** summoned by magic. Here with usual 1st syllable stress in an inverted foot; US, CN /CŎN jurd/, *rarely* [CUN-] ; UK /CUN jurd/ [CŎN-].

115. **Sagittary** /SAJ ih tĕr ee/; UK /-tuh ree/ or /-tree/ an inn.

140. **antres** /ANT urz/ caves.

144. **Anthropophagi** /an ~~throh~~ PŎF uh jī/ cannibals. Sometimes /ĝī/ is used.

153. **dilate** /dih-, dī LAYT/ tell in detail.

189. **God be with you** (F1). Some eds. substitute **God b'wi' you**, or Q1's **God b'uy you** or some other variation. In any case it should be reduced to 3 syllables /gŏd BWEE yōō/, /gŏd BĪ yōō/; US *also* /gawd-/.

200. **grise** (F1) /grĭss, grīz/ step. Variant of Q1's **greese** /greess, greez/. Other variants are **grece** /greess/, **grize** /grīz/, **grice** /grĭss/.

217. **equivocal** /ih KWIV uh kł/; US *also* /ee-/ arguing both sides of an issue.

231. **agnize** /ag NĪZ/ recognize.

272. **housewives** (F1). Q1 has the archaic variant *****huswives** with /HUZ ivz/ traditional, /HUSS wīvz/ a newer, spelling pronunciation. The former is the most common form in the UK, the latter in the US. In CN both are used equally. In North America /HUSS wivz/ is also sometimes used.

273. **indign** /in DĪN/ unworthy.

315. **guinea hen** /ĜIN ee/.

322. **hyssop** /HISS up/ a fragrant herb.

322. **tine** wild grasses. Some eds. prefer **thyme** (F1 *Time*) /tīm/ an herb.

325. **corrigible** US /COR ih jih bł/; E. COAST US, UK /CŎR-/ corrective.

327. **poise** counterbalance. Some eds. prefer **peise** with the same meaning. US /peez/, *sometimes* [payz]; UK /peez, payz/. Dialect evidence shows that /ee/ was the form found in southern England and /ay/ in the north.

332. **scion** /SĪ un/ living plant grafted onto root stock.

338. *****perdurable** eternal. Elsewhere in Shk /PUR dyur uh bł/; US *also* [-dur-], but today usually /pur DYOOR uh bł/; US *also* [-DŌŌR-, -DUR-].

345. **sequestration** /see kwih STRAY shun/ [sek wih-] separation.

349. **acerb** (Q1) /uh SURB/ bitter. Some eds. prefer F1's **bitter**.

349. **coloquintida** /cŏl uh KWIN tih duh/ colocynth, used as a purgative.

ă-bat, ăir-**marry**, air-**pair**, ạr-**far**, ĕr-**merry**, ĝ-**get**, ī-**high**, ĭr-**mirror**, ł-**littl**e, ṇ-**listen**, ŏ-**hot**, oh-**go**, ōō-**wood**, ōō-**moon**, oor-**tour**, ŏr-**or**, ow-**how**, ṯh-**that**, ᵵh-**thin**, ŭ-**but**, UR-**fur**, ur-**under**. ( )- suppress the syllable   [ ]- less common   see p. xi for complete list.

371. ***Traverse** US, CN /truh VURSS/ [TRAV urss];
UK /truh VURSS, TRAV urss/ [TRAV URSS] forward.

390. ***surety** certainty. Here may be 2 or 3 syllables (the latter is more
common in mod. Eng.) US /SHUR (ih) tee, SHOOR-/; CN /SHUR-/ [SHOOR-];
UK /SHOR-/ [SHUR-] [SHOOR-].

Act 2 Scene 1

4. **Descry** /dih SKRĪ/ see.

9. **hold the mortise** /MORT iss/ hold their joints together.

17. **enchafed** /en CHAYF id/ excited, stormy.

26. **Veronesa, Veronessa** /vĕr uh NESS uh/ ship from Verona, Italy.

39. **th' aerial blue** here should be /ṬHᵞAIR yɫ/ blue of the sky.

62. ***paragons** US /PĂIR uh gŏnz/ [-gunz]; CN /-gŏnz/; UK /-gunz/ [-gṇz] surpasses.

63. **blazoning** /BLAY z(uh) ning/ praising.

64. **vesture** /VES chur/ covering.

65. **ingener** (*Ingeniuer* F1) designer. Archaic variant of **engineer**. In Shk's time it
may have been /IN jih nur/ or mod. /in jih NEER/. Q1 has *beare all excellency*.

73. **divine** here should be /DIV īn/.

77. **se'nnight's** /SEN its, -īts/ week's.

81. **renew'd** here should be US /REE nōōd/; UK, SOUTH. US /-nyōōd/.

112. ***huswifery** /HUZ if ree/ is traditional, /-wīf ree, -wiff ree/ are newer,
based on spelling. Some eds. prefer **housewifery** /HOWSS-/.

112. ***huswives** /HUZ ivz/ is traditional, /HUSS wīvz/ is a newer, spelling pronunciation. The former is the most common form in the UK, the latter in the US. In CN
both are used equally. In North America /HUSS wivz/ is also sometimes used. Here
means **hussies**.

120. **assay** /uh-, ass SAY/ try. Some eds. prefer **essay** /es SAY/.

126. **frieze** /freez/ coarse wool cloth.

170. **gyve thee** (F2) /jīv/ trap thee. Q1 has **catch you**.

177. **clyster-pipes** /KLISS tur pīps/ enema pipes.

193. **unknown** here should be /UN nohn/.

228. **satiety** (F1) /suh TĪ uh tee/ fullness. Q1 has the archaic variant **saciety** /suh SĪ uh tee/.

238. **voluble** /VŎL yuh bł/ quick-witted.

238. **conscionable** /CŎN shun uh bł/ bound by conscience.

246. **requisites** /REK wih zits/ requirements.

263. **th'incorporate conclusion** /t̯h^{y}in COR pur rut, -rayt/ i.e., sexual union. /-ut/ is more usual for an adj .

288. **howbeit** here should be /how BEE (i)t/ although.

292. **peradventure** perhaps. /PUR ad VEN chur/;
US *rarely* [PĔR-, PUR ad ven chur];
UK, CN *also* [PUR-, PĔR ad ven chur, pĕr ad VEN chur].

293. **accomptant** (F1) /uh COWNT unt, -n̯t/ accountable. Archaic variant of Q1's **accountant**, pronounced the same way.

297. **inwards** /IN wurdz/ internal parts. /IN urdz/ is still a dialect form in the US.

309. **egregiously** /ih GREE jus lee/ notoriously.

Act 2 Scene 2

3. **perdition** /pur DISH un/; UK *also* [PUR DISH un] destruction.

7. *****nuptial** wedding. US, UK /NUP chł/ [-shł]; in CN both are used equally.

ă-bat, ăir-**ma**rry, air-**pair**, a̯r-**far**, ĕr-**merry**, ĝ-**get**, ī-**high**, ĭr-**mirror**, ł-**little**, n̯-**listen**,
ŏ-**hot**, oh-**go**, ōō-**wood**, ōō-**moon**, oor-**tour**, ōr-**or**, ow-**how**, t̯h-**that**, ŧħ-**thin**, Ŭ-**but**,
UR-**fur**, ur-und**er**. ( )- suppress the syllable   [ ]- less common   see p. xi for complete list.

Act 2 Scene 3

23. **parley** /PAR lee/ conference with an enemy. Newer [-lay] not recommended.

26. **alarum** US, CN /uh LAHR um/ [-LĂIR-]; UK /uh LĂIR um, uh LAHR um/ a call to arms.

30. **stope** /stohp/ tankard. Archaic variant of **stoup** /sto͞op/.

54. **Potations** /poh TAY shunz/ drinks.

64. **rouse** /rowz/ drink.

69, 70. **canakin, cannikin, canikin** /KAN uh kin/ small drinking vessel.

83. **Almain** /AL mayn/ German.

90. **breeches** /BRITCH iz/ is traditional, /BREECH iz/ is newer. The former pronunciation is more common in the UK and the latter in the US, CN.

91. **sixpence** /SIKS punss, -p n̩ss/; US *also* /SIKS penss/.

92. **lown** /lown/ rogue.

96. **auld** /awld/ dialect variant of **old**.

124. **equinox** /EK wih nŏks/ [EEK-] equal days and nights, i.e., exact counterpart. The latter pronunciation is older.

130. **horologe** /HŌR uh lohj/ [-lŏj]; E. COAST US /HŎR-/; UK *also* /HŎR-/ early timekeeping device.

140. **ingraft** US /in GRĂFT/; E. NEW ENG., UK /-GRAHF-/ ingrained. Some eds. prefer **engraffed** /en-/.

154. **mazzard, mazard** /MAZ urd/ head.

161. **Diablo** /dee AHB loh/ devil.

171. **the Ottomites** /ŎT uh mīts/ the Turks.

176. **propriety** /pruh PRĪ (ih) tee/ own nature.

181. **Devesting** /duh VEST ing/ archaic variant of **Divesting** /dī-, dih/ undressing.

206. **collied** /CŎL eed/ blackened.

207. **Assays** /uh-, ass SAYZ/ attempts. Some eds. prefer **Essays** /es SAYZ/.

210. **rout** /rowt/ riot.

218. **affin'd** /uh FĪND/ biased.

264. ***bestial** beastlike. /BEST yɫ/; US *also* [-chɫ]. US, CN /BEES-/ not recommended.

275. **imperious** /im PEER yus/ imperial, proud.

280. ***fustian** /FUSS tee un/; US *also older* /FUSS chun/ nonsense. Normal development would favor the latter.

292. **pleasance** (F1) /PLEZ unss/ pleasantness, delight. Q1 has **pleasure**.

319. ***importune** /im POR chun/ ask insistently. About half the respondents in the Survey reported a form with 3rd syllable stress in all countries, but that will not fit the meter in verse and is a relatively recent innovation (cf. *fortune*).

338. **Probal to thinking** /PROH bɫ/ reasonable.

373. **dilatory** here should be 4 syllables US /DILL uh tor e/;
UK /DILL uh tur ee/ slow.

375. **cashier'd** here should be /KASH eerd/ dismissed.

380. **billeted** /BILL it id/ assigned quarters.

Act 3 Scene 1

23. **quillets** /KWIL its/ quibbles, puns and word play.

36. **access** here should be /ak SESS/.

38. **converse** /cun VURSS/ conversation.

40. ***Florentine** US /FLŌR in teen/ [-tīn]; E. COAST US /FLŎR-/;
UK /FLŎR in tīn/ [-teen] person from Florence.

ă-bat, ăir-marry, air-pair, ạr-far, ĕr-merry, ĝ-get, ī-high, ĭr-mirror, ɫ-little, ņ-listen, ŏ-hot, oh-go, o͞o-wood, o͞o-moon, oor-tour, ŏr-or, ow-how, ţh-that, t̶h̶-thin, Ŭ-but, UR-fur, ur-under. ( )- suppress the syllable [ ]- less common   see p. xi for complete list.

Act 3 Scene 3

13. **politic** /PŎL (ih) tik/ as policy demands.

74. **By'r lady** (Q1) /bīr-, bur LAY dee/ by Our Lady, a mild oath. **Trust me** (F1).

90. **Perdition** /pur DISH un/; UK *also* [PUR DISH un] damnation.

123. **close dilations** /clohss/ 'secret thoughts' or 'involuntary delays.'

139. ***uncleanly** /un CLEN lee/ or newer /-CLEEN lee/.

168. **wronger** US /RAWNG ur/; UK /RŎNG-/ someone who does someone wrong.

182. **exsufflicate** /ek SUFF lih kayt, -ut/ exaggerated. /-ut / is more usual for an adj.

183, 198. **jealious** (F1) /JEL yus/ archaic variant of Q1's **jealous**.

210. **close as oak** /clohss/ securely.

232. **Foh** indicates an expression of disgust made with the lips /pff/! or /pfuh/! Sometimes vocalized as /foh/ or **faugh** /faw/.

251. **importunity** /im por-, im pur TYŌŌN ih tee/; US *also* /-TŌŌN-/ insistent requests.

260. **haggard** /HAG urd/ wild hawk.

274. ***Prerogativ'd** privileged. US, UK /pur RŎG uh tiv/ [prih-]; CN /prih-/. /pree-/ is also sometimes used in the US and CN, but is considered non-standard in the UK.

294. ***conjur'd** solemnly entreated. Here should be /cun JOORD/, the older, now rare pronunciation.

319. **Be not acknown on't** /ak NOHN/ say you know nothing about it.

330. **mandragora** here should be /man DRAG uh ruh/ a narcotic.

335. **Avaunt** /uh VAWNT/ begone!

346. **Pioners** soldiers who dug trenches and planted mines. It is not certain whether Shk pronounced this /PĪ uh nurz/ or as in mod. **Pioneers** /pī uh NEERZ/.

360. **ocular** /ŎK y(uh) lur/ visual.

375. **God buy you** good-bye. See 1.3.189.

431. **demonstrate** here should be /dem ŎN strayt/.

450. **aspics'** /ASS piks/ asps'.

453. **Pontic Sea** /PŎN tik/ Black Sea.

456. **Propontic** /proh-, pruh PŎN tik/ Sea of Marmora.

456. **Hellespont** /HEL iss pŏnt/ the Dardenelles.

Act 3 Scene 4

16. **catechize** (UK **catechise**) /KAT uh kīz/ to instruct through a series of questions and answers.

26. **crusadoes** /crōō SAY dohz/ coins.

28–185. **jealious** (F1) /JEL yus/ archaic variant of Q1's **jealous**.

40. **sequester** removal. Here 1st syllable stress is indicated.

51. **rheum** /rōōm/ tear.

67. **perdition** /pur DISH un/; UK *also* [PUR DISH un] loss.

70. **sibyl** /SIB ł/; UK *also* /SIB il/ prophetess.

108. *****importune** /im POR chun/ ask insistently. About half the respondents in the Survey reported a form with 3rd syllable stress in all countries, but that will not fit the meter in verse and is a relatively recent innovation (cf. *fortune*).

117. *****futurity** the future. US /fyōō TOOR ih tee, -CHOOR-/ [-TYOOR-, -TUR-, -CHUR-]; UK /-TYOOR-/ [-CHOOR-], however, the latter is considered non-standard in the UK.

122. **alms** charity for the poor. /ahmz/ is older; /ahlmz, awlmz/ are newer. In the UK the latter are non-standard.

141. **unhatch'd** here should be /UN hatcht/.

142. **demonstrable** here should be /DEM un struh bł/, still common in the UK.

ă-bat, ăir-marry, air-pair, ạr-far, ĕr-merry, ĝ-get, ī-high, ĭr-mirror, ł-little, ņ-listen, ŏ-hot, oh-go, ōō-wood, ōō-moon, oor-tour, ōr-or, ow-how, ţh-that, ŧħ-thin, ŭ-but, UR-fur, ur-under. ( )- suppress the syllable   [ ]- less common   see p. xi for complete list.

146. **endues** /in DYOOZ/; US *also* [-DŌOZ] endows.

153. **suborn'd** /sub ORND/ pursuaded someone to give false evidence.

154. **indicted** /in DĪT id/ charged with wrongdoing.

178. **continuate** (F1) /cun TIN y(ŏo) wut/ uninterrupted. Q1 has **convenient**.

Act 4 Scene 1

2. **unauthorized** here /un aw ~~THOR~~ īzd/ is possible after an epic caesura, but the mod. pronunciation is also possible in the compressed form /un AW ~~thr~~īzd/.

9. **venial** /VEEN yɬ/ pardonable.

26. **importunate** /im POR chuh nut/; UK *also* /-tyoo nut/ insistant.

27. **dotage** /DOHT ij/ love-sickness.

36. **belie** /bih-, bee LĪ/ slander.

37. ***fulsome** revolting. /FU̱LL sum/; US *rarely* [FŬL-].

37. **Handkerchiefs** (F1). **Handkerchers** (Q1) /HANK ur churz/.

71. **secure** here 1st syllable stress is indicated.

79. **'scuses** /SKYŌO siz/ excuses.

82. **gibes** /jībz/ sarcastic comments.

94. ***huswife** /HUZ if/ is traditional, /HUSS wīf/ is a newer, spelling pronunciation. The former is the most common form in the UK, the latter in the US. In CN both are used equally. In North America /HUSS wif/ is also sometimes used. Here means **hussy**.

99. **excess** here should be /ek SESS/, the most common UK form.

101. **conster** /CŎN stur/ construe. Some eds. prefer **construe** which here should be stressed on the 1st syllable.

108. **caitiff** /KAYT if/ scoundrel.

113. ***importunes** /im POR chunz/ asks insistently. About half the respondents in the Survey reported a form with 3rd syllable stress in all countries, but that will not fit the meter in verse and is a relatively recent innovation (cf. *fortune*).

139. **lolls** /lŏllz/ droops.

146. **fitchew** /FITCH o͞o/ polecat, i.e., whore.

198. **patent** US /PAT n̩t/; UK /PAYT n̩t/ [PAT-] license.

205. **expostulate** /ek SPŎS chuh layt/; UK *also* /-tyoo layt/ discuss, object.

225. **unkind** here should be /UN kīnd/.

260. **avaunt** /uh VAWNT/ begone!

Act 4 Scene 2

28. **procreants** /PROH cree unts/ people having sex.

61. **cestern** /SESS turn/ archaic variant of **cistern** /SISS turn/.

63. ***cherubin** angel. US, CN /CHĔR uh bin/ [-yuh-]; UK uses both equally. /KĔR-/ not recommended.

121. **callet** /KAL ut/ whore.

175. **thou daff'st** /dăfst/ archaic variant of **doffest** /DŎF ist/; US *also* /DAWF-/ you thrust aside.

187. **votarist** /VOHT uh rist/ nun.

221. **depute** /duh PYo͞oT/ appoint.

224. **Mauritania** /mor ih TAYN ee uh/.

227. **determinate** /dih-, dee TUR mih nut/ more to the purpose.

233. **harlotry** (F1) /HAR luh tree/, **harlot** (Q1) /HAR lut/ both mean 'whore.'

ă-bat, ăir-marry, air-pair, ạr-far, ĕr-merry, ĝ-get, ī-high, ĭr-mirror, l̩-little, n̩-listen, ŏ-hot, oh-go, o͞o-wood, o͞o-moon, oor-tour, ōr-or, ow-how, t̪h-that, t̶h̶-thin, ŭ-but, UR-fur, ur-under. ( )- suppress the syllable   [ ]- less common   see p. xi for complete list.

Act 4 Scene 3

26, 33. **Barbary** /BAR buh ree/.

75. **'ud's pity** (Q1) /udz/ reduced form of *God's*. F1 has **why**.

Act 5 Scene 1

11. **quat** (F1) /kwŏt/ pimple. Q1 *gnat*.

38. ***mischance** in verse normally with 2nd syllable stress.

106. **gastness** US /GĂST niss/; UK, E. NEW ENG. /GAHST niss/ terror.

123. **Fough** (Q1). Some eds. prefer **Foh!** indicates an expression of disgust made with the lips /pff/! or /pfuh/! Sometimes rendered as /faw/ or /foh/. Q2 has **now**. Omitted F1.

129. **foredoes me** /for DUZ/ ruins me.

Act 5 Scene 2

5. **alablaster** a type of white rock. US /AL uh blăss tur/; E. NEW ENG., UK /-blahss-/ [-blăss-]. Archaic variant of **alabaster** /-băss-, -bahss-/.

12. **Promethean** /proh-, pruh MEETH yun/ i.e., divine.

45. **portents** here should be /por TENTS/ omens.

133. **belie** /bih-, bee LĪ/ slander.

145. **chrysolite** /CRISS uh līt/ topaz.

150. **iterance** (F1) /IT (uh) runss/. Some eds prefer Q1's **iteration** /it ur AY shun/. Both mean 'repetition.'

209. **reprobance** (F1) /REP ruh bunss/ state of damnation. Q1 has *reprobation*.

214. ***recognizance** /rih KŎG nih zunss, -zṇss/; *rarely older* [rih KŎN ih-] keepsake.

216. ***antique** ancient. Here /AN teek/, *rarely older* [AN tik].

273. **compt** (F1) /cownt/ accounting, i.e., Judgement Day. Variant of Q1's **count** which some eds. prefer, and which was pronounced the same way.

301. ***demi-devil** /DEM ee-/ half-devil.

318. **caitiff** /KAYT if/ scoundrel.

335. **close prisoner** /clohss/ a securely kept prisoner.

345. **jealious** (F1) /JEL yus/ archaic variant of Q1's **jealous**.

348. **subdu'd** here should be stressed on the 1st syllable.

349. **Albeit** /awl BEE (i)t/ although.

351. **medicinable** (F1) /MED sin uh bł/ medicinal.

352. **Aleppo** /uh LEP oh/ city in present-day Syria.

354. **traduc'd** slandered. /truh DY$\overline{OO}$ST/; US *also* /-D$\overline{OO}$ST/. /-J$\overline{OO}$ST/ is considered non-standard in the UK.

ă-bat, ăir-**marry**, air-**pair**, ạr-**far**, ĕr-**merry**, ĝ-**get**, ī-**high**, ĭr-**mirror**, ł-**little**, ṇ-**listen**, ŏ-**hot**, oh-**go**, $\overline{oo}$-**wood**, $\overline{oo}$-**moon**, oor-**tour**, ōr-**or**, ow-**how**, ṯh-**that**, ŧħ-**thin**, ŭ-**but**, UR-**fur**, ur-**under**. ( )- suppress the syllable   [ ]- less common   see p. xi for complete list.

Richard II

People in the Play

Aumerle /oh MURL/.

Bagot /BAG ut/.

Berkeley US /BURK lee/; UK /BARK-/.

Bullingbrook Shk also spelled this name **Bullinbrook, Bullingbrooke, Bullinbrooke**, and pronounced it /BULL in brook/. Pope was the 1st to change it to **Bolingbroke** in the early 18th century. Today pronounced US, CN /BOHL ing brook/ [BULL-, BŎL-]; UK /BŎL-/, *rarely* [BULL-].

Bushy /BUSH ee/.

Carlisle /car LĪL/.

Exton, Sir Pierce of /EK stun/.

Fitzwater here should have 2nd syllable stress.

Gaunt /gawnt/.

Gloucester /GLŎS tur/; US *also* /GLAWSS-/.

Herford, Hereford (Bullingbrook) in the US both would be /HUR furd/. In the UK the county is normally /HĚR ih furd/ which in this play should be 2 syllables /HĚR furd/.

Lancaster US /LANG kăst ur, -kᵘss tur/; UK /LANG kᵘss tur/ [-kahst ur, -kăst ur].

Langley (York) /LANG lee/. This name is not spoken.

Mowbray, Mowbrey both pronounced /MOH bree/ [-bray]. The latter is the traditional form.

Norfolk (Mowbray) /NOR fᵘk/.

Northumberland /north UM bur lund/.

Salisbury 2 or 3 syllables, depending on meter US /SAWLZ b(ĕ)r ee/; UK /SAWLZ b(u)r ee/ [SĂLZ-].

Scroop /skroop/. Some eds. prefer mod. **Scrope**, pronounced the same way.

People in the Play (cont.)

Surrey US /SUR ee/; UK, E. COAST US /SUH ree/.

Westminster here should be /WEST min stur/.

Willoughby /WILL uh bee/

Wiltshire /WILT shur/ [-sheer]. Mentioned throughout.

Places in the Play

Bristow /BRIST oh/ archaic variant of F1's **Bristol** /BRIST ł/.

*Ravenspurgh here should be 3 syllables /RAV in SPURG, -SPUR/ or /RAY vin-/. Sometimes spelled **Ravenspur** /-SPUR/.

Act 1 Scene 1

34. **appellant** /uh PELL unt/ challenger.

39. **miscreant** /MIS cree unt/ scoundrel.

70. **kinred** /KIN rid/ archaic variant of **kindred**.

93. **elsewhere** here with 1st syllable stress, the US form, also sometimes used in the UK.

96. **Complotted** /cum PLŎT id/ plotted.

106. ***chastisement** punishment. Here stress should be on the 1st syllable /CHĂSS tiz munt/; US *also* /-tīz-/.

126. **Callice, Callis** /KAL iss/ northern coastal city in France. Both are archaic variants of **Calais** which here should be /KAL ay/, the normal UK form; Fr. /KAH lay/.

143. **rancor** (UK **rancour**) /RANK ur/ ill-will. /-or/ not recommended.

144. **recreant** /REK ree unt/ faithless.

192. ***parley** /PAR lee/ conference with an enemy. Newer [-lay] not recommended.

ă-bat, ăir-marry, air-pair, ạr-far, ĕr-merry, ĝ-get, ī-high, ĭr-mirror, ł-little, ṇ-listen, ŏ-hot, oh-go, o͞o-wood, o͞o-moon, oor-tour, ŏr-or, ow-how, ţh-that, t̶h̶-thin, ŭ-but, UR-fur, ur-under. ( )- suppress the syllable   [ ]- less common   see p. xi for complete list.

193. **slavish** /SLAY vish/ slave-like.

199. **Coventry** US /KUV ṇ tree/; UK /KŎV ṇ tree/ [KUV-].

Act 1 Scene 2

45, 56. **Coventry** US /KUV ṇ tree/; UK /KŎV ṇ tree/ [KUV-].

51. **courser's** /COR surz/ warhorse's.

53. **caitive** /KAYT iv/ base. Variant of **caitiff** /KAYT if/.

53. **recreant** /REK r(ee) yunt/ coward.

66. **Plashy** /PLASH ee/ modern **Pleshey** /PLUSH ee/.

Act 1 Scene 3

4, 52. **the appellant('s)** /ṭhʸuh PELL unt/ challenger.

28. **habiliments** /huh BIL ih munts/ equipment.

35–113. **Derby** US /DUR bee/; UK /DAR bee/.

70. **regenerate** reborn. /rih-, ree JEN ur ut, -ayt/.   /-ut/ would be the usual form for an adj.

81. **casque** /kăsk/; UK *also* [kahsk] helmet.

90. **enfranchisement** /en FRAN chiz munt/ liberty.

95. *jocund /JŎCK und/; US, CN *rarely* [JOHK-] merry.

97. **espy** /ess SPĪ/ see.

106, 111. **recreant** /REK ree unt/ cowardly or unfaithful.

117. **combatants** here should be stressed on the 1st syllable, as is usual in the UK, /CŎM buh tunts/ [CUM-].

134. **untun'd** here should be stressed on the 1st syllable.

138. **kinred's** /KIN ridz/ archaic variant of **kindred's**.

150. **determinate** /dih-, dee TUR mih nayt/ determine.

162. **viol** /VĪ ł/ 6-stringed instrument.

167. **portcullis'd** /port CŬLL ist/ barred.

187. **low'ring, louring** threatening.   /LOWR ing/ with the vowel of *how*.

189. **complot** here should be /CŎM plŏt/ plot.

196. **sepulchre** tomb. Here should be /suh-, sep PŬL kur/.

223. **taper** /TAY pur/ slender candle.

235. **low'r, lour** frown. /lowr/ with the vowel of *how*.

257. **dolor** (UK **dolour**) /DOH lur/; UK *also* /DŎL ur/ pain. /-or/ not recommended.

262. **travel** /TRAV ł/ some eds. prefer ***travail** /TRAV ayl/ labor. In Shk's time *travail* was pronounced /TRAV ł/.

289. **strow'd** /strohd/ archaic variant of **strewed**.

295. **Caucasus** /KAW kuh suss/ Asian mountains.

Act 1 Scene 4

8. **rheum** /rōōm/ tears.

44. **liberal *largess, largesse** generous gift. Here should have 1st syllable stress after /LIB rł/: US /LAR jess/ [-zhess]; CN, UK /LAR zhess/ [-jess]. Forms with /j/ are older.

46. **revenue** sometimes in verse /ruh VEN yōō/, but here as in mod. Eng. US /REV in ōō/; UK, SOUTH. US /-yōō/.

58. **Ely** /EE lee/.

ă-bat, ăir-**marry**, air-**pair**, ạr-**far**, ĕr-**merry**, ĝ-**get**, ī-**high**, ĭr-**mirror**, ł-**little**, ṇ-**listen**, ŏ-**hot**, oh-**go**, ōō-**wood**, ōō-**moon**, oor-**tour**, ōr-**or**, ow-**how**, ţh-**that**, ŧħ-**thin**, ŭ-**but**, UR-**fur**, ur-**under**. ( )- suppress the syllable   [ ]- less common   see p. xi for complete list.

Act 2 Scene 1

2. **unstay'd** here should be /UN stayd/ unchecked.

10. **glose, gloze** /glohz/ flatter.

19. **Lascivious** /luh SIV yus/ lustful.

38. **insatiate** /in SAYSH yut, -yayt/ never satisfied. /-ut/ is more usual for an adj.

38. ***cormorant** /COR m(uh) runt/; US *rarely* [-ant] a fishing bird, i.e., devouring.

42. ***demi-paradise** /DEM ee-/ half (i.e., nearly) paradise.

55. **sepulchre** /SEP ł kur/ tomb.

116. **ague's** /AY gy$\overline{oo}$z/ malarial fever.

130. **president** example. Archaic variant of ***precedent**, both /PRESS ih dunt/. It is not clear whether /PREZ-/ was used in Shk's time.

> 151, 257. ***bankrout** /BANK rowt/ [-rut] archaic variant of **bankrupt.**

156. **kerns** /kurnz/ Irish foot soldiers.

161, 226. **revenues** sometimes in verse /ruh VEN y$\overline{oo}$z/, but here as in mod. Eng. US /REV in $\overline{oo}$z/; UK, SOUTH. US /-y$\overline{oo}$z/.

182. **kinred** /KIN rid/ archaic variant of **kindred.**

202. ***letters-patents** US /PAT n̩ts/ [PAYT-]; UK /PAYT-/ [PAT-] documents conferring a right or power.

204. ***homage** /HŎM ij/; US *also* /ŎM ij/ acknowledgement of allegiance.

216. **Ely** /EE lee/.

218. ***trow** US, CN /troh, trow/; UK /trow/ [troh] believe. Shk's rhymes elsewhere indicate /oh/.

277. **Le Port Blanc** (following Q1–5) angl. /luh port BLANK/; Fr. /luh por BLAH^N/. Some eds. prefer **Port le Blanc** (following F1) angl. /PORT luh BLANK/; Fr. /por luh BLAH^N/.

278, 285. **Britain, Brittaine** /BRIT n̩/ Brittany. In Shk's time /-ayn/ was also used. For clarity *Britt'ny* may be substituted.

279. **Rainold, Reinold** /REN łd/.

279. **Cobham** /CŎB um/.

280. **Arundel** /ĂIR un dł/.

281. **Exeter** /EK sih tur/.

283. **Erpingham** /UR ping um/, though in the US /UR ping ham/ would be usual.

291. **slavish** /SLAY vish/ referring to slaves.

Act 2 Scene 2

10. **unborn** here should be /UN born/.

18. **perspectives** here should be /PUR spek tivz/.

19, 21. **awry** /uh RĪ/ askew.

54. **Beaumond** /BOH mund/ older form of **Beamont** US /BOH mŏnt/;
UK /-munt/ [mŏnt].

58. **Worcester** /W͞o͞oS tur/.

76. **comfortable** here /CUMF tur bł/ in an inverted foot is the best choice.

77. **belie** /bih-, bee LĪ/ show to be false.

90, 120. **Plashy** /PLASH ee/ mod. **Pleshey** /PLUSH ee/.

115. **kinred** /KIN rid/ archaic variant of **kindred**.

119. **Berkeley** here 3 syllables are indicated US /BURK uh lee/; UK /BARK-/.

142. ***presages** here should be /pree-, prih SAY jiz/ intuitions.

ă-bat, ăir-**marry**, air-**pair**, a̱r-**far**, ĕr-**merry**, ĝ-**get**, ī-**high**, ĭr-**mirror**, ł-**little**, n̪-**listen**, ŏ-**hot**, oh-**go**, o͞o-**wood**, o͞o-**moon**, oor-**tour**, ōr-**or**, ow-**how**, t̪h-**that**, t̶h̶-**thin**, Ŭ-**but**, UR-**fur**, ur-**under**. ( )- suppress the syllable   [ ]- less common   see p. xi for complete list.

Act 2 Scene 3

1–68. Berkeley US /BURK lee/; UK /BARK-/.
---

3. **Gloucestershire** /GLŎSS tur shur/ [-sheer]; US *also* /GLAWSS-/.

7. **delectable** here should be /DEE lek tuh bł/ or /DEL ek tuh bł/.

9. **Cotshall** /CŎTS ł/ local pronunciation of the **Cotswold** hills in Gloucestershire /CŎTS wohld/ [CŎTS ohld, -włd].

22. **Worcester** /W͞o͞oS tur/.

56. ***estimate** US /ES tih mut/ [-mayt]; UK /-mayt/ [-mut] reputation.

61. **unfelt** here should be /UN felt/.

65. **the *exchequer** /ţhʸeks CHEK ur/ treasury.

75. **rase** /rayss/ erase. Some eds. prefer a variant **raze** /rayz/ which can also mean 'erase.'

104. **palsy** /PAWL zee/; UK *also* [PŎL-] paralysis or shaking.

104. ***chastise** punish. Here should be /CHĂSS tīz/, the usual US pronunciation, also used in CN; in the UK 2nd syllable stress is usual.

130. ***letters-patents** US /PAT ņts/ [PAYT-]; UK /PAYT-/ [PAT-] documents conferring a right or power.

165. **complices** /CŎMP lih siz/ accomplices.

Act 3 Scene 1

9. **lineaments** /LIN yuh munts/ distinctive features.

22. **signories** /SEEN yur eez/ domains.

25. **Ras'd out** (*rac't* Q1) /rayst/ erased. Some eds. prefer F1's **Razed** /rayzd/ which could mean 'erase' or 'cut, slash.' **Rac'd** /rayst/ from *arace* 'pluck off' is also possible.

25. **imprese** /IM preez/ heraldic device or devices. Variant of **impress** /IM press/.

43. **Glendower** here should be /GLEN dowr/. Some eds. prefer the Welsh **Glyndŵr**, normally /glin DOOR/, but here /GLIN dōōr/.

43. **complices** /CŎMP lih siz/ accomplices.

Act 3 Scene 2

1. **Barkloughly** /bark LECK lee/ or inversion is possible to allow 1st syllable stress. Based on Holinshed's error for *Hertlowli*, now **Harlech** (angl. /HAR leck/) in Wales. Some eds. prefer **Harlechly** /HAR leck lee/.

13. **comfort** here mod. /CUM furt/ in an inverted foot.

32. **succors** (UK **succours**) /SUCK urz/ helps. /-orz/ not recommended.

49. **the antipodes** (Q1) /ţh^yan TIP uh deez/ people on the opposite side of the world, i.e., Irish. Omitted F1.

118. **distaff-women** US /DIS stăf/; E. NEW ENG., UK /DIS stahff/ women who spin.

170. **thorough** (Q1) archaic variant of *through* which is often pronounced as mod. *thorough* in Shk, but here it should be 1 syllable, making F1's, Q2–5's **through** the better choice.

185. ***servile** /SUR vīl/, *rarely* [SUR vł] slave-like.

188. **chid'st** /chīdst/ chidest.

190. **ague** /AY gyōō/ malarial fever.

Act 3 Scene 3

18. **I know it, uncle, and oppose not myself** here 1st syllable stress for *oppose* is indicated.

33. **brazen** /BRAY zun, -zņ/ brass.

33. ***parley** /PAR lee/ conference with an enemy. Newer [-lay] not recommended.

67. **occident** /ŎK sih dunt/ west.

ă-bat, ăir-marry, air-pair, ạr-far, ĕr-merry, ĝ-get, ī-high, ĭr-mirror, ł-little, ņ-listen, ŏ-hot, oh-go, ōō-wood, ōō-moon, oor-tour, ōr-or, ow-how, ţh-that, ŧh-thin, ʊ-but, UR-fur, ur-under. ( )- suppress the syllable   [ ]- less common   see p. xi for complete list.

85. **omnipotent** /ŏm NIP uh tunt/ all-powerful.

100. **pasters'** US /PĂSS turz/; UK, E. NEW ENG. /PAHSS turz/ archaic variant of **pastures'**.

114. **Enfranchisement** /en FRAN chiz munt/ freedom from banishment.

149. **almsman's** poor person. /AHMZ munz/ is older; /AHLMZ-, AWLMZ-/ are newer. In the UK the latter are non-standard.

154. **obscure** here should be /ŎB skyoor/; US *also* [-skyur].

178. **glist'ring** /GLIS tring/ glistening.

178. **Phaëton** /FAY ih tun, -tŏn/ son of the sun god. /-ŏn/ is usual in the US and is increasingly common in the UK. Some eds. prefer **Phaëthon** /--t̶h̶un, -t̶h̶ŏn/. /-un/ would be the traditional form (cf. *Solomon*).

Act 3 Scene 4

29. **apricocks** /AYP rih kŏcks/; US, CN *also* /AP-/ dialect variant of **apricots**.

38. **noisome** /NOY sum/ noxious, disagreeable.

63. **Superfluous** here a normal line requires US /so͞o pur FLO͞O us/; UK, SOUTH. US *also* [syo͞o -], rather than the usual mod. pronunciation with 2nd syllable stress.

92. *****mischance** in verse normally with 2nd syllable stress.

93. **embassage** /EM buh sij/ ambassador's message.

Act 4 Scene 1

13, 82. **Callice, Callis** /KAL iss/ city on northern coast of France. Both are archaic variants of **Calais** which here should be /KAL ay/, the normal UK form; Fr. /KAH lay/.

22. *****chastisement** punishment. Here stress should be on 1st syllable /CHĂSS tiz munt/; US *also* /-tīz-/.

33. **valure** archaic variant of **valor** (UK **valour**) all pronounced /VAL ur/.

54. **hollowed** (Q1), **holloa'd** /HŎL ud, -ohd/ cried out, as in a hunt. Omitted F1.

89. **signories** /SEEN yur eez/ domains.

94. ***ensign** flag. US, CN /EN sṇ/, US *rarely* [-sīn]; UK /-sṇ, -sīn/.

95. **pagans** /PAYG unz/ non-Christians.

95. **Saracens** /SĂIR uh sṇz, -sunz/ Muslims.

104. **appellants** /uh PELL unts/ accusers.

119. **noblesse** /noh BLESS/ nobility.

131, 233. ***heinous** /HAYN us/ hateful. /HEEN us/ is non-standard though common in the UK.

---

136. **prophesy** /PRŎF uh sī/ to predict the future.

140. ***tumultuous** full of turmoil. US /tōō MŬLL chwus/ [-tywus]; SOUTH. US *also* /tyōō-/; CN /tyōō-, tōō MUL chwus, -tywus/; UK /tyōō MŬLL tywus/ [-chwus], *rarely* [tōō MŬLL-]. In the UK /chōō MŬLL-/ is considered non-standard.

144. **Golgotha** here should be /GŎL guh t̶h̶uh/; US *also* /GAWL-/ hill where Jesus died.

159. ***sureties** bails, pledges. Here should be 2 syllables, though in mod. Eng., 3 syllables are more common US /SHUR (ih) tee, SHOOR-/; CN /SHUR-/ [SHOOR-]; UK /SHOR-/ [SHUR-] [SHOOR-].

202. **revenues** here should be /ruh VEN yōōz/.

220. **unking'd** here should be /UN kingd/.

230. **record** here should be /rek-, rik ORD/.

239, 240. **Pilate(s)** /PĪ lut(s)/ Roman governor of Palestine.

267. ***bankrout** (Q4–5) /BANK rowt/ [-rut] archaic variant of F1's **bankrupt**.

297. **unseen** here should be /UN seen/.

ă-bat, ăir-marry, air-pair, ąr-far, ĕr-merry, ĝ-get, ī-high, ĭr-mirror, ł-little, ṇ-listen, ŏ-hot, oh-go, ōō-wood, ōō-moon, oor-tour, ŏr-or, ow-how, t̶h̶-that, t̶h̶-thin, ŭ-but, UR-fur, ur-under. ( )- suppress the syllable [ ]- less common   see p. xi for complete list.

Act 5 Scene 1

25. **Which our *profane* hours here have thrown down.** Scans as a headless line with /PROH fayn/. Some eds. replace **thrown** with **stricken** which produces a normal line with usual mod. /proh FAYN/.

42. **betid** /bih-, bee TID/ happened, past tense of *betide*.

44. *****lamentable** here should be /LAM un tuh bł/ the usual UK pronunciation.

52. **Pomfret** US /PŎM frit/; UK /PUM frit/ [PŎM-].

80. **Hollowmas** US /HŎL oh muss/ [-mass]; UK /-mass/ [-muss] variant of *****Hallowmas** US /HŎL-, HAL oh muss/ [-mass]; UK /HAL oh mass/ [-muss]. All Saints Day, Nov. 1. The older form is /-muss/.

Act 5 Scene 2

32. **combating** here should be /CŎM buh ting/; UK *also* [CUM-].

40. **aye** /ay/ ever. /ī/ is often used, but not recommended.

45. **fealty** /FEEL tee/ faithfulness.

49. **as lief** /leef/ as soon.

52. **justs** /justs/ archaic variant of *****jousts**, now /jowsts/ in all countries; but US *rarely* [justs]; UK *rarely* [jo͞osts]. The oldest form is /justs/, the newest /jowsts/.

79, 102. **appeach** /uh PEECH/ inform against.

Act 5 Scene 3

6. **frequent** here should be /free-, frih KWENT/ visit.

12, 20. **dissolute** /DIS uh lo͞ot/ lacking moral restraint. At one time many RP speakers in the UK used /lyo͞o-/ for syllables beginning *lu-*, but today their number is dwindling.

34, 59. *****heinous** /HAYN us/ hateful. /HEEN us/ is non-standard though common in the UK.

75. **suppliant** /SUP lyunt/ someone who asks humbly for something.

119. **pardonne-moy** Fr. /par DUN uh MWAH/ excuse me. Some eds. prefer
pardonnez-moi /par DUN ay MWAH/.

138. **consorted** /cun SORT id/ assembled.

Act 5 Scene 4

10. **Pomfret** US /PŎM frit/; UK /PUM frit/ [PŎM-].

Act 5 Scene 5

17. ***postern** small back or side gate. US, CN /PŎST urn/ [POHST urn];
UK /PŎST urn/, *rarely* [POHST urn].

20. **thorough** archaic variant of *through* which is often pronounced as mod.
thorough in Shk, but here it should be 1 syllable, making **through** the better choice.

26. **refuge** following the iambic beat would give /ref-, rih FYŌŌJ/, but the foot may
be inverted to allow /REF yōōj/.

34. **penury** /PEN yur ee/; UK *also* /PEN yoor ee/ poverty.

62. **holp** /hohlp/ helped.

66. ***brooch** /brohch/ ornament. US [brōōch] not recommended.

76. **ern'd** /urnd/ grieved.

78, 81. **Barbary** /BAR buh ree/ horse from North Africa. Line 81 would be
/BAR bree/.

79. **bestrid** /bih-, bee STRID/ mounted.

85. **eat** /et/ dialect variant of **eaten**.

94. **jauncing** /JAWN sing/ prancing.

113. **valure** archaic variant of **valor** (UK **valour**) all pronounced /VAL ur/.

ă-bat, ăir-marry, air-pair, ạr-far, ĕr-merry, ĝ-get, ī-high, ĭr-mirror, ł-little, ṇ-listen,
ŏ-hot, oh-go, ōō-wood, ōō-moon, oor-tour, ōr-or, ow-how, țh-that, t̶h̶-thin, ŭ-but,
UR-fur, ur-under. ( )- suppress the syllable [ ]- less common   see p. xi for complete list.

Act 5 Scene 6

3. **Ciceter, Ci'cester** /SIS ih tur/ older form of *Cirencester*, still occasionally used.

3. **Gloucestershire** /GLŎSS tur shur/ [-sheer]; US *also* /GLAWSS-/.

14. **Brocas, Broccas** /BRŎCK us, BROH kus/.

15. **consorted** /cun SORT id/ plotting.

33. **Burdeaux** city in France, possibly pronounced /BUR dŏcks/ in Shk's time. Archaic variant of **Bordeaux, Bourdeaux** which here should be /BOR doh/.

43. *thorough* **shades** archaic variant of *through*, used when the meter demands 2 syllables. It is often pronounced as *thorough* on stage, but using /-o͞o/ in the final syllable will bring it closer to mod. *through*. Some eds. prefer Q1's **through shades**, though it should still be 2 syllables. Others prefer Q2–5's, F1's **through the shades**.

52. **bier** /beer/ coffin.

Richard III

People in the Play

Berkeley US /BURK lee/; UK /BARK lee/.

Bourchier /BOW chur/ his name is not spoken.

Bra(c)kenbury US /BRACK in bĕr ee/; UK /BRACK in bur ee/ or /-bree/.

Breton see **Britain**, "Places in the Play."

Buckingham /BUCK ing um/, though in the US /BUCK ing ham/ is common.

Cardinal (Bourchier) 2 or 3 syllables depending on meter /CARD (ih) nł/, /CARD n̩ ł/. 2 syllables is usual in the US, 3 syllables in the UK.

Catesby 2 or 3 syllables depending on meter /KAYTS bee, KAY tiz bee/.

Derby (Stanley) US /DUR bee/; UK /DAR bee/.

Dorset /DOR sit/.

Ely /EE lee/.

Gloucester (Richard) /GLŎS tur/; US *also* /GLAWSS-/. At 3.4.46 expanded to 3 syllables /-uh tur/.

Henry 2 or 3 syllables depending on meter /HEN (ur) ree/.

Lancaster US /LANG kăst ur, -kᵘss tur/;
UK /LANG kᵘss tur/ [-kahst ur, -kăst ur].

Lovel, Lovell /LUV ł/.

Margaret /MAR guh rit/ or /MAR grit/ depending on meter.

Marquess (Dorset) Some eds. prefer **Marquis**, both pronounced /MAR kwiss/.

Norfolk /NOR fᵘk/.

ă-bat, ăir-**marry**, air-**pair**, a̡r-**far**, ĕr-**merry**, ĝ-**get**, ī-**high**, ĭr-**mirror**, ł-**little**, n̩-**listen**, ŏ-**hot**, oh-**go**, o͞o-**wood**, o͞o-**moon**, oor-**tour**, ōr-**or**, ow-**how**, t̪h-**that**, t̶h̶-**thin**, ŭ-**but**, UR-**fur**, ur-**under**. ( )- suppress the syllable   [ ]- less common   see p. xi for complete list.

People in the Play (cont.)

Plantagenet /plan TAJ ih nit/.

Rotherham /RŎTH ur um/ his name is not spoken.

Scrivener /SKRIV nur/ notary. This word is not spoken.

Surrey US /SUR ee/; UK, E. COAST US /SUH ree/.

Tressel /TRESS ł/.

Tyrrel, Tirrel /TĬR ł/.

Urswick /URZ ik, URZ wik/ his name is not spoken.

Vaughan always 2 syllables /VAW un/.

Warwick US /WŌR ik/; E. COAST US, UK /WŎR-/. Place names in the US often have /-wik/ but this is not recommended for Shk. Mentioned throughout the play.

Wiltshire, Sheriff of /WILT shur/ [-sheer] not spoken.

Woodvil(l)e, Anthony (Rivers) /WŏŏD vil/. US /AN ~~thuh~~ nee/; UK /AN tuh nee/ [-~~thuh~~ nee].

Places in the Play

Britain /BRIT ṇ/ Brittany. In Shk's time /-ayn/ was also used. Some eds. prefer **Bretagne** which here should be /BRET ahnʸ/. For clarity *Britt'ny* may be substituted. This word is also used for 'person from Brittany,' in which meaning some eds. prefer mod. **Breton** US /BRET ṇ/; UK /BRET ŏn/ [-ṇ, -un]. Sometimes the Fr. ending /-ohⁿ/ is used in the UK.

Pomfret US /PŎM frit/; UK /PUM frit/ [PŎM-].

Tewksbury here 3 syllables US /TŌŌKS bĕr ee/; SOUTH. US /TYŌŌKS-/; UK /TYŌŌKS bur ee/. UK [CHŌŌKS-] is considered non-standard.

Act 1 Scene 1

stage direction: solus /SOH lŭss/ alone.

3. **low'r'd, loured** frowned. /lowrd/ with the vowel of *how*.

7. **alarums** US, CN /uh LAHR umz/ [-LĂIR-]; UK /uh LĂIR umz, uh LAHR umz/ calls to arms.

13. **lascivious** /luh SIV yus/ lustful.

18. **curtail'd** here should be /CUR tayld/ cut short.

27. **descant** here should be /DES kănt/ comment on.

> 38, 132. **mew'd up** /my o͞od/ caged.

74. **suppliant** /SUP lee unt/ someone who asks humbly for something.

92. **jealous** (F1) /JELL ee yus/ archaic variant of (Q1–6's) **jealous,** but here 3 syllables are needed for a regular line

106. **abjects** /ab JEKTS/ miserable subjects.

158. **close** /clohss/ hidden.

Act 1 Scene 2

3. **obsequiously** /ub-, ŏb SEE kw(ee) yus lee/ mournfully.

8. **invocate** /IN voh kayt/ call upon.

> 29–225. **Chertsey** /CHUR see/ a monastery.

40. ***halberd** US, CN /HAL burd, HAWL-/; UK /HAL-/ [HAWL-] spear with blades on the end.

46. **Avaunt** /uh VAWNT/ begone!

53. ***heinous** /HAYN us/ hateful. /HEEN us/ is non-standard though common in the UK.

56. **Open their congeal'd mouths** here should be /CŎN jeeld/. Some eds. prefer **Ope their congealed** /cun JEEL id/.

58, 165. **exhale(s)** here with 2nd syllable stress, /eks HAYL/, the normal UK form.

> ă-bat, ăir-marry, air-pair, ạr-far, ĕr-merry, ĝ-get, ī-high, ĭr-mirror, l̟-little, ṇ-listen, ŏ-hot, oh-go, o͞o-wood, o͞o-moon, oor-tour, ōr-or, ow-how, t̠h-that, t̶h̶-thin, ŭ-but, UR-fur, ur-under. ( )- suppress the syllable   [ ]- less common   see p. xi for complete list.

84. **excuse** here should be /EK skyo͞oss/.

94. ***falchion** type of sword. /FĂL chun/ [-shun]; *older* /FAWL chun/.

107. **holp** /hohlp/ helped.

150. ***basilisks** legendary reptile whose glance was fatal. US /BĂSS ih lisks/ [BAZ ih lisks]; UK /BAZ-/ [BĂSS-]; CN both used equally.

187. **Tush** (Q1–6) /tŭsh/ expression of disdain. Omitted F1 and *Riverside*.

191. **accessary** here US /AK sess ĕr ee/; UK /-uh ree/ or /AK sess ree/.

217. ***divers** various. Should be stressed on the 1st syllable US, CN /DĬ vurss, -vurz/; UK /DĬ vurss/ [-vurz].

217. **unknown** here should be /UN nohn/.

249. **moi'ty, moiety** /MOY tee/ portion.

251. **denier** coin of little value. Here should have 2nd syllable stress /duh NEER/ is older; /dun YAY/ is newer, based on Fr.

254. **marv'llous** (F1), **marv'lous,** **marvellous** (*merueilous* Q1, *maruailous* Q2–6) marvellously. Here should be two syllables, either /MARV ĭss/ or /MARV lus/.

Act 1 Scene 3

46. **dissentious** /dih SEN shus/ causing arguments.

67. **children** (F1). Q2–5 have **kinred** /KIN rid/ archaic variant of Q1's **kindred**.

86. **advocate** /AD vuh kut/ someone who supports a person or cause.

88. **suspects** /suh SPECTS/ suspicions.

101. ***Iwis** /ih WISS/; US, CN *also* /ee WISS/ indeed.

101. ***grandam** (F1) /GRAN dam/; US *rarely* [-dum] grandmother. This spelling could also be pronounced as indicated in Q1–6's **granam** /GRAN um/ (cf. *grandma* /GRAM uh/).

114. **avouch't** /uh VOWCHT/ affirm it.

129. **Saint Albons** archaic variant of **St. Albans**, both pronounced
US /saynt AWL bunz/; UK /sint-, sn̩t-/.

138. **mewed up** /myo͞od/ caged.

143. **cacodemon** evil spirit. /kack uh DEE mun/, /KACK uh dee mun/.

185. **prophesied** /PRŎF uh sīd/ predicted the future.

186. **Northumberland** /nor̶t̶h̶ UM bur lund/.

213. **unlook'd** /UN lo͞okt/.

254. ***malapert** /MAL uh purt/; US *also* [mal uh PURT] saucy.

263–9. ***aery('s), eyrie, aerie** high nest. /AIR ee, EER-/; E. COAST US *also* [ĂIR-].
/ĪR ee/ not recommended. /AIR ee/ is the oldest pronunciation.

316. **scathe** (Q1–5) /skayt̶h̶/ harm. Variant of F1, Q6's **scath** /skat̶h̶/.

329. **allies** here with 2nd syllable stress.

346. ***obdurate** unmoveable. Here should have 2nd syllable stress
/ŏb-, ub DYOOR it/; US *also* /-DYUR-/ [-DUR-]. 1st syllable stress is more usual
today.

349. **Tut, tut** (F1) some eds. prefer Q1–6's **Tush** /tŭsh/ expression of disdain.

Act 1 Scene 4

26. **anchors.** Some eds. substitute ***ouches** /OW chiz/ jewelry, or **ingots**
/ĪNG guts/.

49. **renowned** (F1) /rih-, ree NOWN id/. Q1–5 have the archaic variant **renowmed**
/rih-, ree NOW mid/.

50. **scourge** /SKURJ/ punishment.

59. ***Environ'd** /en VĪ rund/; US *also* [-urnd] surrounded.

154. **costard** /CŎST urd/ head.

ă-bat, ăir-**marry**, air-**pair**, a̩r-**far**, ĕr-**merry**, ĝ-**get**, ī-**high**, ĭr-**mirror**, ł-**little**, n̩-**listen**,
ŏ-**hot**, oh-**go**, o͞o-**wood**, o͞o-**moon**, oor-**tour**, ōr-**or**, ow-**how**, t̩h-**that**, t̶h̶-**thin**, ŭ-**but**,
UR-**fur**, ur-**under**. ( )- suppress the syllable   [ ]- less common   see p. xi for complete list.

155, 270. malmsey-butt cask of Malmsey, a sweet wine. /MAHM zee/ is the older pronunciation, but today the /l/ is sometimes pronounced. This, however, is considered non-standard in the UK.

---

187. convict /cun VICT/ convicted.

198. edict /EE dict/ decree.

207. Unrip'st /un RIPST/, **Unripped'st** /un RIPTST/.

272. Pilate /PĪ lut/ Roman governor of Palestine.

Act 2 Scene 1

3. embassage /EM buh sij/ ambassador's message.

13. supreme here should be US /SOO preem/; UK, SOUTH. US *also* [SYOO-].

27. inviolable /in VĪL uh bł/ unbreakable.

30. allies here with 2nd syllable stress.

41. cordial US /COR jł/; UK /COR dył/ restorative medicine.

90. *countermand US, CN /COWNT ur mănd/; UK /-mahnd/ the revoking of a command.

Act 2 Scene 2

1–31. *grandam (F1) /GRAN dam/; US *rarely* [-dum] grandmother. This spelling could also be pronounced as indicated in Q1–6's **granam** /GRAN um/ (cf. *grandma* /GRAM uh/).

14. *importune /im POR chun/ ask insistently. About half the respondents in the Survey reported a form with 3rd syllable stress in all countries, but that will not fit the meter in verse and is a relatively recent innovation (cf. *fortune*).

28. visor (F1). Q1–6 have ***vizard** /VIZ urd/ mask. /- ̣ard/ not recommended.

60. moi'ty, moiety /MOY tee/ portion.

65. widow-dolor (UK **dolour**) /DOH lur/; UK *also* /DŎL ur/ pain. Q1–6 have *widdowes dolours*. /-or/ not recommended.

117. **rancor** (UK **rancour**) /RANK ur/ ill-will. /-or/ not recommended.

121–154. Ludlow /LUD loh/.

---

133. **compact** here should be /cŏm-, cum PACT/ agreement.

151. **consistory** here should be /CŎN sis tree, -tuh ree/; US *also* /-tor ee/ council chamber, i.e., source of wisdom.

Act 2 Scene 3

4. **by'r lady** /bīr-, bur LAY dee/ by Our Lady (i.e., Mary).

13. ***nonage** /NŎN ij/; US, UK *rarely older* [NOH nij]; UK *rarely* [NUN ij] minority, period of youth.

20. **politic** /PŎL ih tik/ cunning.

30. **solace** /SŎL us/ comfort.

42. **instinct** here /in STINCT/.

Act 2 Scene 4

2. **Northampton** /nor ~~TH~~AMP tun/.

10–32. ***Grandam** (F1) /GRAN dam/; US *rarely* [-dum] grandmother. This spelling could also be pronounced as indicated in Q1–6's **Granam** /GRAN um/ (cf. *grandma* /GRAM uh/).

35. **parlous** (F1) /PAR lus/ clever. Archaic variant of Q1–6's **perilous** which here would have to be /PĔR (ih) lus/.

50. **hind** /hīnd/ doe.

Act 3 Scene 1

39. ***obdurate** unmoveable. Here should be /ŏb-, ub DYOOR ut/; US *also* /-DYUR-/ [-DUR-]. 1st syllable stress is more usual today.

ă-bat, ăir-**marry**, air-**pair**, ạr-**far**, ĕr-**merry**, ĝ-**get**, ī-**high**, ĭr-**mirror**, ł-**little**, ṇ-**listen**, ŏ-**hot**, oh-**go**, o͞o-**wood**, o͞o-**moon**, oor-**tour**, ōr-**or**, ow-**how**, ṭh-**that**, ~~th~~-**thin**, ŭ-**but**, UR-**fur**, ur-**under**. ( )- suppress the syllable [ ]- less common   see p. xi for complete list.

62. ***sojourn** reside temporarily. Here stress should fall on the 1st syllable US, CN /SOH jurn/; UK /SŎJ urn/ [-URN, SOH-, SUJ-].

72, 74. **record** here should be /rek-, rik ORD/.

77. **retail'd** passed on. Here should be /rih-, ree TAYLD/.

81. **characters** 'written records' or 'moral qualtities.' Here with 2nd syllable stress.

86. **valure** (Q1) archaic variant of **valor** (UK **valour** Q 3–6, F1), all pronounced /VAL ur/.

145. ***grandam** (F1) /GRAN dam/; US *rarely* [-dum] grandmother. This spelling could also be pronounced as indicated in Q1–6's **granam** /GRAN um/ (cf. *grandma* /GRAM uh/).

154. **perilous** (Q1–6, F1) /PĔR (ih) lus/. Q7, F4 have the archaic variant **parlous** /PAR lus/. Here should be disyllabic.

192, 200. **complots** plots. The 1st instance should be /cum PLŎTS/, the second /CŎM plŏts/.

195. **Herford, Hereford**. In the US both would be /HUR furd/. In the UK the county is normally /HĔR ih furd/ which here should be 2 syllables /HĔR furd/.

Act 3 Scene 2

11. **rased, razed off** /RAY zid/ torn, cut off. **Raced** /RAY sid/ from *arace* 'pluck off' is also possible.

60. **fortnight** /FORT nīt/; US *also* [FORT nit] 2 weeks. Virtually obsolete in the US.

75. **rood** /rōōd/ cross.

84. ***jocund** /JŎCK und/; US, CN *rarely* [JOHK-] merry.

87. **rancor** (UK **rancour**) /RANK ur/ ill-will. /-or/ not recommended.

stage direction after 94: ***Pursuivant** herald, attendant. US /PUR swiv unt/ [PUR siv unt]; UK /PUR swiv unt/, *rarely* [PUR siv unt].

101. **allies** here with 2nd syllable stress.

106. **Gramercy** /gruh MUR see/ thanks.

Act 3 Scene 3

24. **expiate** /EK spee ut, -ayt/ arrived.

Act 3 Scene 4

31. **Holborn** US /HOHL burn/; UK /HOH burn/ [HOHL-] Ely's home district in London.

71. **Consorted** /cun SORT id/ kept company with.

71. **harlot** /HAR lut/ whore.

82. **rase, raze** /rayz/ tear, cut off. **Race** /rayss/ from *arace* 'pluck off' is also possible.

88. ***pursuivant** herald, attendant. US /PUR swiv unt/ [PUR siv unt]; UK /PUR swiv unt/, *rarely* [PUR siv unt].

89. **triumphing** here should be /trī UM fing/.

104. **prophesy** /PRŎF uh sī/ to predict the future.

Act 3 Scene 5

5. **tragedian** /truh JEE dee un/ or /-dyun/ tragic actor.

11. **stratagems** /STRAT uh jumz/ schemes.

32. **suspects** /suh SPECTS/ suspicions.

33. ***covert'st** most secret. US, CN /KOHV urtst/ [KUV-]; UK /KUV-/ [KOHV-], *rarely* [KŎV-].

44. **extreme** here should be /EK streem/.

57. **timorously** /TIM (uh) rus lee/ in a frightened manner.

61. **Misconster** /mis CŎN stur/ misconstrue.

ă-bat, ăir-marry, air-pair, ạr-far, ĕr-merry, ĝ-get, ī-high, ĭr-mirror, ł-little, ṇ-listen, ŏ-hot, oh-go, ōō-wood, ōō-moon, oor-tour, ŏr-or, ow-how, ţh-that, ŧh-thin, ŭ-but, UR-fur, ur-under. ( )- suppress the syllable   [ ]- less common   see p. xi for complete list.

81. **bestial** beastlike. /BEST yⱡ/; US *also* [-chⱡ].   US, CN /BEES-/ not recommended.

87. **insatiate** /in SAYSH yut, -yayt/ never satisfied.   /-ut/ is more usual for an adj.

91. **lineaments** /LIN yuh munts/ distinctive features.

95. **orator** US, CN /OR uh tur/; UK, E. COAST US /ŎR-/.   Sometimes /OR ayt ur/ is used, but it is not recommended.   /-tor/ not recommended.

98, 105. **Baynard's** /BAY nurdz/ Richard's London home.

109. ***recourse** access.   Here should be /rih CORSS/, the usual UK pronunciation; US *also* /ree-/.

Act 3 Scene 6

1. **the indictment** /th^y in DĪT munt/ charge of wrongdoing.

7. ***precedent** (F1) /PRESS ih dunt/.   Q1–6's **president** is an archaic variant, pronounced the same way, or possibly /PREZ-/.

Act 3 Scene 7

5, 6. **contract** engagement.   Here should be /cŏn TRACT/.

7. **Th'unsatiate** (Q1–6) /th^y un SAYSH yut, -yayt/ never satisfied.   Some eds. prefer F1's **insatiate** /in-/.   /-ut/ is more usual for an adj.

12. **lineaments** /LIN yuh munts/ distinctive features.

25. **statuës, (statuas** F1, Q1–6) here should be 3 syllables /STACH oo uz/; UK *also* /STAT yoo uz/.

30. **Recorder** here should be /REK ur dur/ a city official.

32. **saith** says.   Here should be 1 syllable US /sayth/, *rarely* [seth]; UK /seth/ [sayth].   The older form is /seth/.

49. **descant** /DES kănt/ melody sung above the main tune.

55. **leads** /ledz/ roof.

72. **lulling** /LŬLL ing/ archaic variant of **lolling** /LŎL ing/.

74. ***courtezans, courtesans** rich men's whores. US /CORT ih zunz, -zanz/, *rarely* [cort ih ZANZ]; CN /CORT ih zanz/ [-zunz], *rarely* [cort ih ZANZ]; UK /CORT ih zanz, cort ih ZANZ/.

90. **perfit** /PUR fit/ (Q1–6) archaic variant of F1's **perfect**. It could also be /PAR fit/ in Shk's time.

118. **supreme** here should be US /SOO preem/; UK, SOUTH. US *also* [SYOO-].

130. **recure** cure. /ree-, rih KYOOR/; US *also* [-KYUR].

136. **empery** /EM pur ee/ status as emperor.

137. **consorted** /cun SORT id/ in company with.

158. **revenue** sometimes in verse /ruh VEN yoo/, but here as in mod. Eng. US /REV in oo/; UK, SOUTH. US /-yoo/.

160. **defects** here should be /dih-, dee FECTS/.

179. **contract** /cun TRACT/ engaged to be married.

181. **betroth'd** /bih-, bee TROHṬHD/ engaged to be married.

192. **expostulate** /ek SPŎS chuh layt/; UK *also* /-tyoo layt/ discuss, object.

213. **egally** /EE guh lee/ archaic variant of **equally**.

226. **Albeit** /awl BEE (i)t/ although.

234. **impure** here should be /IM pyoor/.

Act 4 Scene 1

31. **Westminster** here should be /WEST min stur/.

54. ***cockatrice** /CŎCK uh triss, -trīss/ a monster whose gaze kills.

84. **timorous** /TIM (uh) rus/ frightened.

ă-bat, ăir-marry, air-pair, ạr-far, ĕr-merry, ĝ-get, ī-high, ir-mirror, ł-little, ṇ-listen, ŏ-hot, oh-go, oo-wood, oo-moon, oor-tour, ōr-or, ow-how, ṭh-that, ŧh-thin, ŭ-but, UR-fur, ur-under. ( )- suppress the syllable [ ]- less common   see p. xi for complete list.

Act 4 Scene 2

35. **close** /clohss/ secret.

35. **exploit** here should be /ek SPLOYT/.

38. **orators** US, CN /OR uh turz/; UK, E. COAST US /ŎR-/. Sometimes /OR ayt urz/ is
used, but it is not recommended. /-torz/ not recommended.

52. **keeping close** /clohss/ keeping hidden, imprisoned.

90. **Herford, Hereford** in the US both would be /HUR furd/. In the UK the county
is normally /HĔR ih furd/ which here should be 2 syllables /HĔR furd/.

96. **prophesy** /PRŎF uh sī/ to predict the future.

103. **Exeter** /EK sih tur/.

105. **Rouge-mount** /RŌŌZH mownt/. Some eds. prefer **Rougemont, Ruge-mont**
/RŌŌZH mŏnt/ red mountain.

122. **Brecknock** /BRECK nuk/. Some eds. prefer **Brecon** /BRECK un/.

Act 4 Scene 3

4-17. **Dighton** /DĪT n̩/.

4. **suborn** /sub ORN/ bribe.

6. **Albeit** /awl BEE (i)t/ although.

11. **alablaster** a type of white rock. US /AL uh blăss tur/; E. NEW ENG.,
UK /-blahss-/ [-blăss-]. Archaic variant of **alabaster** /-băss-, -bahss-/.

36. **close** /clohss/ securely.

38. **Abraham's** here should be /AY brumz/.

40. **Britain** /BRIT n̩/ from Brittany. In Shk's time /-ayn/ was also used. Some eds.
prefer mod. **Breton** US /BRET n̩/; UK /BRET ŏn/ [-n̩, -un]. Sometimes the Fr.
ending /-ohⁿ/ is used in the UK.

52. **servitor** /SURV ih tur/ servant. /-tor/ not recommended.

Act 4 Scene 4

10. **unblown** here should be /UN blohn/.

13, 128. **aery, airy** /AIR ee/ of the air.

23. ***entrails** /EN traylz/; US *also* [-trɨz] guts.

28. **abstract** /AB stract/ summary.

28. **record** here should be /rek-, rik ORD/.

36. **seniory** /SEEN yur ee/ seniority.

45. **holp'st** /hohlpst/ helped.

69. **Th' adulterate** /ɪh ͨuh DULL trayt, -trut/ adulterous. /-ut/ would be usual
for an adj.

79. **prophesy** /PRŎF uh sī/ to predict the future.

101. **caitiff** /KAYT if/ scoundrel.

114. ***mischance** in verse normally with 2nd syllable stress.

128. ***intestate** (Q1–6) /in TESS tayt/; US *also* /-tut/ dead with nothing to bequeath.
F1 has **intestine** /in TESS tin/; UK *also* [-teen] internal.

129. **orators** US, CN /OR uh turz/; UK, E. COAST US /ŎR-/. Sometimes
/OR ayt urz/ is used, but it is not recommended. /-torz/ not recommended.

149. ***alarum** US, CN /uh LAHR um/ [-LĂIR-]; UK /uh LĂIR um, uh LAHR um/
a call to arms.

166. **rood** /rōōd/ cross.

174. **comfortable hour** here should be /CUM fur tuh bł OW ur/.

186. **extreme** here should be /EK streem/.

190. **complete armor** here should be /CŎM pleet/ full armor.

ă-bat, ăir-marry, air-pair, ạr-far, ĕr-merry, ĝ-get, ī-high, ĭr-mirror, ł-little, ņ-listen,
ŏ-hot, oh-go, ōō-wood, ōō-moon, oor-tour, ōr-or, ow-how, ŧh-that, ŧ̶ḣ-thin, ŭ-but,
UR-fur, ur-under. ( )- suppress the syllable   [ ]- less common   see p. xi for complete list.

229. **entrails** /EN traylz/; US *also* [-trĭz] guts.

251. **Lethe** /LEETH ee/ river of forgetfulness in Hades.

276. **handkercher** (Q1–6) /HANK ur chur/. Archaic variant of F1's **handkerchief** which some eds. prefer.

297. **increase** here should be /in CREESS/ offspring.

331. **chastised** punished. Here should be /CHĂSS tīz ed/. The usual US pronuncia-tion, also used in CN, has 1st syllable stress; in the UK 2nd syllable stress is usual.

335. **retail** pass on. Here should be /rih-, ree TAYL/.

434. **puissant** powerful. The traditional forms are /PWISS ṇt/, /PYŌŌ sṇt/, but these are now rare. In all countries one of several Frenchified pronunciations is the most common: /PWEE sṇt/ in the US, /-sahnt/ in CN, and /-sah^{n}t/ in the UK, but all three may be found in each country.

444–538. **Salisbury** 2 or 3 syllables, depending on meter US /SAWLZ b(ĕ)r ee/; UK /SAWLZ b(u)r ee/ [SĂLZ-].

---

464. **runagate** /RUN uh gayt/ fugitive. Some eds. prefer **renegade**.

482. **Safe-conducting** /sayf CŎN duct ing/.

498. **Devonshire** /DEV un shur/ [-sheer].

499. **advertised** informed. Here should be /ad VUR tih zed, -sed/.

500. **Courtney, Courtenay** /CORT nee/.

500. **prelate** /PREL ut/ high-ranking churchman.

501. **Exeter** /EK sih tur/.

519. **Yorkshire** /YORK shur/ [-sheer].

521. **Britain** /BRIT ṇ/ from Brittany. In Shk's time /-ayn/ was also used. Some eds. prefer mod. **Breton** US /BRET ṇ/; UK /BRET ŏn/ [-ṇ, -un]. Sometimes the Fr. ending /-oh^n/ is used in the UK.

522. **Dorsetshire** /DOR sit shur/ [-sheer].

527. **Hois'd** /hoyzd/ archaic variant of *hoisted*. Some eds. prefer **Hoist**.

Act 4 Scene 5

10, 13. **Pembroke** US /PEM brohk/; UK /PEM brōōk/ [-bruck, -brohk].

10. **Ha'rford-west** /HAR furd WEST/. Variant form of **Haverford-west** /HAV (ur) furd WEST/ which here should be 3 syllables.

13. **Talbot** US /TAL but/ [TAWL-]; UK /TAWL but/ [TŎL-, TAL-].

15. **Rice ap Thomas** /RĪSS ap-/. Some eds. prefer Welsh **Rhys-ap-Thomas** /REES ahp-/.

Act 5 Scene 1

15. **allies** here with 2nd syllable stress.

19. ***respite** day to which something is postponed. Here should be US /RESP it/, *rarely* [-īt]; CN /RESP it/ [-īt]; UK /RESP īt/ [-it]. /RESP it/ is older, but /-īt/ has been in use since the 17th century.

Act 5 Scene 2

11. **centry** (F1) /SEN tree/ a variant of Q1–6's **center** (UK **centre**).

12. **Leicester** /LESS tur/ .

13. **Tamworth** /TAM WURTH/ [-wurth]. /TAM uth/ is non-standard in the UK.

Act 5 Scene 3

9. **descried** /dih SKRĪD/ found out.

11. **battalia** order of battle. /buh TAYL yuh/ is older; /buh TAHL yuh/ is newer.

The Complete Oxford begins 5.4 here—line nos. in parentheses.

---

29. (5.4.5) **Pembroke** US /PEM brohk/; UK /PEM brōōk/ [-bruck, -brohk].

ă-bat, ăir-marry, air-pair, ạr-far, ĕr-merry, ĝ-get, ī-high, ĭr-mirror, ł-little, ņ-listen, ŏ-hot, oh-go, ōō-wood, ōō-moon, oor-tour, ōr-or, ow-how, țh-that, ŧħ-thin, ŭ-but, UR-fur, ur-under. ( )- suppress the syllable   [ ]- less common   see p. xi for complete list.

> *The Complete Oxford* begins 5.5 here—line nos. in parentheses.

59. (5.5.12) ***pursuivant-at-arms** herald. US /PUR swiv unt/ [PUR siv unt]; UK /PUR swiv unt/, *rarely* [PUR siv unt].

65. (5.5.18) **staves** /stayvz/ staffs.

> 68, 271 (5.5.21, 225) **Northumberland** /~~north~~ UM bur lund/.

89. (5.5.42) **the arbitrement, arbitrament** /th^yahr BIT ruh munt/ settlement.

105. (5.5.58) ***peize, peise** weigh. US /peez/, *sometimes* [payz]; UK /peez, payz/. Dialect evidence shows that /ee/ was the form found in southern England, and /ay/ in the north.

129. (5.5.83) **prophesied** /PRŎF uh sīd/ predicted the future.

132. (5.5.86) ***fulsome** cloying. /FULL sum/; US *rarely* [FŬL-].

180. (5.5.138) **midnight** here with 2nd syllable stress.

232. (5.5.186) ***jocund** /JŎCK und/; US, CN *rarely* [JOHK-] merry.

242. (5.5.196) ***bulwarks** structures for defense. US, CN /BULL wurks/ [BŬL-]; UK /BULL WURKS, -wurks/. The vowels /or/, /ahr/ not recommended in the final syllable and are non-standard in the UK.

258. (5.5.212) **fat shall pay.** Some eds. substitute **foison pays** /FOY zun, -zn/ harvest, plenty.

> *The Complete Oxford* begins 5.6 here—line nos. in parentheses.

283. (5.6.13) **low'r, lour** threaten. /lowr/ with the vowel of *how*.

289. (5.6.19) **Caparison** /kuh PĂIR ih sn/ cover with an ornamental cloth.

299. (5.6.29) **In the main battle, whose *puissance on either side** power (i.e., army). After the epic caesura *puissance* may be 2 syllables if *either* is pronounced as a single syllable, or if *either* is 2 syllables, *puissance* should be 3 in a 6-foot line. In both cases it must be stressed on the 1st syllable. The traditional forms are /PWISS nss/, /PYŌO (ih) snss/, but these are now rare. In all countries one of several Frenchified pronunciations is the most common: /PWEE snss/ in the US, /-sahnss/ in CN, and /-sah^{n}ss/ in the UK, but all 3 may be found in each country.

305. (5.6.35) **Dickon** /DICK un/.

317, 333. (5.6.47, 63) **Britains** /BRIT n̩z/ men from Brittany. Some eds. prefer mod. **Bretons** US /BRET n̩z/; UK /BRET ŏnz/ [-n̩z, -unz]. Sometimes the Fr. ending /-ohⁿz/ is used in the UK.

323. (5.6.53) **paltry** /PAWL tree/ worthless.

330. (5.6.60) **exploit** here should be /ek SPLOYT/.

335. (5.6.65) **record** here should be /rek-, rik ORD/.

338.(5.6.68) **yeomen** /YOH min/ freemen who own small farms.

341. (5.6.71) **staves** /stayvz/ staffs.

Act 5 Scene 5 (*The Complete Oxford* 5.7)

10. **Leicester** /LESS tur/.

13. **Ferrers** /FĔR urz/.

38. **increase** here should be /in CREESS/ harvest.

ă-bat, ăir-ma**rr**y, air-pair, a̡r-far, ĕr-me**rr**y, ĝ-get, ī-high, ĭr-mirror, ł-little, n̩-listen, ŏ-hot, oh-go, o͞o-wood, ōō-moon, oor-t**our**, ōr-**or**, ow-**how**, ţh-that, t̶h̶-thin, Ŭ-but, UR-**fur**, ur-und**er**.   ( )- suppress the syllable   [ ]- less common   see p. xi for complete list.

Romeo and Juliet

People in the Play

Abram /AY brum/ his name is not spoken. Some eds. prefer **Abraham**.

Apothecary US /uh PŎ̶T̶H̶ uh kĕr ee/; UK /-kuh ree/ druggist.

***Balthasar** (Q1, 4) /BAL thuh zar/ *rarely* /bal t̶huh ZAR, bal T̶H̶AZ ur/. His name is not spoken. Some eds. prefer Q2-3, F1's **Peter**.

Benvolio 3 or 4 syllables depending on meter /ben VOHL (ee) yoh/.

Capulet 2 or 3 syllables depending on meter /KAP y(uh) let, -lit/.
  Capels /KAP łz/.

Escalus (Prince) /ES kuh lus/ his name is not spoken.

Juliet /JŌOL yit, -yet/ or a triple ending /JŌOL ee yit, -yet/. If the meter allows it, the mod. variant /jōo lee ET/ may also be used.

Lawrence, Laurence US /LŌR unss/; E. COAST US /LAH runss/; UK /LŎR runss/.

Mercutio 3 or 4 syllables depending on meter /MUR KYŌO sh(ee) yoh/.

Montague /MŎNT uh gyōo/. /MUNT-/ is an older pronunciation, now obsolete.

***Petruchio** /puh TRŌOK (ee) yoh/ is preferred over /puh TRŌOCH (ee) yoh/ in all countries. Some eds. prefer the Ital. spelling **Petruccio** /pay TRŌOCH oh/. His name is not spoken.

Romeo 2 or 3 syllables depending on meter /ROHM (ee) yoh/.

***Rosaline** US /RŎZ uh linn, -līn/; CN, UK /RŎZ uh līn/ [-linn]. Mentioned throughout.

Tybalt /TIB łt/.

Places in the Play

Mantua 2 or 3 syllables depending on meter US /MAN ch(oo) wuh/;
UK /MAN ty(oo) wuh/ [MAN ch(oo) wuh].

Verona /vĕr-, vur ROH nuh/.

Act 1 Scene 1

2. **colliers** /CŎL yurz/; UK *also* /CŎL ee yurz/ charcoal producers.

66. **hinds** /hīndz/ menial laborers.

73, 94. ***partisans** /PART ih zanz/ [-sanz, -zunz]; UK *also* /part ih ZANZ/ a spear with a blade on the end.

120. **drive** archaic past tense pronounced /driv/ in the dialects. Some eds. prefer **drove**.

125. ***covert** hiding place. US, CN /KOHV urt/ [KUV-]; UK /KUV urt/ [KOHV urt], *rarely* [KUV ur], an older form.

136. **Aurora's** /uh ROR uz/; UK *also* [aw-] goddess of dawn.

145. ***importun'd** /im POR chund/ asked insistently. About half the respondents in the Survey reported a form with 3rd syllable stress in all countries, but that will not fit the meter in verse and is a relatively recent innovation (cf. *fortune*).

149. **close** /clohss/ secret.

219. **severity** /suh VĔR ih tee/.

232. **strooken** /STRŎŎK in/ or perhaps simply a variant spelling of **strucken**.

Act 1 Scene 2

47. **holp** /hohlp/ helped.

51. ***plantan** today spelled **plantain** a medicinal plant. /PLĂNT ayn/ [-un]; UK *also* [PLAHNT ayn]. Variants with /-un/ are older.

56. **God-den** /gud-, gŏŏd EN/ good evening. Some eds. prefer **Good e'en**.

57. **God gi' god-den** /god-, gud gih gud EN/ or /gŏŏd EN/ good evening. Some eds. prefer **God gi' good e'en**.

64. **Martino** /mar TEE noh/.

ă-bat, ăir-**marry**, air-**pair**, ạr-**far**, ĕr-**merry**, ĝ-**get**, ī-**high**, ĭr-**mirror**, ł-**little**, ṇ-**listen**, ŏ-**hot**, oh-**go**, ŏŏ-**wood**, ōō-**moon**, oor-**tour**, ōr-**or**, ow-**how**, ṭh-**that**, ~~th~~-**thin**, ŭ-**but**, UR-**fur**, ur-**under**. ( )- suppress the syllable   [ ]- less common   see p. xi for complete list.

65. **Anselme** /AN selm/.

66. **Vitruvio** /vih TRŌOV ee oh/.

66. **Placentio** /pluh SEN shee yoh/; Ital. /plah CHEN tsee oh/.

66. **Valentine** /VAL in tīn/.

69. **Livia** /LIV ee uh/.

69. **Valentio** /vuh LEN shee yoh/; Ital. /vah LEN tsee oh/.

70. *****Lucio** /LŌOCH ee yoh/ is newer and much more common, based on Ital. Older and less common are angl. [LŌOS-], US *rarely* [LŌOSH-].   At one time many RP speakers in the UK used /lyōo-/ for words beginning *lu-,* but today their number is dwindling.

70. **Helena** /HELL in uh/.

91. **heretics** /HĔR ih tiks/ dissenters.

Act 1 Scene 3

9. **thou s'hear** a northern English, and Scottish dialect form of *shall* is *sall* which in its weak form reduces to *s'*.   It is doubtful that Shk intended this.   The mod. reader may meet the metrical demands by saying *thou sh't hear* /țhowsht HEER/.

15, 21. **Lammas-tide, -eve** /LAM us/ Aug. 1.

15. **fortnight** /FORT nīt/; US *also* [FORT nit] 2 weeks.   Virtually obsolete in the US.

32. **teachy** /TETCH ee/ fretful. Still common in the UK as **tetchy**.

33. *****trow** US, CN /troh, trow/; UK /trow/ [troh] trust.   Shk's rhymes elsewhere indicate /oh/.

36. **rood** /rōod/ cross.

43. **by my holidam** an oath referring to a 'holy object' or the 'holy lady,' i.e., Mary. Other variants are **halidam, halidom, halidame, halidome, holidame**.   Probably these were all variant spellings of /HAL ih dum, HŎL ih dum/ (note *hal-* can also be /HŎL-/ in the US in *Halloween*).

53. **cock'rel's** /CŎCK rłz/ young cock's.

83. **lineament** /LIN yuh munt/ distinctive feature.

86. **margent** /MAR junt/ archaic variant of **margin**.

Act 1 Scene 4

3. **prolixity** /proh LIK sih tee/ long-windedness.

5. **Tartar's** /TAR turz/ people of Central Asia.

5. **lath** US /lăth/; UK, E. NEW ENG. /lahth/ [lăth] narrow strip of wood.

8. **entrance** here /ENT ur unss/ is indicated.

55. **agot-stone** a type of jewel. Archaic variant of **agate**, both pronounced /AG ut/.

57. **atomi** (Q1) tiny creatures. /AT uh mī/ the plural of Lat. *atomus*. Some eds. prefer **atomy**, which could be /AT uh mee/ or **atomies** (Q3–4, F1) /AT uh meez/.

79. **tithe-pig's** /tīth/ pig paid as part of the parish dues.

81. **benefice** /BEN ih fiss/ the living of a churchman.

84. **ambuscadoes** /am buh SKAY dohz/ archaic variant of *ambuscades* ambushes.

85. **fadom** /FAD um/ archaic variant of **fathom** /FĂTH um/.

89. **plats** /plats/ braids. Variant form of **plaits** /plats/; US *also* /playts/.

Act 1 Scene 5

33. **By'r lady** (F4) /bīr-, bur LAY dee/ by Our Lady, a mild oath. **Berlady** (Q2–4, F1) is pronounced the same way. **By Lady** (Q1) /bī-, buh-/.

35. ***nuptial** wedding. US, UK /NUP chł/ [-shł]; in CN both are used equally.

35. **Lucentio** /loo SEN shee yoh/; Ital. /loo CHEN tsee oh/. At one time many RP speakers in the UK used /lyoo-/ for words beginning *lu-*, but today their number is dwindling.

ă-bat, ăir-m**a**rry, air-p**a**ir, ạr-f**a**r, ĕr-m**e**rry, ĝ-get, ī-high, ĭr-m**i**rror, ł-little, ṇ-listen, ŏ-hot, oh-go, o͞o-wood, o͞o-moon, oor-tour, ŏr-or, ow-how, th-that, th-thin, ŭ-but, UR-f**u**r, ur-und**e**r. ( )- suppress the syllable   [ ]- less common   see p. xi for complete list.

36. **Pentecost** /PEN tih cŏst/; US *also* /-cawst/ 7th Sunday after Easter.

46. **Ethiop's** /EE̶T̶H̶ yŏps/ some eds. prefer **Ethiope's** /EE̶T̶H̶ yohps/ person from Ethiopia.

56. **antic face** /AN tik/ grotesque mask. Q3–4, F1's *antique* does not mean 'ancient' here.

77. **goodman** /GooD mun/ title of a man under the rank of gentleman.

84. **scath** /ska̶t̶h̶/ harm. Variant of **scathe** /skaẗh/.

86. **princox** /PRIN cŏcks, PRING-/ insolent boy.

122. **towards** /TOH wurds, -urdz/ about to take place.

129. **Tiberio** /tī BEER ee yoh/.

Act 2 prologue

9. **access** here should be /ak SESS/.

14. **extreme** here should be /EK streem/.

Act 2 Scene 1

12. **purblind** /PUR blīnd/ blind or partly blind.

13. **Abraham** here should be /AY brum/.

14. **Cophetua** /kuh FETCH (oo) wuh/; UK *also* /kuh FET y(oo) wuh/ subject of an old ballad.

20. ***demesnes** parklands. US, CN /duh MAYNZ/ [-MEENZ]; UK uses both equally.

31. **consorted with** /cun SORT id/ in fellowship with.

34, 36. **medlar(s)** /MED lur/ an apple-like fruit.

38. **open-arse** /OHP in a̲rss/, or RP /ahss/ which in the US would be **open-ass** /OHP in ăss/, slang for *medlar*. Q2–3, F1 *open, or*; Q1 *open Et caetera*.

38. **pop'rin pear, popp'rin** /PŎP rin/ type of pear from Flanders.

Act 2 Scene 2 (*The Complete Oxford* continues this as 2.1—line nos. in parentheses)

78. (2.1.120) **prorogued** /pruh-, proh ROHG id/ postponed.

117. (2.1.159) **contract** here should be /cŏn TRACT/.

158. (2.1.203) **falc'ner's** US /FĂLK nurz/ [FAWLK-]; CN /FAWLK-/;
UK /FAWLK-, FĂLK-/ [FŎLK-].

167. (2.1.212) **My niesse, niësse, nyas** (*Neece* Q2–3, F1) nestling hawk. All are
pronounced /NĪ uss/. **My deere** (Q4), **My sweete** (F2), **Madame** (Q1).

179. (2.1.224) **gyves** /jīvz/ chains, fetters.

188. (2.1.233) **sire's close cell** (F1, Q2-3) /clohss/ hidden, secluded. Q1 has
father's cell.

Act 2 Scene 3 (*The Complete Oxford* 2.2)

7. ***osier** US /OH zhur/ [OH zyur]; UK /OH zyur/ willow.

11. ***divers** various. Here should be stressed on the 1st syllable
US, CN /DĪ vurss, -vurz/; UK /DĪ vurss/ [-vurz].

31. **Benedicite** Ang.Lat. /ben uh DISS ih tee/;
Church Lat. /bay nay DEE chee tay/ bless you.

37. **unstuff'd** here should be /UN stuft/.

69. ***Maria** /muh RĪ uh/ is the older, angl. form, /muh REE uh/ is newer.

83. **badst** /badst/ 2nd person sing. past tense of *bid* 'asked.' See *bade* in "The Most
Common 'Hard' Words."

92. **rancor** (UK **rancour**) /RANK ur/ ill-will. /-or/ not recommended.

Act 2 Scene 4 (*The Complete Oxford* 2.3)

22. **minim rests** /MIN im/ the shortest rests in music.

ă-bat, ăir-marry, air-pair, ạr-far, ĕr-merry, ĝ-get, ī-high, ĭr-mirror, ł-little, ṇ-listen,
ŏ-hot, oh-go, ōō-wood, ōō-moon, oor-tour, ōr-or, ow-how, ţh-that, ~~th~~-thin, ŭ-but,
UR-fur, ur-under. ( )- suppress the syllable   [ ]- less common   see p. xi for complete list.

26. **passado** /puh SAH doh/ step and thrust in fencing.

26. **punto reverso** angl. /POON toh/ or /PUN toh rih VUR soh/;
Ital. /POON toh ray VĔR soh/ backhanded stroke in fencing.

26. **hay** /hay/ cry when scoring a hit in fencing. Some eds. prefer **hai** which could
also be /hī/.

28. **antic** /AN tik/. Q1–4, F1 *antique* does not mean 'ancient' here.

29. **phantasimes, phantasims** (*phantacies* Q2–4, F1) /FAN taz imz/ affected young
gentlemen. Some eds. prefer Q1's **fantasticoes** /fan TASS tih kohz/.

31. ***lamentable** US /luh MEN tuh bł/ [LAM en tuh bł]; CN, UK /LAM un tuh bł/
[luh MEN-].

33. ***fashion-mongers** fops. US /FASH un mŏng gurz/ or /-mawng-/ [-mung-];
CN /-mung-, -mŏng-/; UK /-mung-/.

39. ***Petrarch** /ṔET rahrk/; US *also* [PEET-] Italian poet.

41. **Dido** /DĪ doh/ Queen of Carthage.

41. **dowdy** /DOW dee/ shabby-looking woman.

41. **Cleopatra** US /clee oh PAT ruh/; UK *also* /-PAHT ruh/.

42. **hildings** /HILL dingz/ good-for-nothings.

42. **harlots** /HAR luts/ whores.

42. **Thisby, Thisbe** /T̶H̶IZ bee/ in Gk. mythology the beloved of Pyramus.

44. **bon jour** angl. /bohn ZHOOR, -JOOR/; Fr. /boh^n zhoor/ good day.

53. **bow** /bow/.

83. **cheverel** /SHEV ur ł/ kid leather, i.e., easily stretched. Archaic variant of
cheveril, pronounced the same way.

92. **lolling** /LŎLL ing/ with tongue hanging out.

93. **bable** presumably /BAB ł/ a fool's short stick, i.e., penis. Archaic variant of
bauble /BAW bł/.

129. **indite** /in DĪT/ invite.

153. **flirt-gills, flirt-jills** /FLURT jilz/ loose women.

154. **skains-mates** /SKAYNZ mayts/ companions. Some eds. prefer the variant **skeans-** /SKEENZ-/.

190. **top-gallant** mast above the mainmast. Sailors say /tuh GAL unt/, landsmen /tŏp GAL unt/.

203. **as lieve** /leev/ 'as soon,' still used in some US dialects. Some eds. prefer **lief** /leef/.

206. **clout** /clowt/ cloth.

206. **versal** /VUR sł/ universal.

Act 2 Scene 5 (*The Complete Oxford* 2.4)

6. **low'ring, louring** frowning. /LOWR ing/ with the vowel of *how*.

26, 52. **jaunce(-ing)** /jawnss/ jolting journey.

62. **I *trow** US, CN /troh, trow/; UK /trow/ [troh] I daresay. Shk's rhymes elsewhere indicate /oh/.

63. **poultice** /POHL tiss/ cloth with medicine on it.

Act 2 Scene 6 (*The Complete Oxford* 2.5)

18. ***gossamers** /GŎSS uh murz/ spiders' threads.

21. **confessor** here should be /CŎN fess ur/. /-or/ not recommended.

26. **blazon** /BLAY zun, -zņ/ proclaim.

33. **excess** here should be /ek SESS/, the most common UK form.

Act 3 Scene 1

9. **drawer** /DRAW ur/ tapster, the person who draws the liquor at a tavern.

ă-bat, ăir-marry, air-pair, ạr-far, ĕr-merry, ĝ-get, ī-high, ĭr-mirror, ł-little, ņ-listen, ŏ-hot, oh-go, ōō-wood, ōō-moon, oor-tour, ŏr-or, ow-how, ţh-that, ŧħ-thin, ŭ-but, UR-fur, ur-under. ( )- suppress the syllable [ ]- less common   see p. xi for complete list.

29. **riband** /RIB und/ archaic variant of **ribbon**.

45–130. **consort(est)** /cun SORT/ double meaning: 'keep company with' and 'play music with.'

---

74. **Alla stoccato** /ah lah stuh KAH toh/ or angl. /al uh-/. Ital. is *stoccata* at the thrust. Some eds. prefer **stoccado** /stuh KAH doh/.

80. **pilcher** /PIL chur/ scabbard.

85. **passado** /puh SAH doh/ step and thrust in fencing.

123. **lenity** /LEN ih tee/ leniency.

161. **martial** /MAR shł/ warlike.

190. **amerce** /uh MURSS/ lay a heavy fine.

Act 3 Scene 2

2 **Phoebus'** /FEE bus/ god of the sun.

3. **Phaëton** /FAY ih tun, -tŏn/ son of the sun god. /-ŏn/ is usual in the US and is increasingly common in the UK. Some eds. prefer **Phaëthon** /--thun, -thŏn/. /-un/ would be the traditional form (cf. *Solomon*).

5. **close curtain** /clohss/ concealing curtain.

37. **weraday** (Q2) /WĔR uh day/ alas. Some eds. prefer Q3–4's, F1's **weladay** /WEL uh day/, Q1's **alack the day**.

47. ***cockatrice** /CŎCK uh triss, -trīss/ a monster whose gaze kills.

51. **weal** /weel/ welfare.

56. **sounded** archaic variant of **swooned**. In Shk's time either /SOWN did/ or /SŌŌN did/.

57. ***bankrout** /BANK rowt/ [-rut] archaic variant of **bankrupt**.

60. **bier** /beer/ coffin.

76. **ravening** /RAV (i)n ing/ devouring.

88. ***aqua-vitae** distilled liquor, e.g., brandy. US /AHK-, AK wuh VEE tī/, *rarely* [-VĪ tee]; CN /AK wuh VEE tī/ [AHK-]; UK /AK wuh VEE tī/ [-VEE tuh]. /AK wuh VĪ tee/ is the oldest surviving form. /-VEE tay/ not recommended.

Act 3 Scene 3

49. **confessor** here should be /CŎN fess ur/. /-or/ not recommended.

70. **unmade** here should be /UN mayd/.

79. **errant** /ĔR unt/ archaic variant of **errand**.

98. **conceal'd** here should be /CŎN seeld/.

123. **usurer** /YOO zhur ur/; UK *also* [-zhyoor ur, -zhoor ur] someone who lends money for interest.

143. **mishaved** /MISS hay vid/ **misbehaved**.

Act 3 Scene 4

11. **mewed up** /myood/ caged.

Act 3 Scene 5

4. ***pomegranate** today given a variety of pronunciations: US, CN /PŎM uh gran it/; US *also* [PŎM-, PUM gran it, PUM ih gran it]; UK /PŎM uh gran it/ [PŎM gran it]. Here, however, it should be 3 syllables.

9. ***jocund** /JŎCK und/; US, CN *rarely* [JOHK-] merry.

13. **exhal'd** here with 2nd syllable stress, /eks HAYLD/, the normal UK form. Q3–4, F1 have **exhales**.

20. **reflex** here should be /ree-, rih FLEKS/ reflection.

62. **renowm'd** /rih-, ree NOWMD/ archaic variant of **renowned** /rih-, ree NOWND/.

ă-bat, ăir-ma**rry**, air-**pair**, ạr-**far**, ĕr-**merry**, ĝ-**get**, ī-**high**, ĭr-**mirror**, ł-**little**, ṇ-**listen**, ŏ-**hot**, oh-**go**, oo-**wood**, ōō-**moon**, oor-**tour**, ōr-**or**, ow-**how**, ţh-**that**, ᵼh-**thin**, ŭ-**but**, UR-**fur**, ur-**under**. ( )- suppress the syllable [ ]- less common   see p. xi for complete list.

89. **runagate** /RUN uh gayt/ fugitive.

129. ***conduit** fountain. Here must be 2 syllables /CŎN dwit/;
UK *also* [CUN dwit, CŎN dywit, CŎN dit, CUN dit].

168. **hilding** /HILL ding/ good-for-nothing.

172. **God-i-goden** (F1), *Godigeden* (Q2–4), *goddegodden* (Q1)
/gŏd-, gud ee guh DEN/. Some eds. prefer **God-'i-good e'en**. Here perhaps
rather than the usual 'good evening' it means 'for God's sake.'

180. ***demesnes** estates. US, CN /duh MAYNZ/ [-MEENZ]; UK uses both equally.

180. **nobly lien'd** (*liand* Q2) well-connected. The Q2 spelling indicates 2 syllables,
angl. /LĪ und/; or following Fr. /LEE und/. Q3–4, F1's **allied** would have to be compressed with *nobly* /NOH blʸuh LĪD/. Q1 has **trained**. Other eds. prefer **lined**,
'lianc'd /LĪ unst/ allianced, **limb'd**, **ligned** angl. /līnd/; Fr. /leend/.

183. **puling** /PYŌOL ing/ whining.

209. **stratagems** /STRAT uh jumz/ schemes.

219. **dishclout** /DISH clowt/ dish cloth.

221. **Beshrow** /bih-, bee SHROH/ curse. Archaic variant of **beshrew** /-SHRŌO/.

Act 4 Scene 1

48. **prorogue** /pruh-, proh ROHG/ postpone.

63. **umpeer** /UM peer/ archaic variant of **umpire**.

88. **unstain'd** here should be /UN staynd/.

97. **surcease** /sur SEESS/ cease.

100. **wanny** /WŎN ee/ pale. Other choices are **paly** (Q4), **many** (Q2–3, F1).

110. **bier** /beer/ coffin.

Act 4 Scene 2

14. **harlotry** /HAR luh tree/ whore.

20. **prostrate** /PRŎS trayt/; US *rarely* [-trut] lying face down.

39. **Tush** /tŭsh/ expression of disdain.

43. **huswife** /HUZ if/ is traditional, /HUSS wīf/ is a newer, spelling pronunciation. The former is the most common form in the UK, the latter in the US. In CN both are used equally. In North America /HUSS wif/ is also sometimes used. Some eds. prefer mod. **housewife**.

Act 4 Scene 3

3. **orisons** prayers. US, CN /OR ih zunz, -zn̥z/ [-sunz, -sn̥z]; E. COAST US /ŎR-/; UK /ŎR ih zunz, -zn̥z/.

8. **behoofeful** /bih-, bee HOOF fu̥ll/ needful. Variant of **behoveful** /-HOHV-/, **behooveful** /-HOOV-/.

39. **receptacle** here should be /REE sep tuh kł/.

50. **Environed** /en VĪ run ed/; US *also* [en VĪ urn ed] surrounded.

Act 4 Scene 4

6. **cot-quean** /CŎT kween/ man who acts as housewife.

Act 4 Scene 5 (*The Complete Oxford* 4.4—line nos. in parentheses)

4. (4.4.31) **pennyworths, penn'worths** bargains. Both pronounced /PEN urths/.

15. (4.4.42) **weraday** /WĔR uh day/ alas. Some eds. prefer **weladay** /WEL uh day/.

16. (4.4.43) **aqua-vitae** distilled liquor, e.g., brandy. US /AHK-, AK wuh VEE tī/, *rarely* [-VĪ tee]; CN /AK wuh VEE tī/ [AHK-]; UK /AK wuh VEE tī/ [-VEE tuh]. /AK wuh VĪ tee/ is the oldest surviving form. /-VEE tay/ not recommended.

17–50. (4.4.44–81) **lamentable** here should be /LAM un tuh bł/ the usual UK pronunciation.

47. (4.4.78) **solace** /SŎL us/ comfort.

ă-bat, ăir-marry, air-pair, a̯r-far, ĕr-merry, ĝ-get, ī-high, ĭr-mirror, ł-little, n̥-listen, ŏ-hot, oh-go, o͞o-wood, o͞o-moon, oor-tour, ōr-or, ow-how, t̪h-that, t̶h̶-thin, ŭ-but, UR-fur, ur-under. ( )- suppress the syllable [ ]- less common   see p. xi for complete list.

56. (4.4.71 [sic]) **detestable** here should be /DEE tess tuh bł/ or /DET es tuh bł/.

88. (4.4.115) **dirges** /DUR jiz/ funeral songs.

94. (4.4.121) **low'r, lour** frown. /lowr/ with the vowel of *how*.

133. (4.4.159) **Rebeck, Rebec** /REE beck/ a 3-stringed fiddle.

Act 5 Scene 1

2. ***presage** here should be /pree-, prih SAYJ/ foretell.

29. **Tush** /tŭsh/ expression of disdain.

49. **penury** /PEN yur ee/; UK *also* /PEN yoor ee/ poverty.

52. **caitiff wretch** /KAYT if/ scoundrel.

85. **cordial** US /COR jł/; UK /COR dył/ healing medicine.

Act 5 Scene 3

16, 20. **obsequies** /ŎB suh kweez/ burial services.

22. **mattock** /MAT uk/ digging tool.

38. **inexorable** /in EK sur uh bł/; US *also* /-EG zur-/ unyielding.

45. **detestable** here should be /DEE tess tuh bł/ or /DET es tuh bł/.

68. **conjuration** (following Q1) /cŏn jur RAY shun/ [cun-]; solemn entreaty.
Q3, F1 have **commiseration** /kuh miz ur RAY shun/ pity.

84. **lanthorn** archaic variant of **lantern**. Probably pronounced /LAN turn/, but possibly /LANT horn/ or /LAN thurn, -thorn/.

94. ***ensign** emblem. US, CN /EN sn̩/, US *rarely* [-sīn]; UK /-sn̩, -sīn/.

105. ***paramour** US, CN /PĂIR uh moor/ [-mor]; UK /-mor/ [-moor] lover.

141, 207. **sepulchre** /SEP ł kur/ tomb.

145. **unkind** here should be /UN kīnd/.

146. ***lamentable** here should be /LAM un tuh bł/ the usual UK pronunciation.

148. **comfortable** here should be /CUM fur tuh bł/ giving comfort.

181. **descry** /dih SKRĪ/ see.

185. **mattock** /MAT uk/ digging tool.

221. ***mischance** in verse normally with 2nd syllable stress.

238. **Betroth'd** /bih-, bee TROHṬHD/ engaged to be married.

253. **prefixed** here should be /pree-, prih FIK sid/ appointed.

289. **pothecary** US /PŎTH uh kĕr ee/; UK /-kuh ree/ apothecary, druggist.

292. **scourge** /SKURJ/ severe punishment.

297. **jointure** /JOYN chur/ marriage settlement.

ă-bat, ăir-marry, air-pair, ạr-far, ĕr-merry, ĝ-get, ī-high, ĭr-mirror, ł-little, ṇ-listen, ŏ-hot, oh-go, ōō-wood, ōō-moon, oor-tour, ōr-or, ow-how, ṭh-that, th-thin, ŭ-but, UR-fur, ur-under. ( )- suppress the syllable [ ]- less common   see p. xi for complete list.

The Taming of the Shrew

People in the Play

Sometimes some of these names are given an Italian pronunciation in performance. These pronunciations are indicated here as accurately as possible within the limits of this notation. Shakespeare, however, probably intended them to be anglicized. The *-tio, -sio, -cio* endings in Shk's day represented /-se(ee) yoh/ or /-sh(ee) yoh/, or simply /-shoh/ (*Hortensio, Litio, Lisio, Licio, Lucentio, Vincentio*).

Baptista Minola /bap TISS tuh MIN uh luh/; Ital. /bahp TEES tah MEEN oh lah/.

*Bianca 2 or 3 syllables depending on meter US /bee AHNG kuh/ [bee ANG kuh]; UK /bee ANG kuh/, *rarely* [bee AHNG kuh]; CN both are used equally; Ital. /bee AHNG kah/. If two syllables /BYAHNG kuh/ or /BYANG kuh/.

Biondello 3 or 4 syllables depending on meter /b(ee) yun DELL oh/; Ital. /bee yohn DEL loh/.

Cambio assumed name of Lucentio. 2 or 3 syllables depending on meter /KAM b(ee) yoh/; Ital. /KAHM-/.

Christophero see Sly.

*Gremio 2 or 3 syllables depending on meter /GREEM (ee) yoh/ is the older angl. form, /GREM (ee) yoh/ is a newer angl. form. The former is preferred in the UK, the latter in the US. Ital. /GRAYM-/ is also sometimes used.

Grumio 2 or 3 syllables depending on meter /GROOM (ee) yoh/.

*Hortensio 3 or 4 syllables depending on meter /hor TEN s(ee) yoh/; US, CN *rarely* [-sh(ee) yoh]; Ital. /or TEN see yoh/. Normal development would favor /-sh-/.

*Katherina 3 or 4 syllables depending on meter US /kat-, kath (ur) REEN uh/, /kuh TREEN uh/; CN /kat-/, *rarely* [kath -]; UK /kat-/ [kath-]; Ital. /kaht (ay) REE nah/. (F1 has **Katerina**, occasionally).
    Katherine 2 or 3 syllables depending on meter /KATH (u)r rin/, /KAT-/.

*Litio (F1) assumed name of Hortensio. 2 or 3 syllables depending on meter US, CN /LISH (ee) yoh/; UK /LISH-, LISS-/; Ital. forms are also used [LITS-, LEETS-]. Some eds. prefer **Lisio** (which also appears in F1), or **Licio** (F2), both angl. as /LISS-, LISH-/; *Licio* would be Ital. /LITCH-, LEECH-/.

People in the Play (cont.)

Lucentio 3 or 4 syllables depending on meter /lōō SEN sh(ee) yoh/;
Ital. /lōō CHEN ts(ee) yoh/. At one time many RP speakers in the UK used /lyōō-/
for words beginning *lu-*, but today their number is dwindling.

Minola see **Baptista**.

*Petruchio 3 or 4 syllables depending on meter /puh TRŌŌK (ee) yoh/ is preferred
over /puh TRŌŌCH (ee) yoh/ in all countries. Some eds. prefer the Ital. spelling
Petruccio /pay TRŌŌCH oh/. Shk probably meant to indicate the pronunciation
/ch/, not /k/ (cf. *Machiavel* sometimes spelled *Match-*).

Sly, Christopher sometimes referred to as **Christophero** /crih STŎF (ur) roh/. See
Induction 2.73.

*Tranio 2 or 3 syllables depending on meter. The Ital. pronunciation is
more common than the angl. form US, CN /TRAH n(ee) yoh/ [TRAY-];
UK /TRAH-/, *rarely* [TRAY-].

Vincentio 3 or 4 syllables depending on meter /vin SEN sh(ee) yoh/;
Ital. /veen CHEN ts(ee) yoh/.

Places in the Play

*Padua 2 or 3 syllables depending on meter /PAD y(oo) wuh/ [PAJ (oo) wuh].
An Ital. vowel /PAHD-/ is not recommended, since the Ital. form is *Padova*.

Pisa /PEE zuh/.

Induction Scene 1

5. **paucas pallabris** angl. /PAW kus puh LAB riss, -riz/. Sly's confusion of
Sp. *pocas palabras* /POH kahss pah LAH brahss/ and Lat. *pauca verba*
Ang.Lat. /PAW kuh VUR buh/; Class.Lat. /POW kah WĔR bah/. Both mean 'few
words,' i.e., 'enough said.'

6. **Sessa** /SESS uh/ uncertain meaning, perhaps 'hurry,' 'let it go,' 'cease.'

9. **denier** coin of little value. /duh NEER, DEN yur/ are older;
/DEN yay, dun YAY/ are newer, based on Fr.

ă-bat, ăir-marry, air-pair, ạr-far, ĕr-merry, ĝ-get, ī-high, ĭr-mirror, l̵-little, ṇ-listen,
ŏ-hot, oh-go, ōō-wood, ōō-moon, oor-tour, ōr-or, ow-how, ṭh-that, ŧh-thin, ŭ-but,
UR-fur, ur-under. ( )- suppress the syllable   [ ]- less common   see p. xi for complete list.

9. **Saint Jeronimy** /jur RŎN ih mee/.

12. **thirdborough** constable. US /THURD bur oh, -uh/;
E. COAST US /-buh roh, -buh ruh/; UK /-buh ruh/. F1 has **headborough**.

13. **borough** town. US /BUR oh/ [-uh]; E. COAST US /BUH roh/ [-ruh]; UK /BUH ruh/.

17, 18. **Brach** /bratch/ female dog. Some eds. prefer **Breathe** in line 17.

18. **Clowder** /CLOW dur/ name of a dog.

51. **dulcet** /DULL sit/ sweet.

57. **ewer** /Y$\overline{OO}$ ur/ pitcher.

101. **veriest** /VĔR yist/ most exceeding.

105. **Barthol'mew** here should be stressed /BAR ~~thl~~ my$\overline{oo}$/ or as in Shk's time
/BAR tł my$\overline{oo}$/.

108.***obeisance** /oh BAY snss/; US *also* [-BEE-] curtsy.

127. **close** /clohss/ secret.

135. ***homage** /HŎM ij/; US *also* /ŎM ij/ acknowledgement of service to a lord.

Induction Scene 2

20. **bear-herd** /BAIR urd/ bearkeeper. A more recent, spelling pronunciation
/BAIR hurd/ is also used.

22. **Wincot** /WINK ut/.

32. **abject** /AB jekt/ contemptible.

39. **Semiramis** /suh MĬR uh miss/ lusty queen of Assyria.

40. **bestrow** /bih-, bee STROH/ archaic variant of **bestrew** /-STR$\overline{OO}$/.

50. ***Adonis** US, CN /uh DŎN iss/, *rarely* [-DOHN-]; UK /uh DOHN iss/,
rarely [-DŎN-] Venus's lover.

51. **Cytherea** /s~~ith~~ uh REE uh/ Venus.

54. **Io** /Ī oh/ maiden loved by Jupiter.

57. **Daphne** /DAFF nee/ nymph changed to a laurel tree.

71. **savors** (UK **savours**) /SAY vurz/ smells.

73. **Christopher** (F1) does not fit the meter. **Christophero** (F2) /cris TŎF (ur) roh/.

105. **goodman** /GŌōD mun/ husband.

110. **Al'ce** /ălss/ variant of **Alice**.

123. **absent** /ub-, ab SENT/ keep away from.

138. **comonty** /CŎM un tee/ Sly's error for **comedy**. Some eds. prefer **commodity**.

138. **gambold** /GAM błd/ frisk. Archaic variant of **gambol** /GAM bł/.

Act 1 Scene 1

3. ***Lombardy** /LŎM bar dee/ [LUM-] region in Northern Italy.

13. **Bentivolii** /ben tih VOH lee ī/ a 15th-century family.

24. **saciety** /suh SĪ (uh) tee/ fullness. Archaic variant of **satiety** /suh TĪ (uh) tee/.

25. **Mi perdonato** /mee pĕr doh NAH toh/ Ital. pardon me. Some eds. substitute **Mi perdonate** /mee pĕr doh NAH tay/.

31. **Stoics** /STOH iks/ philosophers who showed no emotion.

33. **Ovid** /ŎV id/ Roman poet.

33. **abjur'd** /ab-, ub JOORD/; US *also* /-JURD/ renounced.

36. ***poesy** US /POH (ih) see/ [-zee]; UK, CN /- zee/ [-see] poetry.

41. **Gramercies** /gruh MUR seez/ thanks.

48. ***importune** /im POR chun/ ask insistently. About half the respondents in the Survey reported a form with 3rd syllable stress in all countries, but that will not fit the meter in verse and is a relatively recent innovation (cf. *fortune*).

ă-bat, ăir-**marry**, air-**pair**, ạr-**far**, ĕr-**merry**, ĝ-**get**, ī-**high**, ĭr-**mirror**, ł-**little**, ṇ-**listen**, ŏ-**hot**, oh-**go**, ōō-**wood**, ōō-**moon**, oor-**tour**, ōr-**or**, ow-**how**, ţh-**that**, ~~th~~-**thin**, ŭ-**but**, UR-**fur**, ur-**under**. ( )- suppress the syllable   [ ]- less common   see p. xi for complete list.

62. ***Iwis** /ih WISS/; US, CN *also* /ee WISS/ indeed.

68. **Husht, master, here's some good pastime toward** /TOH wurd, -urd/ about to take place.

69. **That wench is stark mad or wonderful froward** /FROH wurd, FROH urd/ difficult to deal with. Both 68 and 69 are four-foot lines, 68 with an epic caesura after *master*.

84. **Minerva** /mih NUR vuh/ goddess of wisdom.

87. **mew** /myōō/ cage.

101. **commune** here should be /CŎM yōōn/ speak intimately.

115. **parle** /parl/ conference with an enemy.

126. **Tush** /tŭsh/ expression of disdain.

127. ***alarums** US, CN /uh LAHR umz/ [-LĂIR-]; UK /uh LĂIR umz, uh LAHR umz/ calls to arms.

131. **as lief** /leef/ as soon.

154. **queen of Carthage** /CAR thij/ Dido, ruler of Carthage in N. Africa.

162.   **Redime**   **te**   **captum**   **quam**   **queas**   **minimo**
Ang.Lat. /RED (ih) mee tee KAP tum   kwam   KWEE ass MIN ih moh/
Class.Lat. /RED (ih) may tay KAHP tōōm kwahm KWAY ahs MIN ih moh/
           Ransom yourself from captivity as cheaply as you can.

163. **Gramercies** /gruh MUR seez/ thanks.

168. **Agenor** /uh JEE nur/ Europa's father. /-nor/ not recommended.

169. **Cretan** /CREET n̩, -un/ of Crete.

169. **strond** /strŏnd/ shore. Archaic variant of **strand**. Here rhymes with *hand*.

183. **mew'd** /myōōd/ caged.

198. **Basta** angl. /BAS tuh/; Ital. /BAH stah/ enough.

204. ***Florentine** US /FLŌR in teen/ [-tīn]; E. COAST US /FLŎR-/;
UK /FLŎR in tīn/ [-teen] person from Florence.

205. **Neapolitan** /nee uh PŎL ih tun/ man from Naples.

232. **descried** /dih SKRĪD/ found out.

Act 1 Scene 2

1–190. **Verona** /vĕr-, vur ROH nuh/.

4. ***trow** US, CN /troh, trow/; UK /trow/ [troh] trust. Shk's rhymes elsewhere indicate /oh/.

24. **Con tutto   il   core,   ben trovato**
    /cŏn TOO toh eel COR ay ben troh VAH toh/
    with all my heart, well met.
Some eds. substitute **cuore** /KWOR ay/ for *core*.

25. **Alla   nostra   casa   ben venuto,   molto   honorato**
    /ah lah NŎS trah KAH sah ben ven OO toh, MŎL toh ŏn or AH toh

    signor   mio   Petrucio
    SEEN yor MEE oh pay TROOCH oh, -yoh/
    welcome to my house, my most honored Signor Petrucio.

28. **'leges** /LEJ iz/ alleges.

69. **Florentius'** /fluh REN shus/ he married an ugly wife.

70. **Sibyl** /SIB ł/; UK *also* /SIB il/ prophetess in Gk mythology.

70, 90. **shrowd** /shrohd/ sharp-tongued. Archaic variant of **shrewd**.

71. **Xantippe** /zan TIP ee/ wife of Socrates noted for her nagging. Some eds. prefer the spelling **Xanthippe** also pronounced /zan TIP ee/, now often given a spelling pronunciation /-THIP-/. /gzan-/ not recommended.

79. **aglet-baby** /AG lit/ small figure on a lacing cord.

90. **froward** /FROH wurd, FROH urd/ difficult to deal with.

124. **defects** here should be /dih-, dee FEKTS/.

ă-bat, ăir-marry, air-pair, ạr-far, ĕr-merry, ĝ-get, ī-high, ĭr-mirror, ł-little, ṇ-listen, ŏ-hot, oh-go, ōō-wood, ōō-moon, oor-tour, ōr-or, ow-how, ʈh-that, ŧh-thin, ŭ-but, UR-fur, ur-under. ( )- suppress the syllable   [ ]- less common   see p. xi for complete list.

127. **access** here should be /ak SESS/.

150. ***largess, largesse** generous gift. Here should have 1st syllable stress US /LAR jess/ [-zhess]; CN, UK /LAR zhess/ [-jess]. Forms with /j/ are older.

164. ***Trow you** US, CN /troh, trow/; UK /trow/ [troh] know. Shk's rhymes elsewhere indicate /oh/.

190. **Antonio's** /an TOHN yohz/; Ital. /ahn-/.

202. **chafed** /CHAY fid/ enraged.

206.* **'larums** US, CN /LAHR umz/ [-LĂIR-]; UK /LĂIR umz, LAHR umz/ calls to arms.

210. **Tush** /tŭsh/ expression of disdain.

242. **Leda's** /LEE duz/ mother of Helen of Troy.

256. **Alcides'** /al SĪ deez/ Hercules'.

259, 267. **access** here should be /ak SESS/.

268. **ingrate** here should be /in GRAYT/ ungrateful.

275. ***quaff** /kwŏf/; UK *rarely* [kwahf] drink freely. /kwăf/ is also used, but is not recommended.

280. **your ben venuto** /ben ven O͞O toh/ your welcome, i.e., host.

Act 2 Scene 1

3. **gawds, gauds** /gawdz/ trinkets. Some eds. prefer F1's **goods**.

18. **envy** here with 2nd syllable stress /en VEE/.

26. **hilding** /HILL ding/ good-for-nothing.

47. **a gentleman of Verona** here *gentlemen* is compressed to 2 syllables and *Verona* is pronounced normally /vĕr-, vur ROH nuh/; but if *gentleman* is 3 syllables, then *Verona* could be reduced to /VROH nuh/.

60. **Mantua** US /MAN choo wuh/; UK /MAN tyoo wuh/ [MAN choo wuh].

68. **Antonio's** /an TOHN yohz/; Ital. /ahn-/.

73. **Backare, Bacare** (F1), **Baccare** (F2) fake Latin for 'back off!' Accent could be on the 2nd or 1st syllable. Angl. /BACK uh ree/, /back AIR ee/ or with Ital. or Lat. ending /BACK ah ray/, /back AH ray/.

80. **Rheims** angl. /reemz/; Fr. /răⁿss/ city in France.

97. **access** here should be /ak SESS/.

108. **Holla** /huh LAH/ a call to attract attention.

131. **I am as** *peremptory* **as she proud-minded** insisting on obedience. If contracted to *I'm,* then /pur EM tur ee/ which is more common today. If *I am* is spoken as 2 words then /PĔR um tree/ which is also used today. Both forms appear elsewhere in Shk.

135. **extreme** here should be /EK streem/.

150. **bow'd** /bohd/ bent.

163. **discomfited** /dis CUM fit id/ defeated.

175. **volubility** /vŏl yuh BIL ih tee/ ability to talk easily, with quick wit.

180. **banes** /baynz/ proclamation in church of an intended marriage. Archaic variant of **banns** /banz/.

198. **join'd stool** /JOYND sto͞ol/ a well-crafted stool. Some eds. prefer **joint stool**.

227. **craven** /CRAY vin, -vn̩/ coward.

247. **askaunce** at a sideways angle. Archaic variant of **askance** US /uh SKĂNSS/; UK, E. NEW ENG. /uh SKAHNSS/ [uh SKĂNSS]. The archaic vowel was pronounced /-AW-/ and gave rise to RP /-AH-/.

263. **extempore** /ek STEM p(uh) ree/ composed on the spur of the moment.

293. **froward** difficult to deal with. /FROH wurd, FROH urd/ before an epic caesura.

295. **Grissel** /GRISS ł/ Griselda, a submissive wife.

ă-bat, ăir-marry, air-pair, ạr-far, ĕr-merry, ĝ-get, ī-high, ĭr-mirror, ł-little, n̩-listen, ŏ-hot, oh-go, o͞o-wood, o͞o-moon, oor-tour, ŏr-or, ow-how, ţh-that, ŧh-thin, ŭ-but, UR-fur, ur-under. ( )- suppress the syllable [ ]- less common   see p. xi for complete list.

296. **Lucrece** Lucretia, Roman who commited suicide after being raped. Here should be /LOO creess/. At one time many RP speakers in the UK used /lyoo-/ for words beginning *lu-,* but today their number is dwindling.

313. **meacock** /MEE cŏck/ milksop.

348. **ewers** here should be 1 syllable /yoorz/ pitchers.

348. **lave** /layv/ wash.

349. **Tyrian** /TĬR yun/ purple, dark red.

351. **arras** /ĂIR us/ tapestry.

354. **Valens** archaic variant of **valence** short draperies edging a bed canopy. US /VAYL unss/ [VAL-]; UK /VAL unss].

357. **milch-kine** /MILCH kīn/ milk cows.

370. **jointer** /JOYNT ur/ marriage settlement. Archaic variant of **jointure** /JOYN chur/.

374–8. **argosy, -ies** /ARG uh see/ large merchant ship.

375. **Marsellis** /mar SELL iss/ archaic variant of **Marseilles**. The usual mod. pronunciation /mar SAY/ will not fit, but another modern variant from the UK will [mar SAY łz].

378. *****galliasses** /GAL ee us iz/ [GAL ee ass iz] large galley ships.

390. **cavil** /KAV ł/; UK *also* /KAV il/ quibble.

Act 3 Scene 1

4–87. **pedant** /PED ṇt/ dull teacher.

6. *****prerogative** /pur RŎG uh tiv/ [prih-, pree-] precedence. /pree-/ non-standard in the UK.

18. *****breeching scholar** a still-whippable schoolboy. /BRITCH ing/ is traditional, /BREECH ing/ is newer. The former pronunciation is more common in the UK and the latter in the US, CN.

28 – 9. **Hic ibat Simois; hic est Sigeia tellus;**
Ang.Lat. /hick Ī bat SIM oh iss hick est sī JEE yuh TEL us;
Class.Lat. /heek IB aht SIM oh iss heek est see GAY ih ah TEL o͞os
Here flowed the Simois; here is the Sigeian land

Hic steterat Priami regia celsa senis
Ang.Lat. /hick STET ur at PRĪ am ī REE jee uh SEL suh SEEN iss/
Class.Lat. /heek STET ĕr aht PREE ah mee RAY ĝee ah KEL sah SEN iss/
Here stood the lofty palace of old Priam.

30, 41. **conster** /CŎN stur/ explain the meaning. Some eds. prefer **construe** which here should be /CŎN stro͞o/.

37. ***pantaloon** foolish old man. US, UK /PANT uh lo͞on/ [pant uh LO͞ON]; CN /pant uh LOON/ [PANT uh lo͞on].

50. **Pedascule** Ang.Lat. /puh DASS kyoo lee/; Class.Lat. /ped AHSS ko͞o lay/ tutor.

52. **Aeacides** /ee ASS ih deez/ descendent of Aeacus.

67–79. **gamouth** musical scale. Archaic variant of **gamut**, both pronounced /GAM ut/, or the former possibly /GAM u͟t͟h/.

76. **ut** /ut, o͞ot/ the lowest note on the scale, modern *do*.

Act 3 Scene 2

10. **rudesby** /RO͞ODZ bee/ rude person.

16. **banes** /baynz/ proclamation in church of an intended marriage. Archaic variant of **banns** /banz/.

44. ***breeches** /BRITCH iz/ is traditional, /BREECH iz/ is newer. The former pronunciation is more common in the UK and the latter in the US, CN.

48. **chapeless** /CHAYP liss/; US *also* /CHAP liss/ without a metal tip on the sheath.

51. **mose** /mohz/ uncertain, perhaps a discharge from the nostrils.

51. **lampass, lampas** /LAMP us/; UK *also* /LAMP uz/ swelling of the gums.

ă-bat, ăir-marry, air-pair, ạr-far, ĕr-merry, ĝ-get, ī-high, ĭr-mirror, ɬ-little, ṇ-listen, ŏ-hot, oh-go, o͞o-wood, o͞o-moon, oor-tour, ŏr-or, ow-how, ṯh-that, t̶h̶-thin, ŭ-but, UR-fur, ur-under. ( )- suppress the syllable [ ]- less common   see p. xi for complete list.

53. **spavins** /SPAV inz/ swelling of the hock.

65. **caparison'd** /kuh PĂIR ih sṇd/ covered with an ornamental cloth.

67. **kersey** /KUR zee/ coarse woolen cloth.

119. **accoutrements** /uh CO͞OT ruh munts, uh CO͞OT ur munts/ furnishings, i.e., clothes.

The *Complete Oxford* begins Scene 3.3 here—line nos. in parentheses

---

160. (3.3.33) **gogs-wouns** /gŏgz WO͞ONZ/ God's (i.e., Jesus') wounds.

172. (3.3.45)*****quaff'd** /kwŏft/; UK *rarely* [kwahft] drank freely. /kwăft/ is also used, but is not recommended.

172. (3.3.45) **muscadel** /muss kuh DEL/ strong sweet wine. Some eds. prefer **muscatel** /muss kuh TEL/.

181. (3.3.54) **rout** /rowt/ crowd of guests.

230. (3.3.102) **chattels** /CHAT łz/ property.

Act 4 Scene 1

11. **Holla** /huh LAH/ a call to attract attention.

43. *****cony-catching** rabbit catching, i.e., trickery. /KOH nee/, *rarely older* [KUN ee].

47. *****fustian** /FUSS tee un/; US *also older* /FUSS chun/ coarse cloth of cotton and linen. Normal development would favor the latter.

50. **Gills, Jills** /jilz/ i.e., girls.

66. **Inprimis** /in PRĪ miss/ in the first place. Archaic variant of *****imprimis** /im PRĪ miss/ (traditional), /im PREE miss/ (restored Latin). The latter is now more common.

133. **Gabr'el's** /GAYB rłz/ variant of *Gabriel's,* still current today.

142. **Soud** uncertain, perhaps indicates Petruchio's humming. Some eds. prefer **Food.**

147. **awry** /uh RĪ/ askew.

182. **continency** /CŎN tih nun see/ sexual self-restraint.

188. **politicly** /PŎL (ih) tik lee/ shrewdly.

193. **haggard** /HAG urd/ wild hawk.

197. **eat** appears twice in this line. The 1st is /et/, a dialect variant of **ate** which is also commonly /et/ in the UK.

211. **shew** archaic variant of **show**. Here meant to rhyme with *shrew*, but *shew* and *shrew* each had variants with /ōō/ and /oh/ in Elizabethan Eng.

Act 4 Scene 2

20. **cullion** 'scoundrel,' literally 'testicle.' Normally /CŬL yun/, here expanded to /CŬL ee yun/.

39. **haggard** /HAG urd/ wild hawk.

63. **mercantant** merchant. /MUR kun tunt/ in a broken-backed line. F1 has the variant **marcantant** /MAR-/. Some eds. prefer the Ital. form **mercatante** angl. /mur kuh TAN tee/; Ital. /měr kah TAHN tay/.

63. **pedant** /PED ṇt/ teacher.

76. **Tripoli** /TRIP (uh) lee/ city in North Africa.

77–81. **Mantua** 2 or 3 syllables depending on meter US /MAN ch(oo) wuh/; UK /MAN ty(oo) wuh/ [MAN ch(oo) wuh].

98. **incomparable** here should be /in CŎM pur ruh bł/.

Act 4 Scene 3

5. **alms** charity for the poor. /ahmz/ is older; /ahlmz, awlmz/ are newer. In the UK the latter are non-standard.

6. **elsewhere** a normal line indicates 2nd syllable stress, a form still used in the UK, but unknown in the US. The foot may, however, be inverted to allow 1st syllable stress.

ă-bat, ăir-marry, air-pair, ạr-far, ĕr-merry, ĝ-get, ī-high, ĭr-mirror, ł-little, ṇ-listen, ŏ-hot, oh-go, ōō-wood, ōō-moon, oor-tour, ŏr-or, ow-how, ţh-that, ťh-thin, ʊ-but, UR-fur, ur-under. ( )- suppress the syllable   [ ]- less common   see p. xi for complete list.

36. **amort** /uh MORT/ downcast.

56. **fardingales** /FAR ding gaylz/ hooped petticoats. Archaic variant of **farthin-gales** /FAR t̪hing gaylz/.

64. **porringer** US /PŌR in jur/; E. COAST US, UK /PŎR-/ a dish for porridge.

81. **paltry** /PAWL tree/ worthless.

87. **masquing** US /MĂSK ing/; UK, E. NEW ENG. /MAHSK-/ [MĂSK-] fit only for a masked dance or pantomime.

88. ***demi-canon** /DEM ee-/ large canon.

102. **nor more commendable** here /CŎM en duh bł/ in a regular line, or mod. /cuh MEN duh bł/ after an epic caesura.

110. **skein** /skayn/ loose coil.

112. **bemete** /bih-, bee MEET/ measure, i.e., beat.

127. ***Ergo** /UR go/ is older, /ĔR go/ is newer. The former is more common in the UK, the latter in the US, CN, but both forms appear in all countries.

134. **Inprimis** /in PRĪ miss/ in the first place. Archaic variant of ***Imprimis** /im PRĪ miss/ (traditional), /im PREE miss/ (restored Latin). The latter is now more common.

152. **mete-yard** /MEET yard/ measuring stick.

170. **habiliments** /huh BILL ih munts/ clothes.

Act 4 Scene 4

4. **Genoa** /JEN oh uh/ Italian city.

11. **throughly** archaic variant of *thoroughly*. /T̶H̶ROO lee/ is the normal pronunciation on stage, but to enhance clarity a syncopated form of the modern pronunciation may be used: *thor'ghly*.

49. **affied** /uh FĪD/ betrothed.

59. **scrivener** /SKRIV nur/ notary.

The Complete Oxford begins Scene 4.5 here—line nos. in parentheses.

93. (4.5.19) **cum privilegio**   **ad   imprimendum   solum**
  Ang.Lat.   /kŭm priv ih LEE j(ee) oh   ad   im prim EN dum   SOH lum/
  Class.Lat. /kōōm pree wih LAYG ee yoh ahd im prim EN dōōm SOH lōōm/
       with exclusive rights to print.

Act 4 Scene 5 (*The Complete Oxford* 4.6)

41. **Allots** /uh LŎTS/ gives.

78. **froward** /FROH wurd, FROH urd/ difficult to deal with.

79. *****untoward** unmannerly. Here should be /un TOH wurd, -urd/ to rhyme with
froward, though the most common pronunciation in CN, UK is /un tuh WÂRD/ (as in
war).

Act 5 Scene 1

13. **toward** /TOH wurd, -urd/ about to take place.

67. **copatain hat** hat shaped like a sugar loaf. This unusual word is usually
/CŎP uh tayn/ today, but normal development would yield the ending /-tin/
(cf. *captain*). Some eds. prefer the variant **copintank** /CŎP in tank/.

75. **'cerns** /surnz/ concerns.

78. **Bergamo** angl. /BUR guh moh/; Ital. /BĔR gah moh/ city in Italy.

99. *****cony-catch'd** i.e., tricked. /KOH nee/, *rarely older* [KUN ee].

106. **dotard** /DOHT urd/ senile old man.

117. **eyne** /īn/ dialect form of *eyes.*

Act 5 Scene 2

9. **banket** /BANK it/ light meal, often of fruit. Archaic variant of **banquet**.

ă-bat, ăir-**marry**, air-**pair**, ạr-**far**, ĕr-**merry**, ĝ-**get**, ī-**high**, ĭr-**mir**ror, ł-**little**, ṇ-**listen**,
ŏ-**hot**, oh-**go**, ōō-**wood**, ōō-**moon**, oor-**tour**, ōr-**or**, ow-**how**, ţh-**that**, t̶h̶-**thin**, ʊ-**but**,
UR-**fur**, ur-**under**. ( )- suppress the syllable   [ ]- less common   see p. xi for complete list.

64. **veriest** /VĔR yist/ most exceeding.

99. **by my holidam** an oath referring to a 'holy object' or the 'holy lady,' i.e., Mary. Other variants are: **halidam, halidom, halidame, halidome, holidame.** Probably these were all variant spellings of /HAL ih dum, HŎL ih dum/ (note that *hal-* can also be /HŎL-/ in *Halloween*).

104. **Swinge** /swinj/ beat.

119–183. **froward** /FROH wurd, FROH urd/ difficult to deal with.

122. **bable** presumably /BAB ł/, archaic variant of **bauble** /BAW bł/.

136. **unkind** here should be /UN kīnd/.

139. **meads** /meedz/ meadows.

145. **deign** /dayn/ think it appropriate.

182. **toward** /TOH wurd, -urd/ obedient.

182–3 are 4-beat lines in a dactylic form (a strong beat followed by 2 weak ones).

188. **shrow** /shroh/ archaic variant of **shrew** which here should rhyme with *so*.

The Tempest

People in the Play

Alonso /uh LŎN zoh/.

Antonio 3 or 4 syllables depending on meter /an TOHN (ee) yoh/; Ital. /ahn-/.

Ariel 2 or 3 syllables depending on meter /AIR (ee) yĭ/; E. COAST US *sometimes* [ĂIR-]. /-el/ is newer.

Boatswain /BOH sṇ/ is usual, though /BOHT swayn/ is sometimes used by landsmen.

Caliban /KAL ih ban/.

Gonzalo /gŏn-, gun ZAH loh/.

Miranda /mih RAN duh/; US *also* /mur-/.

Prospero /PRŎS pur oh/ or /PRŎS proh/ depending on meter.
  Prosper /PRŎS pur/.

Sebastian US /suh BĂS chun/; UK /suh BĂST yun/.

Stephano, Stefano /STEF uh noh/.

Trinculo /TRINK yoo loh, -yuh-/.

Places in the Play

Milan here should be /MILL un/.

Act 1 Scene 1

4–34. ***yare(ly)** /yair/; US *also* /yặr/ quickly, smartly.

5. ***Heigh!** US /hay, hī/; CN /hī/, *rarely* [hay]; UK /hay/. Shk intended /hay/.

6. **topsail** sailors use /TŎP sĭ/; landsmen /TŎP sayl/.

ă-bat, ăir-marry, air-pair, ặr-far, ĕr-merry, ĝ-get, ī-high, ĭr-mirror, ĭ-little, ṇ-listen, ŏ-hot, oh-go, ōō-wood, ōō-moon, oor-tour, ōr-or, ow-how, ţh-that, ŧħ-thin, Ŭ-but, UR-fur, ur-under. ( )- suppress the syllable [ ]- less common   see p. xi for complete list.

25. ***mischance** 2nd syllable stress in verse, but in this prose passage the alternative modern pronunciation with 1st syllable stress is possible.

34. **topmast** /TŎP must/ is used by sailors; landsmen say US /TŎP măst/; UK, E. NEW ENG. /-mahst/.

40. **blasphemous** /BLĂSS fuh mus/; UK, E. NEW ENG. *also* [BLAHSS-] speaking irreverently.

48. ***unstanch'd** unsatisfied. Variant of **unstaunched** /un STAWNCHT/. The *stanch* variant was pronounced with the vowel of *tan* in Elizabethan Eng. The *staunch* variant in words of this sort (*graunt, chaunt*) gave rise to RP /-AH-/.

Act 1 Scene 2

2. **allay** /uh LAY/ calm.

30. **perdition** /pur DISH un/; UK *also* [PUR DISH un] loss.

31. **Betid** /bih TID/; US *also* /bee-/ happened, past tense of *betide*.

50. **abysm** /uh BIZM/ variant of **abyss** /uh BISS/ which some eds prefer.

63. **holp** /hohlp/ helped.

71. **signories** /SEEN yur eez/ lands.

79. **Being once perfected how to grant suits** *Being* has 2 syllables, and *perfected* is /PUR fik tid/ expert in.

87. ***verdure** vigor. US, CN /VUR jur, -dyoor, -dyur/; UK /-dyoor/ [-dyur, -jur].

97. **sans** /sănz/ without.

98. **revenue** here should be /ruh VEN yo͞o/.

105. ***prerogative** /pur RŎG uh tiv/ [prih-, pree-] rights. /pree-/ non-standard in the UK.

113, 124. ***homage** /HŎM ij/; US *also* /ŎM ij/ acknowledgement of allegiance.

114. **coronet** small crown. Here should be US /COR (uh) net, -nit/; E. COAST US, UK /CŎR-/.

123. **in *lieu o'** US, CN /lo͞o, lyo͞o/; UK /lyo͞o/ [lo͞o] in return for.

125. **extirpate** here /ek STUR payt/ drive off.

128. **midnight** here with 2nd syllable stress.

152. ***cherubin** angel. US, CN /CHĔR uh bin/ [-yuh-]; UK uses both equally. /KĔR-/ not recommended.

161. **Neapolitan** /nee uh PŎL ih tun/ man from Naples.

180. ***prescience** foreknowledge. Here 3 syllables /PRESS ee unss/. /PRESH unss/ is sometimes used, especially in the US, but would have to be /PRESH ee unss/ to fit the meter.

199. **topmast** /TŎP must/ is used by sailors; landsmen say US /TŎP măst/; UK, E. NEW ENG. /-mahst/.

200. **boresprit** /BOR sprit/ archaic variant of ***bowsprit** US /BOW sprit/ [BOH-]; UK /BOH sprit/ the spar jutting forward from the bow of a ship to carry forward sail.

219. **thou badst** /badst/ 2nd person sing. past tense of *bid* 'asked.'

229. **Bermoothes** /bur MO͞OTͪH uz/ archaic variant of **Bermudas**.

258–340. **Sycorax** /SIK ur racks/.

261, 265. **Argier** /ahr JEER/, archaic variant of **Algiers** /al JEERZ/.

276. **unmitigable** /un MIT ih guh bł/ that cannot be softened.

295. ***entrails** /EN traylz/; US *also* [-trłz] guts.

370. **aches** Shk pronounced this with 2 syllables /AY chiz/.

373. **Setebos** US /SET uh bohss, -bŏs/, *rarely* [-bŭs]; UK /-bŏss/ [-bŭs, -bohss]. Normal development would favor /-us/. /-ohss/ is a newer pronunciation.

386. ***chanticleer** a rooster. US /CHĂNT-, SHĂNT ih kleer/; UK /CHĂNT-/, *rarely* [CHAHNT-, SHAHNT-]; *rarely* with 3rd syllable stress in both countries.

393. **Allaying** /uh LAY ing/ diminishing.

397. **fadom** /FAD um/ archaic variant of **fathom** /FĂTͪH um/.

ă-bat, ăir-marry, air-pair, ạr-far, ĕr-merry, ĝ-get, ī-high, ĭr-mirror, ł-little, ṇ-listen, ŏ-hot, oh-go, o͞o-wood, o͞o-moon, oor-tour, ŏr-or, ow-how, tͪh-that, th̶-thin, ŭ-but, UR-fur, ur-under. ( )- suppress the syllable   [ ]- less common   see p. xi for complete list.

476. ***surety** guarantee. Here should be 2 syllables, though in mod. Eng., 3 syllables are more common US /SHUR (ih) tee, SHOOR-/; CN /SHUR-/ [SHOOR-]; UK /SHOR-/ [SHUR-] [SHOOR-].

478. **advocate** /AD vuh kut/ someone who supports a person or cause.

Act 2 Scene 1

19. **Dolor** (UK **Dolour**) /DOH lur/; UK *also* /DŎL ur/ pain. /-or/ not recommended.

31. **cock'rel** /CŎCK rɫ/ young cock.

71–258. **Claribel** /CLĂIR ih bel/.

72–259. **Tunis** US /TOO niss/; UK, SOUTH. US /TYOO-/. /CHOO-/ non-standard in the UK.

---

76. ***paragon** US /PĂIR uh gŏn/ [-gun]; CN /-gŏn/; UK /-gun/ [-gn̩] most perfect example.

77–102 . **Dido('s)** /DĪ doh/ Queen of Carthage.

---

80. **Aeneas** /ih NEE yus/; UK *also* /EE NEE yus/ Prince of Troy.

83-86. **Carthage** /CAR thij/ ancient city in North Africa.

129. ***importun'd** /im POR chund/ urged. About half the respondents in the Survey reported a form with 3rd syllable stress in all countries, but that will not fit the meter in verse and is a relatively recent innovation (cf. *fortune*).

141. **chirurgeonly** /kī RUR jun lee/ in a surgeon-like manner.

148. **contraries** /CŎN truh reez/ the opposite of what is usual.

150. ***magistrate** /MAJ ih strayt/; US *also* [-strut].

152. **contract** here Shk may have intended /cŏn TRACT/, but the foot may be inverted to allow mod. /CŎN tract/.

153. ***Bourn** /born, boorn/ boundary. North American [burn] not recommended. *Borne* (F1). Normal development would favor /born/.

153. **tilth** /tilth/ plowland.

164. **foison** /FOY zun, -zn̩/ plenty.

223, 228. *sloth US, CN /slaw~~th~~/ [sloh~~th~~]; UK /sloh~~th~~/ [slŏ~~th~~] laziness.

257. cubit /KYŌŌ bit/ about 20 inches.

266. chough, chuff /chuf/ jackdaw.

285. aye /ay/ ever. /ī/ is often used, but not recommended.

291. president archaic variant of *precedent, both /PRESS ih dunt/. It is not clear whether /PREZ-/ was used in Shk's time.

Act 2 Scene 2

9. *mow /moh/ [mow] grimace. Both were used in Shk's time, but his rhymes elsewhere indicate /moh/.

21. bumbard /BUM burd/ leather bottle. Archaic variant of bombard, formerly pronounced the same way, but usually /BŎM bard/ today.

38, 111. *gaberdine loose garment of course cloth. US /GAB ur deen/, *rarely* [gab ur DEEN]; UK /gab ur DEEN/ [GAB ur deen]; in CN both are used equally.

48. Mall /mawl/ is the usual pronunciation for this spelling, but here probably /mŏll/, as in *Molly*. Some eds. prefer Moll /mŏll/.

48. Margery /MARJ ur ee/.

52. savor (UK savour) /SAY vur/ smell.

58. salvages archaic variant of savages. May have been /SAL vuh jiz/ for some, but it was more likely only another way of spelling /SAV uh jiz/ (cf. *halve* which had already lost its Middle English /l/ to become /hav/).

58. Inde, Ind the Indies. Shk's rhymes indicate /īnd/ elsewhere, but perhaps /ind/ is the better choice here, being closer to *India*.

66–136. ague /AY gyōō/ malarial fever.

113. Neapolitans /nee uh PŎL ih tunz/ men from Naples.

ă-bat, ăir-marry, air-pair, ạr-far, ĕr-merry, ĝ-get, ī-high, ĭr-mirror, ł-little, ṇ-listen, ŏ-hot, oh-go, ōō-wood, ōō-moon, oor-tour, ōr-or, ow-how, ţh-that, ~~th~~-thin, ŭ-but, UR-fur, ur-under. ( )- suppress the syllable   [ ]- less common   see p. xi for complete list.

128. **Swom** most eds. prefer **Swum** or **Swam**. The meaning here is 'swam,' but in older forms of Eng. the past tense could be written all 3 ways. Whether *swom* was meant to indicate /swum/ or /swŏm/ is unclear. For simplicity use /swam/; for an archaic flavor use /swum/ which is still used in dialects on both sides of the Atlantic.

170. **marmazet** /MAR muh zet/ small monkey. Archaic variant of **marmoset**, pronounced the same way, as well as /MAR muh set/ [mar muh ZET, -SET].

172. **scamels** /SKAY młz, SKAM łz/ perhaps an error. May be a type of shellfish or seabird. Some eds. prefer **seamews** /SEE my$\overline{oo}$z/ or **seamels** /SEE młz/, both 'seagulls.' Others suggest **staniels** /STAN young płz/ inferior hawks,

Act 3 Scene 1

44. **defect** here should be /dih-, dee FEKT/.

Act 3 Scene 2

26. **justle** /JUSS ł/ archaic variant of **jostle** /JŎSS ł/.

63. **pied** /pīd/ having 2 or more colors in splotches.

80. **murrain** US, CN /MUR in/; E. COAST US, UK /MUH rin/ plague.

91. **wezand, weasand** /WEE zṇd/ wind pipe.

96. **utensils** here should be /Y$\overline{OO}$ ten słz/.

100. ***nonpareil** one without equal. /nŏn puh RELL/ is the oldest form, still common in the US, but now vanished from the UK and CN, where it has been replaced with /nŏn puh RAYL/ [-RAY], based on mod. Fr. /-RAYL/ is also common in the US. /-RĪ, -RĪL/ are occasionally heard, but not recommended. Sometimes 1st syllable stress is used.

101, 102. **Sycorax** /SIK ur racks/.

117. ***jocund** /JŎCK und/; US, CN *rarely* [JOHK-] merry.

121. **scout** jeer at. Some eds. prefer F1's **cout** /kowt, coht/ as a dialect form of *colt* cheat.

151. **taborer** /TAY bur ur/ player of a small drum. /-bor-/ not recommended.

Act 3 Scene 3

1. **By'r lakin** /bīr-, bur LAY kin/ by Our Lady (i.e., Mary).

3. **forth-rights** here should be /FOR~~TH~~ rīts/ straight paths.

10. **frustrate** /FRUSS trayt, -trut/ frustrated.

14. **throughly** archaic variant of *thoroughly*. /~~TH~~ROO lee/ is the normal pronunciation on stage, but to enhance clarity a syncopated form of the modern pronunciation may be used: *thor'ghly*.

15 ***travail** here should be /TRAV ayl/ hard work. Some eds. prefer **travel**. In Shk's time both were pronounced /TRAV ł/.

21. **drollery** /DROHL (uh) ree/ a puppet show, or comic play.

30. **certes** /SUR teez/ certainly.

41. **viands** /VĪ undz/ food. /VEE undz/ not recommended.

65. **dowle, dowl** /dowl/ small feather.

77. **perdition** /pur DISH un/; UK *also* [PUR DISH un] destruction.

stage direction after 82: ***mows** grimaces. /mohz/ and /mowz/ were both used in Shk's time and are still used today. Shk's rhymes elsewhere indicate /mohz/.

106. **gins** /ĝinz/ begins.

Act 4 Scene 1

26. ***opportune** here 2nd syllable stress is indicated /ŏp POR tyo͞on/; US *also* /-to͞on/.

30. **Phoebus'** /FEE bus/ god of the sun.

47. ***mow** grimace. Here should be /moh/ for the rhyme, though /mow/ was also used in Shk's time and is still sometimes used today.

51. **dalliance** /DAL ee unss/ sportiveness.

ă-bat, ăir-marry, air-pair, ạr-far, ĕr-merry, ĝ-get, ī-high, ĭr-mirror, ł-little, ṇ-listen, ŏ-hot, oh-go, o͞o-wood, o͞o-moon, oor-tour, ōr-or, ow-how, ṭh-that, ŧh-thin, ŭ-but, UR-fur, ur-under. ( )- suppress the syllable   [ ]- less common   see p. xi for complete list.

53. **abstenious** /ab STEEN ee us/ archaic variant of **abstemious** /ab STEEM ee us/.

56. **ardor** (UK **ardour**) /A̧RD ur/ warm emotion.

57. **Now come my Ariel! Bring a** *corollary* one too many. If *Ariel* is 3 syllables, then /cuh RŎL (uh) ree/, the normal UK form. If *Ariel* is 2 syllables, then the US form /COR uh lĕr ee/ fits. Note E. COAST US also has /CŎR-/.

60–167. **Ceres** /SEER eez/ goddess of the harvest.

---

60. **leas** /leez/ meadows.

63. **meads** /meedz/ meadows.

63. **stover** /STOH vur/ hay for winter use.

64. **pioned** /PĪ un ed/ perhaps 'dug out.' Some eds. prefer **peonied** /PEE uh need/ full of peonies.

65. **spungy** archaic variant of **spongy**, both pronounced /SPUN jee/.

74. **amain** /uh MAYN/ with full speed.

78. **saffron** /SAFF run/ yellow.

89. **Dis** /dis/ Pluto.

93. **Paphos** place on Cyprus sacred to Venus. US /PAY fus, -fŏs/; UK /-fŏs/ [-fus]. Normal development would favor /-us/. A newer ending /-ohss/ is also used, especially in the US. A more recent restored pronunciation with /PAH-/ is also used.

110. **Earth's increase** Earth's offspring, the harvest. Here /in CREESS/, used elsewhere, is possible, but produces the only broken-backed line in this song. Using the older genetive form /UR t̶h̶iz IN creess/ is also possible.

110. **foison** /FOY zun, -zn̩/ harvest.

121. **confines** here should be /cŏn-, cun FĪNZ/.

128. **Naiades** Shk's variant of ***Naiads** /NĪ adz/ [NAY-] river nymphs. Normal development would favor /NAY udz/.

128. **windring** /WĪND ring/ winding, wandering. Some eds. prefer **wand'ring, winding**.

170. **varlots** attendents. Archaic variant of **varlets**, both pronounced /VAR luts/.

175. **tabor** /TAY bur/ small drum. /-bor/ not recommended.

176. **unback'd** here should be /UN backt/ never having had a rider.

179. **lowing** /LOH ing/ bleating.

180. **goss** /gŏss/; US *also* /gawss/ variant of **gorse**.

206. ***mischance** in verse normally with 2nd syllable stress.

219. **aye** /ay/ ever. /ī/ is often used, but not recommended.

Act 5 Scene 1

11. **boudge** /BUJ/, or possibly /bōōj/. Archaic variant of **budge**.

36. ***demi-puppets** /DEM ee-/ meaning either 'partially subject to Prospero's will' or 'small dolls.'

39. **mushrumps** (F1) /MUSH rumps/. Some eds. prefer **mushrooms**.

43. ***azur'd** blue. US /AZH oord/ [AZ yoord, AZH urd]; UK /AZH oord, AZ yoord/ [AY zyoord, -zhyoord].   Normal development would favor /AZH urd, AY zhurd/.

49. **op'd** /ohpt/ opened.

51. **abjure** /ab-, ub JOOR/; US *also* /-JUR/ renounce.

55. **fadoms** /FAD umz/ archaic variant of **fathoms** /FĂ<u>T</u>H umz/.

89. **cowslip's** /COW slips/ a yellow flower.

140. **Irreperable** here /ih REP ur uh bł/; US *also* /ir-/.

145. **supportable** here should be /SUP ort uh bł/.

158. **justled** /JUSS łd/ archaic variant of **jostled** /JŎSS łd/.

209. **Claribel** /CLĂIR ih bel/.

ă-bat, ăir-marry, air-pair, ạr-far, ĕr-merry, ĝ-get, ī-high, ĭr-mirror, ł-little, ṇ-listen, ŏ-hot, oh-go, ōŏ-wood, ōō-moon, oor-tour, ōr-or, ow-how, ţh-that, th-thin, ŭ-but, UR-fur, ur-under. ( )- suppress the syllable   [ ]- less common   see p. xi for complete list.

209. **Tunis** US /T$\overline{OO}$ niss/; UK, SOUTH. US /TY$\overline{OO}$-/. /CH$\overline{OO}$-/ non-standard in the UK.

217. **prophesied** /PRŎF uh sīd/ predicted the future.

218. **blasphemy** /BLĂSS fuh mee/; UK, E. NEW ENG. *also* /BLAHSS-/ irreverent speech.

224. ***yare** /yair/; US *also* /yạr/ ready, smart.

258, 259. **Coraggio** /koh RAH joh/ or /-jee oh/ Ital. 'courage.'

261 **Setebos** the evil god of Caliban's mother. US /SET uh bohss, -bŏss/, *rarely* [-bus]; UK /-bŏss/ [-bus, -bohss]. Normal development would favor /-us/. /-ohss/ is a newer pronunciation.

263. ***chastise** punish. Here /chăss TĪZ/, the usual UK pronunciation, produces a regular iambic rhythm. In the US 1st syllable stress is usual.

272. ***demi-devil** /DEM ee-/ half-devil.

309. ***nuptial** wedding. Here should be 3 syllables. Shk probably intended /NUP shee ł/, but   today /NUP chuh wł, NUP shuh wł/ are common, though considered non-standard in the UK.

310. **Of these our dear-beloved solemnized.** /suh LEM nīz ed/ in Shk's day which would mean *beloved* has 2 syllables. A better choice may be /bee-, bih LUV id/ and /SŎL um nīzd/.

Twelfth Night

People in the Play

Sometimes some of these names are given an Italian pronunciation in performance. These pronunciations are indicated both as accurately as possible within the limits of this notation. In most cases, however, we have indicated them to be anglicized.

Sir Andrew Aguecheek /AY gyo͞o cheek/.

Antonio 3 or 4 syllables depending on meter /an TOHN (ee) yoh/; Ital. /ahn-/.

Cesario 3 or 4 syllables depending on meter /suh ZAH r(ee) yoh/; Ital. /chay-/.

Curio /KYUR ee yoh, KYOOR-/; Ital. /KO͞OR-/.

Fabian occurs in verse once and should be 2 syllables. /FAY b(ee) yun/. In prose it may be 3.

Feste /FESS tee/.

*Jaques usually /JAY kweez/ in Shk. His name is not spoken. See AYL, "People in the Play."

Malvolio in verse always 3 syllables /mal VOH l(ee) yoh/.

*Maria /muh RĪ uh/ is the older, angl. form, /muh REE uh/ is newer. In CN the latter is more frequent, in the UK, US both are used equally. Note that some scholars prefer the form /muh RĪ uh/ in this play, but /muh REE uh/ for the character in LLL.

Olivia always 3 syllables in verse /oh LIV (ee) yuh/.

Orsino /or SEE noh/.

Sebastian US /suh BĂS chun/; UK /suh BĂST yun/.

Valentine /VAL in tīn/.

*Viola angl. /VĪ uh luh/ is more common than [VEE oh luh] based on Ital.

ă-bat, ăir-ma**rry**, air-p**air**, a̧r-f**ar**, ĕr-me**rry**, ĝ-get, ī-high, ĭr-mi**rror**, ᶅ-lit**tle**, ɳ-lis**ten**, ŏ-hot, oh-go, o͞o-wood, o͞o-moon, oor-tour, ôr-or, ow-how, t̞h-that, t̶h̶-thin, ŭ-but, UR-fur, ur-und**er**. ( )- suppress the syllable   [ ]- less common   see p. xi for complete list.

Places in the Play

Illyria 3 or 4 syllables depending on meter /ih LĬR (ee) yuh/.

Act 1 Scene 1

2. **excess** here should be /ek SESS/, the most common UK form.

Act 1 Scene 2

4. ***Elysium** the realm of the blessed in the afterlife. US /ih LEEZH ee um/ [-LIZ-, -LIZH-, -LEESS-, -LISS-]; UK /-LIZ-/; *also* /ee-/ in all countries. The oldest forms still in use are /-LIZ-/, /-LIZH-/. The historic form is /ih LIZH um/ here expanded to 4 syllables /ih LIZH ee um/.

15. **Arion** /uh RĪ un/ Gk. poet. Sometimes newer /-ŏn/ is used, but is not recommended.

40. **abjur'd** /ab-, ub JOORD/; US *also* /-JURD/ renounced.

56, 62. **eunuch** /YOO nuk/ castrated male.

Act 1 Scene 3

14. ***quaffing** /KWŎF ing/; UK *rarely* [KWAHF-] drinking freely. /KWĂF-/ is also used, but is not recommended.

26. **viol-de-gamboys** a cello-like instrument. An unusual variant of *viol-de-gamba* /VĪ ł duh GAM buh/, or with the Italian vowel, /GAHM buh/. The ending *-oys* may have been just an alternative way of spelling the sound /-uz/, i.e., /GAM buz/.

31. **allay** /uh LAY/ put to rest.

40. **coystrill, coistrel** /COY strł/ knave.

42. **Castiliano vulgo** /kas til YAN oh VUL goh/, /-YAHN oh/ meaning uncertain, perhaps 'speak of the devil.'

90, 91. **Pourquoi** /poor KWAH/ Fr. 'why.'

102. **distaff** cleft staff used in spinning thread. US /DIS stăf/; E. NEW ENG., UK /DIS stahf/.

103. ***huswife** hussy. /HUZ if/ is traditional, /HUSS wĩf/ is a newer, spelling pronunciation. The former is the most common form in the UK, the latter in the US. In CN both are used equally. In North America /HUSS wif/ is also sometimes used. Some eds. prefer **housewife**.

113. **masques** US /măsks/; UK, E. NEW ENG. /mahsks/ [măsks] masked dancing and pantomime.

115. **kickshawses** (F3) /KICK shaw ziz/ gewgaws.

> 120–33. **galliard** /GAL yurd/; UK *also newer* /GAL ee ard/ a lively dance.

127. **Mistress Mall's** /mawlz/ would be the usual pronunciation with this spelling, but here probably /mŏllz/, as in *Molly*.

129. ***coranto** courant, a type of dance. US /coh-, cuh RAHN toh/ [-RAN-]; UK /cŏr AHN toh, -AN toh/.

130. **sink-a-pace** some eds. prefer **cinquepace** 'lively dance,' both pronounced /SINK uh payss/ or sometimes /SINK payss/.

135. **dun-color'd**. Some eds. prefer ***divers-coloured** variously colored. US, CN /DĪ vurss, -vurz/ [dī-, dih VURSS]; UK /DĪ vurss/ [-vurz, dī VURSS].

Act 1 Scene 4

16. **access** here should be /ak SESS/.

28. ***nuntio's, nuncio's** messenger's. US /NŌŌN see ohz/ [NUN-]; UK /NUN see ohz/, *rarely* [NŌŌN see ohz]. Normal development would favor [NUN shohz], now rare.

30. **belie** /bih-, bee LĪ/ misrepresent.

32. **rubious** /RŌŌB yus/ ruby red.

34. **semblative** /SEM bluh tiv/ resembling.

> ă-bat, ăir-marry, air-pair, ạr-far, ĕr-merry, ĝ-get, ī-high, ĭr-mirror, ł-little, ṇ-listen, ŏ-hot, oh-go, ŏŏ-wood, ōō-moon, oor-tour, ŏr-or, ow-how, ţh-that, ŧħ-thin, ŭ-but, UR-fur, ur-under. ( )- suppress the syllable   [ ]- less common   see p. xi for complete list.

Act 1 Scene 5

35. **Quinapalus** /kwin AP uh lus/ name made up by Feste.

50. **syllogism** /SIL uh jizm/ a framework for logically analyzing an argument.

55. **Misprision** /mis PRIZH un, -ņ/ misunderstanding.

56.   **Cucullus   non   facit   monachum**
Ang.Lat.   /kyōō KŬL us nŏn   FAY sit MŎN uh kum/
Class.Lat. /kōō KōōL ōōs nŏn   FAH kit MŎN ah kōōm/.
        the hood does not make the monk.

57. **motley** /MŎT lee/ costume of different colored cloth worn by fools.

62. **catechize** /KAT uh kīz/ to instruct through a series of questions and answers.

81. **twopence** /TUP ņss, -unss/.

97. ***indue** /in DYŌŌ/; US *also* [-DŌŌ] endow. Some eds. prefer **endue** /en-/.

97. **leasing** /LEE zing/ lying.

115. ***pia mater** here 'the brain.' Ang.Lat. /PĪ uh MAYT ur/ is older;
Class.Lat. /PEE uh MAHT ur/ is newer and much more common. Forms that mix
old and new are also used.

132. **draught** US, CN /drăft/; UK, E. NEW ENG. /drahft/ drink.

157. **peascod** /PEEZ cŏd/ peapod.

175. **comptible** /COWNT ih bł/ sensitive to. Some eds. prefer **'countable**. They
were pronounced the same way in Elizabethan Eng.

209. ***homage** /HŎM ij/; US *also* /ŎM ij/ dues owed to a superior lord.

217. **profanation** /prŏf uh NAY shun/ desecration.

228. **heresy** /HĚR ih see/ dissent from the dominant thinking.

245. ***divers** various. US, CN /DĪ vurss, -vurz/ [dī-, dih VURSS];
UK /DĪ vurss/ [-vurz, dī VURSS].

254. ***nonpareil** one without equal. /nŏn puh RELL/ is the oldest form, still common in the US, but now vanished from the UK and CN, where it has been replaced
with /nŏn puh RAYL/ [-RAY], based on mod. Fr. /-RAY/ is also common in the US.

/-RĪ, -RĪL/ are occasionally heard, but not recommended. Sometimes 1st syllable stress is used.

270. **cantons** /KANT unz/ songs. Archaic variant of **cantos**.

272. **Hallow** /huh LOH/ or /HAL-, HŎL oh/ a shout. Some eds. prefer **Halloo** /huh LOO/.

272. **reverberate** /ree-, rih VUR bur ut, -ayt/ echoing. /-ut/ is more usual for an adj.

293. **blazon** /BLAY zun, -zṇ/ details of a coat of arms.

Act 2 Scene 1

11. **determinate** /dih-, dee TUR mih nut/ intended.

17. **Rodorigo, Roderigo** /rŏd ur REE goh/.

18. **Messaline** /MESS uh leen/.

Act 2 Scene 3

2. **deliculo surgere** Ang.Lat. /dih LICK yuh loh SUR jur ee/ abbreviated form of the proverb "To get up at dawn is very healthful." *Deliculo* is either Tobey's or Shk's error for **diluculo** Ang.Lat. /dih LUCK yuh loh/;
Class.Lat. /dee LOO kŏŏ loh SOOR ĝĕr ay/.

14. **stoup** /stoop/ tankard.

23. **Pigrogromitus** name made up by Feste. /pī groh-, pig roh GRŎM ih tus, pig roh groh MĪ tus/.

23. **Vapians** /VAY pee unz/.

24. **equinoctial** /ek wih NŎK shḷ/ [eek-] equator.

24. **Queubus** /KYOO bus/.

25, 31. **sixpence** /SIKS punss, -pṇss/; US *also* /SIKS penss/.

ă-bat, ăir-marry, air-pair, ạr-far, ĕr-merry, ĝ-get, ī-high, ĭr-mirror, ḷ-little, ṇ-listen, ŏ-hot, oh-go, ŏŏ-wood, ōō-moon, oor-tour, ōr-or, ow-how, ţh-that, ŧħ-thin, ŭ-but, UR-fur, ur-under. ( )- suppress the syllable [ ]- less common   see p. xi for complete list.

25. ***leman** sweetheart. US /LEE mun/ [LEM un, LAY mun]; CN /LAY mun/, *sometimes* [LEM un, LEE mun]; UK /LEM-/ [LEE mun], *rarely* [LAY mun]. /LAY mun/ is newer and not recommended.

26. **impeticos** /im PET ee kohz/ or /im PET ih kohz/ comic word meaning 'to pocket.'

26. **gratillity, gratility** /gruh TIL ih tee/ an invented variant of *gratuity.*

28. **Mermidons** a tavern. /MUR mih dunz, -dŏnz/; /-ŏn/ is usual in the US, /-un/ is more common in the UK. Archaic variant of **Myrmidons**, pronounced the same way.

33. **testril** /TEST rł/ sixpence.

53. **mellifluous** /muh LIF loo us/ sweetly flowing.

56. **dulcet** /DULL sit/ sweet.

62. ***By'r lady** /bīr-, bur LAY dee/ by Our Lady (i.e., Mary).

72. **caterwauling** /KAT ur wawl ing/ yowling.

75. **Cataian** /cat-, cuh TAY un/ a person from China, i.e., scoundrel. Variant of **Cathayan** /cath-, cuh THAY un/ which some eds. prefer. Others suggest **Catharan** /CATH uh run, kuh THAIR un/ puritan.

76. **Peg a' Ramsey, Peg o' Ramsey** a term of contempt. *a'* and *o'* are /uh/ of.

77. **consanguineous** /cŏn sang GWIN ee us/ related by blood.

90. **coziers'** US /KOH zhurz/ [KOH zyurz]; UK /KOH zyurz/ cobblers'.

120. **stope** /stohp/ tankard. Archaic variant of **stoup** /sto͞op/.

135. **an ayword** /AY wurd/ byword. Most eds. prefer **nayword** /NAY wurd/. Notice that *an ayword* would be pronounced nearly the same as *a nayword.*

150. **swarths** /sworths/ archaic and dialect variant of ***swaths** rows of mowed grass or grain, i.e., large amounts /swŏths/; UK *also* [swayths, swahths, swawths]. /swăths/ not recommended. The oldest forms are with /ŏ/ or UK /aw/. Some eds. prefer **swathes** /swaythz/.

155. **epistles** /ih-, ee PISS łz/ letters. /ee-/ non-standard in the UK.

177. **Penthesilea** queen of the Amazons. /pen ~~thuh~~ sih LEE uh/ is older; /-LAY uh/ is the restored pronunciation.

Act 2 Sceen 4

3. **antique** ancient. Here /AN teek/, *rarely older* [AN tik]. Some eds. prefer **antic** /AN tik/ quaint.

46. **chaunt** archaic variant of **chant** US /chănt/; E. NEW ENG, UK /chahnt/. The archaic vowel was pronounced /-AW-/, and gave rise to RP /-AH-/.

60. **strown** /strohn/ archaic variant of F1's **strewn**, here rhymes with *thrown*.

74. **taffata, taffeta** /TAF ut uh/ a silk-like cloth.

112. **damask** /DAM usk/ pink or light red.

114. **sate** archaic variant of **sat**. May have been /sayt/ or /sat/.

124. **denay** /dee-, dih NAY/ archaic variant of *denial*.

Act 2 Scene 5

5. **niggardly** /NIG urd lee/ miserly.

19. **contemplative** daydreaming. In verse always /cun TEMP luh tiv/ but in this prose passage may be /CŎN tem play tiv/.

20. **Close** /clohss/ keep hidden.

33. **'Slight** /zlīt/ by God's light.

40. **Strachy, Strachey** /STRAY chee/.

40. **yeoman** /YOH mun/ an attendant.

70. ***prerogative** /pur RŎG uh tiv/ [prih-, pree-] right, privilege. /pree-/ nonstandard in the UK.

83. **gin** /jin/ snare.

ă-bat, ăir-marry, air-pair, ạr-far, ĕr-merry, ĝ-get, ī-high, ĭr-mirror, l̦-little, ṇ-listen, ŏ-hot, oh-go, ōō-wood, ōō-moon, oor-tour, ōr-or, ow-how, ţh-that, ~~th~~-thin, ŭ-but, UR-fur, ur-under. ( )- suppress the syllable [ ]- less common see p. xi for complete list.

105. **Lucrece** Lucretia, Roman who commited suicide after being raped. The 2nd instance should be /L$\overline{OO}$ creess/, the 1st is prose and may be the usual mod. /l$\overline{oo}$ CREESS/. At one time many RP speakers in the UK used /ly$\overline{oo}$-/ for words beginning *lu-,* but today their number is dwindling.

108. ***fustian** /FUSS tee un/; US *also older* /FUSS chun/ nonsensical. Normal development would favor the latter.

113. **staniel** /STAN yɫ/ inferior hawk, i.e., useless person. Some eds. prefer F1's **stallion**.

123. **Sowter** /SOWT ur/ hound's name.

129. **consonancy** /CŎN suh nun see/ agreement.

148. ***inure** /in YOOR/; US *also* [in OOR], US, CN *rarely* [in YUR] accustom.

149. **slough** /sluff/ skin.

160. **champian** /CHAM pee un/ open country. Variant of ***champaign** /sham PAYN/ [SHAM payn]; US *sometimes* [CHAM payn]. The latter form is the oldest.

161. **politic** /PŎL ih tik/ shrewd.

163. **point-devise, -device** /POYNT dih V$\overline{I}$SS/ fastidious.

181. **Sophy** /SOH fee/ Shah of Persia.

196. ***aqua-vitae** distilled liquor, e.g., brandy. US /AHK-, AK wuh VEE tī/, *rarely* [-V$\overline{I}$ tee]; CN /AK wuh VEE tī/ [AHK-]; UK /AK wuh VEE tī/ [-VEE tuh]. /AK wuh V$\overline{I}$ tee/ is the oldest surviving form. /-VEE tay/ not recommended.

205. **Tartar** /TAR tur/ hell.

Act 3 Scene 1

2,10. **tabor** /TAY bur/ small drum. /-bor/ not recommended.

12. **chev'ril, cheveril** /SHEV rɫ/ or /SHEV ur rɫ/ kidskin, i.e., pliable.

34. **pilchers** /PIL churz/ sardines. Archaic variant of **pilchards** /PIL churdz/.

51. **Pandarus** /PAN duh rus/ a pimp.

51. **Phrygia** /FRIJ uh, FRIJ ee uh/. Normal development would favor the former.

52, 55. **Cressida** /CRESS ih duh/.

56. **conster** /CŎN stur/ explain.

64. **haggard** /HAG urd/ wild hawk.

71. **Dieu vous garde, monsieur** /dyö vōō GARD mö syö/ Fr. 'God save you, sir.'

72. **Et vous aussi, votre serviteur** /ay vōōz oh SEE, voht ^ruh sěr vee tör/
Fr. 'And you too, your servant.'

124. *****grize** /grīz/ step, degree. Variant of **grise** /grīss, grīz/, **grece** /greess/, **grice** /grīss/.

151. **maugre** /MAW gur/ in spite of.

Act 3 Scene 2

13. **'Slight** /zlīt/ by God's light.

31. **as lief** /leef/ as soon.

42. **martial** /MAR shł/ warlike.

48. **bed of Ware** /wair/ famous large bedstead.

52. **cubiculo** /kyōō BIK yuh loh/ from Ital. 'little bedchamber.'

65. *****presage** indication. US, UK /PRESS ij/ [pree-, prih SAYJ];
CN /pree-, prih SAYJ/ [PRESS ij].

70. **renegado** renouncer of his religion. /ren uh GAY doh/ is older, /-GAH doh/ is newer.

75. **pedant** /PED ṇt/ dull teacher.

ă-bat, ăir-marry, air-pair, ạr-far, ĕr-merry, ĝ-get, ī-high, ĭr-mirror, ł-little, ṇ-listen, ŏ-hot, oh-go, ōō-wood, ōō-moon, oor-tour, ōr-or, ow-how, țh-that, ᵵh-thin, ŭ-but, UR-fur, ur-under. ( )- suppress the syllable [ ]- less common   see p. xi for complete list.

Act 3 Scene 3

18. **reliques, relics** /REL iks/ ancient monuments.

31. **Albeit** /awl BEE (i)t/ although.

Act 3 Scene 4

68. **slough** /sluff/ skin.

74. **lim'd** /līmd/ caught in a trap made of lime paste.

116. **Sathan** archaic form of **Satan**, both pronounced /SAYT n̩, -un/ the devil.

117. **collier** /CŎL yur/; UK *also* /CŎL ee yur/ coal miner.

196. ***cockatrices** /CŎCK uh triss iz, -trīss iz/ monsters whose gaze kills.

202. **unchary** /un CHAIR ee/; E. COAST US *also* /-CHĂIR-/ carelessly.

224. ***yare** /yair/; US *also* /yạr/ prompt.

238. ***implacable** /im PLAK uh bł/ cannot be appeased.

240. **sepulchre** /SEP ł kur/ tomb.

261. **mortal arbitrement, arbitrament** /ạr BIT ruh munt/ trial by combat to the death.

274. **firago** /fih RAH goh, -RAY-/ female warrior. Variant of ***virago** /vih RAH goh/; US *also older* [-RAY-]. US, CN [VĬR uh goh] not recommended.

275. **scabbard** /SKAB urd/ sword sheath.

279. **Sophy** /SOH fee/ Shah of Persia.

287. **Capilet** /KAP ih let/. Some eds. prefer **Capulet** /-yuh-, -uh-/.

289. **perdition** /pur DISH un/; UK *also* [PUR-] destruction.

307. **duello** /do͞o EL oh/; UK, SOUTH. US *also* /dyo͞o-/ duelling code.

385. **paltry** /PAWL tree/ worthless.

391. **'Slid** /zlid/ by God's eyelid.

Act 4 Scene 1

31. **twopence** /TUP n̩ss, -unss/.

44. ***malapert** /MAL uh purt/; US *also* [mal uh PURT] saucy.

51. **Rudesby** /RŌODZ bee/ rude person.

62. **Lethe** /LEE̶T̶H̶ ee/ river of forgetfulness in Hades.

Act 4 Scene 2

> **2–101. Sir Topas** probably an older spelling of **Topaz**, both pronounced /TOH paz/.
> Sometimes a spelling pronunciation /TOH păss/ is used, but this is not
> recommended.

> **2, 21. curate** /KYOOR ut/; US *also* /KYUR ut/ priest.

8. **studient** /STŌOD yunt/; UK, SOUTH. US /STYŌOD-/. Archaic variant of **student**.

12. **Bonos dies** angl. /BOH nohss/ or /BOH nus DĬ eez/. Feste's version of Lat.
Bonus dies, Class.Lat. /BŎN ōos DIH ess/ or Sp. *Buenos días*
/BWAY nohss DEE ahss/ good day.

13. **Prague** /prahg/.

14. **King Gorboduc** /GOR buh duck/ legendary king of England.

25. **hyperbolical** /hī pur BŎL ih kł/ raving.

31. **Sathan** archaic form of **Satan**, both pronounced /SAYT n̩, -un/ the devil.

37. **barricadoes** /băir ih KAY dohz/ is older, /-KAH dohz/ is newer. Archaic
variant of *barricades*.

37. **clerestories** /CLEER stor eez/ windows in upper wall.

42. **thou errest** /UR ist, ĔR ist/. The former is older.

50, 58. ***Pythagoras** US /pih T̶H̶AG uh rus/ [pī-]; UK /pī-/ Gk. philosopher.

> ă-bat, ăir-marry, air-pair, a̱r-far, ĕr-merry, ĝ-get, ī-high, ĭr-mirror, ł-little, n̩-listen,
> ŏ-hot, oh-go, ōo-wood, ōō-moon, oor-tour, ōr-or, ow-how, ṯh-that, t̶h̶-thin, Ŭ-but,
> UR-fur, ur-under. ( )- suppress the syllable   [ ]- less common   see p. xi for complete list.

52, 60. **grandam** /GRAN dam/; US *rarely* [-dum] grandmother. Informally /GRAN um/.

75. **perdie, perdy** /PUR DEE/ by God, indeed. Some eds. prefer the variant **pardie** /par DEE/.

100. **God buy you** good-bye. Some eds. substitute **God b'wi' you** /gŏd BWEE yōō/ or some other variation of that phrase.

126. **lath** US /lăth/; UK, E. NEW ENG. /lahth/ [lăth] narrow strip of wood.

131. **goodman** /GōōD mun/ title of a man under the rank of gentleman.

Act 4 Scene 3

24. **chantry** US /CHĂNT ree/; UK, E. NEW ENG. /CHAHN tree/ chapel.

27. **jealious** /JEL yus/ archaic variant of **jealous**.

Act 5 Scene 1

36. **Primo, secundo, tertio** firstly, secondly, thirdly. Perhaps part of a child's game or dice game. Ang.Lat. /PRĪ moh, suh KUN doh, TUR shee oh/ or /-shoh/; restored Latin /PREE moh, sek KōōN doh, TĔR shee oh/.

55. **draught** US, CN /drăft/; UK, E. NEW ENG. /drahft/ depth of water needed by a ship to float.

56. **scathful** /SKATH full/ harmful. Variant of **scatheful** /SKAYTH-/.

109. **fulsome** distasteful. /FULL sum/; US *rarely* [FŬL-].

113. **ingrate** here should be /in GRAYT/ ungrateful.

120. **savors nobly** (UK **savours**) /SAY vurz/ has the characteristics of nobility.

132. **jocund** /JŎCK und/; US, CN *rarely* [JOHK-] merry.

147. **propriety** /pruh PRĪ ih tee/ identity.

182. **incardinate** /in CAR dih nut, -ayt/ Aguecheek's mistake for **incarnate** /in CAR nit/ [-nayt] in the flesh. /-ut/ is usual for adjs.

200–1. passy-measures pavin /PĂSS ee-/, /PAV in/ slow stately dance. Archaic variant of ***pavan** US /puh VAHN/ [-VAN]; UK /-VAHN, -VAN/.

217. natural perspective Shk probably intended /NATCH rĺ PUR spek tiv/, but it could also be /NATCH ur ĺ pur SPEK tiv/ with an epic caesura.

232. Messaline /MESS uh leen/.

246. record here should be /rek-, rik ORD/.

263. betroth'd /bih-, bee TROHṬHD/ engaged to be married.

276. *durance /DYOOR unss/; US *also* /DŌōR-/ [DUR-] imprisonment.

284. Belzebub /BEL zih bub/ a devil. Archaic variant of **Beelzebub** /bee EL zih bub/.

285. stave's /stayvz/ staff's.

287. epistles /ih-, ee PISS ĺz/ letters. /ee-/ non-standard in the UK.

296. vox /vŏks/ voice, dramatic reading.

299. perpend /pur PEND/ consider.

314. savors (UK **savours**) /SAY vurz/ has the characteristic of.

372. Sir Topas probably an older spelling of **Topaz**, both pronounced /TOH paz/. Sometimes a spelling pronunciation /TOH păss/ is used, but this is not recommended.

376. whirligig /WHUR lee ĝig/ spinning top.

382. convents /cun VENTS/ suits.

ă-bat, ăir-marry, air-pair, ạr-far, ĕr-merry, ĝ-get, ī-high, ĭr-mirror, ĺ-little, ṇ-listen, ŏ-hot, oh-go, ōō-wood, ōō-moon, oor-tour, ōr-or, ow-how, ṭh-that, ᵵh-thin, Ŭ-but, UR-fur, ur-under. ( )- suppress the syllable [ ]- less common   see p. xi for complete list.

The Winter's Tale

People in the Play

Antigonus /an TIG uh nus/.

Archidamus /ark ih DAY mus/ this name is not spoken.

Autolycus /aw TŎL ih kus/.

Camillo /kuh MILL oh/.

Cleomines, Cleomenes /clee ŎM ih neez/.

Dion /DĪ un/ is traditional, but sometimes newer pronunciations /DĪ ŏn/ or /DEE ŏn, -un/ are used.

Dorcas /DOR kus/.

Emilia usually 3 syllables /ih MEEL (ee) yuh/. An older pronunciation /-MILL-/ is now rare.

Florizel US /FLŌR ih zel/; E. COAST US, UK /FLŎR-/.

Hermione 3 or 4 syllables depending on meter /hur MĪ (uh) nee/.

Jailer, (UK Gaoler) both /JAY lur/.

Leontes /lee ŎN teez/.

Mamillius 3 or 4 syllables depending on meter /muh MILL (ee) yus/.

Mopsa /MŎP suh/.

Paulina /paw LĪ nuh/ but sometimes newer /-LEE-/ is used.

Perdita /PUR dit uh/.

Polixenes 3 or 4 syllables depending on meter /puh LIX (ih) neez/.

Places in the Play

Bohemia /boh HEEM (ee) yuh/ part of the present-day Czech Republic.

*****Delphos** where the sacred oracle lies. US /DEL fohss/ [-fŏss, -fus];
UK /-fŏss/ [-fohss, -fus]. Normal development would favor /-us/. /-ohss/ is a newer pronunciation.

Sicilia /sih SILL (ee) yuh/. 4.4.589 *And shall appear in Sicilia* points to /SISS ł yuh/ or /sih sih LEE uh/.

Act 1 Scene 1

15. **insufficience** /in suh FISH unss/.

Act 1 Scene 2

5. *****perpetuity** eternity. /PUR puh TYOO ih tee/; US *also* [-TOO-]. /-CHOO-/ is also used but is considered non-standard in the UK.

13. **sneaping** /SNEEP ing/ biting cold.

17. **sev'nnight** variant of *se'nnight* /SEN nit, -nīt/ week.

19. **gainsaying** /gayn SAY ing/ denying.

37. **distaffs** cleft staff used in spinning thread. US /DIS stăfs/;
E. NEW ENG., UK /DIS stahfs/.

41. **gest** /jest/ stage of a royal journey.

42. **Prefix'd** appointed. Here may be /prih-, pree FIKST/ or with inverted foot, newer /PREE fikst/.

66. **verier** /VĔR yur/ more outrageous.

110. **tremor cordis** fluttering of the heart. Ang.Lat. /TREE mur COR diss/; restored Latin /TREM ur COR diss/. The latter is more common today.

125. **virginalling** /VUR jin ł ing/ playing, fingering.

ă-bat, ăir-marry, air-pair, ạr-far, ĕr-merry, ĝ-get, ī-high, ĭr-mirror, ł-little, ṇ-listen, ŏ-hot, oh-go, ŏŏ-wood, ōō-moon, oor-tour, ōr-or, ow-how, ṭh-that, ᵗh-thin, ŭ-but, UR-fur, ur-under. ( )- suppress the syllable   [ ]- less common   see p. xi for complete list.

134. ***bourn** /born, boorn/ boundary. North American [burn] not recommended. Normal development would favor /born/.

137. **collop** /CŎL up/ small slice of meat, part of my own flesh.

142. **credent** /CREED ṇt/ believable.

155. ***unbreech'd** not old enough for men's clothes. /un BRITCHT/ is traditional, /-BREECHT/ is newer. The former pronunciation is more common in the UK and the latter in the US, CN.

169. **July's** here should be /JOO līz/.

204. **barricado** fortification. /băir ih KAY doh/ is older, /-KAH doh/ is newer.

227. **extraordinary** here US /ek struh OR dih něr ee/; UK /-dih nuh ree/.

228. **purblind** /PUR blīnd/ blind or partly blind.

244. **hoxes** /HŎK siz/ hamstrings.

271. **cogitation** /cŏj ih TAY shun/ thought.

301. **lout** /lowt/ oaf.

316. **bespice** /bih-, bee SPĪSS/ to spice.

318. **draught** US, CN /drăft/; UK, E. NEW ENG. /drahft/ drink.

318. **cordial** US /COR jł/; UK /COR dył/ healing medicine.

339. **allied** here with 2nd syllable stress.

372. ***Wafting his eyes** shifting his eyes. US, CN /WŎFT ing/; SOUTH. US /WĂFT-/; UK /WŎFT-/ [WĂFT-,WAHFT-]. /WĂFT/ is newer and considered non-standard by many.

388. ***basilisk** legendary reptile whose glance was fatal. US /BĂSS ih lisk/ [BAZ ih lisk]; UK /BAZ-/ [BĂSS-]; CN both used equally.

395. **does behove** /bih-, bee HOHV/ is an advantage to.

421. **savor** (UK **savour**) /SAY vur/ smell.

438, 464. ***posterns** small back or side gates. US, CN /PŎST urnz/ [POHST-]; UK /PŎST urnz/, *rarely* [POHST urnz].

Act 2 Scene 1

46. **pandar, pander** /PAN dur/ pimp.

52. ***posterns** small back or side gates. US, CN /PŎST urnz/ [POHST urnz];
UK /PŎST urnz/, *rarely* [POHST urnz].

72, 73. **calumny** /CAL um nee/ slander.

84. ***precedent** /PRESS ih dunt/ example.

90. **federary** confederate. Before an epic caesura US /FED uh rĕr ree/; UK /-ruh ree/,
but it may also be syncopated to *feder'ry* /FED uh ree/ (cf. UK *secret'ry*).

99. **throughly** archaic variant of *thoroughly*. /T̶H̶ROO lee/ is the normal
pronunciation on stage, but to enhance clarity a syncopated form of the modern
pronunciation may be used: *thor'ghly*.

120. **deserv'd** here with 1st syllable stress.

157. **dungy** /DUNG ee/ filthy.

162. **Commune** speak intimately. Here may be the usual mod. /cuh MYOON/, or if
the foot is inverted /CŎM yoon/, found elsewhere in Shk.

163. ***prerogative** /pur RŎG uh tiv/ [prih-, pree-] right. /pree-/ non-standard in the
UK.

192. ***credulity** gullibility. /cruh DYOO lih tee/; US *also* /-DOO-/; /-JOO-/ is
considered non-standard in the UK.

Act 2 Scene 2

10. **th' access** here should be /t̶hʸ ak SESS/.

28. **unsafe** here should be /UN sayf/.

28. **lunes** /loonz/ fits of madness. At one time many RP speakers in the UK used
/lyoo-/ for words beginning *lu-,* but today their number is dwindling.

37. **advocate** /AD vuh kut/ someone who supports a person.

ă-bat, ăir-marry, air-pair, a̩r-far, ĕr-merry, ĝ-get, ī-high, ĭr-mirror, ł-little, n̩-listen,
ŏ-hot, oh-go, o͞o-wood, o͞o-moon, oor-tour, ōr-or, ow-how, t̩h-that, t̶h-thin, ŭ-but,
UR-fur, ur-under. ( )- suppress the syllable   [ ]- less common   see p. xi for complete list.

Act 2 Scene 3

4. **harlot** /HAR lut/ lewd.

8. **moi'ty, moiety** /MOY tee/ portion.

37. **medicinal** here should be /MED sin ł/.

56. **Less *appear* so, in comforting your evils.** Here 1st syllable stress is indicated for *appear*. Possibly 2 weak stresses were intended in the 1st foot with *-pear* scanned as 2 syllables (see p. 24).

75. **dotard** /DOHT urd/ senile old man.

91. **callat, callet** /KAL ut/ whore.

109. ***lozel, losel** /LOH zł/ [LŎZ ł] scoundrel.

115. **heretic** /HĔR ih tik/ dissenter.

119. **savors** (UK **savours**) /SAY vurz/ smacks of, smells of.

160. **Margery** /MARJ ur ee/. a hen-like woman.

198. **accompt** /uh COWNT/ archaic variant of **account**, pronounced the same way.

Act 3 Scene 1

20. **contents** here should be /cŏn TENTS/.

Act 3 Scene 2

11. **indictment** /in DĪT munt/ charge of wrongdoing.

37. **spectators** here should be /spek TAY turz/, a common UK pronunciation, virtually unknown in the US.

39. **moi'ty, moiety** /MOY tee/ portion.

56. **gainsay** /GAYN say/ deny.

170. **glisters** /GLIS turz/ glistens.

Act 3 Scene 3

62. ancientry /AYN shun tree/ old people.

70. barne /barn/ archaic dialect form meaning 'child.' Some eds. prefer **bairn** /bairn/ which today is a Scottish form.

77. hallow'd /HAL-, HŎL ohd/ or /huh LOHD/ shouted. Some eds. prefer **halloo'd** /huh LO͞OD/.

79. Hilloa, loa /hih LOH, LOH/ a call to attract attention.

88. chafes /chayfs/ rages.

92. mainmast /MAYN mᵘst/ is used by sailors; landsmen say US, CN /-măst/; UK, E. NEW ENG. /-mahst/.

124. close /clohss/ secret.

Act 4 Scene 1

2. unfolds here with 1st syllable stress.

9. oe'rwhelm here should be /OR whelm/.

14. glistering /GLIS tring/ glistening.

20. spectators here should be /spek TAY turz/, a common UK pronunciation, virtually unknown in the US.

26. prophesy /PRŎF uh sī/ to predict the future.

Act 4 Scene 2

1. importunate /im POR chuh nut/; UK *also* /-tyoo nut/ insistant.

8. allay /uh LAY/ relief.

ă-bat, ăir-**marry**, air-**pair**, ạr-**far**, ĕr-**merry**, ĝ-**get**, ī-**high**, ĭr-**mirror**, ł-**little**, ṇ-**listen**, ŏ-**hot**, oh-**go**, o͞o-**wood**, o͞o-**moon**, oor-**tour**, ōr-**or**, ow-**how**, ţh-**that**, ᵵh-**thin**, ŭ-**but**, UR-**fur**, ur-**under**. ( )- suppress the syllable   [ ]- less common   see p. xi for complete list.

Act 4 Scene 3

2, 10. ***heigh!** US /hay, hī/; CN /hī/, *rarely* [hay]; UK /hay/. Here /hay/ was intended as indicated in F1, line 6 *hey,* and also the internal rhyme with *jay* in line 10.

2. **doxy** /DŎK see/ beggar's wench.

9. **chaunts** archaic variant of **chants** US /chănts/; E. NEW ENG, UK /chahnts/. The archaic vowel was pronounced /-AW-/ and gave rise to RP /-AH-/.

20. **bouget** may have been /BOW jit/ to rhyme with *avouch it.* Archaic variant of **budget** /BUJ it/ leather bag.

22. **avouch** /uh VOWCH/ affirm.

27. **caparison** /kuh PĂIR ih sn̩/ ornamental cloth covering for a horse.

27. **revenue** sometimes in verse /ruh VEN yōō/, but in this prose passage may be mod. Eng. US /REV in ōō/; UK, SOUTH. US /-yōō/.

35. **springe** /sprinj/ snare.

36. **compters** /COWNT urz/ archaic variant of **counters** discs to help calculate. They were pronounced the same way in Elizabethan Eng.

45. **saffron** /SAFF run/ yellow food coloring used in baking.

48. **pruins** probably /PRŌŌ inz/, archaic and dialect variant of **prunes.**

Act 4 Scene 4

50. ***nuptial** wedding. US, UK /NUP chł/ [-shł]; in CN both are used equally.

65. **unknown** here should be /UN nohn/.

75. **savor** (UK **savour**) /SAY vur/ smell.

82, 98. **gillyvors** /JIL ee vurz/ dialect form of **gillyflowers** /JIL ee flow urz/ carnations.

87. **piedness** /PĪD niss/ having many colors.

93. **scion** /SĪ un/ living plant grafted onto root stock.

104. **savory** (UK **savoury**) /SAY v(uh) ree/ a type of herb.

104. **marjorum** type of herb. Archaic variant of **marjoram**, both pronounced /MAR jur rum/.

116. **Proserpina** /proh- pruh SUR pih nuh/ abducted by Pluto.

118. **Dis's** god of the underworld. Here exceptionally the possessive form is 2 syllables after /s/, /DIS iz/ (see p. 28).

122. **Cytherea's** /si~~th~~ uh REE uz/ Venus's.

122. **primeroses** may have been pronounced /PRĪM roh ziz/ or as its mod. variant **primroses** /PRIM roh ziz/.

124. **Phoebus** /FEE bus/ god of the sun.

127. **flow'r-de-luce** /FLOWR duh lōōss/ lily flower. Main stress may also fall on the 3rd syllable, the usual US form. At one time many RP speakers in the UK used /lyōō-/ for words beginning *lu-*, but today their number is dwindling.

134. **Whitsun** /WHIT sn̩/ Pentecost, the 7th Sunday after Easter.

138. **alms** charity for the poor. /ahmz/ is older; /ahlmz, awlmz/ are newer. In the UK the latter are non-standard.

146–178. **Doricles** US /DŌR ih kleez/; E. COAST US, UK /DŎR-/.

---

149. **unstain'd** here should be /UN staynd/.

157. **green-sord** /sord/ archaic variant of **sward** /swōrd/.

182. **tabor** /TAY bur/ small drum. /-bor/ not recommended.

190. ***lamentably** US /luh MEN tuh blee/ [LAM en-]; CN, UK /LAM un tuh blee/ [luh MEN-].

192. **milliner** /MILL ih nur/ seller of fancy goods.

198, 200. ***Whoop** /whōōp/ [hōōp, hŏŏp, whŏŏp].

207. **caddises, caddisses** /KAD iss iz/ ribbons for garters.

207. ***cambrics** fine linen cloths. /KAM briks/, or older [KAYM briks].

ă-bat, ăir-marry, air-pair, ạr-far, ĕr-merry, ĝ-get, ī-high, ĭr-mirror, ł-little, n̩-listen, ŏ-hot, oh-go, ōō-wood, ōō-moon, oor-tour, ōr-or, ow-how, ţh-that, ~~th~~-thin, ŭ-but, UR-fur, ur-under. ( )- suppress the syllable [ ]- less common see p. xi for complete list.

209. **chaunts** archaic variant of **chants** US /chănts/; E. NEW ENG, UK /chahnts/. The archaic vowel was pronounced /-AW-/ and gave rise to RP /-AH-/.

213. **scurrilous** US /SKUR ih lus/; E. COAST US, UK /SKUH rih lus/ vulgar.

220. **damask** /DAM usk/ pink or light red.

224. **quoifs** tight-fitting caps. Variant of **coifs**, both pronounced /coyfs/.

224. **stomachers** ornamental chest covering. Mod. /STUM uh kurz/. In Shk's time /STUM uh cheerz/, rhyming with *dears*, though the rhyme could also have been based on variant pronunciations /-kairz/-/dairz/.

245. **kill-hole** oven hole. Some eds. prefer **kiln hole**, now usually pronounced /kiln/, though /kill/ is older.

254. **behooves** /bih-, bee HO͞OVZ/ is necessary, proper for. UK prefers the spelling **behoves** /bih HOHVZ/.

260. **ballet** /BAL ut/ archaic variant of **ballad**.

263, 268 **usurer('s)** /YO͞O zhur urz/; UK *also* [-zhyoor urz, -zhoor urz] someone who lends money for interest.

265. ***carbonado'd** slashed for roasting. /car buh NAH dohd/; UK *rarely older* [-NAY dohd].

277. **fadom** /FAD um/ archaic variant of **fathom** /FĂT͟H um/.

323. **ware-a** /WAIR uh/ referring to 'wares.' *Dear-a* could also have been /air/ in Shk's time.

327. **Saltiers** uncertain. Perhaps confused with ***satyrs** US, CN /SAYT urz/, *rarely* [SAT urz]; UK /SAT urz/ [SAYT-] lusty goat-like creatures. It may also show confusion with **saltiers** (also spelled **saltires**) /SAL-, SAWL teerz, -tīrz/ heraldic crosses. Other eds. suggest that it may be **saultiers** 'leapers,' which could have been /SAWL teerz, -turz/ or perhaps /SAWT-/.

328. **gallimaufry** /gal ih MAW free/ stew, hodgepodge.

328. **gambols** /GAM błz/ frolics.

339. **by th' squier** /skwīr/ archaic variant of **square** carpenter's square, i.e., precisely.

368. ***protestation** US /proh tess-, prŏt ess TAY shun/;
CN /prŏt ess-/ [proh tess-]; UK /prŏt ess-/.

378. **perdition** /pur DISH un/; UK *also* [PUR DISH un] destruction.

395. ***nuptial** wedding. US, UK /NUP chł/ [-shł]; in CN both are used equally.

399. **rheums** /rōōmz/ diseases.

406. **unfilial** /un FIL ee ł/ contrary to the duty of a child.

417. **contract** here should be /cŏn TRACT/.

424. **thou cop'st with** /cohpst/ thou hast to do with.

431. **Farre** /far/ archaic variant of **far**, here 'farther.'

431. **Deucalion** father of the human race. /dyōō KAY lee un/; US *also* /dōō-/.
Sometimes newer /-ŏn/ is used, but is not recommended.

490. **close** /clohss/ hidden.

491. **unknown** here should be /UN nohn/.

491. **fadoms** /FAD umz/ archaic variant of **fathoms** /FĂṬH umz/.

500. ***opportune** here should be /ŏp POR tyōōn/; US *also* /-tōōn/.

567. **unpath'd** here with 1st syllable stress.

567. **undream'd** here with 1st syllable stress.

597. **trompery, trumpery** /TRUMP ur ee/ worthless stuff.

598. ***pomander** scent ball. US /POH man dur/ [PŎM un dur, poh MAN dur];
CN /poh MAN dur/ [POH man dur, PŎM un dur, poh MAHN dur];
UK /poh MAN dur/. All the variants have existed for centuries, but etymologically
the best choice is /PŎM un dur/ (from Fr. *pomme d'amber*, cf. *pomegranate* from
Fr. *pomme granate*).

598. ***brooch** /brohch/ ornament. US [brōōch] not recommended.

ă-bat, ăir-marry, air-**pair**, ạr-**far**, ĕr-**merry**, ĝ-**get**, ī-**high**, ĭr-**mirror**, ł-**little**, ṇ-**listen**,
ŏ-**hot**, oh-**go**, ōō-**wood**, ōō-**moon**, oor-**tour**, ōr-**or**, ow-**how**, ṭh-**that**, t̶h̶-**thin**, ŭ-**but**,
UR-**fur**, ur-**under**. ( )- suppress the syllable [ ]- less common   see p. xi for complete list.

607. **pettitoes** /PET ee tohz/ trotters of a pig.

616. **whoobub** archaic variant of **hubbub** /HUB ub/, very likely pronounced the same way.

617. **choughs, chuffs** /chufs/ jackdaws.

635. **pennyworth** bargain. The older form is /PEN urth/, but in this prose passage the newer, spelling pronunciation /PEN ee wurth, -WURTH/ may be used.

641. **flea'd** /fleed/ archaic and dialect variant of **flayed** /flayd/ skinned.

650. __*covert__ hiding place. US, CN /KOHV urt/ [KUV-]; UK /KUV urt/ [KOHV urt], *rarely* [KUV ur], an older form.

655. **undescried** /un dih SKRĪD/ unseen.

672. **requisite** /REK wiz it/ required.

677. **extempore** /ek STEM pur ree/ on the spur of the moment.

708–56. **farthel** /FAR thł/ bundle. Variant of **fardel** /FAR dł/.

---

736. **cap-a-pe** from head to toe. Archaic variant of __*cap-à-pie__. Traditionally /kap uh PEE/, still the most common form in the US, CN, and also used in the UK. A newer form /-PAY/ is preferred in the UK and also used in the US. Stress may also fall on the 1st syllable. A Frenchified version /kap uh pee AY/ is also increasingly used. The spelling pronunciation /-PĪ/ is not recommended.

740, 742. **advocate('s)** /AD vuh kut/ someone who supports a person.

773. **germane** US /jur MAYN/; UK /JUR MAYN/ [JUR mayn] related to.

786. __*aqua-vitae__ distilled liquor, e.g., brandy. US /AHK-, AK wuh VEE tī/, *rarely* [-VĪ tee]; CN /AK wuh VEE tī/ [AHK-]; UK /AK wuh VEE tī/ [-VEE tuh]. /AK wuh VĪ tee/ is the oldest surviving form. /-VEE tay/ not recommended.

788. **prognostication** a prediction. US /prŏg nŏss tih KAY shun/;
UK /prug-/ [prŏg-].

800. **Close with him** /clohz/ make the deal.

812. **moi'ty, moiety** /MOY tee, MOY uh tee/ portion.

Act 5 Scene 1

4. More penitence than done trespass. *Penitence* was meant to be syncopated /PEN (ih) tunss/ and *trespass* is pronounced normally with 1st syllable stress.

87. access here should be /ak SESS/.

108. proselytes /PRŎS ih līts/ converts.

153. *paragon US /PĂIR uh gŏn/ [-gun]; CN /-gŏn/; UK /-gun/ [-gn̩] most perfect example.

157. Smalus /SMAY lus/.

202. *divers various. Here should be stressed on the 1st syllable US, CN /DĪ vurss, -vurz/; UK /DĪ vurss/ [-vurz].

221. advocate /AD vuh kut/ someone who supports a person or cause.

Act 5 Scene 2

3, 116. farthel /FAR t̩hl̩/ bundle. Variant of **fardel** /FAR dl̩/.

21. Rogero /roh JĔR oh, ruh JĔR oh/. Some eds. prefer **Ruggiero** /ro͞oj YĔR oh/.

56. *conduit fountain or water channel. Here must be 2 syllables /CŎN dwit/; UK *also* [CUN dwit, CŎN dywit, CŎN dit, CUN dit].

64. avouches /uh VOWCH iz/ affirms.

87. dolor (UK **dolour**) /DOH lur/; UK *also* /DŎL ur/ pain. /-or/ not recommended.

91. swounded archaic variant of **swooned**. In Shk's time the vowel could be either /ow/ or /o͞o/.

97. Julio (Giulio) Romano /JOOL ee yoh roh MAHN oh/.

160. *boors US, CN /bo͞orz/, *sometimes* [borz]; UK /bo͞orz, borz/ peasants.

ă-bat, ăir-marry, air-pair, a̩r-far, ĕr-merry, ĝ-get, ī-high, ĭr-mirror, ł-little, n̩-listen, ŏ-hot, oh-go, o͞o-wood, o͞o-moon, oor-tour, ŏr-or, ow-how, t̩h-that, t̸h-thin, Ŭ-but, UR-fur, ur-under. ( )- suppress the syllable   [ ]- less common   see p. xi for complete list.

Act 5 Scene 3

67. **fixure** /FIK shur/; UK *also* /-syoor/ fixedness.   Some eds. prefer **fixture**.

77. **cordial** US /COR jł/; UK /COR dył/ cheering.

155. **dissever'd** /dih SEV urd/ severed.

APPENDIX A: COMMON WORDS WITH MORE THAN ONE STANDARD PRONUNCIATION IN TODAY'S ENGLISH

Some common words have two or more pronunciations within Standard American or British English today, or the same word may vary between countries. Here is a list of some that occur in Shakespeare. All of the pronunciations given in the chart are acceptable as Standard English within the listed country, that is, large numbers of educated speakers pronounce the words in the given way, though some may be newer forms based on spelling.

It is important to remember that speakers from one part of the country often look with scorn on pronunciations they do not use. An example is *catch* which many Americans know only as /ketch/ while others say /katch/; there are many within each group who believe theirs is the only correct pronunciation.

There are also groups of words that vary between North America and the UK. The British and some New Englanders generally use /ah/ before /f, th, s/, and also before /n/ followed by a consonant in words like *laugh, bath, fast, can't* where most North Americans use /ă/. These words are not included in this list.

Evidence for the pronunciations listed here comes primarily from the surveys conducted for this study (indicated by an asterisk) supplemented by older dialect studies and the dictionaries.

	United States	UK (RP)
accomplish	/uh CŎMP lish/	/-CUMP-/ [-CŎMP-]
again(st)	/uh GEN(ST)/; rarely [uh GAYN(ST)]	/uh GEN(ST)/ [uh GAYN(ST)]
***agile**	/AJ ł/ [-īl]	/AJ īl/
***balk**	/bawk, bawlk/	/bawk/ [bawlk]
battery	/BAT ur ee/	/BAT ree/
been	/bin, ben/; rarely [been]	/been/ [bin]
borrow	/BAHR oh/ [-uh, BŌR-]	/BŎR oh/
braggart	/BRAG urt/	/-ut/ [-aht]
***buoy**	/BOO ee/ [boy]	/boy/
calm	/kahm, kahlm, kawlm/	/kahm/ [kahlm]
catch	/katch, ketch/	/katch/
***celestial**	/suh LEST ee ł, -chł/	/suh LEST ył/
circumstance	/SUR kum stanss/	/SUR kum st^{u}nss/ [-stahnss, -stanss]
clerk	/clurk/	/clahk/
***compost**	/CŎM pohst/ [-pŏst]	/CŎM pŏst/
counterfeit	/COWN tur fit/	/COWN tuh fit/ [-feet]
***deity**	/DEE ih tee/	/DAY ih tee/ [DEE-]
desolation, desolate	/DESS-/; rarely [DEZ-]	/DESS-/
***direct**	/dur-, dih REKT/ [dī-]	/dih REKT/ [dī-]
***disdain**	/dis DAYN/ [diz-]	/dis DAYN/ [diz-]

disguise	/dis SKĪZ/	/dis SKĪZ/ [diz ĜĪZ]
dog	/dawg, dŏg/	/dŏg/
either	/EE ţhur/ [Ī ţhur]	/Ī ţhuh/ [EE-]
***exile**	/EK sīl, EGG zīl/	/EK sīl/ [EGG zīl]
experiment	/ek SPĔR ih ment, -SPĬR-/	/ek SPĔR ih ment/
***falcon**	/FAL kun/ [FAWL-]	/FAL kun, FAWL-/
***fantasy**	/FANT uh see/	/FANT uh see/ [-zee]
***fertile**	/FURT ł/ [-īl]	/FUR tīl/
figure	/FIG yur/	/FIG uh/
***forehead**	/FOR hed/ [FOR id]; E. Coast [FAHR-]	/FŎR id/ [FOR hed]
***fragile**	/FRAJ ł/ [-īl]	/FRAJ īl/
gone	/gawn, gŏn/	/gŏn/
herbs	/urbz/ [hurbz]	/HURBZ/
***homicide**	/HŎM ih sīd/; rarely [HOHM-]	/HŎM ih sīd/
***hostile**	/HŎST ł/ [-īl]	/HŎST īl/
***hover**	/HUV ur/	/HŎV uh/ [HUV uh]
human, huge, etc.	/HYŌŌ-/, [YŌŌ-]	/HYŌŌ-/
***(after-) inquiry**	/ING kwur ee/ [ing KWĪ ree]	/ing KWĪ ree/
***interest**	/IN trist/ [IN tur ist]	/INT rist/ [IN tuh rist]
issue	/ISH ōō/	/ISH ōō/ [ISS yōō, ISH yōō]
***jury**	/JUR ee, JŌŌR ee/	/JŌŌR ee/
***leisure**	/LEE zhur/ [LEZH ur]	/LEZH uh/
***lever**	/LEV ur/ [LEE vur]	/LEE vuh/
***luxury**	/LUCK shur ee, LUG zhur ee/	/LUCK shuh ree/
madman	/MAD man/	/MAD mun/
medicine	/MED ih sin/	/MED sṇ/ [MED sin, MED ih sin]
melancholy	/MEL un cŏl ee/	/MEL un cuh lee/ [-cŏl-]
***minority**	/mih NŎR it ee/ [mī-]; E. COAST /-NAHR-/	/mī NŎR it ee/ [mih-]
***mongrel**	/MŎNG grł/ [MAWNG-, MUNG-]	/MUNG grł/
***negotiate**	/nuh GOH shee ayt/; rarely [-see ayt]	/nuh GOH shee ayt/ [-see ayt]
neither	/NEE ţhur/ [NĪ ţhur]	/NĪ ţhuh/ [NEE-]
***oaths**	/ohŧhs, ohţhz/	/ohŧhs, ohţhz/
often	/AWF ṇ, -tun/	/ŎF ṇ/ [-tun]

on	/ŏn, awn/	/ŏn/
orange	/OR inj, ornj/; E. COAST /AHR inj/	/ŎR inj/
*poor	/po͞or, por/	/po͞or, por/
*posterior	/pŏs STEER ee ur/ [pohst-]	/pŏs STEER ee uh/
princess	/PRIN sess/	/prin SESS/
privacy	/PRĪ vuh see/	/PRIV uh see/
*process	/PRŎS ess/ [PROH sess]	/PROH sess/ [PRŎS ess]
*progress	/PRŎG ress/ [PROH gress]	/PROH gress/ [PRŎG ress]
rather	/RĂṮH ur/ [RUH ṯhur, RAH-]	/RAH ṯhuh/
roof	/ro͞of/ [ro͝of, ruff]	/ro͞of/ [ro͝of]
room	/ro͞om/ [ro͝om, rum]	/ro͞om/ [ro͝om]
root	/ro͞ot/ [ro͝ot, rut]	/ro͞ot/; /ro͝ot/ is non-standard
*sliver	/SLIV ur/	/SLIV uh/ [SLĪ vuh]
sorrow	/SAHR oh/[-uh, SŌR-]	/SŎR oh/
sorry	/SAHR ee/ [SŌR ee]	/SŎR ee/
*sterile	/STĚR ł/ [-īl]	/STĚR īl/
suggest	/sug JEST/	/suh JEST/
syrup	/SĬR up, SUR-/	/SĬR up/
tomorrow	/to͞o MAHR oh, -uh/ [tuh-, -MŌR-]	/to͞o MŌR oh/, /tuh-/
*tournament	/TUR nuh munt/ [TOOR-, TOR-]	/TOOR nuh munt/ [TOR-, TUR-]
toward (prep.)	/tword, tord/ [tuh-, to͞o WÂRD]	/tuh-, to͞o WÂRD/ [tord]
*trespass	/TRESS păss, -pus/	/TRESS pus/; /-păss, -pahss/ are non-standard
were	/WUR/	/WUR/ [wair]
with	/wiṯh/ [wiṯh]	/wiṯh/; /wiṯh/ is non-standard
wrath	/răṯh/; E. NEW ENG. /ah/	/rŏṯh/ [rawṯh]; /rahṯh, răṯh/ are non- standard

ă-bat, ăir-marry, air-pair, ạr-far, ĕr-merry, ĝ-get, ī-high, ĭr-mirror, ł-little, ṇ-listen, ŏ-hot, oh-go, o͝o-wood, o͞o-moon, oor-tour, ŏr-or, ow-how, ṯh-that, ṯh-thin, ŭ-but, UR-fur, ur-under. ( )- suppress the syllable [ ]- less common   see p. xi for complete list.

APPENDIX B: COMMON ARCHAIC FORMS IN SHAKESPEARE

alevan /uh LEV un/   eleven

beshrow /bee-, bih SHROH/   **beshrew** to curse

burthen /BURṬH in/   burden

fadom /FAD um/   fathom

fift /fift/   fifth

lanthorn /LAN turn/, or possibly   lantern
/LAN ~~thorn, -thurn~~, LANT horn/.
Although a popular misconception
led to the spelling with -*horn*, it
was probably still pronounced
/LAN turn/ (cf. the breed of
chicken *Leghorn,* still /LEG urn/
today).

moe /moh/   more

murther/MUR ṭhur/   murder

sate /sat/ or possibly /sayt/   sat

shrike /shrīk/   shriek

shrowd /shrohd/   shrewd

sixt /sikst/   sixth

sound /sownd, so͞ond/   swoon

strook, -en /stro͞ok, struck/   struck, stricken

vild /vīld/   vile

wrastle /RĂSS ł/   wrestle

336

APPENDIX C: PRONUNCIATION IN ELIZABETHAN ENGLAND

It is difficult to describe Shakespeare's speech in terms of modern pronunciation for several reasons. First because of the dialect differences in today's English. A statement like "vowel *x* sounded much like the vowel in present-day *awe*" is often misleading because *awe* is pronounced differently in London, New York, and Toronto. There were also many dialects of Elizabethan English, both regionally and socially. Finally, no one really knows exactly how English was spoken in Shakespeare's day. We can come close because there were several writers in the sixteenth and seventeenth centuries who wrote in some detail on how words were pronounced. At times, however, it is difficult to interpret their descriptions.

It is clear, however, that the consonants were much the same as they are today. Those Elizabethans interested in "proper" English still pronounced the *gh* inherited from Old English in *night, weigh, neighbor* (pronounced as in German *ich*, that is, like an extended /h/ in *he*) and in *bough, daughter* (pronounced as in Scottish *loch*). Words with initial *kn-* or *gn-* like *knot* and *gnat*, were pronounced with /k/ and /g/ before /n/ until sometime in the seventeenth century. Words spelled *wh-* were pronounced with a breath /hw-/, which is still retained in some US dialects, particularly in the South, and in Scottish English, whereas in most American speech and in Standard British it has become simple /w-/. Words spelled *th* that were borrowed from Latin or French were pronounced with /t/ (*author, orthography, Katherine*). *Sure* could be pronounced either /SIH-oor/ or /shoor/, and *sugar, suit, sue* varied in a similar way. Elizabethan English also had /r/ after most vowels in words like *bark, dear, her*, which today has been lost in Standard British and most dialects in England, as well as in some East Coast American dialects. What exactly Shakespeare's /r/ sounded like is difficult to say for certain, but it was probably much like that found in North America and southwestern England today, though it may have been trilled as in Scottish at the beginning of words.

The vowels were much the same too, with some notable exceptions. The diphthongs heard in words like *mouse* and *mice* were pronounced more like /UH-oo/, /UH-ee/, rather than modern /AH-oo/, /AH-ee/. The long *a* in words like *trail, day, mate* was pronounced like the vowel of modern *get, fed*, but held longer. Words with long *e* spelled *ea* (*meat, eat, speak*) were pronounced as they are today with /ee/ by some Elizabethans, but another, perhaps more formal pronunciation, equal to the vowel just described in *trail, day*, was also used by some segments of the population.* It is also possible that for some the vowel in *meat* had the quality of /ĕ/ in *met*, but was held longer, and so was distinct from two other long vowels, /ee/ as in *meet* and the vowel in *mate*, which had the quality of /ă/ in *mat*, held longer (Cercignani 1981, 154–161). Long *o* was slightly diphthongized as it is today in many northern US dialects or was a monophthong rather like standard British *awe* (or in North American English the vowel before /r/ in *oar*), not as in Standard British *owe* where the diphthong has become /EH-oo/. Most of the words spelled *oi, oy* could be pronounced as in modern /oy/ or as Elizabethan long *i* /UH-ee/, so *point* and *pint* were

---

* In modern English the words *break, steak, great, yea* are still pronounced with long *a* today, as are all *ea* words of this sort in Irish English.

homonyms. Modern short *u* in words spelled with *o* could be /o͞o/ in Elizabethan English (*blood, done, dost, doth, love, come*), but could also be /uh/.

Words spelled *-ir-, -er-, -ur-* which today are all pronounced alike with the vowel of *her*, may have maintained their distinct Middle English vowel sounds into this era, so *fir* may have still been /fĭr/, *refer* /-fĕr/, and *fur* /fur/. Many words spelled *-er-* which are now pronounced /ur/ were then pronounced /ahr/: *heard, German, person, merchant* (and still are in UK *derby, clerk*). *War, warm, reward* had the short *a* of *wax* or possibly the sound /ah/. Words which today have /ahr/ (*harm, arm, barn*) may also have had the short /ă/. The /ah/ used in Standard British in *staff, father, fast* was probably /ă/ as well, perhaps held longer.

In addition there were some differences in syllables that did not bear the main stress:

fortune, actual	/-tih-oon/, /-tih-oo͏ł/ or /-tyoon/, /-tyoo͏ł/
educate	/-dih-oo-/, /-dyoo-/
action, martial	/-sih-un/, /-sih-ŭł/ or /-syun/, /-sył/ or mod. /-shun/, /-shł/
occasion, measure	/-zih-un/, /-zih-oor/ or /-zyun/, /-zyur/ or mod. /-zhun/, /-zhur/.
nature, venture, pasture	/-tur/ as in *enter* or /-tih-oor/.
verdure, ordure	/-dur/ as in *order* or /-dih-oor/
temperate, fortunate	rhymed with *hate* or with *hat*
embassage, pilgrimage	rhymed with *age* or with *badge*
Titania, Bianca, Hermia	ended in the vowel of *cat* or the vowel of *say*, still heard in some US dialects in *Ioway* (*Iowa*)

There are also many examples of individual words that differed from modern English. *One* and *gone* rhymed with *moan, Rome* was /ro͞om/, *whore* was /ho͞or/ (still found in Canada), *schedule* was /SED yool/. *Eunuch* had several pronunciations, one of the most common being /EV nook/. In stressed positions *should, would, could* were pronounced with /l/.

Some other differences like word stress are discussed in the introduction.

ă-bat, ăir-marry, air-pair, ạr-far, ĕr-merry, ĝ-get, ī-high, ĭr-mirror, ł-little, ṇ-listen, ŏ-hot, oh-go, o͞o-wood, o͞o-moon, oor-tour, ōr-or, ow-how, t̪h-that, t̶h̶-thin, ŭ-but, UR-fur, ur-under. ( )- suppress the syllable   [ ]- less common   see p. xi for complete list.

References

DICTIONARIES

The American Heritage Dictionary of the English Language, 3rd ed. 1992. Boston: Houghton Mifflin.

BBC English Dictionary. 1992. London: BBC English and HarperCollins.

Collins Cobuild English Language Dictionary. 1987. London: Collins.

English Pronouncing Dictionary, 14th ed. 1988. Ed. A. C. Gimson and Susan Ramsaran. Cambridge, UK: Cambridge University Press.

Everyman's English Pronouncing Dictionary, 12th ed. 1964. Ed. Daniel Jones. London: J. M. Dent.

Irvine, Theodora. 1945. *A Pronouncing Dictionary of Shakespearean Proper Names*. New York.: Barnes and Noble.

Kökeritz, Helge. 1959. *Shakespeare's Names*. New Haven, Conn.: Yale University Press.

Longman Pronunciation Dictionary. 1990. Ed. J. C. Wells. London: Longman.

Merriam-Webster's Collegiate Dictionary, 10th ed. 1993. Springfield, Mass.: Merriam-Webster.

Onions, C. T. *A Shakespeare Glossary*. 1986. Revised Robert D. Eagleson. Oxford: Clarendon.

The Oxford English Dictionary, 2nd ed. 1989. 20 vols. Oxford: Clarendon.

A Pronouncing Dictionary of American English. 1953. Ed. John Samuel Kenyon and Thomas Albert Knott. Springfield, Mass.: Merriam.

A Pronouncing Dictionary of English Place-Names. 1981. Ed. Klaus Forster. London: Routledge and Kegan Paul.

Pronouncing Dictionary of Proper Names. 1993. Ed. John K. Bollard. Detroit: Omnigraphics.

The Random House Dictionary of the English Language, 2nd ed. 1987. New York: Random House.

A Universal Critical and Pronouncing Dictionary of the English Language. 1856. Ed. Joseph E. Worcester. London: Henry G. Bohn.

Webster's New International Dictionary of the English Language. 1934. Springfield, Mass.: Merriam.

Webster's Third New International Dictionary of the English Language. 1961. Springfield, Mass.: Merriam.

EDITIONS OF SHAKESPEARE'S WORKS

The basic text for the *Guide* is *The Riverside Shakespeare*. 1974. Ed. G. Blakemore Evans. Boston: Houghton Mifflin.

Based on *Riverside* 1974 are

A Complete and Systematic Concordance to the Works of Shakespeare. 1968–1980. Ed. Marvin Spevak. 9 vols. Hildesheim, Germany: Olms.

The Harvard Concordance to Shakespeare. 1973. Ed. Marvin Spevack. Cambridge, Mass.: Belknap Press of Harvard University Press.

Other editions that were used in the search for alternative readings include:

The Arden Shakespeare. 1951–. Ed. Una Ellis-Fermor, Harold F. Brooks, Harold Jenkins, and Brian Morris. London: Methuen. Recent volumes published by Routledge.

The Complete Oxford Shakespeare. 1987. Ed. Stanley Wells and Gary Taylor. 3 vols. Oxford: Clarendon.

The New Cambridge Shakespeare. 1984–. Ed. Philip Brockbank and Brian Gibbons. Cambridge: Cambridge University Press.

A New Variorum Edition of Shakespeare. 1871–. Ed. Horace Howard Furness. Philadelphia: Lippincott. A revised series is being published by the Modern Language Association of America.

The Oxford Shakespeare. 1982–. Ed. Stanley Wells. Oxford: Clarendon.

The Parallel King Lear 1608–1623. 1989. Prepared by Michael Warren. Berkeley: University of California.

The Three-Text Hamlet. 1991. Ed. Paul Bertram and Bernice W. Kliman. New York: AMS.

William Shakespeare: The Complete Works. 1986. Ed. Stanley Wells and Gary Taylor. Oxford: Clarendon.

William Shakespeare: A Textual Companion. 1987. Stanley Wells et. al. Oxford: Clarendon.

ON SHAKESPEARE'S TEXTS

Thompson, Ann, et al. 1992. *Which Shakespeare? A User's Guide to Editions.* Milton Keynes, UK: Open University.

Wells, Stanley. 1979. *Modernizing Shakespeare's Spelling.* Oxford: Oxford University Press.

_____. 1984. *Re-editing Shakespeare for the Modern Reader.* Oxford: Clarendon.

ON LATIN AND GREEK PRONUNCIATION

Allen, W. Sidney. 1968. *Vox Graeca.* Cambridge, UK: Cambridge University Press.

_____. *Vox Latina.* 1978. Cambridge, UK: Cambridge University Press.

Else, Gerald F. 1967. The Pronunciation of Classical Names and Words in English. *Classical Journal* 62:210–214.

Kelly, H. A. 1986. Pronouncing Latin Words in English. *Classical World* 80:33–37.

Moore-Smith, G. C. 1930. The English Language and the 'Restored' Pronunciation of Latin. In *A Grammatical Miscellany offered to Otto Jespersen,* 167–78. Copenhagen: Levin and Munksgaard.

Sargeaunt, John. 1920. *The Pronunciation of English Words Derived from the Latin.* Society for Pure English Tract No. IV. Oxford: Clarendon.

Tucker, R. Whitney. 1973. Why Don't Scholars Speak English? *Classical Journal* 69: 145–8.

ON REGIONAL BRITISH AND NORTH AMERICAN PRONUNCIATIONS

Bähr, Dieter. 1981. *Die englische Sprache in Kanada.* Tübingen, Germany: Gunter Narr.

Dictionary of American Regional English. 1985–. Ed. Frederick G. Cassidy and Joan Houston Hall. 3 vols. to date. Cambridge, Mass.: Belknap Press of Harvard University Press.

The English Dialect Dictionary. 1898–1904. Ed. Joseph Wright. 6 vols. London: Henry Frowde.

The Linguistic Atlas of New England. 1941–3. Ed. Hans Kurath et al. 6 vols. Providence, R.I:
American Council of Learned Societies and Brown University.
Survey of English Dialects. 1962. Ed. Harold Orton et al. 4 vols. Leeds: E. J. Arnold.
Wells, J. C. 1982. *Accents of English.* 3 vols. Cambridge, UK: Cambridge University Press.

ON ELIZABETHAN PRONUNCIATION

Cercignagni, Fausto. 1981. *Shakespeare's Works and Elizabethan Pronunciation.* Oxford:
Clarendon.
Dobson, E. J. 1968. *English Pronunciation 1500–1700.* 2 vols. Oxford: Clarendon.
Kökeritz, Helge. 1953. *Shakespeare's Pronunciation.* New Haven: Yale University Press.
Prins, A. A. 1974. *A History of English Phonemes.* Leiden: Leiden University Press.
Viëtor, Wilhelm. 1906. *Shakespeare's Pronunciation: A Shakespeare Phonology.* Marburg,
Germany: N. G. Elwert.

ON READING SHAKESPEARE'S VERSE

Kökeritz, Helge. 1969. Elizabethan Prosody and Historical Phonology. In *Approaches to
English Historical Linguistics,* ed. Roger Lass. New York: Holt, Rinehart, and Winston,
208–227.
Linklater, Kristin. 1992. *Freeing Shakespeare's Voice: The Actor's Guide to Talking the Text.*
New York: Theatre Communications Group.
Sipe, Dorothy L. 1968. *Shakespeare's Metrics.* Vol. 166. Yale Studies in English. New Ha-
ven, Conn.: Yale University Press.
Spain, Delbert. 1988. *Shakespeare Sounded Soundly.* Santa Barbara, Calif.: Capra.
Wright, George T. 1985. Shakespeare's Poetic Techniques. In *William Shakespeare: His
World, His Work, His Influence,* ed. John F. Andrews. Vol. 2, 3 vols. New York: Scrib-
ner, 363–387.
_____. 1988. *Shakespeare's Metrical Art.* Berkeley: University of California Press.

Subject Index

About the Author

DALE COYE is Assistant Professor of General Education and English at the College of New Jersey. He is the former artistic director of the Princeton Summer Theatre and the author of several plays and revues, including theatre pieces for elementary and high school students (http://members.aol.com/dalecoye).